Thoughtful Data Science

A Programmer's Toolset for Data Analysis and
Artificial Intelligence with Python, Jupyter Notebook,
and PixieDust

David Taieb

BIRMINGHAM - MUMBAI

Thoughtful Data Science

Acquisition Editors: Frank Pohlmann, Suresh M Jain
Project Editors: Savvy Sequeira, Kishor Rit
Content Development Editor: Alex Sorrentino
Technical Editor: Bhagyashree Rai
Proofreader: Safis Editing
Indexers: Priyanka Dhadke
Graphics: Tom Scaria
Production Coordinator: Sandip Tadge

First published: July 2018

Production reference: 1300718

Published by Packt Publishing Ltd.
Livery Place
35 Livery Street
Birmingham B3 2PB, UK.
ISBN 978-1-78883-996-9
www.packtpub.com

To Alexandra, Solomon, Zachary, Victoria and Charlotte:

Thank you for your support, unbounded love, and infinite patience. I would not have been able to complete this work without all of you.

To Fernand and Gisele:

Without whom I wouldn't be where I am today. Thank you for your continued guidance all these years.

mapt.io

Mapt is an online digital library that gives you full access to over 5,000 books and videos, as well as industry leading tools to help you plan your personal development and advance your career. For more information, please visit our website.

Why subscribe?

- Spend less time learning and more time coding with practical eBooks and Videos from over 4,000 industry professionals

- Learn better with Skill Plans built especially for you

- Get a free eBook or video every month

- Mapt is fully searchable

- Copy and paste, print, and bookmark content

PacktPub.com

Contributors

About the author

David Taieb is the Distinguished Engineer for the Watson and Cloud Platform Developer Advocacy team at IBM, leading a team of avid technologists on a mission to educate developers on the art of the possible with data science, AI and cloud technologies. He's passionate about building open source tools, such as the PixieDust Python Library for Jupyter Notebooks, which help improve developer productivity and democratize data science. David enjoys sharing his experience by speaking at conferences and meetups, where he likes to meet as many people as possible.

I want to give special thanks to all of the following dear friends at IBM who contributed to the development of PixieDust and/ or provided invaluable support during the writing of this book: Brad Noble, Jose Barbosa, Mark Watson, Raj Singh, Mike Broberg, Jessica Mantaro, Margriet Groenendijk, Patrick Titzler, Glynn Bird, Teri Chadbourne, Bradley Holt, Adam Cox, Jamie Jennings, Terry Antony, Stephen Badolato, Terri Gerber, Peter May, Brady Paterson, Kathleen Francis, Dan O'Connor, Muhtar (Burak) Akbulut, Navneet Rao, Panos Karagiannis, Allen Dean, and Jim Young.

About the reviewers

Margriet Groenendijk is a data scientist and developer advocate for IBM. She has a background in climate research, where, at the University of Exeter, she explored large observational datasets and the output of global scale weather and climate models to understand the impact of land use on climate. Prior to that, she explored the effect of climate on the uptake of carbon from the atmosphere by forests during her PhD research at the Vrije Universiteit in Amsterdam.

Now adays, she explores ways to simplify working with diverse data using open source tools, IBM Cloud, and Watson Studio. She has experience with cloud services, databases, and APIs to access, combine, clean, and store different types of data. Margriet uses time series analysis, statistical data analysis, modeling and parameter optimisation, machine learning, and complex data visualization. She writes blogs and speaks about these topics at conferences and meetups.

va barbosa is a developer advocate for the Center for Open-Source Data & AI Technologies, where he helps developers discover and make use of data and machine learning technologies. This is fueled by his passion to help others, and guided by his enthusiasm for open source technology.

Always looking to embrace new challenges and fulfill his appetite for learning, va immerses himself in a wide range of technologies and activities. He has been an electronic technician, support engineer, software engineer, and developer advocate.

When not focusing on the developer experience, va enjoys dabbling in photography. If you can't find him in front of a computer, try looking behind a camera.

Packt is searching for authors like you

If you're interested in becoming an author for Packt, please visit authors.packtpub. com and apply today. We have worked with thousands of developers and tech professionals, just like you, to help them share their insight with the global tech community. You can make a general application, apply for a specific hot topic that we are recruiting an author for, or submit your own idea.

Table of Contents

Preface

"Developers are the most-important, most-valuable constituency in business today, regardless of industry."

– Stephen O'Grady, author of *The New Kingmaker*s

First, let me thank you and congratulate you, the reader, for the decision to invest some of your valuable time to read this book. Throughout the chapters to come, I will take you on a journey of discovering or even re-discovering data science from the perspective of a developer and will develop the theme of this book which is that data science is a team sport and that if it is to be successful, developers will have to play a bigger role in the near future and better collaborate with data scientists. However, to make data science more inclusive to people of all backgrounds and trades, we first need to *democratize it by making data simple and accessible* — this is in essence what this book is about.

Why am I writing this book?

As I'll explain in more detail in *Chapter 1, Perspectives on Data Science from a Developer*, I am first and foremost a developer with over 20 years, experience of building software components of a diverse nature; frontend, backend, middleware, and so on. Reflecting back on this time, I realize how much getting the algorithms right always came first in my mind; data was always somebody else's problem. I rarely had to analyze it or extract insight from it. At best, I was designing the right data structure to load it in a way that would make my algorithm run more efficiently and the code more elegant and reusable.

However, as the Artificial Intelligence and data science revolution got under way, it became obvious to me that developers like myself needed to get involved, and so 7 years ago in 2011, I jumped at the opportunity to become the lead architect for the IBM Watson core platform UI & Tooling. Of course, I don't pretend to have become an expert in machine learning or NLP, far from it. Learning through practice is not a substitute for getting a formal academic background.

However, a big part of what I want to demonstrate in this book is that, with the right tools and approach, someone equipped with the right mathematical foundations (I'm only talking about high-school level calculus concepts really) can quickly become a good practitioner in the field. A key ingredient to being successful is to simplify as much as possible the different steps of building a data pipeline; from acquiring, loading, and cleaning the data, to visualizing and exploring it, all the way to building and deploying machine learning models.

It was with an eye to furthering this idea of making data simple and accessible to a community beyond data scientists that, 3 years ago, I took on a leading role at the IBM Watson Data Platform team with the mission of expanding the community of developers working with data with a special focus on education and activism on their behalf. During that time as the lead developer advocate, I started to talk openly about the need for developers and data scientists to better collaborate in solving complex data problems.

Note: During discussions at conferences and meetups, I would sometimes get in to trouble with data scientists who would get upset because they interpreted my narrative as me saying that data scientists are not good software developers. I want to set the record straight, including with you, the data scientist reader, that this is far from the case.

The majority of data scientists are excellent software developers with a comprehensive knowledge of computer science concepts. However, their main objective is to solve complex data problems which require rapid, iterative experimentations to try new things, not to write elegant, reusable components.

But I didn't want to only talk the talk; I also wanted to walk the walk and started the PixieDust open source project as my humble contribution to solving this important problem. As the PixieDust work progressed nicely, the narrative became crisper and easier to understand with concrete example applications that developers and data scientists alike could become excited about.

When I was presented with the opportunity to write a book about this story, I hesitated for a long time before embarking on this adventure for mainly two reasons:

- I have written extensively in blogs, articles, and tutorials about my experience as a data science practitioner with Jupyter Notebooks. I also have extensive experience as a speaker and workshop moderator at a variety of conferences. One good example is the keynote speech I gave at ODSC London in 2017 titled, *The Future of Data Science: Less Game of Thrones, More Alliances* (`https://odsc.com/training/portfolio/future-data-science-less-game-thrones-alliances`). However, I had never written a book before and had no idea of how big a commitment it would be, even though I was warned many times by friends that had authored books before.

- I wanted this book to be inclusive and target equally the developer, the data scientist, and the line of business user, but I was struggling to find the right content and tone to achieve that goal.

In the end, the decision to embark on this adventure came pretty easily. Having worked on the PixieDust project for 2 years, I felt we had made terrific progress with very interesting innovations that generated lots of interest in the open-source community and that writing a book would complement nicely our advocacy work on helping developers get involved in data science.

As a side note, for the reader who is thinking about writing a book and who has similar concerns, I can only advise on the first one with a big, "Yes, go for it." For sure, it is a big commitment that requires a substantial amount of sacrifice but provided that you have a good story to tell with solid content, it is really worth the effort.

Who this book is for

This book will serve the budding data scientist and developer with an interest in developing their skills or anyone wishing to become a professional data scientist. With the introduction of PixieDust from its creator, the book will also be a great desk companion for the already accomplished Data Scientist.

No matter the individual's level of interest, the clear, easy-to-read text and real-life scenarios would suit those with a general interest in the area, since they get to play with Python code running in Jupyter Notebooks.

To produce a functioning PixieDust dashboard, only a modicum of HTML and CSS is required. Fluency in data interpretation and visualization is also necessary since this book addresses data professionals such as business and general data analysts. The later chapters also have much to offer.

What this book covers

The book contains two logical parts of roughly equal length. In the first half, I lay down the theme of the book which is the need to bridge the gap between data science and engineering, including in-depth details about the Jupyter + PixieDust solution I'm proposing. The second half is dedicated to applying what we learned in the first half, to four industry cases.

Chapter 1, Perspectives on Data Science from a Developer, I attempt to provide a definition of data science through the prism of my own experience, building a data pipeline that performs sentiment analysis on Twitter posts. I defend the idea that it is a team sport and that most often, silos exist between the data science and engineering teams that cause unnecessary friction, inefficiencies and, ultimately, a failure to realize its full potential. I also argue the point of view that data science is here to stay and that eventually, it will become an integral part of what is known today as computer science (I like to think that someday new terms will emerge, such as *computer data science* that better capture this duality).

Chapter 2, Data Science at Scale with Jupyter Notebooks and PixieDust, I start diving into popular data science tools such as Python and its ecosystem of open-source libraries dedicated to data science, and of course Jupyter Notebooks. I explain why I think Jupyter Notebooks will become the big winner in the next few years. I also introduce the PixieDust open-source library capabilities starting from the simple `display()` method that lets the user visually explore data in an interactive user interface by building compelling charts. With this API, the user can choose from multiple rendering engines such as Matplotlib, Bokeh, Seaborn, and Mapbox. The `display()` capability was the only feature in the PixieDust MVP (minimum viable product) but, over time, as I was interacting with a lot of data science practitioners, I added new features to what would quickly become the PixieDust toolbox:

- **sampleData()**: A simple API for easily loading data into pandas and Apache Spark DataFrames

- **wrangle_data()**: A simple API for cleaning and massaging datasets. This capability includes the ability to destructure columns into new columns using regular expressions to extract content from unstructured text. The `wrangle_data()` API can also make recommendations based on predefined patterns.

- **PackageManager**: Lets the user install third-party Apache Spark packages inside a Python Notebook.

- **Scala Bridge**: Enables the user to run the Scala code inside a Python Notebook. Variables defined in the Python side are accessible in Scala and vice-versa.

- **Spark Job Progress Monitor**: Lets you track the status of your Spark Job with a real-time progress bar that displays directly in the output cell of the code being executed.

- **PixieApp**: Provides a programming model centered around HTML/CSS that lets developers build sophisticated dashboards to operationalize the analytics built in the Notebook. PixieApps can run directly in the Jupyter Notebook or be deployed as analytic web applications using the PixieGateway microservice. PixieGateway is an open-source companion project to PixieDust.

The following diagram summarizes the PixieDust development journey, including recent additions such as the PixieGateway and the PixieDebugger which is the first visual Python debugger for Jupyter Notebooks:

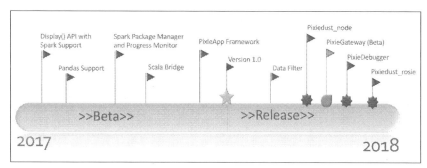

PixieDust journey

One key message to take away from this chapter is that PixieDust is first and foremost an open-source project that lives and breathes through the contributions of the developer community. As is the case for countless open-source projects, we can expect many more breakthrough features to be added to PixieDust over time.

Chapter 3, PixieApp under the Hood, I take the reader through a deep dive of the PixieApp programming model, illustrating each concept along the way with a sample application that analyzes GitHub data. I start with a high-level description of the anatomy of a PixieApp including its life cycle and the execution flow with the concept of routes. I then go over the details of how developers can use regular HTML and CSS snippets to build the UI of the dashboard, seamlessly interacting with the analytics and leveraging the PixieDust display() API to add sophisticated charts.

The PixieApp programming model is the cornerstone of the tooling strategy for bridging the gap between data science and engineering, as it streamlines the process of operationalizing the analytics, thereby increasing collaboration between data scientists and developers and reducing the time-to-market of the application.

Chapter 4, Deploying PixieApps to the Web with the PixieGateway Server, I discuss the PixieGateway microservice which enables developers to publish PixieApps as analytical web applications. I start by showing how to quickly deploy a PixieGateway microservice instance both locally and on the cloud as a Kubernetes container. I then go over the PixieGateway admin console capabilities, including the various configuration profiles and how to live-monitor the deployed PixieApps instances and the associated backend Python kernels. I also feature the chart sharing capability of the PixieGateway that lets the user turn a chart created with the PixieDust `display()` API into a web page accessible by anyone on the team.

The PixieGateway is a ground-breaking innovation with the potential of seriously speeding up the operationalization of analytics — which is sorely needed today — to fully capitalize on the promise of data science. It represents an open-source alternative to similar products that already exist on the market, such as the Shiny Server from R-Studio (`https://shiny.rstudio.com/deploy`) and Dash from Plotly (`https://dash.plot.ly`)

Chapter 5, Best Practices and Advanced PixieDust Concepts, I complete the deep-dive of the PixieDust toolbox by going over advanced concepts of the PixieApp programming model:

- **@captureOutput decorator**: By default, PixieApp routes require developers to provide an HTML fragment that will be injected in the application UI. This is a problem when we want to call a third-party Python library that is not aware of the PixieApp architecture and directly generate the output to the Notebook. `@captureOutput` solves this problem by automatically redirecting the content generated by the third-party Python library and encapsulating it into a proper HTML fragment.

- **Leveraging Python class inheritance for greater modularity and code reuse**: Breaks down the PixieApp code into logical classes that can be composed together using the Python class inheritance capability. I also show how to call an external PixieApp using the `pd_app` custom attribute.

- **PixieDust support for streaming data**: Shows how PixieDust `display()` and PixieApp can also handle streaming data.

- **Implementing Dashboard drill-down with PixieApp events**: Provides a mechanism for letting PixieApp components publish and subscribe to events generated when the user interacts with the UI (for example, charts, and buttons).

- **Building a custom display renderer for the PixieDust display() API**: Walks through the code of a simple renderer that extends the PixieDust menus. This renderer displays a custom HTML table showing the selected data.

- **Debugging techniques**: Go over the various debugging techniques that PixieDust offers including the visual Python debugger called PixieDebugger and the `%%PixiedustLog` magic for displaying Python logging messages.

- **Ability to run Node.js code**: We discuss the `pixiedust_node` extension that manages the life cycle of a Node.js process responsible for executing arbitrary Node.js scripts directly from within the Python Notebook.

Thanks to the open-source model with its transparent development process and a growing community of users who provided some valuable feedback, we were able to prioritize and implement a lot of these advanced features over time. The key point I'm trying to make is that following an open-source model with an appropriate license (PixieDust uses the Apache 2.0 license available here `https://www.apache.org/licenses/LICENSE-2.0`) does work very well. It helped us grow the community of users, which in turn provided us with the necessary feedback to prioritize new features that we knew were high value, and in some instances contributed code in the form of GitHub pull requests.

Chapter 6, Image Recognition with TensorFlow, I dive into the first of four industry cases. I start with a high-level introduction to machine learning, followed by an introduction to deep learning—a subfield of machine learning—and the TensorFlow framework that makes it easier to build neural network models. I then proceed to build an image recognition sample application including the associated PixieApp in four parts:

- *Part 1*: Builds an image recognition TensorFlow model by using the pretrain ImageNet model. Using the TensorFlow for poets tutorial, I show how to build analytics to load and score a neural network model.

- *Part 2*: Creates a PixieApp that operationalizes the analytics created in *Part 1*. This PixieApp scrapes the images from a web page URL provided by the user, scores them against the TensorFlow model and then graphically shows the results.

- *Part 3*: I show how to integrate the TensorBoard Graph Visualization component directly in the Notebook, providing the ability to debug the neural network model.

- *Part 4*: I show how to retrain the model with custom training data and update the PixieApp to show the results from both models.

I decided to start the series of sample applications with deep learning image recognition with TensorFlow because it's an important use case that is growing in popularity and demonstrating how we can build the models and deploy them in an application in the same Notebook represents a powerful statement toward the theme of bridging the gap between data science and engineering.

Chapter 7, Big Data Twitter Sentiment Analysis, I talk about doing natural language processing at Twitter scale. In this chapter, I show how to use the IBM Watson Natural Language Understanding cloud-based service to perform a sentiment analysis of the tweets. This is very important because it reminds the reader that reusing managed hosted services rather building the capability in-house can sometimes be an attractive option.

I start with an introduction to the Apache Spark parallel computing framework, and then move on to building the application in four parts:

- *Part 1*: Acquiring the Twitter data with Spark Structured Streaming
- *Part 2*: Enriching the data with sentiment and most relevant entity extracted from the text
- *Part 3*: Operationalizing the analytics by creating a real-time dashboard PixieApp.
- *Part 4*: An optional section that re-implements the application with Apache Kafka and IBM Streaming Designer hosted service to demonstrate how to add greater scalability.

I think the reader, especially those who are not familiar with Apache Spark, will enjoy this chapter as it is a little easier to follow than the previous one. The key takeaway is how to build analytics that scale with Jupyter Notebooks that are connected to a Spark cluster.

Chapter 8, Financial Time Series Analysis and Forecasting, I talk about time series analysis which is a very important field of data science with lots of practical applications in the industry. I start the chapter with a deep dive into the NumPy library which is foundational to so many other libraries, such as pandas and SciPy. I then proceed with the building of the sample application, which analyzes a time series comprised of historical stock data, in two parts:

- *Part 1*: Provides a statistical exploration of the time series including various charts such as autocorrelation function (ACF) and partial autocorrelation function (PACF)
- *Part 2*: Builds a predictive model based on the ARIMA algorithms using the statsmodels Python library

Time series analysis is such an important field of data science that I consider to be underrated. I personally learned a lot while writing this chapter. I certainly hope that the reader will enjoy it as well and that reading it will spur an interest to know more about this great topic. If that's the case, I also hope that you'll be convinced to try out Jupyter and PixieDust on your next learnings about time series analysis.

Chapter 9, US Domestic Flight Data Analysis Using Graphs, I complete this series of industry use cases with the study of Graphs. I chose a sample application that analyzes flight delays because the data is readily available, and it's a good fit for using graph algorithms (well, for full disclosure, I may also have chosen it because I had already written a similar application to predict flight delays based on weather data where I used Apache Spark MLlib: `https://developer.ibm.com/clouddataservices/2016/08/04/predict-flight-delays-with-apache-spark-mllib-flightstats-and-weather-data`).

I start with an introduction to graphs and associated graph algorithms including several of the most popular graph algorithms such as Breadth First Search and Depth First Search. I then proceed with an introduction to the `networkx` Python library that is used to build the sample application.

The application is made of four parts:

- *Part 1*: Shows how to load the US domestic flight data into a graph.
- *Part 2*: Creates the `USFlightsAnalysis` PixieApp that lets the user select an origin and destination airport and then display a Mapbox map of the shortest path between the two airports according to a selected centrality
- *Part 3*: Adds data exploration to the PixieApp that includes various statistics for each airline that flies out of the selected origin airport
- *Part 4*: Use the techniques learned in *Chapter 8, Financial Time Series Analysis and Forecasting* to build an ARIMA model for predicting flight delays

Graph theory is also another important and growing field of data science and this chapter nicely rounds up the series, which I hope provides a diverse and representative set of industry use cases. For readers who are particularly interested in using graph algorithms with big data, I recommend looking at Apache Spark GraphX (`https://spark.apache.org/graphx`) which implements many of the graph algorithms using a very flexible API.

Chapter 10, Final Thoughts, I end the book by giving a brief summary and explaining my take on Drew's Conway Venn Diagram. Then I talk about the future of AI and data science and how companies could prepare themselves for the AI and data science revolution. Also, I have listed some great references for further learning.

Appendix, PixieApp Quick-Reference, is a developer quick-reference guide that provides a summary of all the PixieApp attributes. This explains the various annotations, custom HTML attributes, and methods with the help of appropriate examples.

But enough about the introduction: let's get started on our journey with the first chapter titled *Perspectives on Data Science from a Developer*.

To get the most out of this book

- Most of the software needed to follow the example is open source and therefore free to download. Instructions are provided throughout the book, starting with installing anaconda which includes the Jupyter Notebook server.

- In *Chapter 7, Big Data Twitter Sentiment Analysis*, the sample application requires the use of IBM Watson cloud services including NLU and Streams Designer. These services come with a free tier plan, which is sufficient to follow the example along.

Download the example code files

You can download the example code files for this book from your account at http://www.packtpub.com. If you purchased this book elsewhere, you can visit http://www.packtpub.com/support and register to have the files emailed directly to you.

You can download the code files by following these steps:

1. Log in or register at http://www.packtpub.com.
2. Select the **SUPPORT** tab.
3. Click on **Code Downloads & Errata**.
4. Enter the name of the book in the **Search** box and follow the on-screen instructions.

Once the file is downloaded, please make sure that you unzip or extract the folder using the latest version of:

- WinRAR / 7-Zip for Windows
- Zipeg / iZip / UnRarX for Mac
- 7-Zip / PeaZip for Linux

The code bundle for the book is also hosted on GitHub at https://github.com/PacktPublishing/Thoughtful-Data-Science. We also have other code bundles from our rich catalog of books and videos available at https://github.com/PacktPublishing/. Check them out!

Download the color images

We also provide a PDF file that has color images of the screenshots/diagrams used in this book. You can download it here: http://www.packtpub.com/sites/default/files/downloads/ThoughtfulDataScience_ColorImages.pdf.

Conventions used

There are a number of text conventions used throughout this book.

`CodeInText`: Indicates code words in text, database table names, folder names, filenames, file extensions, pathnames, dummy URLs, user input, and Twitter handles. For example: "You can use the `{%if ...%}...{%elif ...%}...{%else%}`…`{%endif%}` notation to conditionally output text."

A block of code is set as follows:

```
import pandas
data_url = "https://data.cityofnewyork.us/api/views/e98g-f8hy/rows.csv?accessType=DOWNLOAD"
building_df = pandas.read_csv(data_url)
building_df
```

When we wish to draw your attention to a particular part of a code block, the relevant lines or items are set in bold:

```
import pandas
data_url = "https://data.cityofnewyork.us/api/views/e98g-f8hy/rows.csv?accessType=DOWNLOAD"
building_df = pandas.read_csv(data_url)
building_df
```

Any command-line input or output is written as follows:

```
jupyter notebook --generate-config
```

Bold: Indicates a new term, an important word, or words that you see on the screen, for example, in menus or dialog boxes, also appear in the text like this. For example: " The next step is to create a new route that takes the user value and returns the results. This route will be invoked by the **Submit Query** button."

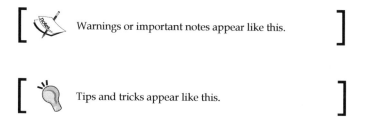

Warnings or important notes appear like this.

Tips and tricks appear like this.

Get in touch

Feedback from our readers is always welcome.

General feedback: Email feedback@packtpub.com, and mention the book's title in the subject of your message. If you have questions about any aspect of this book, please email us at questions@packtpub.com.

Errata: Although we have taken every care to ensure the accuracy of our content, mistakes do happen. If you have found a mistake in this book we would be grateful if you would report this to us. Please visit, http://www.packtpub.com/submit-errata, selecting your book, clicking on the **Errata Submission Form** link, and entering the details.

Piracy: If you come across any illegal copies of our works in any form on the Internet, we would be grateful if you would provide us with the location address or website name. Please contact us at copyright@packtpub.com with a link to the material.

If you are interested in becoming an author: If there is a topic that you have expertise in and you are interested in either writing or contributing to a book, please visit http://authors.packtpub.com.

Reviews

Please leave a review. Once you have read and used this book, why not leave a review on the site that you purchased it from? Potential readers can then see and use your unbiased opinion to make purchase decisions, we at Packt can understand what you think about our products, and our authors can see your feedback on their book. Thank you!

For more information about Packt, please visit packtpub.com.

1
Perspectives on Data Science from a Developer

"Data is a precious thing and will last longer than the systems themselves."

– Tim Berners-Lee, inventor of the World Wide Web

(https://en.wikipedia.org/wiki/Tim_Berners-Lee)

In this introductory chapter, I'll start the conversation by attempting to answer a few fundamental questions that will hopefully provide context and clarity for the rest of this book:

- What is data science and why it's on the rise
- Why is data science here to stay
- Why do developers need to get involved in data science

Using my experience as a developer and recent data science practitioner, I'll then discuss a concrete data pipeline project that I worked on and a data science strategy that derived from this work, which is comprised of three pillars: data, services, and tools. I'll end the chapter by introducing Jupyter Notebooks which are at the center of the solution I'm proposing in this book.

What is data science

If you search the web for a definition of data science, you will certainly find many. This reflects the reality that data science means different things to different people. There is no real consensus on what data scientists exactly do and what training they must have; it all depends on the task they're trying to accomplish, for example, data collection and cleaning, data visualization, and so on.

For now, I'll try to use a universal and, hopefully, consensual definition: *data science refers to the activity of analyzing a large amount of data in order to extract knowledge and insight leading to actionable decisions*. It's still pretty vague though; one can ask what kind of knowledge, insight, and actionable decision are we talking about?

To orient the conversation, let's reduce the scope to three fields of data science:

- **Descriptive analytics**: Data science is associated with information retrieval and data collection techniques with the goal of reconstituting past events to identify patterns and find insights that help understand what happened and what caused it to happen. An example of this is looking at sales figures and demographics by region to categorize customer preferences. This part requires being familiar with statistics and data visualization techniques.

- **Predictive analytics**: Data science is a way to predict the likelihood that some events are currently happening or will happen in the future. In this scenario, the data scientist looks at past data to find explanatory variables and build statistical models that can be applied to other data points for which we're trying to predict the outcome, for example, predicting the likelihood that a credit card transaction is fraudulent in real-time. This part is usually associated with the field of machine learning.

- **Prescriptive analytics**: In this scenario, data science is seen as a way to make better decisions, or perhaps I should say data-driven decisions. The idea is to look at multiple options and using simulation techniques, quantify, and maximize the outcome, for example, optimizing the supply chain by looking at minimizing operating costs.

In essence, descriptive data science answers the question of *what* (does the data tells me), predictive data science answers the question of *why* (is the data behaving a certain way), and prescriptive data science answers the questions of *how* (do we optimize the data toward a specific goal).

Is data science here to stay?

Let's get straight to the point from the start: I strongly think that the answer is yes.

However, that was not always the case. A few years back, when I first started hearing about data science as a concept, I initially thought that it was yet another marketing buzzword to describe an activity that already existed in the industry: **Business Intelligence (BI)**. As a developer and architect working mostly on solving complex system integration problems, it was easy to convince myself that I didn't need to get directly involved in data science projects, even though it was obvious that their numbers were on the rise, the reason being that developers traditionally deal with data pipelines as black boxes that are accessible with well-defined APIs.

However, in the last decade, we've seen exponential growth in data science interest both in academia and in the industry, to the point it became clear that this model would not be sustainable.

As data analytics are playing a bigger and bigger role in a company's operational processes, the developer's role was expanded to get closer to the algorithms and build the infrastructure that would run them in production. Another piece of evidence that data science has become the new *gold rush* is the extraordinary growth of data scientist jobs, which have been ranked number one for 2 years in a row on Glassdoor (`https://www.prnewswire.com/news-releases/glassdoor-reveals-the-50-best-jobs-in-america-for-2017-300395188.html`) and are consistently posted the most by employers on Indeed. Headhunters are also on the prowl on LinkedIn and other social media platforms, sending tons of recruiting messages to whoever has a profile showing any data science skills.

One of the main reasons behind all the investment being made into these new technologies is the hope that it will yield major improvements and greater efficiencies in the business. However, even though it is a growing field, data science in the enterprise today is still confined to experimentation instead of being a core activity as one would expect given all the hype. This has lead a lot of people to wonder if data science is a passing fad that will eventually subside and yet another technology bubble that will eventually pop, leaving a lot of people behind.

These are all good points, but I quickly realized that it was more than just a passing fad; more and more of the projects I was leading included the integration of data analytics into the core product features. Finally, it is when the IBM Watson Question Answering system won at a game of *Jeopardy!* against two experienced champions, that I became convinced that data science, along with the cloud, big data, and **Artificial Intelligence (AI)**, was here to stay and would eventually change the way we think about computer science.

Why is data science on the rise?

There are multiple factors involved in the meteoric rise of data science.

First, the amount of data being collected keeps growing at an exponential rate. According to recent market research from the IBM Marketing Cloud (`https://www-01.ibm.com/common/ssi/cgi-bin/ssialias?htmlfid=WRL12345GBEN`) something like 2.5 quintillion bytes are created every day (to give you an idea of how big that is, that's 2.5 billion of billion bytes), but yet only a tiny fraction of this data is ever analyzed, leaving tons of missed opportunities on the table.

Second, we're in the midst of a cognitive revolution that started a few years ago; almost every industry is jumping on the AI bandwagon, which includes **natural language processing** (NLP) and machine learning. Even though these fields existed for a long time, they have recently enjoyed the renewed attention to the point that they are now among the most popular courses in colleges as well as getting the lion's share of open source activities. It is clear that, if they are to survive, companies need to become more agile, move faster, and transform into digital businesses, and as the time available for decision-making is shrinking to near real-time, they must become fully data-driven. If you also include the fact that AI algorithms need high-quality data (and a lot of it) to work properly, we can start to understand the critical role played by data scientists.

Third, with advances in cloud technologies and the development of **Platform as a Service** (**PaaS**), access to massive compute engines and storage has never been easier or cheaper. Running big data workloads, once the purview of large corporations, is now available to smaller organizations or any individuals with a credit card; this, in turn, is fueling the growth of innovation across the board.

For these reasons, I have no doubt that, similar to the AI revolution, data science is here to stay and that its growth will continue for a long time. But we also can't ignore the fact that data science hasn't yet realized its full potential and produced the expected results, in particular helping companies in their transformation into data-driven organizations. Most often, the challenge is achieving that next step, which is to transform data science and analytics into a core business activity that ultimately enables clear-sighted, intelligent, bet-the-business decisions.

What does that have to do with developers?

This is a very important question that we'll spend a lot of time developing in the coming chapters. Let me start by looking back at my professional journey; I spent most of my career as a developer, dating back over 20 years ago, working on many aspects of computer science.

I started by building various tools that helped with software internationalization by automating the process of translating the user interface into multiple languages. I then worked on a LotusScript (scripting language for Lotus Notes) editor for Eclipse that would interface directly with the underlying compiler. This editor provided first-class development features, such as content assist, which provides suggestions, real-time syntax error reporting, and so on. I then spent a few years building middleware components based on Java EE and OSGI (`https://www.osgi.org`) for the Lotus Domino server. During that time, I led a team that modernized the Lotus Domino programming model by bringing it to the latest technologies available at the time. I was comfortable with all aspects of software development, frontend, middleware, backend data layer, tooling, and so on; I was what some would call a full-stack developer.

That was until I saw a demo of the IBM Watson Question Answering system that beat longtime champions Brad Rutter and Ken Jennings at a game of *Jeopardy!* in 2011. Wow! This was groundbreaking, a computer program capable of answering natural language questions. I was very intrigued and, after doing some research, meeting with a few researchers involved in the project, and learning about the techniques used to build this system, such as NLP, machine learning, and general data science, I realized how much potential this technology would have if applied to other parts of the business.

A few months later, I got an opportunity to join the newly formed Watson Division at IBM, leading a tooling team with the mission to build data ingestion and accuracy analysis capabilities for the Watson system. One of our most important requirements was to make sure the tools were easy to use by our customers, which is why, in retrospect, giving this responsibility to a team of developers was the right move. From my perspective, stepping into that job was both challenging and enriching. I was leaving a familiar world where I excelled at designing architectures based on well-known patterns and implementing frontend, middleware, or backend software components to a world focused mostly on working with a large amount of data; acquiring it, cleansing it, analyzing it, visualizing it, and building models. I spent the first six months drinking from the firehose, reading, and learning about NLP, machine learning, information retrieval, and statistical data science, at least enough to be able to work on the capabilities I was building.

It was at that time, interacting with the research team to bring these algorithms to market, that I realized how important developers and data scientists needed to collaborate better. The traditional approach of having data scientists solve complex data problems in isolation and then throw the results "over the wall" to developers for them to operationalize them is not sustainable and doesn't scale, considering that the amount of data to process keeps growing exponentially and the required time to market keeps shrinking.

Instead, their role needs to be shifting toward working as one team, which means that data scientists must work and think like software developers and vice versa. Indeed, this looks very good on paper: on the one hand, data scientists will benefit from tried-and-true software development methodologies such as Agile—with its rapid iterations and frequent feedback approach—but also from a rigorous software development life cycle that brings compliance with enterprise needs, such as security, code reviews, source control, and so on. On the other hand, developers will start thinking about data in a new way: as analytics meant to discover insights instead of just a persistence layer with queries and **CRUD** (short for, **create**, **read**, **update**, **delete**) APIs.

Putting these concepts into practice

After 4 years as the Watson Core Tooling lead architect building self-service tooling for the Watson Question Answering system, I joined the Developer Advocacy team of the Watson Data Platform organization which has the expanded mission of creating a platform that brings the portfolio of data and cognitive services to the IBM public cloud. Our mission was rather simple: win the hearts and minds of developers and help them be successful with their data and AI projects.

The work had multiple dimensions: education, evangelism, and activism. The first two are pretty straightforward, but the concept of activism is relevant to this discussion and worth explaining in more details. As the name implies, activism is about bringing change where change is needed. For our team of 15 developer advocates, this meant walking in the shoes of developers as they try to work with data—whether they're only getting started or already operationalizing advanced algorithms—feel their pain and identify the gaps that should be addressed. To that end, we built and made open source numerous sample data pipelines with real-life use cases.

At a minimum, each of these projects needed to satisfy three requirements:

- The raw data used as input must be publicly available
- Provide clear instructions for deploying the data pipeline on the cloud in a reasonable amount of time
- Developers should be able to use the project as a starting point for similar scenarios, that is, the code must be highly customizable and reusable

The experience and insights we gained from these exercises were invaluable:

- Understanding which data science tools are best suited for each task
- Best practice frameworks and languages
- Best practice architectures for deploying and operationalizing analytics

The metrics that guided our choices were multiple: accuracy, scalability, code reusability, but most importantly, improved collaboration between data scientists and developers.

Deep diving into a concrete example

Early on, we wanted to build a data pipeline that extracted insights from Twitter by doing sentiment analysis of tweets containing specific hashtags and to deploy the results to a real-time dashboard. This application was a perfect starting point for us, because the data science analytics were not too complex, and the application covered many aspects of a real-life scenario:

- High volume, high throughput streaming data
- Data enrichment with sentiment analysis NLP
- Basic data aggregation
- Data visualization
- Deployment into a real-time dashboard

To try things out, the first implementation was a simple Python application that used the tweepy library (the official Twitter library for Python: `https://pypi.python.org/pypi/tweepy`) to connect to Twitter and get a stream of tweets and textblob (the simple Python library for basic NLP: `https://pypi.python.org/pypi/textblob`) for sentiment analysis enrichment.

The results were then saved into a JSON file for analysis. This prototype was a great way to getting things started and experiment quickly, but after a few iterations we quickly realized that we needed to get serious and build an architecture that satisfied our enterprise requirements.

Data pipeline blueprint

At a high level, data pipelines can be described using the following generic blueprint:

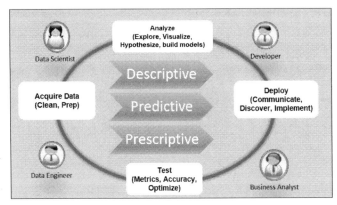

Data pipeline workflow

The main objective of a data pipeline is to operationalize (that is, *provide direct business value*) the data science analytics outcome in a scalable, repeatable process, and with a high degree of automation. Examples of analytics could be a recommendation engine to entice consumers to buy more products, for example, the Amazon recommended list, or a dashboard showing **Key Performance Indicators (KPIs)** that can help a CEO make future decisions for the company.

There are multiple persons involved in the building of a data pipeline:

- **Data engineers**: They are responsible for designing and operating information systems. In other words, data engineers are responsible for interfacing with data sources to acquire the data in its raw form and then massage it (some call this data wrangling) until it is ready to be analyzed. In the Amazon recommender system example, they would implement a streaming processing pipeline that captures and aggregates specific consumer transaction events from the e-commerce system of records and stores them into a data warehouse.

- **Data scientists**: They analyze the data and build the analytics that extract insight. In our Amazon recommender system example, they could use a Jupyter Notebook that connects to the data warehouse to load the dataset and build a recommendation engine using, for example, collaborative filtering algorithm (`https://en.wikipedia.org/wiki/Collaborative_filtering`).

- **Developers**: They are responsible for operationalizing the analytics into an application targeted at line of business users (business analysts, C-Suite, end users, and so on). Again, in the Amazon recommender system, the developer will present the list of recommended products after the user has completed a purchase or via a periodic email.

- **Line of business users**: This encompasses all users that consume the output of data science analytics, for example, business analysts analyzing dashboards to monitor the health of a business or the end user using an application that provides a recommendation as to what to buy next.

 In real-life, it is not uncommon that the same person plays more than one of the roles described here; this may mean that one person has multiple, different needs when interacting with a data pipeline.

As the preceding diagram suggests, building a data science pipeline is iterative in nature and adheres to a well-defined process:

1. **Acquire Data**: This step includes acquiring the data in its raw form from a variety of sources: structured (RDBMS, system of records, and so on) or unstructured (web pages, reports, and so on):

    ○ **Data cleansing**: Check for integrity, fill missing data, fix incorrect data, and data munging

    ○ **Data prep**: Enrich, detect/remove outliers, and apply business rules

2. **Analyze**: This step combines descriptive (understand the data) and prescriptive (build models) activities:

    ° **Explore**: Find statistical properties, for example, central tendency, standard deviation, distribution, and variable identification, such as univariate and bivariate analysis, the correlation between variables, and so on.

    ° **Visualization**: This step is extremely important to properly analyze the data and form hypotheses. Visualization tools should provide a reasonable level of interactivity to facilitate understanding of the data.

    ° **Build model**: Apply inferential statistics to form hypotheses, such as selecting features for the models. This step usually requires expert domain knowledge and is subject to a lot of interpretation.

3. **Deploy**: Operationalize the output of the analysis phase:

    ° **Communicate**: Generate reports and dashboards that communicate the analytic output clearly for consumption by the line of business user (C-Suite, business analyst, and so on)

    ° **Discover**: Set a business outcome objective that focuses on discovering new insights and business opportunities that can lead to a new source of revenue

    ° **Implement**: Create applications for end-users

4. **Test**: This activity should really be included in every step, but here we're talking about creating a feedback loop from field usage:

    ° Create metrics that measure the accuracy of the models

    ° Optimize the models, for example, get more data, find new features, and so on

What kind of skills are required to become a data scientist?

In the industry, the reality is that data science is so new that companies do not yet have a well-defined career path for it. How do you get hired for a data scientist position? How many years of experience is required? What skills do you need to bring to the table? Math, statistics, machine learning, information technology, computer science, and what else?

Well, the answer is probably a little bit of everything plus one more critical skill: domain-specific expertise.

There is a debate going on around whether applying generic data science techniques to any dataset without an intimate understanding of its meaning, leads to the desired business outcome. Many companies are leaning toward making sure data scientists have substantial amount of domain expertise, the rationale being that without it you may unknowingly introduce bias at any steps, such as when filling the gaps in the data cleansing phase or during the feature selection process, and ultimately build models that may well fit a given dataset but still end up being worthless. Imagine a data scientist working with no chemistry background, studying unwanted molecule interactions for a pharmaceutical company developing new drugs. This is also probably why we're seeing a multiplication of statistics courses specialized in a particular domain, such as biostatistics for biology, or supply chain analytics for analyzing operation management related to supply chains, and so on.

To summarize, a data scientist should be in theory somewhat proficient in the following areas:

- Data engineering / information retrieval
- Computer science
- Math and statistics
- Machine learning
- Data visualization
- Business intelligence
- Domain-specific expertise

 If you are thinking about acquiring these skills but don't have the time to attend traditional classes, I strongly recommend using online courses. I particularly recommend this course: https://www.coursera.org/: https://www.coursera.org/learn/data-science-course.

The classic Drew's Conway Venn Diagram provides an excellent visualization of what is data science and why data scientists are a bit of a unicorn:

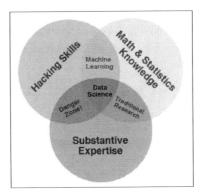

Drew's Conway Data Science Venn Diagram

By now, I hope it becomes pretty clear that the perfect data scientist that fits the preceding description is more an exception than the norm and that, most often, the role involves multiple personas. Yes, that's right, the point I'm trying to make is that *data science is a team sport* and this idea will be a recurring theme throughout this book.

IBM Watson DeepQA

One project that exemplifies the idea that data science is a team sport is the IBM DeepQA research project which originated as an IBM grand challenge to build an artificial intelligence system capable of answering natural language questions against predetermined domain knowledge. The **Question Answering (QA)** system should be good enough to be able to compete with human contestants at the *Jeopardy!* popular television game show.

As is widely known, this system dubbed IBM Watson went on to win the competition in 2011 against two of the most seasoned *Jeopardy!* champions: Ken Jennings and Brad Rutter. The following photo was taken from the actual game that aired on February 2011:

IBM Watson battling Ken Jennings and Brad Rutter at Jeopardy!

Source: https://upload.wikimedia.org/wikipedia/en/9/9b/Watson_Jeopardy.jpg

It was during the time that I was interacting with the research team that built the IBM Watson QA computer system that I got to take a closer look at the DeepQA project architecture and realized first-hand how many data science fields were actually put to use.

The following diagram depicts a high-level architecture of the DeepQA data pipeline:

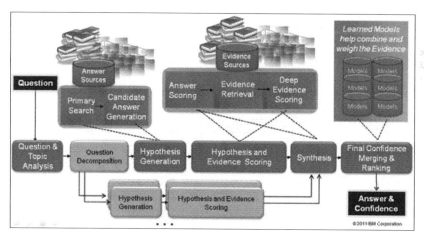

Watson DeepQA architecture diagram

Source: https://researcher.watson.ibm.com/researcher/files/us-mike.barborak/DeepQA-Arch.PNG

As the preceding diagram shows, the data pipeline for answering a question is composed of the following high-level steps:

1. **Question & Topic Analysis (natural language processing)**: This step uses a deep parsing component which detects dependency and hierarchy between the words that compose the question. The goal is to have a deeper understanding of the question and extracts fundamental properties, such as the following:

   ○ **Focus**: What is the question about?

   ○ **Lexical Answer Type (LAT)**: What is the type of the expected answer, for example, a person, a place, and so on. This information is very important during the scoring of candidate answers as it provides an early filter for answers that don't match the LAT.

   ○ **Named-entity resolution**: This resolves an entity into a standardized name, for example, "Big Apple" to "New York".

   ○ **Anaphora resolution**: This links pronouns to previous terms in the question, for example, in the sentence "On Sept. 1, 1715 Louis XIV died in this city, site of a fabulous palace **he** built," the pronoun "he" refers to Louis XIV.

   ○ **Relations detection**: This detects relations within the question, for example, "She divorced Joe DiMaggio in 1954" where the relation is "Joe DiMaggio Married X." These type of relations (Subject->Predicate->Object) can be used to query triple stores and yield high-quality candidate answers.

   ○ **Question class**: This maps the question to one of the predefined types used in *Jeopardy!*, for example, factoid, multiple-choice, puzzle, and so on.

2. **Primary search and Hypothesis Generation (information retrieval)**: This step relies heavily on the results of the question analysis step to assemble a set of queries adapted to the different answer sources available. Some example of answer sources include a variety of full-text search engines, such as Indri (`https://www.lemurproject.org/indri.php`) and Apache Lucene/Solr (`http://lucene.apache.org/solr`), document-oriented and title-oriented search (Wikipedia), triple stores, and so on. The search results are then used to generate candidate answers. For example, title-oriented results will be directly used as candidates while document searches will require more detailed analysis of the passages (again using NLP techniques) to extract possible candidate answers.

3. **Hypothesis and Evidence scoring (NLP and information retrieval)**: For each candidate answer, another round of search is performed to find additional supporting evidence using different scoring techniques. This step also acts as a prescreening test where some of the candidate answers are eliminated, such as the answers that do not match the LAT computed from step 1. The output of this step is a set of machine learning features corresponding to the supporting evidence found. These features will be used as input to a set of machine learning models for scoring the candidate answers.

4. **Final merging and scoring (machine learning)**: During this final step, the system identifies variants of the same answer and merges them together. It also uses machine learning models to select the best answers ranked by their respective scores, using the features generated in step 3. These machine learning models have been trained on a set of representative questions with the correct answers against a corpus of documents that has been pre-ingested.

As we continue the discussion on how data science and AI are changing the field of computer science, I thought it was important to look at the state of the art. IBM Watson is one of these flagship projects that has paved the way to more advances we've seen since it beats Ken Jennings and Brad Rutter at the game of *Jeopardy!*.

Back to our sentiment analysis of Twitter hashtags project

The quick data pipeline prototype we built gave us a good understanding of the data, but then we needed to design a more robust architecture and make our application enterprise ready. Our primary goal was still to gain experience in building data analytics, and not spend too much time on the data engineering part. This is why we tried to leverage open source tools and frameworks as much as possible:

- **Apache Kafka** (`https://kafka.apache.org`): This is a scalable streaming platform for processing the high volume of tweets in a reliable and fault-tolerant way.

- **Apache Spark** (`https://spark.apache.org`): This is an in-memory cluster-computing framework. Spark provides a programming interface that abstracts a complexity of parallel computing.

- **Jupyter Notebooks** (`http://jupyter.org`): These interactive web-based documents (Notebooks) let users remotely connect to a computing environment (Kernel) to create advanced data analytics. Jupyter Kernels support a variety of programming languages (Python, R, Java/Scala, and so on) as well as multiple computing frameworks (Apache Spark, Hadoop, and so on).

For the sentiment analysis part, we decided to replace the code we wrote using the textblob Python library with the Watson Tone Analyzer service (`https://www.ibm.com/watson/services/tone-analyzer`), which is a cloud-based rest service that provides advanced sentiment analysis including detection of emotional, language, and social tone. Even though the Tone Analyzer is not open source, a free version that can be used for development and trial is available on IBM Cloud (`https://www.ibm.com/cloud`).

Our architecture now looks like this:

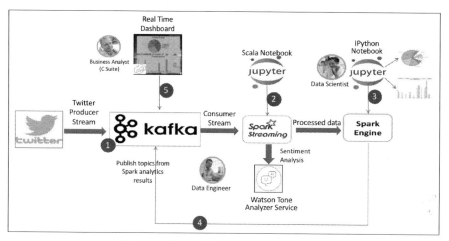

Twitter sentiment analysis data pipeline architecture

In the preceding diagram, we can break down the workflow in to the following steps:

1. Produce a stream of tweets and publish them into a Kafka topic, which can be thought of as a channel that groups events together. In turn, a receiver component can subscribe to this topic/channel to consume these events.

2. Enrich the tweets with emotional, language, and social tone scores: use Spark Streaming to subscribe to Kafka topics from component **1** and send the text to the Watson Tone Analyzer service. The resulting tone scores are added to the data for further downstream processing. This component was implemented using Scala and, for convenience, was run using a Jupyter Scala Notebook.

3. Data analysis and exploration: For this part, we decided to go with a Python Notebook simply because Python offer a more attractive ecosystem of libraries, especially around data visualizations.

4. Publish results back to Kafka.

5. Implement a real-time dashboard as a Node.js application.

With a team of three people, it took us about 8 weeks to get the dashboard working with real-time Twitter sentiment data. There are multiple reasons for this seemingly long time:

- Some of the frameworks and services, such as Kafka and Spark Streaming, were new to us and we had to learn how to use their APIs.

- The dashboard frontend was built as a standalone Node.js application using the Mozaïk framework (`https://github.com/plouc/mozaik`), which made it easy to build powerful live dashboards. However, we found a few limitations with the code, which forced us to dive into the implementation and write patches, hence adding delays to the overall schedule.

The results are shown in the following screenshot:

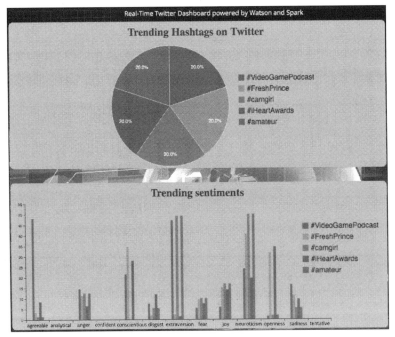

Twitter sentiment analysis real-time dashboard

Lessons learned from building our first enterprise-ready data pipeline

Leveraging open source frameworks, libraries, and tools definitely helped us be more efficient in implementing our data pipeline. For example, Kafka and Spark were pretty straightforward to deploy and easy to use, and when we were stuck, we could always rely on the developer community for help by using, for example, question and answer sites, such as `https://stackoverflow.com`.

Using a cloud-based managed service for the sentiment analysis step, such as the IBM Watson Tone Analyzer (`https://www.ibm.com/watson/services/tone-analyzer`) was another positive. It allowed us to abstract out the complexity of training and deploying a model, making the whole step more reliable and certainly more accurate than if we had implemented it ourselves.

It was also super easy to integrate as we only needed to make a REST request (also known as an HTTP request, see `https://en.wikipedia.org/wiki/Representational_state_transfer` for more information on REST architecture) to get our answers. Most of the modern web services now conform to the REST architecture, however, we still need to know the specification for each of the APIs, which can take a long time to get right. This step is usually made simpler by using an SDK library, which is often provided for free and in most popular languages, such as Python, R, Java, and Node.js. SDK libraries provide higher level programmatic access to the service by abstracting out the code that generates the REST requests. The SDK would typically provide a class to represent the service, where each method would encapsulate a REST API while taking care of user authentication and other headers.

On the tooling side, we were very impressed with Jupyter Notebooks, which provided excellent features, such as collaboration and full interactivity (we'll cover Notebooks in more detail later on).

Not everything was smooth though, as we struggled in a few key areas:

- Which programming language to choose for some of the key tasks, such as data enrichment and data analysis. We ended up using Scala and Python, even though there was little experience on the team, mostly because they are very popular among data scientists and also because we wanted to learn them.

- Creating visualizations for data exploration was taking too much time. Writing a simple chart with a visualization library, such as Matplotlib or Bokeh required writing too much code. This, in turn, slowed down our need for fast experimentation.

- Operationalizing the analytics into a real-time dashboard was way too hard to be scalable. As mentioned before, we needed to write a full-fledged standalone Node.js application that consumes data from Kafka and needed to be deployed as a cloud-foundry application (`https://www.cloudfoundry.org`) on the IBM Cloud. Understandably, this task required quite a long time to complete the first time, but we also found that it was difficult to update as well. Changes in the analytics that write data to Kafka needed to be synchronized with the changes on the dashboard application as well.

Data science strategy

If data science is to continue to grow and graduate into a core business activity, companies must find a way to scale it across all layers of the organization and overcome all the difficult challenges we discussed earlier. To get there, we identified three important pillars that architects planning a data science strategy should focus on, namely, data, services, and tools:

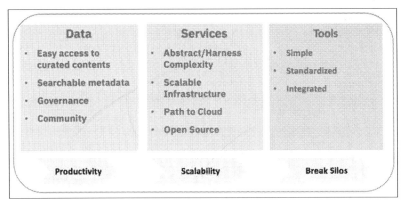

Three pillars of data science at scale

- **Data is your most valuable resource**: You need a proper data strategy to make sure data scientists have easy access to the curated contents they need. Properly classifying the data, set appropriate governance policies, and make the metadata searchable will reduce the time data scientists spend acquiring the data and then asking for permission to use it. This will not only increase their productivity, it will also improve their job satisfaction as they will spend more time working on doing actual data science.

  Setting a data strategy that enables data scientists to easily access high-quality data that's relevant to them increases productivity and morale and ultimately leads to a higher rate of successful outcomes.

- **Services**: Every architect planning for data science should be thinking about a **service-oriented architecture (SOA)**. Contrary to traditional monolithic applications where all the features are bundled together into a single deployment, a service-oriented system breaks down functionalities into services which are designed to do a few things but to do it very well, with high performance and scalability. These systems are then deployed and maintained independently from each other giving scalability and reliability to the whole application infrastructure. For example, you could have a service that runs algorithms to create a deep learning model, another one would persist the models and let applications run it to make predictions on customer data, and so on.

  The advantages are obvious: high reusability, easier maintenance, reduced time to market, scalability, and much more. In addition, this approach would fit nicely into a cloud strategy giving you a growth path as the size of your workload increases beyond existing capacities. You also want to prioritize open source technologies and standardize on open protocols as much as possible.

  Breaking processes into smaller functions infuses scalability, reliability, and repeatability into the system.

- **Tools do matter!** Without the proper tools, some tasks become extremely difficult to complete (at least that's the rationale I use to explain why I fail at fixing stuff around the house). However, you also want to keep the tools simple, standardized, and reasonably integrated so they can be used by less skilled users (even if I was given the right tool, I'm not sure I would have been able to complete the house fixing task unless it's simple enough to use). Once you decrease the learning curve to use these tools, non-data scientist users will feel more comfortable using them.

    Making the tools simpler to use contributes to breaking the silos and increases collaboration between data science, engineering, and business teams.

Jupyter Notebooks at the center of our strategy

In essence, Notebooks are web documents composed of editable cells that let you run commands interactively against a backend engine. As their name indicates, we can think of them as the digital version of a paper scratch pad used to write notes and results about experiments. The concept is very powerful and simple at the same time: a user enters code in the language of his/her choice (most implementations of Notebooks support multiple languages, such as Python, Scala, R, and many more), runs the cell and gets the results interactively in an output area below the cell that becomes part of the document. Results could be of any type: text, HTML, and images, which is great for graphing data. It's like working with a traditional **REPL** (short for, **Read-Eval-Print-Loop**) program on steroids since the Notebook can be connected to powerful compute engines (such as Apache Spark (`https://spark.apache.org`) or Python Dask (`https://dask.pydata.org`) clusters) allowing you to experiment with big data if needed.

Within Notebooks, any classes, functions, or variables created in a cell are visible in the cells below, enabling you to write complex analytics piece by piece, iteratively testing your hypotheses and fixing problems before moving on to the next phase. In addition, users can also write rich text using the popular Markdown language or mathematical expressions using LaTeX (`https://www.latex-project.org/`), to describe their experiments for others to read.

The following figure shows parts of a sample Jupyter Notebook with a Markdown cell explaining what the experiment is about, a code cell written in Python to create 3D plots, and the actual 3D charts results:

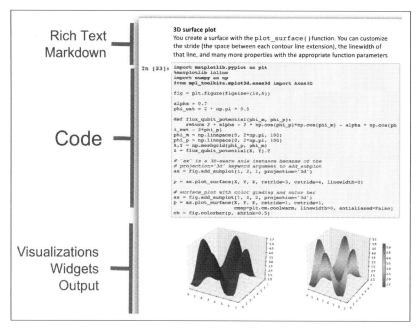

Sample Jupyter Notebook

Why are Notebooks so popular?

In the last few years, Notebooks have seen a meteoric growth in popularity as the tool of choice for data science-related activities. There are multiple reasons that can explain it, but I believe the main one is its versatility, making it an indispensable tool not just for data scientists but also for most of the personas involved in building data pipelines, including business analysts and developers.

For data scientists, Notebooks are ideal for iterative experimentation because it enables them to quickly load, explore, and visualize data. Notebooks are also an excellent collaboration tool; they can be exported as JSON files and easily shared across the team, allowing experiments to be identically repeated and debugged when needed. In addition, because Notebooks are also web applications, they can be easily integrated into a multi-users cloud-based environment providing an even better collaborative experience.

These environments can also provide on-demand access to large compute resources by connecting the Notebooks with clusters of machines using frameworks such as Apache Spark. Demand for these cloud-based Notebook servers is rapidly growing and as a result, we're seeing an increasing number of **SaaS** (short for, **Software as a Service**) solutions, both commercial with, for example, IBM Data Science Experience (`https://datascience.ibm.com`) or DataBricks (`https://databricks.com/try-databricks`) and open source with JupyterHub (`https://jupyterhub.readthedocs.io/en/latest`).

For business analysts, Notebooks can be used as presentation tools that in most cases provide enough capabilities with its Markdown support to replace traditional PowerPoints. Charts and tables generated can be directly used to effectively communicate results of complex analytics; there's no need to copy and paste anymore, plus changes in the algorithms are automatically reflected in the final presentation. For example, some Notebook implementations, such as Jupyter, provide an automated conversion of the cell layout to the slideshow, making the whole experience even more seamless.

For reference, here are the steps to produce these slides in Jupyter Notebooks:

- Using the **View | Cell Toolbar | Slideshow**, first annotate each cell by choosing between **Slide**, **Sub-Slide**, **Fragment**, **Skip**, or **Notes**.
- Use the `nbconvert jupyter` command to convert the Notebook into a Reveal.js-powered HTML slideshow:

  `jupyter nbconvert <pathtonotebook.ipynb> --to slides`

- Optionally, you can fire up a web application server to access these slides online:

  `jupyter nbconvert <pathtonotebook.ipynb> --to slides -post serve`

For developers, the situation is much less clear-cut. On the one hand, developers love REPL programming, and Notebooks offer all the advantages of an interactive REPL with the added bonuses that it can be connected to a remote backend. By virtue of running in a browser, results can contain graphics and, since they can be saved, all or part of the Notebook can be reused in different scenarios. So, for a developer, provided that your language of choice is available, Notebooks offer a great way to try and test things out, such as fine-tuning an algorithm or integrating a new API. On the other hand, there is little Notebook adoption by developers for data science activities that can complement the work being done by data scientists, even though they are ultimately responsible for operationalizing the analytics into applications that address customer needs.

To improve the software development life cycle and reduce time to value, they need to start using the same tools, programming languages, and frameworks as data scientists, including Python with its rich ecosystem of libraries and Notebooks, which have become such an important data science tool. Granted that developers have to meet the data scientist in the middle and get up to speed on the theory and concept behind data science. Based on my experience, I highly recommend using **MOOCs** (short for, **Massive Open Online Courses**) such as Coursera (`https://www.coursera.org`) or EdX (`http://www.edx.org`), which provide a wide variety of courses for every level.

However, having used Notebooks quite extensively, it is clear that, while being very powerful, they are primarily designed for data scientists, leaving developers with a steep learning curve. They also lack application development capabilities that are so critical for developers. As we've seen in the *Sentiment analysis of Twitter Hashtags* project, building an application or a dashboard based on the analytics created in a Notebook can be very difficult and require an architecture that can be difficult to implement and that has a heavy footprint on the infrastructure.

It is to address these gaps that I decided to create the PixieDust (`https://github.com/ibm-watson-data-lab/pixiedust`) library and open source it. As we'll see in the next chapters, the main goal of PixieDust is to lower the *cost of entry* for new users (whether it be data scientists or developers) by providing simple APIs for loading and visualizing data. PixieDust also provides a developer framework with APIs for easily building applications, tools, and dashboards that can run directly in the Notebook and also be deployed as web applications.

Summary

In this chapter, I gave my perspective on data science as a developer, discussing the reasons why I think that data science along with AI and Cloud has the potential to define the next era of computing. I also discussed the many problems that must be addressed before it can fully realize its potential. While this book doesn't pretend to provide a magic recipe that solves all these problems, it does try to answer the difficult but critical question of democratizing data science and more specifically *bridging the gap between data scientists and developers.*

In the next few chapters, we'll dive into the PixieDust open source library and learn how it can help Jupyter Notebooks users be more efficient when working with data. We'll also deep dive on the PixieApp application development framework that enables developers to leverage the analytics implemented in the Notebook to build application and dashboards.

In the remaining chapters, we will deep dive into many examples that show how data scientists and developers can collaborate effectively to build end-to-end data pipelines, iterate on the analytics, and deploy them to end users at a fraction of the time. The sample applications will cover many industry use-cases, such as image recognition, social media, and financial data analysis which include data science use cases like descriptive analytics, machine learning, natural language processing, and streaming data.

We will not discuss deeply the theory behind all the algorithms covered in the sample applications (which is beyond the scope of this book and would take more than one book to cover), but we will instead emphasize how to leverage the open source ecosystem to rapidly complete the task at hand (model building, visualization, and so on) and operationalize the results into applications and dashboards.

 The provided sample applications are written mostly in Python and come with complete source code. The code has been extensively tested and is ready to be re-used and customized in your own projects.

2
Data Science at Scale with Jupyter Notebooks and PixieDust

"The Best Line of Code is the One You Didn't Have to Write!"

– Unknown

In the previous chapter, I gave a developer's perspective on data science based on real experience and discussed three strategic pillars required for successful deployment with in the enterprise: data, services, and tools. I also discussed the idea that data science is not only the sole purview of data scientists, but rather a team sport with a special role for developers.

In this chapter, I'll introduce a solution — based on Jupyter Notebooks, Python, and the PixieDust open source library — that focuses on three simple goals:

- Democratizing data science by lowering the barrier to entry for non-data scientists

- Increasing collaboration between developers and data scientists

- Making it easier to operationalize data science analytics

 This solution only focuses on the tools pillar and not on data and services, which should be implemented independently, although we'll cover some of it when discussing the sample applications starting in *Chapter 6, Image Recognition with TensorFlow*.

Why choose Python?

Like many developers, when it came to building data-intensive projects, using Python wasn't my first choice. To be honest, having worked with Java for so many years, Scala seemed much more attractive to me at first, even though the learning curve was pretty steep. Scala is a very powerful language that elegantly combines object-oriented and functional programming, which is sorely lacking in Java (at least until Java 8 started to introduce lambda expressions).

Scala also provides a very concise syntax that translates into fewer lines of code, higher productivity, and ultimately fewer bugs. This comes in very handy, especially when a large part of your work is to manipulate data. Another reason for liking Scala is the better API coverage when using big data frameworks such as Apache Spark, which are themselves written in Scala. There are also plenty of other good reasons to prefer Scala, such as it's a strong typed system and its interoperability with Java, online documentation, and high performance.

So, for a developer like myself who is starting to get involved in data science, Scala would seem like a more natural choice, but yet, spoiler alert, we ended up focusing on Python instead. There are multiple reasons for this choice:

- Python, as a language, has a lot going on for itself too. It is a dynamic programming language with similar benefits to Scala, such as functional programming, and concise syntax, among others.
- Python has seen, over the last few years, a meteoric rise among data scientists, overtaking longtime rival R as the overall preferred language for data science, as demonstrated by a quick search for the terms `Python Data Science`, `Python Machine Learning`, `R Data Science`, and `R Machine Learning` on Google Trends:

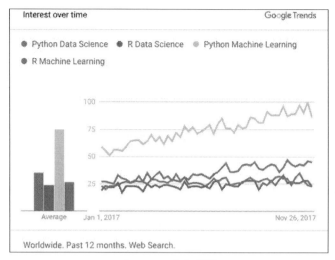

Interest trends for 2017

In a virtuous circle, Python's rising popularity fuels a vast and growing ecosystem of wide-ranging libraries that can be easily imported into your projects using the pip Python package installer. Data scientists now have access to many powerful open source Python libraries for data manipulation, data visualization, statistics, mathematics, machine learning, and natural language processing.

Even beginners can quickly build a machine learning classifier using the popular scikit-learn package (`http://scikit-learn.org`) without being a machine learning expert, or quickly plot rich charts using Matplotlib (`https://matplotlib.org`) or Bokeh (`https://bokeh.pydata.org`).

In addition, Python has also emerged as one of the top languages for developers as shown in this IEEE Spectrum 2017 survey (`https://spectrum.ieee.org/computing/software/the-2017-top-programming-languages`):

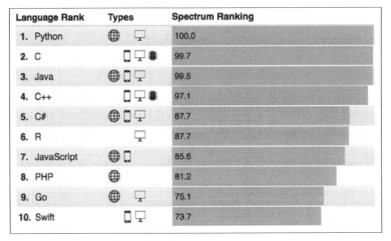

Usage statistics by programming languages

This trend is also confirmed on GitHub where Python is now number three in the total number of repositories, just behind Java and JavaScript:

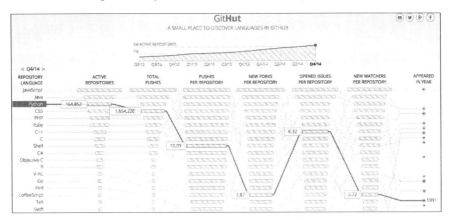

GitHub repositories statistics by programming language

The preceding chart shows some interesting statistics, demonstrating how active the Python developer community is. Python - related repositories that are active on GitHub are the third biggest in size, with similarly healthy total code pushes and opened issues per repository.

Python has also become ubiquitous on the web, powering numerous high-profile websites with web development frameworks, such as Django (`https://www.djangoproject.com`), Tornado (`http://www.tornadoweb.org`) and TurboGears (`http://turbogears.org`). More recently, there are signs that Python is also making its way into the field of cloud services with all major Cloud providers including it in some capacity in their offerings.

Python obviously has a bright future in the field of data science, especially when used in conjunction with powerful tools such as Jupyter Notebooks, which have become very popular in the data scientist community. The value proposition of Notebooks is that they are very easy to create and perfect for quickly running experiments. In addition, Notebooks support multiple high-fidelity serialization formats that can capture instructions, code, and results, which can then very easily be shared with other data scientists on the team or as open source for everyone to use. For example, we're seeing an explosion of Jupyter Notebooks being shared on GitHub, numbering in excess of 2.5 million and counting.

The following screenshot shows the result of a GitHub search for any file with the extension `.ipynb`, which is the most popular format for serialized Jupyter Notebooks (JSON format):

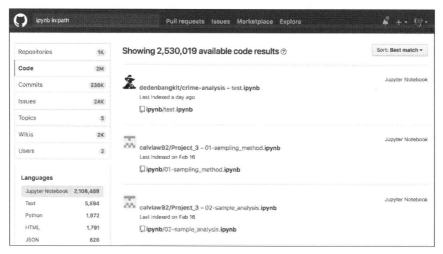

Search results for Jupyter Notebooks on GitHub

This is great, but Jupyter Notebooks are too often thought of as data scientist tools only. We'll see in the coming chapters that they can be much more and that they can also help all types of teams solve data problems. For example, they can help business analysts quickly load and visualize a dataset, enable developers to work with data scientists directly within a Notebook to leverage their analytics and build powerful dashboards, or allow DevOps to effortlessly deploy these dashboards into scalable, enterprise-ready microservices that can run as standalone web applications or embeddable components. It is based on this vision of bringing the tools of data science to non-data scientists that the PixieDust open source project was created.

Introducing PixieDust

Fun fact

I am often asked how I came up with the name PixieDust, for which I answer that I simply wanted to make Notebook simple, as in magical, for non-data scientists.

PixieDust (`https://github.com/ibm-watson-data-lab/pixiedust`) is an open-source project composed primarily of three components designed to address the three goals stated at the beginning of this chapter:

- A helper Python library for Jupyter Notebooks that provides simple APIs to load data from various sources into popular frameworks, such as pandas and Apache Spark DataFrame, and then to visualize and explore the dataset interactively.

- A simple Python-based programming model that enables developers to "productize" the analytics directly into the Notebook by creating powerful dashboards called PixieApps. As we'll see in the next chapters, PixieApps are different from traditional **BI** (short for, **Business Intelligence**) dashboards because developers can directly use HTML and CSS to create an arbitrary complex layout. In addition, they can embed in their business logic access to any variable, class, or function created in the Notebook.

- A secure microservice web server called PixieGateway that can run PixieApps as standalone web applications or as components that can be embedded into any website. PixieApps can easily be deployed from the Jupyter Notebook using a graphical wizard and without requiring any code changes. In addition, PixieGateway supports the sharing of any charts created by PixieDust as embeddable web pages, allowing data scientists to easily communicate results outside of the Notebook.

It is important to note that the PixieDust `display()` API primarily supports two popular data processing frameworks:

- **pandas** (`https://pandas.pydata.org`): By far the most popular Python data analysis package, pandas provides two main data structures: DataFrame for manipulating two-dimensional table-like datasets, and Series for one-dimensional column-like datasets.

 Currently, only pandas DataFrames are supported by PixieDust `display()`.

- **Apache Spark DataFrame** (`https://spark.apache.org/docs/latest/sql-programming-guide.html`): This is a high-level data structure for manipulating distributed datasets across a Spark Cluster. Spark DataFrames are built on top of the lower-level **RDD** (short for, **Resilient Distributed Dataset**) with the added functionality that it supports SQL queries.

Another less commonly used format supported by PixieDust `display()` is an array of JSON objects. In this case, PixieDust will use the values to build the rows and keys are used as columns, for example, as follows:

```
my_data = [
{"name": "Joe", "age": 24},
{"name": "Harry", "age": 35},
{"name": "Liz", "age": 18},
...
]
```

In addition, PixieDust is highly extensible both at the data handling and rendering level. For example, you can add new data types to be rendered by the visualization framework or if you want to leverage a plotting library you particularly like, you can easily add it to the list of renderers supported by PixieDust (see the next chapters for more details).

You will also find that PixieDust contains a few extra utilities related to Apache Spark, such as the following:

- **PackageManager**: This lets you install Spark packages inside a Python Notebook.

- **Scala Bridge**: This lets you use Scala directly in a Python Notebook using the `%%scala` magic. Variables are automatically transferred from Python to Scala and vice versa.

- **Spark Job Progress Monitor**: Track the status of any Spark job by showing a progress bar directly in the cell output.

Before we dive into each of the three PixieDust components, it would be a good idea to get access to a Jupyter Notebook, either by signing up to a hosted solution on the cloud (for example, Watson Studio at `https://datascience.ibm.com`) or installing a development version on your local machine.

 You can install the Notebook server locally by following the instructions here: `http://jupyter.readthedocs.io/en/latest/install.html`.

To start the Notebook server locally, simply run the following command from a Terminal:

```
jupyter notebook --notebook-dir=<<directory path where notebooks are
stored>>
```

The Notebook home page will automatically open in a browser. There are many configuration options to control how the Notebook server is launched. These options can be added to the command line or persisted in the Notebook configuration file. If you want to experiment with all the possible configuration options, you can generate a configuration file using the `--generate-config` option as follows:

```
jupyter notebook --generate-config
```

This will generate the following Python file, `<home_directory>/.jupyter/jupyter_notebook_config.py`, which contains a set of auto-documented options that have been disabled. For example, if you don't want to have the browser automatically opened when the Jupyter Notebook starts, locate the line that contains the `sc.NotebookApp.open_browser` variable, uncomment it, and set it to `False`:

```
## Whether to open in a browser after starting. The specific browser
used is
#  platform dependent and determined by the python standard library
'web browser'
#  module, unless it is overridden using the --browser (NotebookApp.
browser)
#  configuration option.
c.NotebookApp.open_browser = False
```

After making that change, simply save the `jupyter_notebook_config.py` file and restart the Notebook server.

The next step is to install the PixieDust library using the `pip` tool:

1. From the Notebook itself, enter the following command in a cell:

   ```
   !pip install pixiedust
   ```

 Note: The exclamation point syntax is specific to Jupyter Notebook and denotes that the rest of the command will be executed as a system command. For example, you could use `!ls` to list all the files and directories that are under the current working directory.

2. Run the cell using the **Cell** | **Run Cells** menu or the **Run** icon on the toolbar. You can also use the following keyboard shortcuts to run a cell:

   ° *Ctrl + Enter*: Run and keep the current cell selected

   ° *Shift + Enter*: Run and select the next cell

   ° *Alt + Enter*: Run and create new empty cell just below

3. Restart the kernel to make sure the `pixiedust` library is correctly loaded into the kernel.

The following screenshot shows the results after installing `pixiedust` for the first time:

```
1  !pip install pixiedust

Collecting pixiedust
  Downloading https://files.pythonhosted.org/packages/e0/f4/aed791371240b6e325d0a68b9235d2c2ca4da7fcc6081be30b7da0bc7
a36/pixiedust-1.1.9.tar.gz (186kB)
    100% |████████████████████████████████| 194kB 1.9MB/s ta 0:00:01
Requirement already satisfied: mpld3 in /Users/dtaieb/.local/lib/python2.7/site-packages (from pixiedust)
Requirement already satisfied: lxml in /Users/dtaieb/.local/lib/python2.7/site-packages (from pixiedust)
Requirement already satisfied: geojson in /Users/dtaieb/.local/lib/python2.7/site-packages (from pixiedust)
Requirement already satisfied: astunparse in /Users/dtaieb/anaconda/envs/testPDConda/lib/python2.7/site-packages (fro
m pixiedust)
Requirement already satisfied: markdown in /Users/dtaieb/.local/lib/python2.7/site-packages (from pixiedust)
Requirement already satisfied: six<2.0,>=1.6.1 in /Users/dtaieb/anaconda/envs/testPDConda/lib/python2.7/site-packages
 (from astunparse->pixiedust)
Requirement already satisfied: wheel<1.0,>=0.23.0 in /Users/dtaieb/.local/lib/python2.7/site-packages (from astunpars
e->pixiedust)
Building wheels for collected packages: pixiedust
  Running setup.py bdist_wheel for pixiedust ... done
  Stored in directory: /Users/dtaieb/Library/Caches/pip/wheels/0a/5b/93/663556baf63f1e20d34fa1c23d43dd761ac9103db14cb
44339
Successfully built pixiedust
Installing collected packages: pixiedust
Successfully installed pixiedust-1.1.9
```

Installing the PixieDust library on a Jupyter Notebook

I strongly recommend using Anaconda (`https://anaconda.org`), which provides excellent Python package management capabilities. If, like me, you like to experiment with different versions of Python and libraries dependencies, I suggest you use Anaconda virtual environments.

They are lightweight Python sandboxes that are very easy to create and activate (see `https://conda.io/docs/user-guide/tasks/manage-environments.html`):

- Create a new environment: `conda create --name env_name`
- List all environments: `conda env list`
- Activate an environment: `source activate env_name`

I also recommend that, optionally, you get familiar with the source code, which is available at `https://github.com/ibm-watson-data-lab/pixiedust` and `https://github.com/ibm-watson-data-lab/pixiegateway`.

We are now ready to explore the PixieDust APIs starting with `sampleData()` in the next section.

SampleData – a simple API for loading data

Loading data into a Notebook is one of the most repetitive tasks a data scientist can do, yet depending on the framework or data source being used, writing the code can be difficult and time-consuming.

Let's take a concrete example of trying to load a CSV file from an open data site (say `https://data.cityofnewyork.us`) into both a pandas and Apache Spark DataFrame.

Note: Going forward, all the code is assumed to run in a Jupyter Notebook.

For pandas, the code is pretty straightforward as it provides an API to directly load from URL:

```
import pandas
data_url = "https://data.cityofnewyork.us/api/views/e98g-f8hy/rows.
csv?accessType=DOWNLOAD"
building_df = pandas.read_csv(data_url)
building_df
```

The last statement, calling `building_df`, will print its contents in the output cell. This is possible without a print because Jupyter is interpreting the last statement of a cell calling a variable as a directive to print it:

	Permit BIN	Permit Application Job Number	Permit Application Document Number	Permit Application Job Type	Permit Type	Permit SubType	Permit Status Description	Permit Sequence Number	Permit Status Date	Permit Issuance Date	Permit Experation Date
0	1083687	102790106	2	A2	PL		PERMIT ISSUED	6	04/12/2011 12:00:00 AM	04/12/2011 12:00:00 AM	04/11/2012 12:00:00 AM
1	1083690	103338201	1	A2	PL		PERMIT ISSUED	7	04/12/2011 12:00:00 AM	04/12/2011 12:00:00 AM	04/11/2012 12:00:00 AM
2	1082870	102785960	2	A2	PL		PERMIT ISSUED	7	04/12/2011 12:00:00 AM	04/12/2011 12:00:00 AM	04/11/2012 12:00:00 AM
3	1083682	102901852	2	A2	PL		PERMIT ISSUED	9	04/12/2011 12:00:00 AM	04/12/2011 12:00:00 AM	04/11/2012 12:00:00 AM
4	1082862	103345337	1	A2	PL		PERMIT ISSUED	7	04/12/2011 12:00:00 AM	04/12/2011 12:00:00 AM	04/11/2012 12:00:00 AM
5	1005283	103878895	2	A2	PL		PERMIT ISSUED	3	04/12/2011 12:00:00 AM	04/12/2011 12:00:00 AM	04/11/2012 12:00:00 AM
6	1082869	102813822	2	A2	PL		PERMIT ISSUED	7	04/12/2011 12:00:00 AM	04/12/2011 12:00:00 AM	04/11/2012 12:00:00 AM

The default output of a pandas DataFrame

However, for Apache Spark, we need to first download the data into a file then use the Spark CSV connector to load it into a DataFrame:

```
#Spark CSV Loading
from pyspark.sql import SparkSession
try:
    from urllib import urlretrieve
except ImportError:
    #urlretrieve package has been refactored in Python 3
    from urllib.request import urlretrieve

data_url = "https://data.cityofnewyork.us/api/views/e98g-f8hy/rows.
csv?accessType=DOWNLOAD"
urlretrieve (data_url, "building.csv")

spark = SparkSession.builder.getOrCreate()
building_df = spark.read\
  .format('org.apache.spark.sql.execution.datasources.csv.
CSVFileFormat')\
  .option('header', True)\
  .load("building.csv")
building_df
```

The output is slightly different since `building_df` is now a Spark DataFrame:

```
DataFrame[Permit BIN: string, Permit Application Job Number: string, Permit Application Document Number: string, Perm
it Application Job Type: string, Permit Type: string, Permit SubType: string, Permit Status Description: string, Perm
it Sequence Number: string, Permit Status Date: string, Permit Issuance Date: string, Permit Experation Date: string]
```

Default output of a Spark DataFrame

Even though this code is not that big, it has to be repeated every time and, most likely, will require spending the time to do a Google search to remember the correct syntax. The data may also be in a different format, for example, JSON, which will require calling different APIs both for pandas and Spark. The data may also not be well-formed and can contain a bad line in a CSV file or have a wrong JSON syntax. All these issues are unfortunately not rare and contribute to the 80/20 rule of data science, which states that data scientists spends on average 80% of their time acquiring, cleaning, and loading data and only 20% doing the actual analysis.

PixieDust provides a simple `sampleData` API to help improve the situation. When called with no parameters, it displays a list of pre-curated datasets ready for analysis:

```
import pixiedust
pixiedust.sampleData()
```

The results are shown as follows:

Id	Name	Topic	Publisher
1	Car performance data	Transportation	IBM
2	Sample retail sales transactions, January 2009	Economy & Business	IBM Cloud Data Services
3	Total population by country	Society	IBM Cloud Data Services
4	GoSales Transactions for Naive Bayes Model	Leisure	IBM
5	Election results by County	Society	IBM
6	Million dollar home sales in NE Mass late 2016	Economy & Business	Redfin.com
7	Boston Crime data, 2-week sample	Society	City of Boston

PixieDust built-in datasets

The list of prebuilt curated datasets can be customized to fit the organization, which is a good step toward our *data* pillar, as described in the previous chapter.

The user can then simply call the `sampleData` API again with the ID of the prebuilt dataset and get a Spark DataFrame if the Spark framework in the Jupyter Kernel is available or fall back to a pandas DataFrame if not.

In the following example, we call `sampleData()` on a Notebook connected with Spark. We also call `enableSparkJobProgressMonitor()` to display real-time information about the Spark jobs involved in the operation.

> **Note:** Spark jobs are processes that run on a particular node in the Spark cluster with a specific subset of the data. In the case of loading a large amount data from a data source, each Spark job is given a specific subset to work on (the actual size depends on the number of nodes in the cluster and the size of the overall data), running in parallel with the other jobs.

In a separate cell, we run the following code to enable the Spark Job Progress Monitor:

```
pixiedust.enableSparkJobProgressMonitor()
```

The results are as follows:

```
Successfully enabled Spark Job Progress Monitor
```

We then invoke `sampleData` to load the `cars` dataset:

```
cars = pixiedust.sampleData(1)
```

The results are shown as follows:

Loading a built-in dataset with PixieDust sampleData API

The user can also pass an arbitrary URL that points to a downloadable file; PixieDust currently supports JSON and CSV files. In this case, PixieDust will automatically download the file, cache it in a temporary area, detect the format, and load it into a Spark or pandas DataFrame depending on whether Spark is available in the Notebook. Note that the user can also force loading into pandas even if Spark is available using the `forcePandas` keyword argument:

```
import pixiedust
data_url = "https://data.cityofnewyork.us/api/views/e98g-f8hy/rows.
csv?accessType=DOWNLOAD"
building_dataframe = pixiedust.sampleData(data_url, forcePandas=True)
```

The results are as follows:

```
Downloading 'https://data.cityofnewyork.us/api/views/e98g-f8hy/rows.
csv?accessType=DOWNLOAD' from https://data.cityofnewyork.us/api/views/
```

```
e98g-f8hy/rows.csv?accessType=DOWNLOAD
Downloaded 13672351 bytes
Creating pandas DataFrame for 'https://data.cityofnewyork.us/api/
views/e98g-f8hy/rows.csv?accessType=DOWNLOAD'. Please wait...
Loading file using 'pandas'
Successfully created pandas DataFrame for 'https://data.cityofnewyork.
us/api/views/e98g-f8hy/rows.csv?accessType=DOWNLOAD'
```

The `sampleData()` API is also smart enough to recognize URLs that point to compressed files of the ZIP and GZ types. In this case, it will automatically unpack the raw binary data and load the file included in the archive. For ZIP files, it looks at the first file in the archive and, for GZ files, it simply decompresses the content as GZ files are not archives and do not contain multiple files. The `sampleData()` API will then load the DataFrame from the decompressed file.

For example, we can directly load borough information from a ZIP file provided by the London open data website and display the results as a pie chart using the `display()` API, as follows:

```
import pixiedust
london_info = pixiedust.sampleData("https://files.datapress.com/
london/dataset/london-borough-profiles/2015-09-24T15:50:01/London-
borough-profiles.zip")
```

The results are as follows (assuming that your Notebook is connected to Spark, otherwise a pandas DataFrame will be loaded):

```
Downloading 'https://files.datapress.com/london/dataset/london-
borough-profiles/2015-09-24T15:50:01/London-borough-profiles.zip'
from https://files.datapress.com/london/dataset/london-borough-
profiles/2015-09-24T15:50:01/London-borough-profiles.zip
Extracting first item in zip file...
File extracted: london-borough-profiles.csv
Downloaded 948147 bytes
Creating pySpark DataFrame for 'https://files.datapress.com/london/
dataset/london-borough-profiles/2015-09-24T15:50:01/London-borough-
profiles.zip'. Please wait...
Loading file using 'com.databricks.spark.csv'
Successfully created pySpark DataFrame for 'https://files.datapress.
com/london/dataset/london-borough-profiles/2015-09-24T15:50:01/London-
borough-profiles.zip'
```

We can then call `display()` on the `london_info` DataFrame, as shown here:

```
display(london_info)
```

We select **Pie Chart** in the Chart menu and in the **Options** dialog, we drag and drop the `Area name` column in the **Keys** area and the `Crime rates per thousand population 2014/15` in the **Values** area, as shown in the following screenshot:

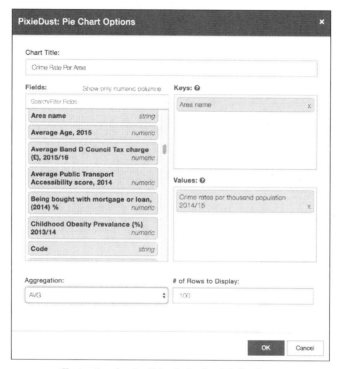

Chart options for visualizing the london_info DataFrame

After clicking on the **OK** button in the **Options** dialog, we get the following results:

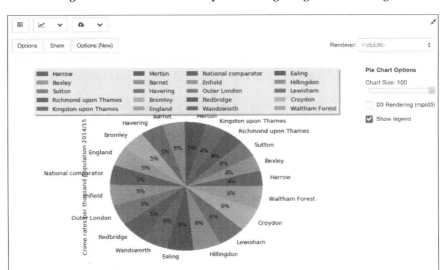

Pie chart created from a URL pointing at a compressed file

Many times, you have found a great dataset, but the file contains errors or the data that's important to you is in the wrong format or buried in some unstructured text that needs to be extracted into its own column. This process is also known as **data wrangling** and can be very time-consuming. In the next section, we will look at an extension to PixieDust called `pixiedust_rosie` that provides a `wrangle_data` method, which helps with this process.

Wrangling data with pixiedust_rosie

Working in a controlled experiment is, most of the time, not the same as working in the real world. By this I mean that, during development, we usually pick (or I should say manufacture) a sample dataset that is designed to behave; it has the right format, it complies with the schema specification, no data is missing, and so on. The goal is to focus on verifying the hypotheses and build the algorithms, and not so much on data cleansing, which can be very painful and time-consuming. However, there is an undeniable benefit to get data that is as close to the real thing as early as possible in the development process. To help with this task, I worked with two IBM colleagues, Jamie Jennings and Terry Antony, who volunteered to build an extension to PixieDust called `pixiedust_rosie`.

This Python package implements a simple `wrangle_data()` method to automate the cleansing of raw data. The `pixiedust_rosie` package currently supports CSV and JSON, but more formats will be added in the future. The underlying data processing engine uses the **Rosie Pattern Language (RPL)** open source component, which is a regular expressions engine designed to be simpler to use for developers, more performant, and scalable to big data. You can find more information about Rosie here: `http://rosie-lang.org`.

To get started, you need to install the `pixiedust_rosie` package using the following command:

```
!pip install pixiedust_rosie
```

The `pixiedust_rosie` package has a dependency on `pixiedust` and `rosie`, which will be automatically downloaded if not already installed on the system.

The `wrangle_data()` method is very similar to the `sampleData()` API. When called with no parameters, it will show you the list of pre-curated datasets, as shown here:

```
import pixiedust_rosie
pixiedust_rosie.wrangle_data()
```

This produces the following results:

Id	Name	Topic	Publisher
1	Car performance data	Transportation	IBM
2	Sample retail sales transactions, January 2009	Economy & Business	IBM Cloud Data Services
3	Total population by country	Society	IBM Cloud Data Services
4	GoSales Transactions for Naive Bayes Model	Leisure	IBM
5	Election results by County	Society	IBM
6	Million dollar home sales in Massachusetts, USA Feb 2017 through Jan 2018	Economy & Business	Redfin.com
7	Boston Crime data, 2-week sample	Society	City of Boston

List of pre-curated datasets available for wrangle_data()

You can also invoke it with the ID of a pre-curated dataset or a URL link, for example, as follows:

```
url = "https://github.com/ibm-watson-data-lab/pixiedust_rosie/raw/
master/sample-data/Healthcare_Cost_and_Utilization_Project__HCUP__-_
National_Inpatient_Sample.csv"
pixiedust_rosie.wrangle_data(url)
```

In the preceding code, we invoke `wrangle_data()` on a CSV file referenced by the `url` variable. The function starts by downloading the file in the local filesystem and performs an automated data classification on a subset of the data, to infer the data schema. A schema editor PixieApp is then launched, which provides a set of wizard screens to let the user configure the schema. For example, the user will be able to drop and rename columns and, more importantly, destructure existing columns into new columns by providing Rosie patterns.

The workflow is illustrated in the following diagram:

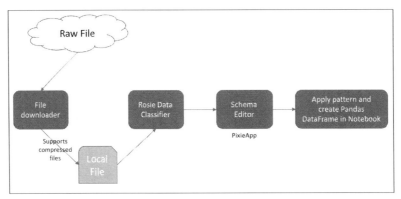

wrangle_data() workflow

The first screen of the `wrangle_data()` wizard shows the schema that has been inferred by the Rosie data classifier as shown in the following screenshot:

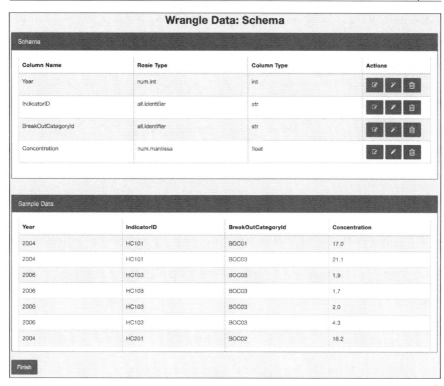

The wrangle_data() schema editor

The preceding schema widget shows the column names, `Rosie Type` (advanced type representation specific to Rosie) and `Column Type` (map to the supported pandas types). Each row also contains three action buttons:

- **Delete column**: This removes the columns from the schema. This column will not appear in the final pandas DataFrame.
- **Rename column**: This changes the name of the column.
- **Transform column**: This transforms a column by destructuring it into new columns.

At any time, the user is able to preview the data (shown in the preceding SampleData widget) to validate that the schema configuration is behaving as intended.

When the user clicks on the transform column button, a new screen is shown that lets the user specify patterns for building new columns. In some cases, the data classifier will be able to automatically detect the patterns, in which case, a button will be added to ask the user whether the suggestions should be applied.

The following screenshot shows the **Transform Selected Column** screen with automated suggestions:

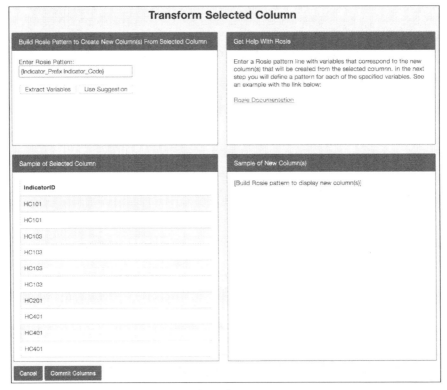

Transform column screen

This screen shows four widgets with the following information:

- Rosie Pattern input is where you can enter a custom Rosie Pattern that represents the data for this column. You then use the **Extract Variables** button to tell the schema editor which part of the pattern should be extracted into a new column (more on that is explained soon).

- There's a help widget that provides a link to the RPL documentation.
- There's a preview of the data for the current column.
- There's a preview of the data with the Rosie Pattern applied.

When the user clicks on the **Extract Variables** button, the widget is updated as follow:

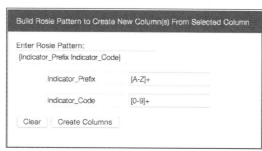

Extracting Rosie variables into columns

At this point, the user has the option to edit the definition and then click on the **Create Columns** button to add the new columns to the schema. The **Sample of New Column(s)** widget is then updated to show a preview of what the data would look like. An error is shown in this widget if the pattern definition contains bad syntax:

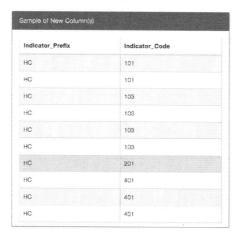

Preview of new columns after applying pattern definitions

When the user clicks on the **Commit Columns** button, the main schema editor screen is displayed again with the new columns added, as shown in the following screenshot:

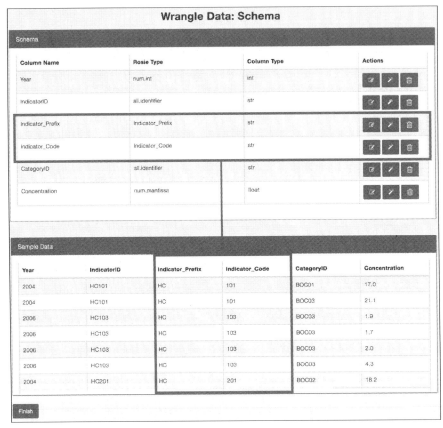

Schema editor with new columns

The final step is to click on the **Finish** button to apply the schema definition to the raw file and create a pandas DataFrame that will be available as a variable in the Notebook. At this point, the user is presented with a dialog box that contains a default variable name that can be edited, as shown in the following screenshot:

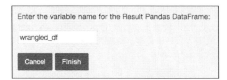

Edit the variable name for the Result Pandas DataFrame

After clicking on the **Finish** button, `pixiedust_rosie` goes over the entire dataset, applying the schema definition. When done, it creates a new cell just below the current one with a generated code that invokes the `display()` API on the newly generated pandas DataFrame, as shown here:

```
#Code generated by pixiedust_rosie
display(wrangled_df)
```

Running the preceding cell will let you explore and visualize the new dataset.

The `wrangle_data()` capability we've explored in this section is a first step toward helping data scientists spend less time cleaning the data and more time analyzing it. In the next section, we will discuss how to help data scientists with data exploration and visualization.

Display – a simple interactive API for data visualization

Data visualization is another very important data science task that is indispensable for exploring and forming hypotheses. Fortunately, the Python ecosystem has a lot of powerful libraries dedicated to data visualization, such as these popular examples:

- Matplotlib: `http://matplotlib.org`
- Seaborn: `https://seaborn.pydata.org`
- Bokeh: `http://bokeh.pydata.org`
- Brunel: `https://brunelvis.org`

However, similar to data loading and cleaning, using these libraries in a Notebook can be difficult and time-consuming. Each of these libraries come with their own programming model and APIs are not always easy to learn and use, especially if you are not an experienced developer. Another issue is that these libraries do not have a high-level interface to commonly used data processing frameworks such as pandas (except maybe Matplotlib) or Apache Spark and, as a result, a lot of data preparation is needed before plotting the data.

To help with this problem, PixieDust provides a simple `display()` API that enables Jupyter Notebook users to plot data using an interactive graphical interface and without any required coding. This API doesn't actually create charts but does all the heavy lifting of preparing the data before delegating to a renderer by calling its APIs according to the user selection.

The `display()` API supports multiple data structures (pandas, Spark, and JSON) as well as multiple renderers (Matplotlib, Seaborn, Bokeh, and Brunel).

As an illustration, let's use the built-in car performance dataset and start visualizing the data by calling the `display()` API:

```
import pixiedust
cars = pixiedust.sampleData(1, forcePandas=True) #car performance data
display(cars)
```

The first time the command is called on the cell, a tabular view is displayed and, as the user navigates through the menus, selected options are stored in the cell metadata as JSON so they can be used again the next time the cell is running. The output layout for all the visualizations follows the same pattern:

- There's an extensible top-level menu for switching between charts.
- There's a download menu for downloading the file in the local machine.
- There's a filter toggle button that lets users refine their exploration by filtering the data. We'll discuss the filter capability in the *Filtering* section.
- There's a Expand/Collapse Pixiedust Output button for collapsing/expanding the output content.
- There's an **Options** button that invokes a dialog box with configurations specific to the current visualization.
- There's a **Share** button that lets you publish the visualization on the web.

 Note: This button can only be used if you have deployed a PixieGateway, which we'll discuss in detail in *Chapter 4, Deploying PixieApps to the Web with the PixieGateway Server*.

- There's a contextual set of options on the right-hand side of the visualization.
- There's the main visualization area.

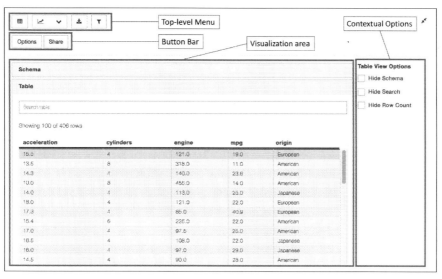

Visualization output layout for the table renderer

To start creating a chart, first select the appropriate type in the menu. Out of the box, PixieDust supports six types of charts: **Bar Chart**, **Line Chart**, **Scatter Plot**, **Pie Chart**, **Map**, and **Histogram**. As we'll see in *Chapter 5*, *Best Practices and Advanced PixieDust Concepts*, PixieDust also provides APIs to let you customize these menus by adding new ones or adding options to existing ones:

PixieDust Charts menu

The first time a chart menu is called, an options dialog will be displayed to configure a set of basic configuration options, such as what to use for the X and Y axes, the type of aggregation, and many more. To save you time, the dialog will be prepopulated with the data schema that PixieDust automatically introspected from the DataFrame.

In the following example, we will create a bar chart showing the average mileage consumption by horsepower:

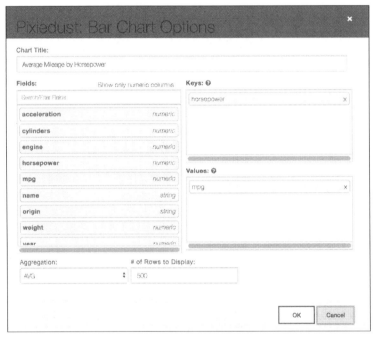

Bar chart dialog options

Clicking **OK** will display the interactive interface in the cell output area:

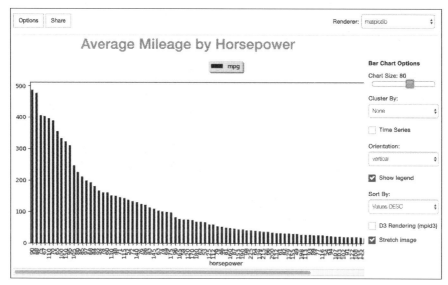

Bar chart visualization

The canvas shows the chart in the center area and some contextual options on the side relevant to the type of chart selected. For example, we can select the field **origin** in the **Cluster By** combobox to show a breakdown by country of origin:

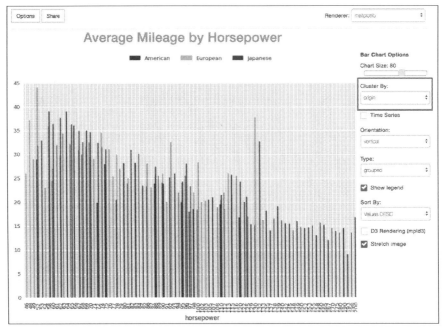

Clustered bar chart visualization

As mentioned before, PixieDust `display()` doesn't actually create the chart, rather it prepares the data based on the selected options and does the heavy lifting of calling the APIs of a renderer engine, with the correct parameters. The goal behind this design is for each chart type to support multiple renderers without any extra coding, providing as much freedom of exploration to the user as possible.

Out of the box, PixieDust supports the following renderers provided that the corresponding libraries are installed. For those that are not installed, a warning will be generated in the PixieDust log and the corresponding renderer will not be displayed in the menu. We'll cover in detail the PixieDust log in *Chapter 5, Best Practices and Advanced PixieDust Concepts.*

- Matplotlib (https://matplotlib.org)
- Seaborn (https://seaborn.pydata.org)

 This library needs to be installed using: !pip install seaborn.

- Bokeh (https://bokeh.pydata.org)

 This library needs to be installed using: !pip install bokeh.

- Brunel (https://brunelvis.org)

 This library needs to be installed using: !pip install brunel.

- Google Map (https://developers.google.com/maps)
- Mapbox (https://www.mapbox.com)

 Note: Google Map and Mapbox require an API key that you can obtain on their respective sites.

You can switch between renderers using the **Renderer** combobox. For example, if we want more interactivity to explore the chart (such as zooming and panning), we can use the Bokeh renderer instead of Matplotlib, which gives us only a static image:

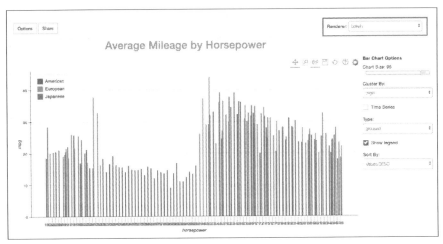

Cluster bar chart using the Bokeh renderer

Another chart type worth mentioning is Map, which is interesting when your data contains geospatial information, such as longitude, latitude, or country/state information. PixieDust supports multiple types of geo-mapping rendering engines including the popular Mapbox engine.

 Before using the Mapbox renderer, it is recommended to get an API key from the Mapbox site at this location: (https://www.mapbox.com/help/how-access-tokens-work). However, if you don't have one, a default key will be provided by PixieDust.

To create a Map chart, let's use the *Million-dollar home sales in NE Mass* dataset, as follows:

```
import pixiedust
homes = pixiedust.sampleData(6, forcePandas=True) #Million dollar home
sales in NE Mass
display(homes)
```

First, select **Map** in the chart drop-down button, then in the options dialog, select LONGITUDE and LATITUDE as the keys and enter the Mapbox access token in the provided input. You can add multiples fields in the **Values** area, and they will be displayed as tooltips on the map:

Options dialog for Mapbox charts

When clicking the **OK** button, you'll get an interactive map that you can customize using the style (simple, choropleth, or density map), color, and basemap (light, satellite, dark, and outdoors) options:

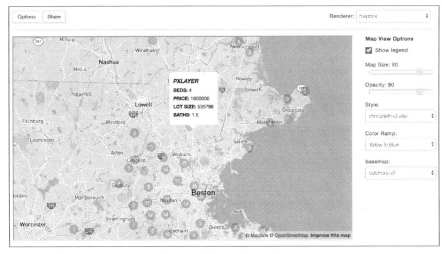

Interactive Mapbox visualization

Each chart type has its own set of contextual options, which are self-explanatory, and I encourage you at this point to play with each and every one of them. If you find issues or have enhancement ideas, you can always create a new issue on GitHub at `https://github.com/ibm-watson-data-lab/pixiedust/issues` or, better yet, submit a pull request with your code changes (there's more information on how to do that here: `https://help.github.com/articles/creating-a-pull-request`).

To avoid reconfiguring the chart every time the cell runs, PixieDust stores the chart options as a JSON object in the cell metadata, which is eventually saved in the Notebook. You can manually inspect this data by selecting the **View | Cell Toolbar | Edit Metadata** menu, as shown in the following screenshot:

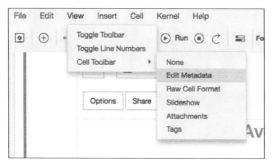

Show Edit Metadata button

An **Edit Metadata** button will be shown at the top of the cell, which, when clicked on, displays the PixieDust configuration:

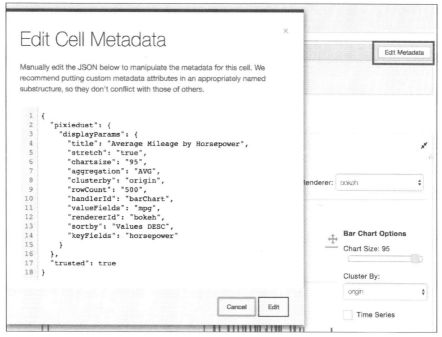

Edit Cell Metadata dialog

This JSON configuration will be important when we discuss PixieApps in the next section.

Filtering

To better explore data, PixieDust also provides a built-in, simple graphical interface that lets you quickly filter the data being visualized. You can quickly invoke the filter by clicking on the filter toggle button in the top-level menu. To keep things simple, the filter only supports building predicates based on one column only, which is sufficient in most cases to validate simple hypotheses (based on feedback, this feature may be enhanced in the future to support multiple predicates). The filter UI will automatically let you select the column to filter on and, based on its type, will show different options:

- **Numerical type**: The user can select a mathematical comparator and enter a value for the operand. For convenience, the UI will also show statistical values related to the chosen column, which can be used when picking the operand value:

Filter on the mpg numerical column of the cars data set

- **String type**: The user can enter an expression to match the column value, which can be either a regular expression or a plain string. For convenience, the UI also shows basic help on how to build a regular expression:

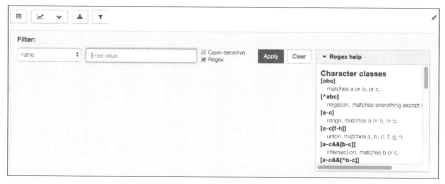

Filter on the name String type of the cars dataset

When clicking on the **Apply** button, the current visualization is updated to reflect the filter configuration. It is important to note that the filter applies to the whole cell and not only to the current visualization. Therefore, it will continue to apply when switching between chart types. The filter configuration is also saved in the cell metadata, so it will be preserved when saving the Notebook and rerunning the cell.

For example, the following screenshot visualizes the cars dataset as a bar chart showing only the rows with mpg greater than 23, which, according to the statistics box, is the mean for the dataset, and clustered by years. In the options dialog, we select the mpg column as the key and origin as the value:

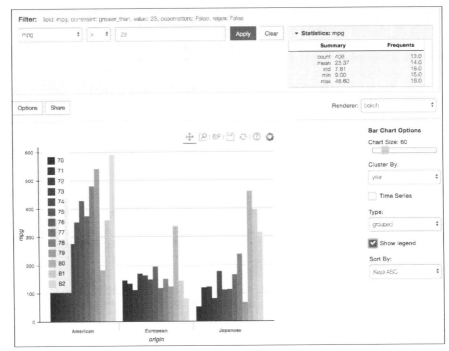

Filtered bar chart for the cars dataset

To summarize, in this section, we've discussed how PixieDust can help with three difficult and time-consuming data science tasks: data loading, data wrangling, and data visualization. Next, we are going to see how PixieDust can help increase collaboration between data scientists and developers.

Bridging the gap between developers and data scientists with PixieApps

Solving hard data problems is only part of the mission given to data science teams. They also need to make sure that data science results get properly operationalized to deliver business value to the organization. Operationalizing data analytics is very much use case - dependent. It could mean, for example, creating a dashboard that synthesizes insights for decision makers or integrating a machine learning model, such as a recommendation engine, into a web application.

In most cases, this is where data science meets software engineering (or as some would say, *where the rubber meets the road*). Sustained collaboration between the teams — instead of a one-time handoff — is key to a successful completion of the task. More often than not, they also have to grapple with different languages and platforms, leading to significant code rewrites by the software engineering team.

We experienced it firsthand in our *Sentiment analysis of Twitter hashtags* project when we needed to build a real-time dashboard to visualize the results. The data analytics was written in Python using pandas, Apache Spark, and a few plotting libraries such as Matplotlib and Bokeh, while the dashboard was written in Node.js (`https://nodejs.org`) and D3 (`https://d3js.org`).

We also needed to build a data interface between the analytics and the dashboard and, since we needed the system to be real-time, we chose to use Apache Kafka to stream events formatted with the analytics results.

The following diagram generalizes an approach that I call the **hand-off pattern** where the data science team builds the analytics and deploys the results in a data interface layer. The results are then consumed by the application. The data layer is usually handled by the data engineer, which is one of the roles we discussed in *Chapter 1, Perspectives on Data Science from a Developer*:

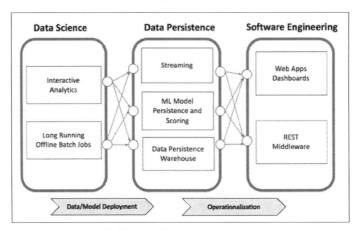

Hand-off between data science and engineering

The problem with this hand-off pattern is that it is not conducive to rapid iteration. Any changes in the data layer need to be synchronized with the software engineering team to avoid breaking the application. The idea behind PixieApps is to build the application while staying as close as possible to the data science environment, which is, in our case, the Jupyter Notebook. With this approach, the analytics are directly called from the PixieApp, which runs embedded in the Jupyter Notebook, hence making it easy for data scientists and developers to collaborate and iterate to make rapid improvements.

PixieApp defines a simple programming model for building single-page applications with direct access to the IPython Notebook Kernel (which is the Python backend process running the Notebook code). In essence, a PixieApp is a Python class that encapsulates both the presentation and business logic. The presentation is composed of a set of special methods called routes that return an arbitrary HTML fragment. Each PixieApp has a default route that returns the HTML fragment for the starting page. Developers can use custom HTML attributes to invoke other routes and dynamically update all or part of the page. A route may, for example, invoke a machine learning algorithm created from within the Notebook or generate a chart using the PixieDust display framework.

The following diagram shows the high-level architecture of how PixieApps interact with the Jupyter Notebook client frontend and the IPython Kernel:

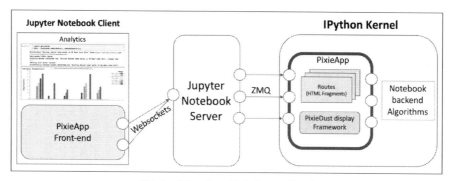

PixieApp interaction with the Jupyter Kernel

As a preview of what a PixieApp looks like, here's a *hello world* sample application that has one button showing a bar chart for the cars DataFrame we created in the previous section:

```
#import the pixieapp decorators
from pixiedust.display.app import *

#Load the cars dataframe into the Notebook
cars = pixiedust.sampleData(1)

@PixieApp    #decorator for making the class a PixieApp
class HelloWorldApp():
    #decorator for making a method a
    #route (no arguments means default route)
    @route()
    def main_screen(self):
        return """
        <button type="submit" pd_options="show_chart=true" pd_
target="chart">Show Chart</button>
        <!--Placeholder div to display the chart-->
        <div id="chart"></div>
        """

    @route(show_chart="true")
    def chart(self):
        #Return a div bound to the cars dataframe
        #using the pd_entity attribute
        #pd_entity can refer a class variable or
```

```
        #a global variable scoped to the notebook
        return """
        <div pd_render_onload pd_entity="cars">
            <pd_options>
                {
                    "title": "Average Mileage by Horsepower",
                    "aggregation": "AVG",
                    "clusterby": "origin",
                    "handlerId": "barChart",
                    "valueFields": "mpg",
                    "rendererId": "bokeh",
                    "keyFields": "horsepower"
                }
            </pd_options>
        </div>
        """
#Instantiate the application and run it
app = HelloWorldApp()
app.run()
```

When the preceding code runs in a Notebook cell, we get the following results:

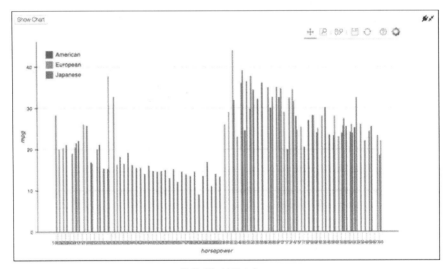

Hello World PixieApp

You probably have a lot of questions about the preceding code, but don't worry. In the next chapters, we'll cover all the PixieApp technical details, including how to use them in end-to-end pipelines.

Architecture for operationalizing data science analytics

In the previous section, we saw how PixieApps combined with the PixieDust display framework offer an easy way to build powerful dashboards that connect directly with your data analytics, allowing for rapid iterations between the algorithms and the user interface. This is great for rapid prototyping, but Notebooks are not suitable to be used in a production environment where the target persona is the line of business user. One obvious solution would be to rewrite the PixieApp using a traditional three tiers web application architecture, for example, as follows:

- React (`https://reactjs.org`) for the presentation layer
- Node.js for the web layer
- A data access library targeted at the web analytics layer for machine learning scoring or running any other analytic jobs

However, this would provide only a marginal improvement over the existing process, which would consist only, in this case, of the ability to do iterative implementation with the PixieApp.

A much better solution would be to directly deploy and run PixieApps as web applications, including the analytics in the surrounding Notebook and, while we're at it, without any code change.

Using this model, Jupyter Notebooks would become the central tool for a simplified development life cycle, as shown in the following diagram:

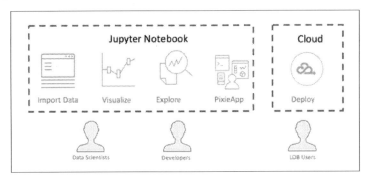

Data science pipeline development life cycle

1. Data scientists use a Python Notebook to load, enrich, and analyze data and create analytics (machine learning models, statistics, and so on)

2. From the same Notebook, developers create a PixieApp to operationalize these analytics

3. Once ready, developers publish the PixieApp as a web application, where it can be easily consumed interactively by line-of-business users without the need to access Notebooks

PixieDust provides an implementation of this solution with the PixieGateway component. PixieGateway is a web application server responsible for loading and running PixieApps. It is built on top of the Jupyter Kernel Gateway (`https://github.com/jupyter/kernel_gateway`), which itself is built on top of the Tornado web framework, and therefore follows an architecture as shown in the following diagram:

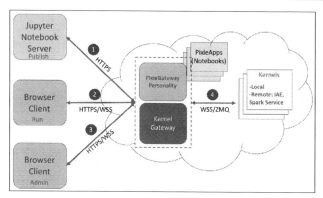

PixieGateway architecture diagram

1. The PixieApp is published into the PixieGateway server directly from the Notebook and a URL is generated. Behind the scene, PixieGateway allocates a Jupyter Kernel to run the PixieApp. Based on configuration, the PixieApp could share the kernel instance with other apps or have a dedicated kernel based on needs. The PixieGateway middleware can scale horizontally by managing the lifecycle of multiple kernels instances, which themselves can either be local to the server or remote on a cluster.

> **Note**: Remote kernels must be Jupyter Kernel Gateways.

Using the publishing wizard, the user can optionally define security for the application. Multiple options are available including Basic Authentication, OAuth 2.0, and Bearer Token.

2. The line of business users accesses the app from their browser using the URL from step 1.

3. PixieGateway provides a comprehensive admin console for managing the server including configuring the applications, configuring and monitoring kernels, access to the logs for troubleshooting, and so on.

4. The PixieGateway manages sessions for each active user and dispatches requests to the appropriate kernels for execution using the IPython messaging protocol (`http://jupyter-client.readthedocs.io/en/latest/messaging.html`) over WebSocket or ZeroMQ depending on whether the Kernel is local or remote.

When productizing your analytics, this solution provides a major improvement over the classic three-tier web application architecture because it collapses the web and the data tier into one **web analytics tiers,** as shown in the following diagram:

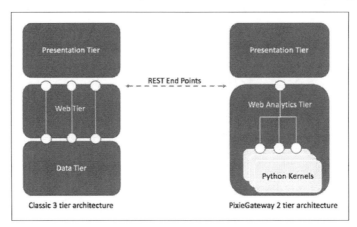

Comparison between classic three tiers and PixieGateway web architecture

In the classic three-tier architecture, developers have to maintain multiple REST endpoints that invoke the analytics in the data tier and massage the data to comply with the presentation tier requirements for correctly displaying the data. As a result, a lot of engineering has to be added to these endpoints, increasing the cost of development and code maintenance. In contrast, in the PixieGateway two-tier architecture, developers do not have to worry about creating endpoints because the server is responsible for dispatching the requests to the appropriate kernel using built-in generic endpoints. Explained another way, the PixieApp Python methods automatically become endpoints for the presentation tier without any code change. This model is conducive to rapid iterations since any change in the Python code is directly reflected in the application after republishing.

PixieApps are great to rapidly build single-page applications and dashboards. However, you may also want to generate simpler one-page reports and share them with your users. To that end, PixieGateway also lets you share charts generated by the display() API using the **Share** button, resulting in a URL linking to a web page containing the chart. In turn, a user can embed the chart into a website or a blog post by copying and pasting the code generated for the page.

Note: We'll cover PixieGateway in details in *Chapter 4, Deploying PixieApps to the Web with the PixieGateway Server*, including how to install a new instance both locally and on the cloud.

To demonstrate this capability, let's use the cars DataFrame created earlier:

Share Chart dialog

If sharing is successful, then the next page will show the generated URL and the code snippet to embed into a web application or blog post:

Confirmation of a shared chart

Clicking on the link will take you to the page:

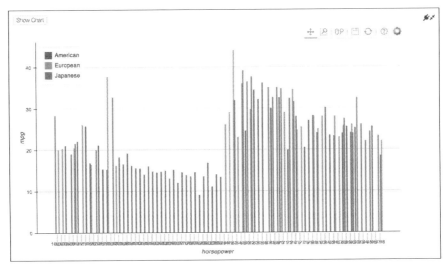

Display chart as a web page

Summary

In this chapter, we discussed the reasons why our data science tooling strategy was centered around Python and Jupyter Notebook. We also introduced the PixieDust capabilities that improve user productivity with features such as the following:

- Data loading and cleaning
- Data visualization and exploration without any coding
- A simple programming model based on HTML and CSS, called PixieApp, for building tools and dashboards that interact directly with the Notebook
- A point and click mechanism to publish charts and PixieApp directly to the web

In the next chapter, we'll do a deep dive on the PixieApp programming model, discussing every aspect of the APIs with numerous code samples.

3
PixieApp under the Hood

"Every vision is a joke until the first man accomplishes it; once realized, it becomes commonplace."

– Robert H Goddard

In this chapter, we will do a technical deep dive into the PixieApp framework. You will be able to use the following information both as a *Getting Started* tutorial and as reference documentation for the PixieApp programming model.

We will start with a high-level description of the anatomy of a PixieApp before diving in to its foundational concepts, such as routes and requests. To help follow along, we will incrementally build a *GitHub Tracking* sample application that applies the capabilities and best practices as they are being introduced, starting from building the data analytics to integrating them into the PixieApp.

By the end of this chapter, you should be able to apply the lessons learned to your own use case, including writing your own PixieApp.

Note: The PixieApp programming model doesn't require any prior experience with JavaScript, however, it is expected that the reader is familiar with the following:

- Python (https://www.python.org)
- HTML5 (https://www.w3schools.com/html)
- CSS3 (https://www.w3schools.com/css)

Anatomy of a PixieApp

The term **PixieApp** stands for **Pixie Application,** and is meant to emphasize its tight integration with the PixieDust capabilities, especially the `display()` API. Its main goal is to make it easy for developers to build a user interface that can invoke the data analytics implemented in the Jupyter Notebook.

A PixieApp follows the **single-page application (SPA)** design pattern (https:// en.wikipedia.org/wiki/Single-page_application), where the user is presented with a welcome screen that is dynamically updated to respond to a user interaction. An update can be a partial refresh, such as updating a graph after the user clicks on a control or a full refresh, such as a new screen in a multistep process. In each case, the update is controlled on the server side by a route that is triggered using a specific mechanism that we'll discuss later. When triggered, the route executes code to handle the request and then emits an HTML fragment, which is applied to the right target DOM element (https://www.w3schools.com/js/js_htmldom.asp) on the client side.

The following sequence diagram shows how the client side and server side interact with each other when running a PixieApp:

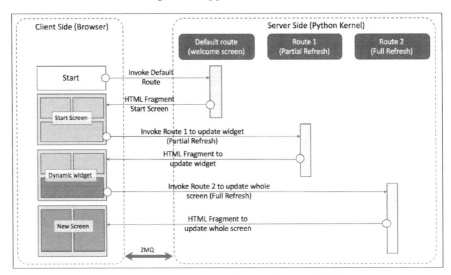

Sequence diagram showing the information flow of a PixieApp

When the PixieApp is started (by calling the `run` method), the default route is invoked, and the corresponding HTML fragment is returned. As the user interacts with the application, more requests are executed, triggering the associated routes which refresh the UI accordingly.

From an implementation perspective, a PixieApp is simply a regular Python class that has been decorated with the `@PixieApp` decorator. Under the cover, the `PixieApp` decorator instruments the class to add methods and fields required to run the app, such as the `run` method.

 More information on Python decorators can be found here:

https://wiki.python.org/moin/PythonDecorators

To get things started, the following code shows a simple *Hello World* PixieApp:

```
#import the pixieapp decorators
from pixiedust.display.app import *

@PixieApp    #decorator for making the class a PixieApp
class HelloWorldApp():
    @route()   #decorator for making a method a route (no arguments
means default route)
    def main_screen(self):
        return """<div>Hello World</div>"""

#Instantiate the application and run it
app = HelloWorldApp()
app.run()
```

 You can find the code here:

https://github.com/DTAIEB/Thoughtful-Data-Science/
blob/master/chapter%203/sampleCode1.py

The preceding code shows the structure of a PixieApp, how to define the routes, and how to instantiate and run the app. Because PixieApps are regular Python classes, they can inherit from other classes, including other PixieApps, which is convenient for larger projects to make the code modular and reusable.

Routes

Routes are used to dynamically update all or part of the client screen. They can be easily defined by using the @route decorator on any class method, based on the following rules:

- A route method is required to return a string that represents the HTML fragment for the update.

 Note: CSS and JavaScript are allowed to be used in the fragment.

- The @route decorator can have one or more keyword arguments, which are required to be of the String type. These keyword arguments can be thought of as request parameters, which are used internally by the PixieApp framework to dispatch the request to the route that is the best match according to the following rules:
    - The routes with most arguments are always evaluated first.
    - All arguments must match for a route to be selected.
    - If the route is not found, then the default route is selected as a fallback.
    - Routes can be configured using a wildcard, that is, *, in which case, any value for the state argument will be a match.

    Following is an example:

    ```
    @route(state1="value1", state2="value2")
    ```

- A PixieApp is required to have one, and only one, default route, which is a route with no argument, that is, @route().

It is very important to configure the routes in a way that doesn't cause conflict, especially if your application has hierarchical states. For example, a route associated with state1="load" could be responsible for loading data and then a second route associated with (state1="load", state2="graph") could be responsible for plotting the data. In this case, a request with both state1 and state2 specified will match the second route because route evaluation happens from most specific to least specific, stopping at the first matching route.

To clarify, the following diagram shows how requests are matched with routes:

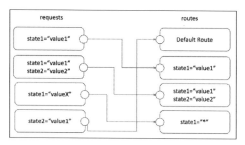

Matching requests to routes

The expected contract for a method defined as a route is to return an HTML fragment, which can contain Jinja2 templating constructs. Jinja2 is a powerful Python template engine that provides a rich set of features to dynamically generate text, including access to Python variables, methods, and control structures, such as `if...else`, the `for` loop, and so on. Covering all its features would be beyond the scope of this book, but let's discuss a few important constructs that are used frequently:

 Note: If you want to know more about Jinja2, you can read the full documentation here:

`http://jinja.pocoo.org/docs/templates`

- **Variables**: You can use the double-curly braces to access variables that are in scope, for example, `"<div>This is my variable {{my_var}}</div>"`. During rendering, the `my_var` variable will be replaced with its actual value. You can also use the `.` (dot) notation to access complex object, for example, `"<div>This is a nested value {{my_var.sub_value}}</div>"`.

- **for loop**: You can use the `{%for ...%}...{%endfor%}` notation to dynamically generate text by iterating over a sequence of items (list, tuple, dictionary, and so on), as in the example:

```
{%for message in messages%}
<li>{{message}}</li>
{%endfor%}
```

- **if statement**: You can use the `{%if ...%}...{%elif ...%}...{%else%}...{%endif%}` notation to conditionally output text, as in the example:

```
{%if status.error%}
<div class="error">{{status.error}}</div>
{%elif status.warning%}
```

```
<div class="warning">{{status.warning}}</div>
{%else%}
<div class="ok">{{status.message}}</div>
{%endif%}
```

It is also important to know how variables and methods come into the scope of the JinJa2 template string returned by the route. PixieApp automatically provides access to three types of variables and methods:

- **Class variables and methods**: These are accessible using the `this` keyword.

 Note: The reason we're not using the more Pythonic `self` keyword is that it is unfortunately already taken by Jinja2 itself.

- **Method arguments**: This is useful when the route arguments use the `*` value and you want to have access to that value at runtime. In this case, you can add arguments to the method itself using the same name as the one defined in the route arguments and the PixieApp framework will automatically pass the correct value.

 Note: The order of the arguments actually doesn't matter. You also do not have to use every argument defined in the route, which is convenient if you are only interested in using a subset of the arguments.

The variable will also be in the scope of the Jinja2 template string, as shown in the example:

```
@route(state1="*", state2="*")
def my_method(self, state1, state2):
    return "<div>State1 is {{state1}}. State2 is {{state2}}</div>"
```

 You can find the code file here:

https://github.com/DTAIEB/Thoughtful-Data-Science/
blob/master/chapter%203/sampleCode2.py

- **Local variables to the method**: PixieApp will automatically put all the local variables defined in the method in scope of the Jinja2 template string, provided that you add the `@templateArgs` decorator to the method, as shown in the example:

```
@route()
@templateArgs
def main_screen(self):
    var1 = self.compute_something()
    var2 = self.compute_something_else()
```

```
return "<div>var1 is {{var1}}. var2 is {{var2}}</div>"
```

 You can find the code here:
https://github.com/DTAIEB/Thoughtful-Data-Science/
blob/master/chapter%203/sampleCode3.py

Generating requests to routes

As mentioned before, PixieApp follows the SPA design pattern. After the first screen is loaded, all subsequent interactions with the server are done using dynamic requests as opposed to URL links as is the case for multipage web applications. There are three ways to generate a kernel request to a route:

- Use the `pd_options` custom attribute to define a list of states to be passed to the server, as in the following example:

  ```
  pd_options="state1=value1;state2=value2;..;staten=valuen"
  ```

- If you already have a JSON object that contains the `pd_options` value—as in the case of invoking `display()`—you would have to transform it into the format expected by the `pd_options` HTML attribute, which can be time-consuming. In this case, it is more convenient to specify `pd_options` as a child element, which allows the options to be passed directly as a JSON object (and avoid the extra work of transforming the data), as in the following example:

  ```
  <div>
      <pd_options>
          {"state1":"value1","state2":"value2",...,
          "staten":"valuen"}
      </pd_options>
  </div>
  ```

- Programmatically by calling the `invoke_route` method, as in the following example:

  ```
  self.invoke_route(self.route_method, state1='value1',
  state2='value2')
  ```

 Note: Remember to use `this`, as opposed to `self`, if you are calling this method from a Jinja2 template string, as `self` is already used by Jinja2 itself.

When the state values passed in `pd_options` need to be dynamically computed based on user selections, you need to use the `$val(arg)` special directive, which acts as a macro that will be resolved at the time the kernel request is executed.

The `$val(arg)` directive takes one argument that can be one of the following:

- The ID of an HTML element on the page, such as an input or a combobox, as in the following example:

```
<div>
    <pd_options>
        {"state1":"$val(my_element_id)","state2":"value2"}
    <pd_options>
</div>
```

- A JavaScript function that must return the desired value, as in the following example:

```
<script>
    function resValue(){
            return "my_query";
    }
</script>
...
<div pd_options="state1=$val(resValue)"></div>
```

 Note: Dynamic value using the `$val` directive are supported by most of the PixieDust custom attributes.

A GitHub project tracking sample application

Let's apply what we learned so far to implementing the sample application. To try things out, we want to use the GitHub Rest APIs (`https://developer.github.com/v3`) to search for projects and load the results into a pandas DataFrame for analysis.

The initial code shows the welcome screen with a simple input box to enter the GitHub query and a button to submit the request:

```
from pixiedust.display.app import *

@PixieApp
class GitHubTracking():
    @route()
    def main_screen(self):
        return """
<style>
    div.outer-wrapper {
```

```
        display: table;width:100%;height:300px;
    }
    div.inner-wrapper {
        display: table-cell;vertical-align: middle;
        height: 100%;width: 100%;
    }
</style>
<div class="outer-wrapper">
    <div class="inner-wrapper">
        <div class="col-sm-3"></div>
        <div class="input-group col-sm-6">
            <input id="query{{prefix}}" type="text"
             class="form-control"
             placeholder="Search projects on GitHub">
            <span class="input-group-btn">
                <button class="btn btn-default"
                  type="button">Submit Query</button>
            </span>
        </div>
    </div>
</div>
"""

app = GitHubTracking()
app.run()
```

 You can find the code file here:

https://github.com/DTAIEB/Thoughtful-Data-Science/
blob/master/chapter%203/sampleCode4.py

A few things to note from the preceding code:

- The Bootstrap CSS framework (https://getbootstrap.com/docs/3.3) and the jQuery JS framework (https://jquery.com) are provided by the Jupyter Notebook. We can readily use them in our code without the need to install them.

- Font Awesome icons (https://fontawesome.com) are also available by default in the Notebook.

- The PixieApp code could be executed in multiple cells of the Notebook. Since we're relying on DOM element IDs, it is important to make sure that two elements do not have the same ID which would cause undesirable side effects. To that end, it is recommended to always include the unique identifier {{prefix}}, provided by the PixieDust framework, for example, "query{{prefix}}".

The results are shown in the following screenshot:

Welcome screen of our GitHub Tracking application

The next step is to create a new route that takes the user value and returns the results. This route will be invoked by the **Submit Query** button.

To keep things simple, the following code doesn't use a Python library to interface with GitHub, such as PyGithub (`http://pygithub.readthedocs.io/en/latest`), instead, we'll directly call the REST APIs as documented in the GitHub website:

> **Note**: When you see the following notation `[[GitHubTracking]]`, this means that the code is meant to be added to the `GitHubTracking` PixieApp class and, to avoid repeating the surrounding code over and over again, it has been omitted. When in doubt, you can always refer to the complete Notebook specified at the end of the section.

```python
import requests
import pandas
[[GitHubTracking]]
@route(query="*")
@templateArgs
def do_search(self, query):
    response = requests.get( "https://api.github.com/search/
repositories?q={}".format(query))
    frames = [pandas.DataFrame(response.json()['items'])]
    while response.ok and "next" in response.links:
        response = requests.get(response.links['next']['url'])
        frames.append(pandas.DataFrame(response.json()['items']))

    pdf = pandas.concat(frames)
    response = requests.get( "https://api.github.com/search/
repositories?q={}".format(query))
    if not response.ok:
```

```
    return "<div>An Error occurred: {{response.text}}</div>"
  return """<h1><center>{{pdf|length}} repositories were found</
center></h1>"""
```

 You can find the code file here:
https://github.com/DTAIEB/Thoughtful-Data-Science/
blob/master/chapter%203/sampleCode5.py

In the preceding code, we created a route called do_search that takes one argument called query, which we use to build an API URL to GitHub. Using the requests Python module (http://docs.python-requests.org) to issue a GET request to this URL, we get a JSON payload that we turn into a pandas DataFrame. According to the GitHub documentation, the Search API paginates with the next page being stored in the link's headers. The code uses a while loop to go over each link and load the next page into a new DataFrame. We then concatenate all the DataFrames into one called pdf. All we have left to do is build the HTML fragment that will display the results. The fragment uses the Jinja2 notation {{...}} to access the pdf variable defined as a local variable, which only works because we used the @templateArgs decorator in the do_search method. Notice that we also use a Jinja2 filter called length to display the number of repositories found: {{pdf|length}}.

 For more information on filters, visit the following:
http://jinja.pocoo.org/docs/templates/#filters

We still need to invoke the do_search route when the user clicks on the **Submit Query** button. For that, we add the pd_options attribute to the <button> element, as highlighted here:

```
<div class="input-group col-sm-6">
    <input id="query{{prefix}}" type="text"
     class="form-control"
     placeholder="Search projects on GitHub">
    <span class="input-group-btn">
        <button class="btn btn-default"
         type="button"
         pd_options="query=$val(query{{prefix}})">
            Submit Query
        </button>
    </span>
</div>
```

We use the $val() directive in the pd_options attribute to dynamically retrieve the value of the input box with ID equals to "query{{prefix}}" and store it in the query argument.

Displaying the search results in a table

The preceding code loads all the data at once, which is not recommended since we could have a huge number of hits. Similarly, displaying it all in one go would make the UI sluggish and non-practical. Thankfully, we can easily build a paginated table without too much effort, using the following steps:

1. Create a route called do_retrieve_page that takes a URL as an argument and returns the HTML fragment for the table body

2. Maintain the first, previous, next, and last URLs as fields in the PixieApp class

3. Create a pagination widget (we'll use Bootstrap since it's available) with First, Prev, Next, and Last button

4. Create a table placeholder with the columns headers to be displayed

We'll now update the code for do_search, as follows:

 Note: The following code is referencing the do_retrieve_page method which we will define a little later. Please do not attempt to run this code as is until you also add the do_retrieve_page method.

```
[[GitHubTracking]]
@route(query="*")
@templateArgs
def do_search(self, query):
    self.first_url = "https://api.github.com/search/
repositories?q={}".format(query)
    self.prev_url = None
    self.next_url = None
    self.last_url = None

    response = requests.get(self.first_url)
    if not response.ok:
        return "<div>An Error occurred: {{response.text}}</div>"

    total_count = response.json()['total_count']
    self.next_url = response.links.get('next', {}).get('url',
                                                        None)
    self.last_url = response.links.get('last', {}).get('url',
                                                        None)
    return """
<h1><center>{{total_count}} repositories were found</center></h1>
<ul class="pagination">
    <li><a href="#" pd_options="page=first_url"
```

```
            pd_target="body{{prefix}}">First</a></li>
        <li><a href="#" pd_options="page=prev_url"
         pd_target="body{{prefix}}">Prev</a></li>
        <li><a href="#" pd_options="page=next_url"
         pd_target="body{{prefix}}">Next</a></li>
        <li><a href="#" pd_options="page=last_url"
         pd_target="body{{prefix}}">Last</a></li>
    </ul>
    <table class="table">
        <thead>
            <tr>
                <th>Repo Name</th>
                <th>Lastname</th>
                <th>URL</th>
                <th>Stars</th>
            </tr>
        </thead>
        <tbody id="body{{prefix}}">
            {{this.invoke_route(this.do_retrieve_page,
             page='first_url')}}
        </tbody>
    </table>
</table>
"""
```

> You can find the code file here:
> https://github.com/DTAIEB/Thoughtful-Data-Science/
> blob/master/chapter%203/sampleCode6.py

The preceding code sample shows a very important property of PixieApps, which is that you can maintain state throughout the life cycle of the application by simply storing the data into class variables. In this case, we use `self.first_url`, `self.prev_url`, `self.next_url`, and `self.last_url`. These variables use the `pd_options` property for each button in the pagination widget and update each time the `do_retrieve_page` route is invoked. The fragment returned by `do_search` now returns a table with a placeholder for the body, identified by `body{{prefix}}`, which becomes the `pd_target` for each button. We also use the `invoke_route` method to make sure that we get the first page when the table is first displayed.

We've seen before that the HTML fragment returned by a route is used to replace the entire page, but in the preceding code, we use the `pd_target="body{{prefix}}"` attribute to signify that the HTML fragment will be injected in the body element of the table that has the `body{{prefix}}` ID. If needed, you can also define multiple targets for a user action, by creating one or more `<target>` elements as children of the clickable source element. Each `<target>` element can itself use all the PixieApp custom attributes to configure kernel requests.

Here is an example:

```
<button type="button">Multiple Targets
    <target pd_target="elementid1"
     pd_options="state1=value1"></target>
    <target pd_target="elementid2"
     pd_options="state2=value2"></target>
</button>
```

Back to our GitHub sample application, the do_retrieve_page method now looks like this:

```
[[GitHubTracking]]
@route(page="*")
@templateArgs
def do_retrieve_page(self, page):
    url = getattr(self, page)
    if url is None:
        return "<div>No more rows</div>"
    response = requests.get(url)
    self.prev_url = response.links.get('prev', {}).get('url',
                                                        None)
    self.next_url = response.links.get('next', {}).get('url',
                                                        None)
    items = response.json()['items']
    return """
{%for row in items%}
<tr>
    <td>{{row['name']}}</td>
    <td>{{row.get('owner',{}).get('login', 'N/A')}}</td>
    <td><a href="{{row['html_url']}}"
     target="_blank">{{row['html_url']}}</a></td>
    <td>{{row['stargazers_count']}}</td>
</tr>
{%endfor%}
        """
```

 You can find the code file here:

https://github.com/DTAIEB/Thoughtful-Data-Science/
blob/master/chapter%203/sampleCode7.py

The page argument is a string that contains the name of the url class variable we want to display. We use the standard getattr Python function (https://docs. python.org/2/library/functions.html#getattr) to get the url value from the page. We then issue a GET request on the GitHub API url to retrieve the payload as JSON format which we pass to the Jinja2 template to generate the set of rows that will be injected in the table. For that, we use the {%for...%} loop control structure available in Jinja2 (http://jinja.pocoo.org/docs/templates/#for) to generate a sequence of <tr> and <td> HTML tags.

The following screenshot shows the search results for the query: pixiedust:

49 repositories were found

First | Prev | Next | Last

Repo Name	Lastname	URL	Stars
pixiedust	ibm-watson-data-lab	https://github.com/ibm-watson-data-lab/pixiedust	304
pixiedust	nutterb	https://github.com/nutterb/pixiedust	123
PixieDust	PixieEngine	https://github.com/PixieEngine/PixieDust	10
pixiedust	mxu	https://github.com/mxu/pixiedust	13
pixiedust-facebook-analysis	IBM	https://github.com/IBM/pixiedust-facebook-analysis	13
pixiedust_incubator	ibm-watson-data-lab	https://github.com/ibm-watson-data-lab/pixiedust_incubator	9
pixiedust_node	ibm-watson-data-lab	https://github.com/ibm-watson-data-lab/pixiedust_node	19
pixiedust-traffic-analysis	IBM	https://github.com/IBM/pixiedust-traffic-analysis	7

Screen showing the list of GitHub repo resulting from a query

In Part 1, we showed how to create the GitHubTracking PixieApp, invoke the GitHub query REST API, and display the results in a table using pagination. You can find the complete Notebook with the source code here:

https://github.com/DTAIEB/Thoughtful-Data-Science/blob/master/chapter%203/GitHub%20Tracking%20Application/GitHub%20Sample%20Application%20-%20Part%201.ipynb

In the next section, we will explore more PixieApp features that will allow us to improve the application by letting the user drill down into a particular repository and visualize various statistics about the repository.

The first step is to add a button to each row of the search results table that triggers a new route for visualizing the selected repository statistics.

The following code is part of the `do_search` function and adds a new column in the table header:

```
<thead>
    <tr>
        <th>Repo Name</th>
        <th>Lastname</th>
        <th>URL</th>
        <th>Stars</th>
        <th>Actions</th>
    </tr>
</thead>
```

To complete the table, we update the `do_retrieve_page` method to add a new cell that contains a `<button>` element, with `pd_options` arguments that match the new route: `analyse_repo_owner` and `analyse_repo_name`. The values of these arguments are extracted from the `row` element used for iterating over the payload received from the GitHub request:

```
{%for row in items%}
<tr>
    <td>{{row['name']}}</td>
    <td>{{row.get('owner',{}).get('login', 'N/A')}}</td>
    <td><a href="{{row['html_url']}}"
     target="_blank">{{row['html_url']}}</a></td>
    <td>{{row['stargazers_count']}}</td>
    <td>
        <button pd_options=
         "analyse_repo_owner={{row["owner"]["login"]}};
         analyse_repo_name={{row['name']}}"
         class="btn btn-default btn-sm" title="Analyze Repo">
            <i class="fa fa-line-chart"></i>
        </button>
    </td>
</tr>
{%endfor%}
```

With this simple code change in place, restart the PixieApp by running the cell again and we can now see the button for each repo, even though we haven't yet implemented the corresponding route, which we'll implement next. As a reminder, when no matching route is found, the default route is triggered.

The following screenshot shows the table with the added buttons:

49 repositories were found

First   Prev   Next   Last

Repo Name	Lastname	URL	Stars	Actions
pixiedust	ibm-watson-data-lab	https://github.com/ibm-watson-data-lab/pixiedust	304	
pixiedust	nutterb	https://github.com/nutterb/pixiedust	123	
PixieDust	PixieEngine	https://github.com/PixieEngine/PixieDust	10	
pixiedust	mku	https://github.com/mku/pixiedust	13	
pixiedust-facebook-analysis	IBM	https://github.com/IBM/pixiedust-facebook-analysis	13	

Adding action buttons for each row

The next step is to create the route associated with the Repo Visualization page. The design for this page is rather simple: from a combobox, the user chooses the type of data they want to visualize on the page. The GitHub REST API provides access to many types of data but, for this sample application, we will use the commit activity data, which is part of the Statistics category (see `https://developer.github.com/v3/repos/statistics/#get-the-last-year-of-commit-activity-data` for a detailed description of this API).

 As an exercise, feel free to improve this sample application by adding visualizations for other types of APIs, such as the Traffic API (`https://developer.github.com/v3/repos/traffic`).

It's also important to note that, even though most of the GitHub APIs work without authentication, the server may throttle the responses if you don't provide credentials. To authenticate the requests, you will need to use your GitHub password or generate a personal access token by selecting the **Developer settings** menu on your GitHub **Settings** page, then click on **Personal access tokens** menu, followed by the **Generate new token button**.

In a separate Notebook cell, we will create two variables for the GitHub user ID and token:

```
github_user = "dtaieb"
github_token = "XXXXXXXXXX"
```

These variables will be used later on to authenticate the requests. Note that, even though these variables are created in their own cell, they are visible to the entire Notebook, including the PixieApp code.

To provide good code modularity and reuse, we'll implement the Repo Visualization page in a new class and have our main PixieApp class inherit from it and automatically reuse its routes. This is a pattern to keep in mind when you start having large projects and want to break it down into multiple classes.

The main route for the Repo Visualization page returns an HTML fragment that has a drop-down menu and a `<div>` placeholder for the visualizations. The drop-down menu is created using Bootstrap `dropdown` class (`https://www.w3schools.com/bootstrap/bootstrap_dropdowns.asp`). To make the code easier to maintain, the menu items are generated using a Jinja2 `{%for..%}` loop over an array of tuples (`https://docs.python.org/3/tutorial/datastructures.html#tuples-and-sequences`) called `analyses` that contains a description and a function for loading the data into a pandas DataFrame. Again here, we create this array in its own cell, which will be referenced in the PixieApp class:

```
analyses = [("Commit Activity", load_commit_activity)]
```

> **Note**: The `load_commit_activity` function will be discussed later on in this section.
>
> For the purpose of this sample application, the array only contains one element related to the commit activity, but any element you may add in the future will automatically be picked up by the UI.

The `do_analyse_repo` route has two arguments: `analyse_repo_owner` and `analyse_repo_name`, which should be sufficient to access the GitHub APIs. We also need to save these arguments as class variables because they will be needed in the route that generates the visualizations:

```
@PixieApp
class RepoAnalysis():
    @route(analyse_repo_owner="*", analyse_repo_name="*")
    @templateArgs
    def do_analyse_repo(self, analyse_repo_owner, analyse_repo_name):
        self._analyse_repo_owner = analyse_repo_owner
        self._analyse_repo_name = analyse_repo_name
        return """
<div class="container-fluid">
    <div class="dropdown center-block col-sm-2">
        <button class="btn btn-primary dropdown-toggle"
          type="button" data-toggle="dropdown">
            Select Repo Data Set
```

```
                <span class="caret"></span>
        </button>
        <ul class="dropdown-menu"
         style="list-style:none;margin:0px;padding:0px">
            {%for analysis,_ in this.analyses%}
                <li>
                    <a href="#"
                     pd_options="analyse_type={{analysis}}"
                     pd_target="analyse_vis{{prefix}}"
                     style="text-decoration: none;background-
color:transparent">
                        {{analysis}}
                    </a>
                </li>
            {%endfor%}
        </ul>
    </div>
    <div id="analyse_vis{{prefix}}" class="col-sm-10"></div>
</div>
"""
```

You can find the code file here:

https://github.com/DTAIEB/Thoughtful-Data-Science/
blob/master/chapter%203/sampleCode8.py

Two things to note in the preceding code are the following:

- The Jinja2 template references the `analyses` array using the `this` keyword, even though the `analyses` variable is not defined as a class variable. This works because of another important PixieApp feature: any variable defined in the Notebook itself can be referenced as if they were class variables of the PixieApp.
- I store `analyse_repo_owner` and `analyse_repo_name` as class variables with a different name, for example, `_analyse_repo_owner` and `_analyse_repo_name`. This is important because using the same name would have a side effect on the route matching algorithm, which also looks at class variables to find arguments. Using the same name would then cause this route to always be found, which is not the desired effect.

The action button link is defined by the `<a>` tag and uses `pd_options` to access a route that has one argument called `analyse_type`, as well as `pd_target` pointing at the `"analyse_vis{{prefix}}"` placeholder, `<div>`, defined below in the same HTML fragment.

Invoking the PixieDust display() API using pd_entity attribute

When using the `pd_options` attribute to create a kernel request, the PixieApp framework uses the current PixieApp class as the target. However, you can change this target by specifying a `pd_entity` attribute. You could, for example, point at another PixieApp or, more interestingly, point at a data structure supported by the `display()` API, such as a pandas or Spark DataFrame. In this case, and provided that you include the correct options as expected by the `display()` API, the generated output will be the chart itself (an image in the case of Matplotlib, Iframe in the case of Mapbox, or an SVG in the case of Bokeh). One simple way to get the correct options is to invoke the `display()` API in its own cell, configure the chart as desired using the menus and then copy the cell metadata JSON fragment available by clicking on the **Edit Metadata** button. (You may first have to enable the button by using the menu **View | Cell Toolbar | Edit Metadata**).

You can also specify `pd_entity` without any value. In this case, the PixieApp framework will use the entity passed as the first argument to the `run` method used to launch the PixieApp application. For example, `my_pixieapp.run(cars)` with `cars` being a pandas or Spark DataFrame created by the `pixiedust.sampleData()` method. The value of `pd_entity` can also be a function call that returns the entity. This is useful when you want to dynamically compute the entity before rendering it. As with other variables, the scope of `pd_entity` can be either the PixieApp class or any variable declared in the Notebook.

For example, we can create a function in its own cell that takes a prefix as an argument and returns a pandas DataFrame. We then use it as a `pd_entity` value in my PixieApp, as shown in the following code:

```
def compute_pdf(key):
    return pandas.DataFrame([
        {"col{}".format(i): "{}{}-{}".format(key,i,j) for i in
range(4)} for j in range(10)
    ])
```

You can find the code file here:

https://github.com/DTAIEB/Thoughtful-Data-Science/
blob/master/chapter%203/sampleCode9.py

In the preceding code, we used Python list comprehensions (https://docs.python.
org/2/tutorial/datastructures.html#list-comprehensions) to quickly
generate mock data based on the key argument.

Python list comprehensions are one of my favorite features of the
Python language as they let you create, transform, and extract data
with an expressive and concise syntax.

I can then create a PixieApp that uses the compute_pdf function as a pd_entity
to render the data as a table:

```
from pixiedust.display.app import *
@PixieApp
class TestEntity():
    @route()
    def main_screen(self):
        return """
        <h1><center>
            Simple PixieApp with dynamically computed dataframe
        </center></h1>
        <div pd_entity="compute_pdf('prefix')"
         pd_options="handlerId=dataframe"
         pd_render_onload></div>
        """
test = TestEntity()
test.run()
```

You can find the code file here:

https://github.com/DTAIEB/Thoughtful-Data-Science/
blob/master/chapter%203/sampleCode10.py

In the preceding code, for simplicity, I hardcoded the key to 'prefix' and I'll
leave it as an exercise to use an input control and the $val() directive to make
it user definable.

Another important thing to notice is the use of the pd_render_onload attribute
in the div that displays the chart. This attribute tells PixieApp to execute the kernel
request defined by the element immediately after it is loaded into the browser DOM.

The results for the preceding PixieApp are shown in the following screenshot:

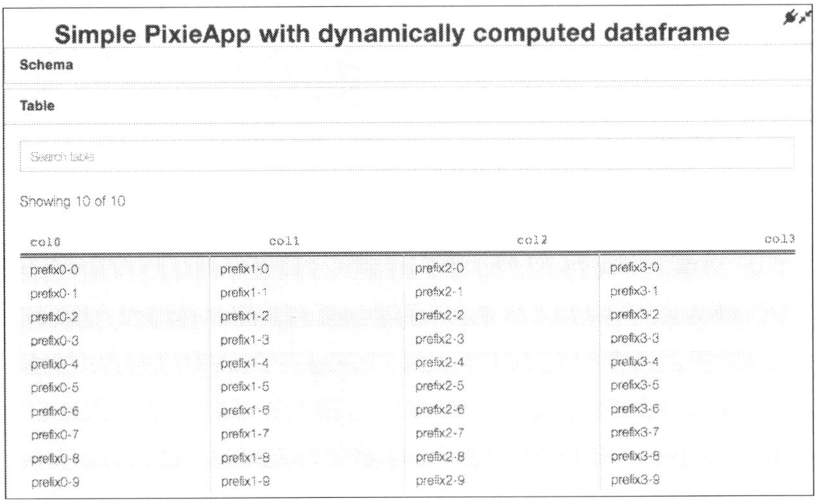

Dynamic DataFrame creation within a PixieApp

Back to our *GitHub Tracking* application, let's now apply the pd_entity value to the DataFrame loaded from the GitHub Statistics API. We create a method called load_commit_activity, responsible for loading the data into a pandas DataFrame and returning it along with the pd_options needed to display the chart:

```
from datetime import datetime
import requests
import pandas
def load_commit_activity(owner, repo_name):
    response = requests.get(
        "https://api.github.com/repos/{}/{}/stats/commit_activity".
format(owner, repo_name),
        auth=(github_user, github_token)
    ).json()
    pdf = pandas.DataFrame([
        {"total": item["total"],
         "week":datetime.fromtimestamp(item["week"])} for item in
response
    ])

    return {
        "pdf":pdf,
        "chart_options": {
```

```
            "handlerId": "lineChart",
            "keyFields": "week",
            "valueFields": "total",
            "aggregation": "SUM",
            "rendererId": "bokeh"
        }
    }
```

 You can find the code file here:

https://github.com/DTAIEB/Thoughtful-Data-Science/
blob/master/chapter%203/sampleCode11.py

The preceding code sends a GET request to GitHub, authenticated with the `github_user` and `github_token` variables set up at the beginning of the Notebook. The response is a JSON payload that we'll use to create a pandas DataFrame. Before we can create the DataFrame, we need to transform the JSON payload in to the right format. Right now, the payload looks like this:

```
[
{"days":[0,0,0,0,0,0,0],"total":0,"week":1485046800},
{"days":[0,0,0,0,0,0,0],"total":0,"week":1485651600},
{"days":[0,0,0,0,0,0,0],"total":0,"week":1486256400},
{"days":[0,0,0,0,0,0,0],"total":0,"week":1486861200}
...
]
```

We need to drop the `days` key as it's not needed for displaying the chart and, for proper chart display, we need to convert the value of the `week` key, which is a Unix timestamp, into a Python `datetime` object. This transformation is done using a Python list comprehension with a simple line of code:

```
[{"total": item["total"], "week":datetime.fromtimestamp(item["week"])}
    for item in response]
```

In the current implementation, the `load_commit_activity` function is defined in its own cell, but we could also have defined it as a member method of the PixieApp. As a best practice, using its own cell is very convenient because we can unit test the function and iterate rapidly on it without incurring the overhead of running the full app every time.

To get the `pd_options` value, we can simply run the function with a sample
repo information and then call the `display()` API in a separate cell:

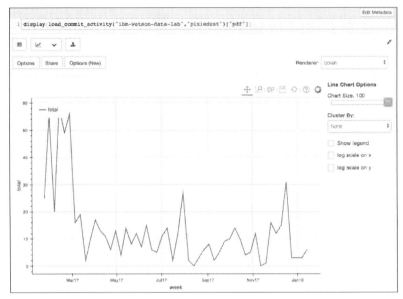

Using display() in a separate cell to get the visualization configuration

To obtain the preceding chart, you need to select **Line Chart** and then, in the
Options dialog, drag and drop the `week` column to the **Keys** box and the `total`
column to the **Values** box. You also need to select Bokeh as the renderer. Once done,
notice that PixieDust will automatically detect that the *x* axis is a datetime and will
adjust the rendering accordingly.

Using the **Edit Metadata** button, we can now copy the chart options JSON fragment:

Capturing the display() JSON configuration

And return it in the `load_commit_activity` payload:

```
return {
        "pdf":pdf,
        "chart_options": {
           "handlerId": "lineChart",
           "keyFields": "week",
           "valueFields": "total",
           "aggregation": "SUM",
           "rendererId": "bokeh"
        }
     }
```

We are now ready to implement the do_analyse_type route in the RepoAnalysis class, as shown in the following code:

```
[[RepoAnalysis]]
@route(analyse_type="*")
@templateArgs
def do_analyse_type(self, analyse_type):
    fn = [analysis_fn for a_type,analysis_fn in analyses if a_type ==
analyse_type]
    if len(fn) == 0:
        return "No loader function found for {{analyse_type}}"
    vis_info = fn[0](self._analyse_repo_owner,
                    self._analyse_repo_name)
    self.pdf = vis_info["pdf"]
    return """
```

```
        <div pd_entity="pdf" pd_render_onload>
            <pd_options>{{vis_info["chart_options"] | tojson}}</pd_
options>
        </div>
        """
```

 You can find the code file here:

https://github.com/DTAIEB/Thoughtful-Data-Science/
blob/master/chapter%203/sampleCode12.py

The route has one argument called `analyse_type`, which we use as a key to find
the load function in the `analyses` array (notice that I again use a list comprehension
to do the search quickly). We then call this function passing the repo owner and
name to get the `vis_info` JSON payload and store the pandas DataFrame into a
class variable called `pdf`. The returned HTML fragment will then use `pdf` as the
`pd_entity` value and `vis_info["chart_options"]` as `pd_options`. Here I use
the `tojson` Jinja2 filter (http://jinja.pocoo.org/docs/templates/#list-of-
builtin-filters) to ensure that it is properly escaped in the generated HTML.
I am also allowed to use the `vis_info` variable even though it's been declared
on the stack because I used the `@templateArgs` decorator for the function.

The last thing to do before testing our improved application is to make sure the
main `GitHubTracking` PixieApp class inherits from the `RepoAnalysis` PixieApp:

```
@PixieApp
class GitHubTracking(RepoAnalysis):
    @route()
    def main_screen(self):
        <<Code omitted here>>

    @route(query="*")
    @templateArgs
    def do_search(self, query):
        <<Code omitted here>>

    @route(page="*")
    @templateArgs
    def do_retrieve_page(self, page):
        <<Code omitted here>>

app = GitHubTracking()
app.run()
```

You can find the code file here:

```
https://github.com/DTAIEB/Thoughtful-Data-Science/
blob/master/chapter%203/sampleCode13.py
```

A screenshot of the Repo Analysis page is shown here:

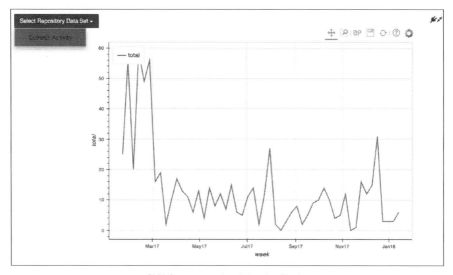

GitHub repo commit activity visualization

If you want to experiment further, you can find the complete Notebook for the *GitHub Tracking application* Part 2 here:

```
https://github.com/DTAIEB/Thoughtful-Data-Science/
blob/master/chapter%203/GitHub%20Tracking%20
Application/GitHub%20Sample%20Application%20-
%20Part%202.ipynb
```

Invoking arbitrary Python code with pd_script

In this section, we look at the `pd_script` custom attribute which lets you run arbitrary Python code whenever a kernel request is triggered. There are a few rules that govern how the Python code is executed:

- The code has access to the PixieApp class using the `self` keyword, as well as any variables, functions, and classes defined in the Notebook, as in the following example:

```
<button type="submit" pd_script="self.state='value'">Click me</
button>
```

- If a `pd_target` is specified, then any statement using the `print` function will be output in the `target` element. This is not the case if no `pd_target` is present. In other words, you cannot use `pd_script` to do a full-page refresh (you would have to use the `pd_options` attribute instead), as in the example:

```
from pixiedust.display.app import *

def call_me():
    print("Hello from call_me")

@PixieApp
class Test():
    @route()
    def main_screen(self):
        return """
        <button type="submit" pd_script="call_me()"
         pd_target="target{{prefix}}">Click me</button>

        <div id="target{{prefix}}"></div>
        """
Test().run()
```

  You can find the code file here:

> https://github.com/DTAIEB/Thoughtful-Data-Science/
> blob/master/chapter%203/sampleCode14.py

- If the code contains more than one line, it is recommended to use the `pd_script` child element, which lets you write the Python code using multiple lines. When using this form, make sure that the code respects the Python language rules for indentation, as in the example:

```
@PixieApp
class Test():
```

```
        @route()
        def main_screen(self):
            return """
            <button type="submit"
             pd_script="call_me()"
             pd_target="target{{prefix}}">
                <pd_script>
                    self.name="some value"
                    print("This is a multi-line pd_script")
                </pd_script>
                Click me
            </button>

            <div id="target{{prefix}}"></div>
            """
    Test().run()
```

 You can find the code file here:

https://github.com/DTAIEB/Thoughtful-Data-Science/
blob/master/chapter%203/sampleCode15.py

One common use case for pd_script is to update some state on the server
before triggering a kernel request. Let's apply this technique to our *GitHub Tracking*
application by adding a checkbox to switch the visualization between a line chart
and a statistical summary of the data.

In the fragment HTML returned by do_analyse_repo, we add the checkbox element
used to switch between the chart and the statistics summary:

```
[[RepoAnalysis]]
...
return """
<div class="container-fluid">
    <div class="col-sm-2">
        <div class="dropdown center-block">
            <button class="btn btn-primary
             dropdown-toggle" type="button"
             data-toggle="dropdown">
                Select Repo Data Set
                <span class="caret"></span>
            </button>
            <ul class="dropdown-menu"
             style="list-style:none;margin:0px;padding:0px">
                {%for analysis,_ in this.analyses%}
```

```
                              <li>
                                  <a href="#"
                                  pd_options="analyse_type={{analysis}}"
                                  pd_target="analyse_vis{{prefix}}"
                                  style="text-decoration: none;background-
color:transparent">
                                      {{analysis}}
                                  </a>
                              </li>
                          {%endfor%}
                      </ul>
                  </div>
                  <div class="checkbox">
                      <label>
                          <input id="show_stats{{prefix}}" type="checkbox"
                            pd_script="self.show_stats=('$val(show_
stats{{prefix}})' == 'true')">
                          Show Statistics
                      </label>
                  </div>
              </div>
              <div id="analyse_vis{{prefix}}" class="col-sm-10"></div>
          </div>
          """
```

In the `checkbox` element, we include a `pd_script` attribute that modifies a variable state on the server based on the state of the `checkbox` element. We use the `$val()` directive to retrieve the value of the `show_stats_{{prefix}}` element and compare it with the `true` `string`. When the user clicks on the checkbox, the state is immediately changed on the server and, the next time the user clicks on the menu, the stats are showing instead of the charts.

We now need to change the `do_analyse_type` route to dynamically configure `pd_entity` and `chart_options`:

```
[[RepoAnalysis]]
@route(analyse_type="*")
@templateArgs
def do_analyse_type(self, analyse_type):
    fn = [analysis_fn for a_type,analysis_fn in analyses if a_type ==
analyse_type]
    if len(fn) == 0:
        return "No loader function found for {{analyse_type}}"
    vis_info = fn[0](self._analyse_repo_owner,
                     self._analyse_repo_name)
```

```
self.pdf = vis_info["pdf"]
chart_options = {"handlerId":"dataframe"} if self.show_stats else
vis_info["chart_options"]
return """
<div pd_entity="get_pdf()" pd_render_onload>
    <pd_options>{{chart_options | tojson}}</pd_options>
</div>
"""
```

You can find the file here:

`https://github.com/DTAIEB/Thoughtful-Data-Science/blob/master/chapter%203/sampleCode16.py`

chart_options is now a local variable that contains options for displaying as a table if show_stats is true and regular line chart options if not.

pd_entity is now set to the get_pdf() method, which is responsible for returning the appropriate DataFrame based on the show_stats variable:

```
def get_pdf(self):
    if self.show_stats:
        summary = self.pdf.describe()
        summary.insert(0, "Stat", summary.index)
        return summary
    return self.pdf
```

You can find the code file here:

`https://github.com/DTAIEB/Thoughtful-Data-Science/blob/master/chapter%203/sampleCode17.py`

We use the pandas describe() method (`https://pandas.pydata.org/pandas-docs/stable/generated/pandas.DataFrame.describe.html`) that returns a DataFrame containing summary statistics, such as count, mean, standard deviation, and so on. We also make sure that the first column of this DataFrame contains the name of the statistic.

The last change we need to make is to initialize the show_stats variable because, if we don't, then the first time we check it, we'll get an AttributeError exception.

Because of the internal mechanics of using the @PixieApp decorator, you can't use the __init__ method to initialize variables; instead, the PixieApp programming model requires you to use a method called setup, which is guaranteed to be called when the application starts:

```
@PixieApp
class RepoAnalysis():
    def setup(self):
        self.show_stats = False
    ...
```

 Note: If you have a class inheriting from other PixieApps, then the PixieApp framework will automatically call all `setup` functions from base classes using their order of appearance.

The following screenshot shows the summary statistics being displayed:

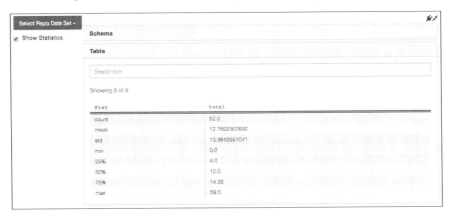

Summary statistics for a GitHub repo

 You can find the complete Notebook for the *GitHub Tracking* application Part 3 here:

```
https://github.com/DTAIEB/Thoughtful-Data-Science/
blob/master/chapter%203/GitHub%20Tracking%20
Application/GitHub%20Sample%20Application%20-
%20Part%203.ipynb
```

Making the application more responsive with pd_refresh

We want to improve the user experience by making the **Show Statistics** button directly show the statistics table instead of having the user to click on the menu again. Similar to the menu that loads the **Commit Activity**, we could add a pd_options attribute to the checkbox with the pd_target attribute pointing at the analyse_vis{{prefix}} element. Instead of duplicating pd_options in each of the controls that triggers a new display, we could add it once to analyse_vis{{prefix}} and have it update itself with the pd_refresh attribute.

The following diagram shows the differences between the two designs:

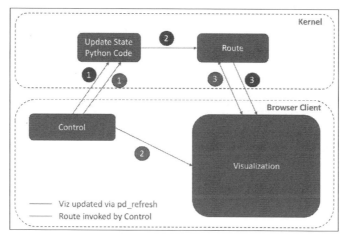

Sequence diagram with and without pd_refresh

In both cases, step 1 is to update some state on the server side. In the case of the route being invoked by the **Control** shown in step 2, the request specification is stored in the control itself, triggering step 3, which is to generate the HTML fragment and inject it in the target element. With pd_refresh, the control doesn't know the pd_options to invoke the route, instead, it simply uses pd_refresh to signal the target element, which in turn will invoke the route. In this design, we only need to specify the request once (in the target element) and user control needs only to update state before triggering a refresh. This makes the implementation much easier to maintain.

To better understand the differences between the two designs, let's compare both implementations in the RepoAnalysis class.

For the **Analysis** menu, the changes are as follows:

Before, the control triggered the `analyse_type` route, passing the `{{analysis}}` selection as part of the kernel request, targeting `analyse_vis{{prefix}}`:

```
<a href="#" pd_options="analyse_type={{analysis}}"
            pd_target="analyse_vis{{prefix}}"
            style="text-decoration: none;background-
color:transparent">
        {{analysis}}
</a>
```

After, the control now stores the selection state as a class field and asks the `analyse_vis{{prefix}}` element to refresh itself:

```
<a href="#" pd_script="self.analyse_type='{{analysis}}'"
 pd_refresh="analyse_vis{{prefix}}"
 style="text-decoration: none;background-color:transparent">
     {{analysis}}
</a>
```

Similarly, the changes for the **Show Statistics** checkbox are as follows:

Before the checkbox simply set the `show_stats` state in the class; the user had to click on the menu again to get the visualization:

```
<div class="checkbox">
    <label>
        <input type="checkbox"
         id="show_stats{{prefix}}"
pd_script="self.show_stats='$val(show_stats{{prefix}})'=='true'">
        Show Statistics
    </label>
</div>
```

After, the visualization is updated as soon as the checkbox is selected, thanks to the `pd_refresh` attribute:

```
<div class="checkbox">
    <label>
        <input type="checkbox"
         id="show_stats{{prefix}}"
  pd_script="self.show_stats='$val(show_stats{{prefix}})'=='true'"
            pd_refresh="analyse_vis{{prefix}}">
        Show Statistics
    </label>
</div>
```

Finally, the changes for the `analyse_vis{{prefix}}` element are as follows:

Before, the element didn't know how to update itself, it relies on other controls to direct a request to the appropriate route:

```
<div id="analyse_vis{{prefix}}" class="col-sm-10"></div>
```

After, the element carries the kernel configuration to update itself; any control can now change state and call refresh:

```
<div id="analyse_vis{{prefix}}" class="col-sm-10"
    pd_options="display_analysis=true"
    pd_target="analyse_vis{{prefix}}">
</div>
```

> You can find the complete Notebook for this section for the *GitHub Tracking* application Part 4 here:
>
> ```
> https://github.com/DTAIEB/Thoughtful-Data-Science/
> blob/master/chapter%203/GitHub%20Tracking%20
> Application/GitHub%20Sample%20Application%20-%20
> Part%204.ipynb
> ```

Creating reusable widgets

The PixieApp programming model provides a mechanism for packaging the HTML and logic of a complex UI construct into a widget that can be easily called from other PixieApps. The steps to create a widget are as follows:

1. Create a PixieApp class that will contain the widget.

2. Create a route with a special `widget` attribute, as in the example:

   ```
   @route(widget="my_widget")
   ```

   It will be the starting route for the widget.

3. Create a consumer PixieApp class that inherits from the widget PixieApp class.

4. Invoke the widget from a `<div>` element by using the `pd_widget` attribute.

Here is an example of how to create a widget and consumer PixieApp class:

```
from pixiedust.display.app import *

@PixieApp
```

```
class WidgetApp():
    @route(widget="my_widget")
    def widget_main_screen(self):
        return "<div>Hello World Widget</div>"

@PixieApp
class ConsumerApp(WidgetApp):
    @route()
    def main_screen(self):
        return """<div pd_widget="my_widget"></div>"""

ConsumerApp.run()
```

You can find the code here:

https://github.com/DTAIEB/Thoughtful-Data-Science/
blob/master/chapter%203/sampleCode18.py

Summary

In this chapter, we've covered the foundational building blocks of the PixieApp programming model that lets you create powerful tools and dashboards directly in the Notebook.

We've also illustrated PixieApp concepts and techniques by showing how to build a *GitHub Tracking* sample application, including detailed code examples. Best practices and more advanced PixieApp concepts will be covered in *Chapter 5, Best Practices and Advanced PixieDust Concepts*, including events, streaming, and debugging.

By now, you should hopefully have a good idea of how Jupyter Notebooks, PixieDust, and PixieApps can help bridge the gap between data scientists and developers by enabling them to collaborate from within a single tool, such as Jupyter Notebook.

In the next chapter, we'll show how to free the PixieApp from the Notebook and publish it as a web application using the PixieGateway microservice server.

4

Deploying PixieApps to the Web with the PixieGateway Server

"Data, I think, is one of the most powerful mechanisms for telling stories. I take a huge pile of data and I try to get it to tell stories."

– *Steven Levitt*, co-author of *Freakonomics*

In the previous chapter, we discussed how Jupyter Notebooks, coupled with PixieDust, accelerate your data science projects with simple APIs that let you load, clean, and visualize data without the need to write extensive code, as well as enable collaboration between data scientists and developers with PixieApps. In this chapter, we'll show how to *liberate* your PixieApps and associated data analytics from the Jupyter Notebook by publishing them as web applications using the PixieGateway server. This operationalization of the Notebook is particularly attractive to the line of business user persona (business analysts, C-Suite executives, and many more) who would like to use the PixieApps but who, unlike data scientists or developers, may not be comfortable using Jupyter Notebooks to do so. Instead, they would prefer to access it as a classic web application or perhaps, similar to a YouTube video, embed it into a blog post or a GitHub page. Using a website or a blog post, it will be easier to communicate the valuable insights and other results extracted from the data analytics from your data.

By the end of this chapter, you will be able to install and configure a PixieGateway server instance both locally for testing or in a Kubernetes container on the cloud for production. For those readers who are not familiar with Kubernetes, we'll cover the basics in the next section.

The other main capability of the PixieGateway server that we'll cover in this chapter, is the ability to easily share a chart created with the PixieDust `display()` API. We'll show how to publish it as a web page accessible by your team with a single click of a button. Finally, we'll cover the PixieGateway admin console that lets you manage your applications, charts, kernels, server logs, and a Python console executing ad-hoc code requests against a kernel.

 Note: The PixieGateway server is a subcomponent of PixieDust, its source code can be found here:

`https://github.com/pixiedust/pixiegateway`

Overview of Kubernetes

Kubernetes (`https://kubernetes.io`) is a scalable open source system for automating and orchestrating the deployment and management of containerized applications, which are very popular among cloud service providers. It is most often used with Docker containers (`https://www.docker.com`) although other types of containers are supported. Before you start, you will need access to a set of computers that have been configured as a Kubernetes cluster; you can find a tutorial on how to create such a cluster here: `https://kubernetes.io/docs/tutorials/kubernetes-basics`.

If you don't have the computer resources, a good solution would be to use a public cloud vendor that provides a Kubernetes service, such as Amazon AWS EKS (`https://aws.amazon.com/eks`), Microsoft Azure (`https://azure.microsoft.com/en-us/services/container-service/kubernetes`), or IBM Cloud Kubernetes Service (`https://www.ibm.com/cloud/container-service`).

To better understand how a Kubernetes cluster works, let's look at the high-level architecture shown in the following diagram:

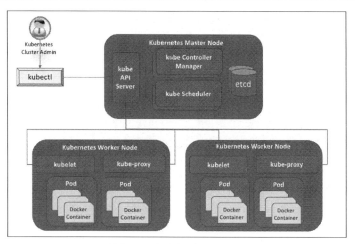

Kubernetes high-level architecture

At the top of the stack, we have the `kubectl` command-line tool that enables users to manage the Kubernetes cluster by sending commands to the **Kubernetes Master Node**. The `kubectl` commands use the following syntax:

```
kubectl [command] [TYPE] [NAME] [flags]
```

Where:

- `command`: This specifies the operation, for example, `create`, `get`, `describe`, and `delete`
- `TYPE`: This specifies the resource type, for example, `pods`, `nodes`, and `services`
- `NAME`: This specifies the name of the resource
- `flags`: This specifies optional flags specific to the operation

 For more information on how to use `kubectl`, visit the following:

https://kubernetes.io/docs/reference/kubectl/overview

Another important component present in the worker node is the **kubelet,** which controls the pod's life cyle by reading the pod configuration from the **kube API Server**. It also is responsible for communication with the master node. The kube-proxy provides load balancing capabilities between all the pods according to the policy specified in the master node, hence ensuring high-availability of the overall application.

In the next section, we will discuss the different ways to install and configure the PixieGateway server, including one method that uses a Kubernetes cluster.

Installing and configuring the PixieGateway server

Before we dive into the technical details, it would be a good idea to deploy a PixieGateway server instance to try things out.

There are mainly two types of installation you can try: local install and server install.

Local install: Use this method for testing and development.

For this part, I strongly recommend using Anaconda virtual environments (`https://conda.io/docs/user-guide/tasks/manage-environments.html`) because they provide good isolation between the environments, enabling you to experiment with different versions and configurations of the Python package.

If you are managing multiple environments, you can get a list of all the available environments by using the following command:

```
conda env list
```

First, select the environment of your choice by using the following command from a Terminal:

```
source activate <<my_env>>
```

You should see the name of your environment in the Terminal, which is an indication that you've correctly activated it.

Next, install the `pixiegateway` package from PyPi by running the following command:

```
pip install pixiegateway
```

 Note: You can find more information about the `pixiegateway` package on PyPi here:

`https://pypi.python.org/pypi/pixiegateway`

Once all the dependencies have been installed, you're ready to start the server. Assuming that you want to use the `8899` port, you can start the PixieGateway server using the following command:

```
jupyter pixiegateway --port=8899
```

Example output should look like this:

```
(dashboard) davids-mbp-8:pixiegateway dtaieb$ jupyter pixiegateway
--port=8899
Pixiedust database opened successfully
Pixiedust version 1.1.10
[PixieGatewayApp] Jupyter Kernel Gateway at http://127.0.0.1:8899
```

 Note: To stop the PixieGateway server, simply use *Ctrl + C* from the Terminal.

You can now open the PixieGateway admin console at the following URL: `http://localhost:8899/admin`.

 Note: When challenged, use `admin` as the user and blank (no password) as the password. We'll review how to configure security and other properties in the *PixieGateway server configuration* section later in this chapter.

Server install using Kubernetes and Docker: Use this install method if you need to run PixieGateway in a production environment where you want to give access to the deployed PixieApps to multiple users over the web.

The following instructions will use IBM Cloud Kubernetes Service, but they can easily be adapted to other providers:

1. Create an IBM Cloud account if you don't already have one and create a container service instance from the catalog.

 Note: A lite version plan is available for testing at no cost.

2. Download and install the Kubernetes CLI (`https://kubernetes.io/docs/tasks/tools/install-kubectl`) and the IBM Cloud CLI (`https://console.bluemix.net/docs/cli/reference/bluemix_cli/get_started.html#getting-started`).

Note: An additional get started article on Kubernetes containers can be found here:

```
https://console.bluemix.net/docs/containers/container_
index.html#container_index
```

3. Log in to the IBM Cloud and then target the org and space where your Kubernetes instance resides. Install and initialize the `container-service` plugin:

```
bx login -a https://api.ng.bluemix.net
bx target -o <YOUR_ORG> -s <YOUR_SPACE></YOUR_SPACE>
bx plugin install container-service -r Bluemix
bx cs init
```

4. Check that your cluster is created and, if not, create one:

```
bx cs clusters
bx cs cluster-create --name my-cluster
```

5. Download the cluster configuration that will be used by the `kubectl` command, which is executed on your local machine, later on:

```
bx cs cluster-config my-cluster
```

The preceding command will generate a temporary YML file that contains the cluster information and an environment variable export statement that you must run before starting to use the `kubectl` command, as in the example:

```
export KUBECONFIG=/Users/dtaieb/.bluemix/plugins/container-
service/clusters/davidcluster/kube-config-hou02-davidcluster.
yml
```

Note: YAML is a very popular data serialization format commonly used for system configuration. You can find more information here:

```
http://www.yaml.org/start.html
```

6. You can now use `kubectl` to create the deployment and services for your PixieGateway server. For convenience, the PixieGateway GitHub repository already has a generic version of `deployment.yml` and `service.yml` that you can directly reference. We'll review how to configure these files for Kubernetes in the *PixieGateway server configuration* section later in this chapter:

```
kubectl create -f https://github.com/ibm-watson-data-lab/
```

```
pixiegateway/raw/master/etc/deployment.yml
```

```
kubectl create -f https://github.com/ibm-watson-data-lab/
pixiegateway/raw/master/etc/service.yml
```

7. It would be a good idea to verify the state of your clusters using the `kubectl get` command:

```
kubectl get pods
```

```
kubectl get nodes
```

```
kubectl get services
```

8. Finally, you'll need the public IP address of the server, which you can find by looking at the `Public IP` column of the output returned using the following command, in the Terminal:

```
bx cs workers my-cluster
```

9. If all goes well, you can now test your deployment by opening the admin console at `http://<server_ip>>:32222/admin`. This time, the default credentials for the admin console are `admin`/`changeme` and we'll show how to change them in the next section.

The `deployment.yml` file used in the Kubernetes install instructions is referencing a Docker image that has the PixieGateway binaries and all its dependencies preinstalled and configured. The PixieGateway Docker image is available at `https://hub.docker.com/r/dtaieb/pixiegateway-python35`.

When working locally, the recommended method is to follow the steps of the local install described earlier. However, for readers who prefer to work with Docker images, it is possible to try out the PixieGateway Docker image locally without Kubernetes, by directly installing it on your local laptop with a simple Docker command:

```
docker run -p 9999:8888 dtaieb/pixiegateway-python35
```

The preceding command assumes that you have already installed Docker and that it is currently running on your local machine. If not, you can download an installer from the following link: `https://docs.docker.com/engine/installation`.

The Docker image will automatically be pulled if not already present and the container will start, starting the PixieGateway server at local port `8888`. The `-p` switch in the command maps the `8888 port` local to the container, to the `9999 port` local to the host machine. With the given configuration, you would access the Docker instance of the PixieGateway server at the following URL: `http://localhost:9999/admin`.

You can find more information about the Docker command line here:

`https://docs.docker.com/engine/reference/commandline/cli`

Note: Another reason why you would use this method is to provide your own custom Docker image for the PixieGateway server. This can be useful if you have built an extension to PixieGateway and want to provide it to your users as an already configured Docker image. Discussion around how to build a Docker image from a base image is beyond the scope of this book, but you can find detailed information here:

`https://docs.docker.com/engine/reference/commandline/image_build`

PixieGateway server configuration

Configuring the PixieGateway server is very similar to configuring the Jupyter Kernel Gateway. Most options are configured using a Python configuration file; to start things off, you can generate a template configuration file using the following command:

```
jupyter kernelgateway --generate-config
```

The `jupyter_kernel_gateway_config.py` template file will be generated under the `~/.jupyter` directory (~ indicates the user home directory). You can find more information about the standard Jupyter Kernel Gateway options here: `http://jupyter-kernel-gateway.readthedocs.io/en/latest/config-options.html`.

Using the `jupyter_kernel_gateway_config.py` file is fine when you are working locally and have easy access to the filesystem. When using the Kubernetes install, it is recommended to configure the options as environment variables, which you can set directly in the `deployment.yml` file by using the predefined `env` category.

Let's now look at each configuration options for the PixieGateway server. A list is provided here using both the Python and Environment method:

Note: As a reminder, Python method means setting the parameter in the `jupyter_kernel_gateway_config.py` Python config file, while the Environment method means setting the parameters in the Kubernetes `deployment.yml` file.

- **Admin console credentials**: Configure the user ID/password for the admin console:
  - ○ **Python**: `PixieGatewayApp.admin_user_id`, `PixieGatewayApp.admin_password`
  - ○ **Environment**: `ADMIN_USERID` and `ADMIN_PASSWORD`

- **Storage connector**: Configure a persistent storage for various resources, such as charts, and Notebooks. By default, PixieGateway uses the local filesystem; for example, it will store the published Notebooks under the `~/pixiedust/gateway` directory. Using the local filesystem is probably fine for a local test environment, but when using a Kubernetes install, you will need to explicitly use persistent volumes (`https://kubernetes.io/docs/concepts/storage/persistent-volumes`), which can be difficult to use. If no persistence strategy is put in place, the persisted files will be deleted when the container is restarted and all your published chart and PixieApps will disappear. PixieGateway provides another option, which is to configure a storage connector that lets you persist the data using the mechanism and backend of your choice.

  To configure a storage connector for charts, you must specify a fully qualified class name in either one of the following configuration variables:
  - ○ **Python**: `SingletonChartStorage.chart_storage_class`
  - ○ **Environment**: `PG_CHART_STORAGE`

  The referenced connector class must inherit from the `ChartStorage` abstract class defined in the `pixiegateway.chartsManager` package (implementation can be found here: `https://github.com/ibm-watson-data-lab/pixiegateway/blob/master/pixiegateway/chartsManager.py`).

  PixieGateway provides an out of the box connector to the Cloudant/CouchDB NoSQL database (`http://couchdb.apache.org`). To use this connector, you'll need to set the connector class to `pixiegateway.chartsManager.CloudantChartStorage`. You'll also need to specify secondary configuration variables to specify the server and credential information (we show the Python/Environment form):
  - ○ `CloudantConfig.host / PG_CLOUDANT_HOST`
  - ○ `CloudantConfig.port / PG_CLOUDANT_PORT`
  - ○ `CloudantConfig.protocol / PG_CLOUDANT_PROTOCOL`
  - ○ `CloudantConfig.username / PG_CLOUDANT_USERNAME`
  - ○ `CloudantConfig.password / PG_CLOUDANT_PASSWORD`

- **Remote Kernels**: Specify the configuration for a remote Jupyter Kernel Gateway.

  At the moment, this configuration option is only supported in Python mode. The variable name you need to use is `ManagedClientPool.remote_ gateway_config`. The expected value is a JSON object that contains the server information, which can be specified in two ways:

  - `protocol`, `host`, and `port`
  - `notebook_gateway` specifies fully qualified URL to the server

  Depending on the kernel configuration, security can also be provided using two ways:

  - `auth_token`
  - `user` and `password`

  This can be seen in the following example:

  ```
  c.ManagedClientPool.remote_gateway_config={
      'protocol': 'http',
      'host': 'localhost',
      'port': 9000,
      'auth_token':'XXXXXXXXXX'
  }

  c.ManagedClientPool.remote_gateway_config={
      'notebook_gateway': 'https://YYYYY.us-south.bluemix.net:8443/
  gateway/default/jkg/',
      'user': 'clsadmin',
      'password': 'XXXXXXXXXX'
  }
  ```

 Notice that, in the preceding example, you need to prefix the variable with `c.`. This is a requirement coming from the underlying Jupyter/ IPython configuration mechanism.

For reference, here are the complete configuration example files using both Python and Kubernetes Environment variables formats:

- The following are the contents of `jupyter_kernel_gateway_config.py`:

  ```
  c.PixieGatewayApp.admin_password = "password"

  c.SingletonChartStorage.chart_storage_class = "pixiegateway.
  chartsManager.CloudantChartStorage"
  ```

```
c.CloudantConfig.host="localhost"
c.CloudantConfig.port=5984
c.CloudantConfig.protocol="http"
c.CloudantConfig.username="admin"
c.CloudantConfig.password="password"

c.ManagedClientPool.remote_gateway_config={
    'protocol': 'http',
    'host': 'localhost',
    'port': 9000,
    'auth_token':'XXXXXXXXXX'
}
```

- The following are the contents of `deployment.yml`:

```
apiVersion: extensions/v1beta1
kind: Deployment
metadata:
  name: pixiegateway-deployment
spec:
  replicas: 1
  template:
    metadata:
      labels:
        app: pixiegateway
    spec:
      containers:
        - name: pixiegateway
          image: dtaieb/pixiegateway-python35
          imagePullPolicy: Always
          env:
            - name: ADMIN_USERID
              value: admin
            - name: ADMIN_PASSWORD
              value: changeme
            - name: PG_CHART_STORAGE
              value: pixiegateway.chartsManager.
CloudantChartStorage
            - name: PG_CLOUDANT_HOST
              value: XXXXXXXX-bluemix.cloudant.com
            - name: PG_CLOUDANT_PORT
              value: "443"
            - name: PG_CLOUDANT_PROTOCOL
              value: https
            - name: PG_CLOUDANT_USERNAME
```

```
   value: YYYYYYYYYY-bluemix
 - name: PG_CLOUDANT_PASSWORD
   value: ZZZZZZZZZZZZ
```

PixieGateway architecture

Now would be a good time to look again at the PixieGateway architecture diagram presented in *Chapter 2, Data Science at Scale with Jupyter Notebooks and PixieDust*. The server is implemented as a custom extension (called Personality) to the Jupyter Kernel Gateway (`https://github.com/jupyter/kernel_gateway`).

In turn, the PixieGateway server provides extension points to customize some behavior that we'll discuss later in this chapter.

The high-level architecture diagram for the PixieGateway server is shown here:

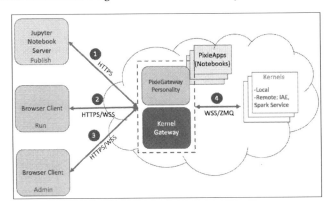

PixieGateway architecture diagram

As the diagram indicates, PixieGateway provides a REST interface for three types of clients:

- **Jupyter Notebook Server**: This calls a dedicated set of REST APIs for sharing charts and publishing PixieApps as web applications
- **Browser client running a PixieApp**: A special REST API manages the execution of Python code in the associated kernel
- **Browser client running the admin console**: A dedicated set of REST APIs for managing various server resources and stats, for example, PixieApps and kernel instances

On the backend, the PixieGateway server manages the life cycle of one or more Jupyter Kernel instances responsible for running the PixieApps. At runtime, each PixieApp is deployed on a kernel instance using a specific set of steps. The following diagram shows a typical topology of all the PixieApp user instances running on the server:

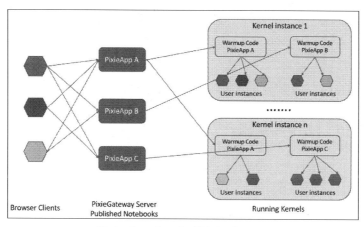

The topology of running PixieApp instances

When a PixieApp is deployed on the server, the code contained in every cell of the Jupyter Notebook is analyzed and broken into two parts:

- **Warmup code**: This is all the code defined in all the cells above the main PixieApp definition. This code is run only once, when the PixieApp application is first started on the kernel, and will not run again until the kernel is restarted, or until it is called explicitly from the run code. This is important because it will help you better optimize performances; for example, you should always put in the warmup section, code that loads a large amount of data that doesn't change much or that may require a long time to initialize.

- **Run code**: This is code that will be run in its own instance for every user session. The run code is typically extracted from the cell that contains the PixieApp class declaration. The publisher automatically discovers this cell by doing a static analysis of the Python code and specifically looking for the following two criteria, which must both be met:
  - The cell contains a class that has the `@PixieApp` annotation
  - The cell instantiates the class and call its `run()` method

For example, the following code must be in its own cell to qualify as the run code:

```
@PixieApp
class MyApp():
    @route()
    def main_screen(self):
    return "<div>Hello World</div>"

app = MyApp()
app.run()
```

As we've seen in *Chapter 3*, *PixieApp under the Hood*, it is possible to declare multiple PixieApps in the same notebook that will be used as child PixieApp or as base classes to the main PixieApp. In this case, we need to make sure that they are defined in their own cell and that you don't try to instantiate them and call their `run()` method.

The rule is that there can be only one main PixieApp class for which the `run()` method will be called and the cell that contains this code is considered the run code by the PixieGateway.

 Note: Cells that are not marked as Code, such as Markdown, Raw NBConvert, or Heading are ignored during the static analysis done by the PixieGateway server. Therefore, it is safe to keep them in your Notebook.

For each client session, PixieGateway will instantiate an instance of the main PixieApp class using the run code (represented as colored hexagons in the preceding diagram). Depending on current load, PixieGateway will decide how many PixieApps should run in a particular kernel instance and, if needed, automatically spawn a new kernel to serve the extra users. For example, if five users are using the same PixieApp, three instances may be running in a particular kernel instance and the two others will be run in another kernel instance. PixieGateway is constantly monitoring the usage patterns to optimize workload distribution by load balancing the instances of PixieApps between multiple kernels.

To help understand how the Notebook code is broken down, the following diagram reflects how the warmup and run code are extracted from the Notebook and transformed to make sure that multiple instances coexist peacefully within the same kernel:

 As a reminder, the cell that contains the main PixieApp must also have code that instantiates it and calls the `run()` method.

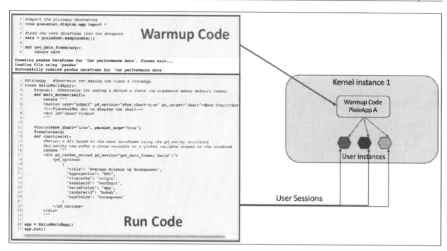

PixieApp life cycle: Warmup and Run Code

Because a given kernel instance can host more than one Notebook with its main PixieApp, we need to make sure that there is no accidental name collision when the warmup code for two main PixieApps is executed. For example, the `title` variable may be used in both PixieApps and, if left alone, the value for the second one would override the value for the first one. To avoid this conflict, all the variable names in the warmup code are made unique by injecting a namespace.

The `title = 'some string'` statement becomes `ns1_title = 'some string'` after publication. The PixieGateway publisher will also update all references to `title` throughout the code to reflect the new name. All of this renaming is automatically done at runtime and there are no specific things that need to be done by the developer.

We will show real code examples later on when we cover the *PixieApp details* page of the admin console.

If you have packaged the code for your main PixieApp as a Python module that is imported in the Notebook, you still need to declare the code for a wrapper PixieApp that inherits from it. This is because the PixieGateway does a static code analysis, looking for the `@PixieApp` notation, and if not found, the main PixieApp will not be properly recognized.

For example, let's assume that you have a PixieApp named `AwesomePixieApp` imported from the `awesome package`. In this case, you would put the following code in its own cell:

```
from awesome import AwesomePixieApp
@PixieApp
class WrapperAwesome(AwesomePixieApp):
    pass
app = WrapperAwesome()
app.run()
```

Publishing an application

In this section, we'll publish the *GitHub Tracking* application that we created in *Chapter 3, PixieApp under the Hood,* into a PixieGateway instance.

You can use the completed notebook from this GitHub location:

```
https://github.com/DTAIEB/Thoughtful-Data-Science/
blob/master/chapter%203/GitHub%20Tracking%20
Application/GitHub%20Sample%20Application%20-%20
Part%204.ipynb
```

From the Notebook, run the application as usual and use the publish button located on the top-left of the cell output, to start the process:

Invoke the publish dialog

The publish dialog has multiple tab menus:

- **Options**:
    - ○ **PixieGateway Server**: For example, `http://localhost:8899`
    - ○ **Page Title**: A short description that will be used as the page title when displayed in the browser

- **Security**: Configure the PixieApp security when accessed through the web:
  - ° **No security**
  - ° **Token**: A security token must be added as a query parameter to the URL, for example, `http://localhost:8899/GitHubTracking?toke n=941b3990d5c0464586d67e48705b9deb`.

 Note: At this time, PixieGateway doesn't provide any authentication/ authorization mechanism. Third party authorization, such as OAuth 2.0 (`https://oauth.net/2`), JWT (`https://jwt.io`), and others will be added in the future.

- **Imports**: Display the list of Python package dependencies automatically detected by the PixieDust publisher. These imported packages will be automatically installed, if not already present, on the kernel where the application is running. When detecting a particular dependency, PixieDust looks at the current system to get the version and install location, for example, PyPi or a custom install URL such as a GitHub repo, for example.
- **Kernel Spec**: This is where you can choose a kernel spec for your PixieApp. By default, PixieDust selects the default kernel available on the PixieGateway server but if, for example, your Notebook relies on Apache Spark, you should be able to pick a kernel that supports it. This option can also be changed after the PixieApp has been deployed using the admin console.

Here's a sample screenshot of the PixieApp publish dialog:

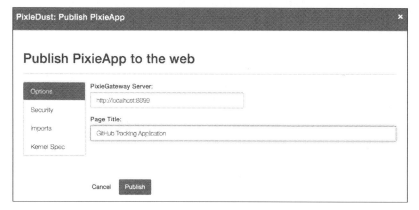

PixieApp publish dialog

Clicking the **Publish** button will start the publishing process. Upon completion (which depending on the size of the Notebook is pretty fast), you'll see the following screen:

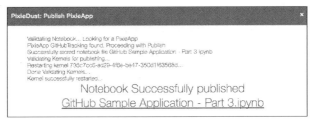

Successful publish screen

You can then test the application by clicking on the provided link, which you can copy and share with users on your team. The following screenshot shows the three main screens of the *GitHub Tracking* application running as a web application on the PixieGateway:

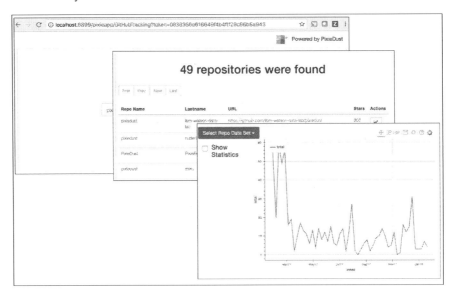

PixieApp running as a web application

Now that you know how to publish a PixieApp, let's review a few developer best practices and rules that will help you optimize PixieApps that are intended to be published as web applications:

- A PixieApp instance is created for each user session, therefore to improve performances, make sure that it doesn't include code that is long-running or that loads a large amount of static data (data that doesn't change often). Instead, place it in the warmup code section and reference it from the PixieApp as needed.

- Don't forget to add the code that runs the PixieApp in the same cell. If not, you'll end up with a blank page when running it on the web. As a good practice, it is recommended to assign the PixieApp instance into its own variable. For example, do this:

```
app = GitHubTracking()
app.run()
```

That's instead of the following

```
GitHubTracking().run()
```

- You can have multiple PixieApp classes declared in the same Notebook, which is needed if you are using child PixieApp or PixieApp inheritance. However, only one of them can be the main PixieApp, which the PixieGateway will run. It is the one that has the extra code that instantiates and runs the PixieApp.

- It's a good idea to add a Docstring (`https://www.python.org/dev/peps/pep-0257`) to your PixieApp class that gives a short description of the application. As we'll see in the *PixieGateway admin Console* section, later in this chapter, this docstring will be displayed in the PixieGateway admin console, as in the following example:

```
@PixieApp
class GitHubTracking(RepoAnalysis):
    """
    GitHub Tracking Sample Application
    """
    @route()
    def main_screen(self):
        return """
    ...
```

Encoding state in the PixieApp URL

In some cases, you may want to capture the state of a PixieApp in the URL as query parameters so that it can be bookmarked and/or shared with other people. The idea is that, when using query parameters, the PixieApp doesn't start from the main screen but rather automatically activates the route corresponding to the parameters. For example, in the *GitHub Tracking* application, you could use `http://localhost:8899/pixieapp/GitHubTracking?query=pixiedust` to bypass the initial screen and jump directly to the table showing the list of repositories that match the given query.

You can have the query parameters automatically added to the URL when the route is activated by adding the `persist_args` special argument to the route.

It would look like this for the `do_search()` route:

```
@route(query="*", persist_args='true')
@templateArgs
def do_search(self, query):
    self.first_url = "https://api.github.com/search/
repositories?q={}".format(query)
    self.prev_url = None
    self.next_url = None
    self.last_url = None
    ...
```

> You can find the code file here:
> `https://github.com/DTAIEB/Thoughtful-Data-Science/blob/master/chapter%204/sampleCode1.py`

The `persist_args` keyword argument does not affect how the route is activated. It is only there to automatically add the proper query arguments to the URL when activated. You can try to make this simple change in the Notebook, republish the PixieApp to the PixieGateway server, and try it out. As soon as you hit the submit button on the first screen, you'll notice that the URL is automatically updated to include the query argument.

> **Note:** The `persist_args` argument also works when running in the Notebook although the implementation is different since we don't have a URL. Instead, the parameters are added to the cell metadata using the `pixieapp` key, as shown in the following screenshot:

Edit Cell Metadata ✕

Manually edit the JSON below to manipulate the metadata for this cell. We recommend putting custom metadata attributes in an appropriately named substructure, so they don't conflict with those of others.

```
1  {
2    "trusted": true,
3    "pixiedust": {
4      "displayParams": {},
5      "pixieapp": {
6        "query": "pixiedust"
7      }
8    }
9  }
```

Cancel Edit

Cell metadata showing the PixieApp parameters

If you are using the `persist_args` feature, you may find that, while doing iterative development, it becomes cumbersome to always go to the cell metadata to remove the parameters. As a shortcut, the PixieApp framework adds a home button in the top-right toolbar to reset the arguments with a single click.

As an alternative, you could also avoid saving the route arguments in the cell metadata altogether when running in the Notebook (but still save them while running on the web). To do that, you would need to use web as the value for the `persist_args` argument instead of `true`:

```
@route(query="*", persist_args='web')
...
```

Sharing charts by publishing them as web pages

In this section, we show how to easily share a chart created by the `display()` API and publish it as a web page.

Using the example from *Chapter 2, Data Science at Scale with Jupyter Notebooks and PixieDust,* let's load the cars performance dataset and create a chart using `display()`:

```
import pixiedust
cars = pixiedust.sampleData(1, forcePandas=True) #car performance data
display(cars)
```

You can find the code file here:
`https://github.com/DTAIEB/Thoughtful-Data-Science/blob/master/chapter%204/sampleCode2.py`

In the PixieDust output interface, select the **Bar Chart** menu, then in the options dialog, select `horsepower` for the **Keys** and `mpg` for the **Values,** as shown in the following screenshot:

PixieDust Chart options

We then use the **Share** button to invoke the chart sharing dialog as shown in the following screenshot, which uses Bokeh as the renderer:

 Note: Chart sharing works with any renderer, and I encourage you to try it with other renderers such as Matplotlib and Mapbox.

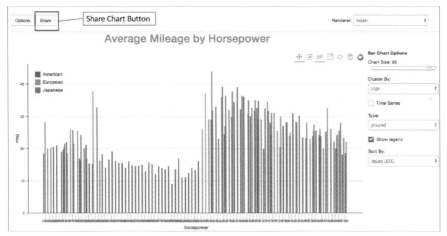

Invoke the Share Chart dialog

In the **Share Chart** dialog, you can specify the PixieGateway server and an optional description for the chart:

 Note that as a convenience, PixieDust will automatically remember the last one used.

Share Chart dialog

Clicking on the **Share** button will start the publishing process that takes the chart content to the PixieGateway and then returns a unique URL to the web page. Similar to the PixieApp, you can then share this URL with the team:

Chart sharing confirmation dialog

The confirmation dialog contains the unique URL for the chart and an HTML fragment that lets you embed the chart in your own web page, such as a blog post, and a dashboard.

Clicking on the link will show the following PixieGateway page:

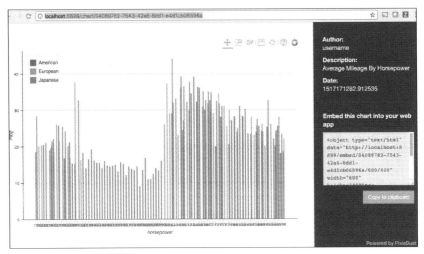

Chart page

The preceding page shows metadata about the chart, for example, **Author**, **Description**, and **Date,** as well as the embedded HTML fragment. Notice that if the chart has interactivity (as is the case for Bokeh, Brunel, or Mapbox), then it is preserved in the PixieGateway page.

For example, in the preceding screenshot, the user can still wheel zoom, box zoom, and pan to explore the chart or download the chart as a PNG file.

Embedding the chart in your own page is also very easy. Simply copy the embedded HTML fragment anywhere in your HTML, as shown in the following example:

```
<!DOCTYPE html>
<html>
    <head>
        <meta charset="utf-8">
        <title>Example page with embedded chart</title>
    </head>
    <body>
        <h1> Embedded a PixieDust Chart in a custom HTML Page</h1>
        <div>
            <object type="text/html" width="600" height="400"
                data="http://localhost:8899/embed/04089782-7543-42a6-
8dd1-e4d1cb06596a/600/400">
                <a href="http://localhost:8899/embed/04089782-7543-
42a6-8dd1-e4d1cb06596a">View Chart</a>
            </object>
        </div>
    </body>
</html>
```

 You can find the code file here:

https://github.com/DTAIEB/Thoughtful-Data-Science/blob/master/chapter%204/sampleCode3.html

Embedded chart objects must use the same level of security or higher as the browser. If not, the browser will throw a Mixed Content error. For example, if the host page is loaded over HTTPS, then the embedded chart must also be loaded over HTTPS, which means that you'll need to enable HTTPS in the PixieGateway server. You can also visit `http://jupyter-kernel-gateway.readthedocs.io/en/latest/config-options.html` to configure an SSL/TLS certificate for the PixieGateway server. Another solution that is easier to maintain would be to configure an Ingress service for the Kubernetes cluster that provides TLS termination.

For convenience, we provide a template ingress YAML file for the PixieGateway service here: `https://github.com/ibm-watson-data-lab/pixiegateway/blob/master/etc/ingress.yml`. You will need to update this file with the TLS host and the secret provided by your provider. For example, if you are using the IBM Cloud Kubernetes Service, you just have to enter the cluster name in the `<your cluster name>` placeholder. You can find more information on how to redirect HTTP to HTTPS here: `https://console.bluemix.net/docs/containers/cs_annotations.html#redirect-to-https`. Ingress services are a great way to improve security, reliability, and protect against DDOS attacks. For example, you can set various limits, such as the number of requests/connections per seconds allowed for each unique IP address or maximum bandwidth allowed. For more information please see `https://kubernetes.io/docs/concepts/services-networking/ingress`.

PixieGateway admin console

The admin console is a great tool to manage your resources and troubleshoot them. You can access it using the `/admin` URL. Notice that you will need to authenticate with the user/password that you configured (see the *PixieGateway server configuration* section for instructions on how to configure the user/password in this chapter; by default the user is `admin` and the password is <blank>).

The user interface for the admin console is composed of multiple menus focused on a specific task. Let's look at them one by one:

- **PixieApps**:
    - Information about all the deployed PixieApps: URL, description, and so on

- ° Security management
- ° Actions, for example, delete, and download

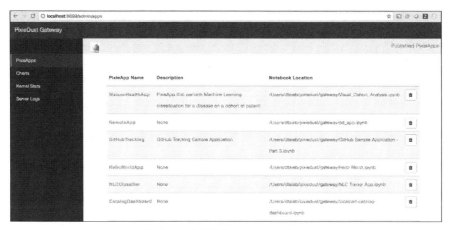

Admin console PixieApp management page

- **Charts:**
    - ° Information about all the published charts: link, preview, and so on
    - ° Actions, for example, delete, download, and embed fragment

Admin console chart management page

- **Kernel Stats**:

  The following screenshot shows the **Kernel Stats** screen:

Admin console Kernel Stats page

This screen shows a live table of all the kernels currently running in the PixieGateway. Each row contains the following information:

  - **Kernel Name**: This is the name of the kernel with a drill-down link, which shows the **Kernel Spec**, **Log**, and **Python Console**.
  - **Status**: This shows the status as `idle` or `busy`.
  - **Busy Ratio**: This is a value between 0 and 100% that denotes the kernel utilization since it was started.
  - **Running Apps**: This is a list of running PixieApps. Each PixieApp is a drill-down link that displays the warmup code and runs code for the PixieApp. This is very useful for troubleshooting errors since you can see what code is being run by the PixieGateway.
  - **Users Count**: This is the number of users with open sessions in this kernel.

- **Server Logs**:

  Full access the tornado server log for troubleshooting

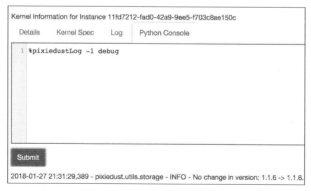

PixieDust Gateway

```
[I 180129 21:31:58 web:2063] 200 GET /stats (127.0.0.1) 1.09ms
[I 180129 21:31:58 web:2063] 200 GET /admin/stats/app/GitHubTracking/kernel/11fd7212-fad0-42a9-9ee5-f703c8ae150c (127.0.0
[I 180129 21:31:58 web:2063] 304 GET /pixiedust.css (127.0.0.1) 9.74ms
[I 180129 21:31:58 web:2063] 304 GET /pixiedust.js (127.0.0.1) 22.60ms
[I 180129 21:34:29 web:2063] 200 GET /admin/stats (127.0.0.1) 5.59ms
[I 180129 21:34:29 web:2063] 304 GET /pixiedust.css (127.0.0.1) 8.53ms
[I 180129 21:34:29 web:2063] 304 GET /pixiedust.js (127.0.0.1) 23.89ms
[I 180129 21:34:30 web:2063] 200 GET /stats (127.0.0.1) 1.03ms
[I 180129 21:34:31 web:2063] 200 GET /admin/stats/kernel/11fd7212-fad0-42a9-9ee5-f703c8ae150c (127.0.0.1) 8.20ms
[I 180129 21:34:31 web:2063] 304 GET /pixiedust.css (127.0.0.1) 9.01ms
[I 180129 21:34:31 web:2063] 304 GET /pixiedust.js (127.0.0.1) 23.22ms
[I 180129 21:34:47 web:2063] 200 POST /executeCode/11fd7212-fad0-42a9-9ee5-f703c8ae150c (127.0.0.1) 1260.49ms
[I 180129 21:35:18 web:2063] 200 POST /executeCode/11fd7212-fad0-42a9-9ee5-f703c8ae150c (127.0.0.1) 20.27ms
[I 180129 21:36:30 web:2063] 200 GET /admin/stats/kernel/11fd7212-fad0-42a9-9ee5-f703c8ae150c (127.0.0.1) 8.44ms
[I 180129 21:36:30 web:2063] 304 GET /pixiedust.css (127.0.0.1) 12.85ms
[I 180129 21:36:30 web:2063] 304 GET /pixiedust.js (127.0.0.1) 23.10ms
[I 180129 21:36:43 web:2063] 200 POST /executeCode/11fd7212-fad0-42a9-9ee5-f703c8ae150c (127.0.0.1) 15.55ms
[I 180129 21:40:18 web:2063] 200 GET /admin/logs (127.0.0.1) 64.33ms
[I 180129 21:40:18 web:2063] 304 GET /pixiedust.css (127.0.0.1) 11.68ms
[I 180129 21:40:18 web:2063] 304 GET /pixiedust.js (127.0.0.1) 22.90ms
```

Admin console server logs page

Python Console

The Python Console is invoked by clicking on the kernel link in the **Kernel Stats** screen. The admin can use it to execute any code against the kernel, which can be useful to troubleshoot issues.

For example, the following screenshot shows how to invoke the PixieDust log:

Kernel Information for Instance 11fd7212-fad0-42a9-9ee5-f703c8ae150c

Details   Kernel Spec   Log   Python Console

```
1 %pixiedustLog -l debug
```

Submit

2018-01-27 21:31:29,389 - pixiedust.utils.storage - INFO - No change in version: 1.1.6 -> 1.1.6.

Display PixieDust log from the PixieGateway admin Python Console

Displaying warmup and run code for a PixieApp

When an execution error happens while loading a page, the PixieGateway will show the full Python traceback in the browser. However, the error may be hard to find because its root cause may be in the warmup code that is executed once when the PixieApp starts. One important debugging technique is to look at the warmup and run code executed by the PixieGateway to spot any anomalies.

If the error is still not obvious, you could, for example, copy the warmup and run code in a temporary Notebook and try to run it from there, with the hope that you can reproduce the error and spot the issue.

You can access the warmup and run code by clicking on the PixieApp link on the **Kernel Stats** screen, which will take you to the following screen:

```
Details for GitHubTracking    Warmup Code    Run Code

 3  from datetime import datetime
 4  import requests
 5  import pixiedust
 6  import pandas
 7
 8  def ns17_load_commit_activity(owner, repo_name):
 9      response = requests.get('https://api.github.com/repos/{}/{}/stats/commit_activity'.format(
10      pdf = pandas.DataFrame([{'total': item['total'], 'week': datetime.fromtimestamp(item['week
11      return {'pdf': pdf, 'chart_options': {'handlerId': 'lineChart', 'keyFields': 'week', 'valu
12  display(ns17_load_commit_activity('ibm-watson-data-lab', 'pixiedust')['pdf'])
13  ns17_analyses = [('Commit Activity', ns17_load_commit_activity)]
14  from pixiedust.display.app import *
15  import requests
16  import pandas
17
```

Display the warmup and run code

Note that the warmup and run code do not contain the original code formatting and therefore can be harder to read. You can mitigate this issue by copying it and pasting the code into a temporary Notebook and reformatting it again.

Summary

After reading this chapter, you should be able to install, configure, and manage a PixieGateway microservice server, publish charts as a web page, and deploy a PixieApp from a Notebook to a web application. Whether you are a data scientist working on analytics in a Jupyter Notebook or a developer writing and deploying applications targeted at the line of a business user, we've shown, in this chapter, how PixieDust can help accomplish your tasks more efficiently and reduce the time it takes to operationalize your analytics.

In the next chapter, we'll look at advanced topics and best practices related to PixieDust and the PixieApp programming model, which will be useful when we go over the industry use cases and sample data pipelines in the remaining chapters.

5
Best Practices and Advanced PixieDust Concepts

"In God we Trust, all others bring data."

– W. Edwards Deming

In the remaining chapters of this book, we will do a deep dive into the architecture of industry use cases, including the implementation of sample data pipelines, heavily applying the techniques we've learned so far. Before we start looking at the code, let's complete our toolbox with a few best practices and advanced PixieDust concepts that will be useful in the implementation of our sample applications:

- Calling third-party Python libraries with `@captureOutput` decorator
- Increasing modularity and code reuse of your PixieApp
- PixieDust support of streaming data
- Adding dashboard drill-downs with PixieApp events
- Extending PixieDust with a custom display renderer
- Debugging:
    - Line-by-line Python code debugging running on the Jupyter Notebook using pdb
    - Visual debugging with PixieDebugger
    - Using the PixieDust logging framework to troubleshoot issues
    - Tips for client-side JavaScript debugging
- Running Node.js inside a Python Notebook

Use @captureOutput decorator to integrate the output of third-party Python libraries

Suppose that you want to reuse your PixieApp in a third-party library that you have been using for a while in order to perform a certain task, such as, for example, computing clusters with the scikit-learn machine learning library (http://scikit-learn.org) and displaying them as a graph. The problem is that most of the time, you are calling a high-level method that doesn't return data, but rather directly draws something on the cell output area, such as a chart or a report table. Calling this method from a PixieApp route will not work because the contract for routes is to return an HTML fragment string that will be processed by the framework. In this case, the method most likely doesn't return anything since it is writing the results directly in the cell output. The solution is to use the `@captureOutput` decorator—which is part of the PixieApp framework—in the route method.

Create a word cloud image with @captureOutput

To better illustrate the `@captureOutput` scenario described earlier, let's take a concrete example where we want to build a PixieApp that uses the `wordcloud` Python library (https://pypi.python.org/pypi/wordcloud) to generate a word cloud image from a text file provided by the user via a URL.

We first install the `wordcloud` library by running the following command in its own cell:

```
!pip install wordcloud
```

 Note: Make sure to restart the kernel when the installation of the `wordcloud` library is complete.

The code for the PixieApp looks like this:

```
from pixiedust.display.app import *
import requests
from wordcloud import WordCloud
import matplotlib.pyplot as plt


@PixieApp
```

```
class WordCloudApp():
    @route()
    def main_screen(self):
        return """
        <div style="text-align:center">
            <label>Enter a url: </label>
            <input type="text" size="80" id="url{{prefix}}">
            <button type="submit"
                pd_options="url=$val(url{{prefix}})"
                pd_target="wordcloud{{prefix}}">
                Go
            </button>
        </div>
        <center><div id="wordcloud{{prefix}}"></div></center>
        """

    @route(url="*")
    @captureOutput
    def generate_word_cloud(self, url):
        text = requests.get(url).text
        plt.axis("off")
        plt.imshow(
            WordCloud(max_font_size=40).generate(text),
            interpolation='bilinear'
        )

app = WordCloudApp()
app.run()
```

 You can find the code here:
https://github.com/DTAIEB/Thoughtful-Data-Science/
blob/master/chapter%205/sampleCode1.py

Notice that by simply adding the @captureOutput decorator to the generate_word_
cloud route, we don't need to return an HTML fragment string any more. We can
simply invoke the Matplotlib imshow() function that sends the image to the system
output. The PixieApp framework will take care of capturing the output and package
it as an HTML fragment string that will be injected in the correct div placeholder.
The result is as follows:

Note: We use the following input URL coming from the `wordcloud` repo on GitHub:

```
https://github.com/amueller/word_cloud/blob/master/
examples/constitution.txt
```

 Another good link to use is:

```
https://raw.githubusercontent.com/amueller/word_cloud/
master/examples/a_new_hope.txt
```

Simple PixieApp that generates a word cloud from a text

Any function that draws directly to the cell output can be used with the @ captureOutput decorator. For example, you can use the Matplotlib show() method or the IPython display() method with the HTML or JavaScript classes. You can even use the display_markdown() method to output rich text using the Markdown markup language (https://en.wikipedia.org/wiki/Markdown) as shown in the following code:

```
from pixiedust.display.app import *
from IPython.display import display_markdown

@PixieApp
class TestMarkdown():
    @route()
    @captureOutput
    def main_screen(self):
        display_markdown("""
# Main Header:
## Secondary Header with bullet
1. item1
2. item2
3. item3
```

```
Showing image of the PixieDust logo
![alt text](https://github.com/pixiedust/pixiedust/raw/master/docs/_
static/PixieDust%202C%20\(256x256\).png "PixieDust Logo")
    """, raw=True)

TestMarkdown().run()
```

This produces the following result:

PixieApp using @captureOutput with Markdown

Increase modularity and code reuse

Breaking up your application into smaller, self-contained components is always a good development practice because it makes the code reusable and easier to maintain. The PixieApp framework provides two ways to create and run reusable components:

- Dynamically invoking other PixieApps with the pd_app attribute
- Packaging part of an application as a reusable widget

Using the pd_app attribute, you can dynamically invoke another PixieApp (we'll call it child PixieApp from here on) by its fully qualified class name. The output of the child PixieApp is placed in the host HTML element (usually a div element) or in a dialog by using the runInDialog=true option. You can also initialize the child PixieApp using the pd_options attribute, in which case the framework will invoke the corresponding route.

To better understand how pd_app works, let's rewrite our WordCloud application by refactoring the code that generates the WordCloud image in its own PixieApp that we'll call WCChildApp.

The following code implements `WCChildApp` as a regular PixieApp, but notice that it doesn't contain a default route. It only has a route called `generate_word_cloud` that is supposed to be called by another PixieApp using a `url` argument:

```
from pixiedust.display.app import *
import requests
from wordcloud import WordCloud
import matplotlib.pyplot as plt

@PixieApp
class WCChildApp():
    @route(url='*')
    @captureOutput
    def generate_word_cloud(self, url):
        text = requests.get(url).text
        plt.axis("off")
        plt.imshow(
            WordCloud(max_font_size=40).generate(text),
            interpolation='bilinear'
        )
```

 You can find the code file here:
https://github.com/DTAIEB/Thoughtful-Data-Science/
blob/master/chapter%205/sampleCode2.py

We can now build the main PixieApp that will invoke the `WCChildApp` when the user clicks on the **Go** button after specifying the URL:

```
@PixieApp
class WordCloudApp():
    @route()
    def main_screen(self):
        return """
        <div style="text-align:center">
            <label>Enter a url: </label>
            <input type="text" size="80" id="url{{prefix}}">
            <button type="submit"
                pd_options="url=$val(url{{prefix}})"
                pd_app="WCChildApp"
                pd_target="wordcloud{{prefix}}">
                Go
            </button>
        </div>
```

```
<center><div id="wordcloud{{prefix}}"></div></center>
"""

app = WordCloudApp()
app.run()
```

 You can find the code file here:
https://github.com/DTAIEB/Thoughtful-Data-Science/
blob/master/chapter%205/sampleCode3.py

In the preceding code, the Go button has the following attributes:

- pd_app="WCChildApp": Use the class name for the child PixieApp. Note that if your child PixieApp lives in an imported Python module, then you'll need to use the fully qualified name.
- pd_options="url=$val(url{{prefix}})": Store the URL entered by the user as an initialization option to the child PixieApp.
- pd_target="wordcloud{{prefix}}": Tell PixieDust to place the output of the child PixieApp in the div with the ID wordcloud{{prefix}}.

The pd_app attribute is a powerful way to modularize your code by encapsulating the logic and presentation of a component. The pd_widget attribute provides another way to achieve similar results, but this time the component is not invoked externally, but rather by inheritance.

Each method has pros and cons:

- The pd_widget technique is implemented as a route and is certainly more lightweight than pd_app, which requires the creation of an entirely new PixieApp instance. Note that both pd_widget and pd_app (through the parent_pixieapp variable) have access to all variables contained in the host app.
- The pd_app attribute provides a cleaner separation between the components and more flexibility than widgets. You could, for example, have a button that dynamically invokes multiple PixieApps based on some user selection.

 Note: As we'll see later in this chapter, this is actually what the PixieDust display uses for the options dialog.

If you find yourself in need of having multiple copies of the same component in a PixieApp, ask yourself whether the component requires its state to be maintained in a class variable. If that's the case, it is preferable to use pd_app, but, if not, then using pd_widget would work as well.

Creating a widget with pd_widget

To create a widget, you can use the following steps:

1. Create a PixieApp class that contains a route tagged with a special argument called widget
2. Make the main class inherit from the PixieApp widget
3. Invoke the widget using the pd_widget attribute on a div element

Again, as an illustration, let's rewrite the WordCloud app with the widget:

```
from pixiedust.display.app import *
import requests
from word_cloud import WordCloud
import matplotlib.pyplot as plt

@PixieApp
class WCChildApp():
    @route(widget='wordcloud')
    @captureOutput
    def generate_word_cloud(self):
        text = requests.get(self.url).text if self.url else ""
        plt.axis("off")
        plt.imshow(
            WordCloud(max_font_size=40).generate(text),
            interpolation='bilinear'
        )
```

 You can find the code file here:
https://github.com/DTAIEB/Thoughtful-Data-Science/blob/master/chapter%205/sampleCode4.py

Notice in the preceding code that url is now referenced as a class variable because we assume that the base class will provide it. The code has to test whether url is None, which would be the case on startup. We implement it this way because pd_widget is an attribute that cannot easily be dynamically generated (you would have to use a secondary route that generates the div fragment with the pd_widget attribute).

The main PixieApp class now looks like this:

```python
@PixieApp
class WordCloudApp(WCChildApp):
    @route()
    def main_screen(self):
        self.url=None
        return """
<div style="text-align:center">
    <label>Enter a url: </label>
    <input type="text" size="80" id="url{{prefix}}">
    <button type="submit"
        pd_script="self.url = '$val(url{{prefix}})'"
        pd_refresh="wordcloud{{prefix}}">
        Go
    </button>
</div>
<center><div pd_widget="wordcloud"
        id="wordcloud{{prefix}}"></div></center>
        """

app = WordCloudApp()
app.run()
```

 You can find the code file here:

https://github.com/DTAIEB/Thoughtful-Data-Science/
blob/master/chapter%205/sampleCode5.py

The div that contains the pd_widget attribute is rendered on start, but since url is still None, no word cloud is actually generated. The Go button has a pd_script attribute that set the self.url to the value provided by the user. It also has a pd_refresh attribute sets to the pd_widget div that will call the wordcloud widget again, but this time with a URL initialized to the correct value.

In this section, we've seen two ways to modularize your code for reuse, as well as the pros and cons for both. I strongly recommend that you play with the code to get a feel of when to use each technique. Don't worry if you feel this is still a little fuzzy; it will hopefully become clearer when we use these techniques in the sample code of the chapters ahead.

In the next section, we change gears and look at streaming data support in PixieDust.

PixieDust support of streaming data

With the rise of **IOT** devices (**Internet of Things**), being able to analyze and visualize live streams of data is becoming more and more important. For example, you could have sensors such as thermometers in machines or portable medical devices like pacemakers, continuously streaming data to a streaming service such as Kafka. PixieDust makes it easier to work with live data inside Jupyter Notebooks by providing simple integration APIs to both the PixieApp and the `display()` framework.

On a visualization level, PixieDust uses Bokeh (`https://bokeh.pydata.org`) support for efficient data source updates to plot streaming data into live charts (note that at the moment, only line chart and scatter plot are supported, but more will be added in the future). The `display()` framework also supports geospatial visualization of streaming data using the Mapbox rendering engine.

To activate streaming visualizations, you need to use a class that inherits from `StreamingDataAdapter`, which is an abstract class that is part of the PixieDust API. This class acts as a generic bridge between the streaming data source and the visualization framework.

> **Note:** I recommend spending time looking at the code for `StreamingDataAdapter` here:
>
> `https://github.com/pixiedust/pixiedust/blob/0c536b45`
> `c9af681a4da160170d38879298aa87cb/pixiedust/display/`
> `streaming/__init__.py`

The following diagram shows how the `StreamingDataAdapter` data structure fits into the `display()` framework:

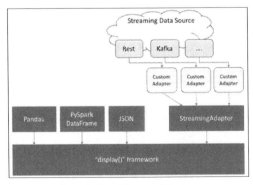

StreamingDataAdapter architecture

When implementing a subclass of `StreamingDataAdapter`, you must override the `doGetNextData()` method provided by the base class, which will be called repeatedly to fetch new data to update the visualization. You can also optionally override the `getMetadata()` method to pass context to the rendering engine (we'll use this method later to configure the Mapbox rendering).

The abstract implementation of `doGetNextData()` looks like this:

```
@abstractmethod
def doGetNextData(self):
    """Return the next batch of data from the underlying stream.
    Accepted return values are:
    1. (x,y): tuple of list/numpy arrays representing the x and y axis
    2. pandas dataframe
    3. y: list/numpy array representing the y axis. In this case,
the x axis is automatically created
    4. pandas serie: similar to #3
    5. json
    6. geojson
    7. url with supported payload (json/geojson)
    """
    Pass
```

> You can find the code file here:
> https://github.com/DTAIEB/Thoughtful-Data-Science/blob/master/chapter%205/sampleCode6.py

The preceding docstring explains the different types of data that is allowed to be returned from `doGetNextData()`.

As an example, we want to visualize the location of a fictitious drone wandering around the earth on a map and in real time. Its current location is provided by a REST service at: `https://wanderdrone.appspot.com`.

The payload uses GeoJSON (`http://geojson.org`), for example:

```
{
    "geometry": {
        "type": "Point",
        "coordinates": [
            -93.824908715741202, 10.875051131034805
        ]
    },
```

```
    "type": "Feature",
    "properties": {}
}
```

You can find the code file here:

`https://github.com/DTAIEB/Thoughtful-Data-Science/`
`blob/master/chapter%205/sampleCode7.json`

To render our drone location in real time, we create a `DroneStreamingAdapter` class
that inherits from `StreamingDataAdapter` and simply return the drone location
service URL in the `doGetNextData()` method as shown in the following code:

```python
from pixiedust.display.streaming import *

class DroneStreamingAdapter(StreamingDataAdapter):
    def getMetadata(self):
        iconImage = "rocket-15"
        return {
            "layout": {"icon-image": iconImage, "icon-size": 1.5},
            "type": "symbol"
        }
    def doGetNextData(self):
        return "https://wanderdrone.appspot.com/"
adapter = DroneStreamingAdapter()
display(adapter)
```

You can find the code file here:

`https://github.com/DTAIEB/Thoughtful-Data-Science/`
`blob/master/chapter%205/sampleCode8.py`

In the `getMetadata()` method, we return the Mapbox specific style properties
(as documented here: `https://www.mapbox.com/mapbox-gl-js/style-spec`) that
uses a rocket Maki icon (`https://www.mapbox.com/maki-icons`) as a symbol for
the drone.

With a few lines of code, we were able to create a real-time geospatial visualization
of a drone location, with the following results:

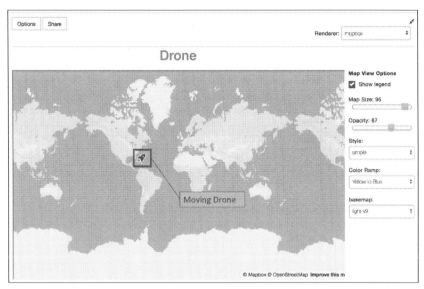

Real-time geospatial mapping of a drone

 You can find the complete Notebook for this example in the PixieDust repo at this location:

`https://github.com/pixiedust/pixiedust/blob/master/notebook/pixieapp-streaming/Mapbox%20Streaming.ipynb`

Adding streaming capabilities to your PixieApp

In the next example, we show how to visualize streaming data coming from an Apache Kafka data source, using the `MessageHubStreamingApp` PixieApp provided out of the box by PixieDust: `https://github.com/pixiedust/pixiedust/blob/master/pixiedust/apps/messageHub/messageHubApp.py`.

 Note: `MessageHubStreamingApp` works with the IBM Cloud Kafka service called Message Hub (`https://console.bluemix.net/docs/services/MessageHub/index.html#messagehub`), but it can easily be adapted to any other Kafka service.

Don't worry if you are not familiar with Apache Kafka as we'll cover aspects of this in *Chapter 7, Big Data Twitter Sentiment Analysis*.

This PixieApp lets the user choose a Kafka topic associated with a service instance and display the events in real-time. Assuming that the events payload from the selected topic uses a JSON format, it presents a schema inferred from sampling the events data. The user can then choose a particular field (must be numerical) and a real-time chart showing the average of the values for this field over time is displayed.

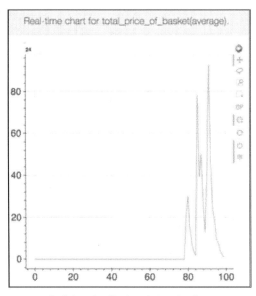

Real-time visualization of streaming data

The key PixieApp attribute needed to provide streaming capabilities is `pd_refresh_rate`, which executes a particular kernel request at specified intervals (pull model). In the preceding application, we use it to update the real-time chart, as shown in the following HTML fragment returned by the `showChart` route:

```
@route(topic="*",streampreview="*",schemaX="*")
def showChart(self, schemaX):
    self.schemaX = schemaX
    self.avgChannelData = self.streamingData.
getStreamingChannel(self.computeAverages)
    return """
<div class="well" style="text-align:center">
```

```
    <div style="font-size:x-large">Real-time chart for {{this.
schemaX}}(average).</div>
</div>

<div pd_refresh_rate="1000" pd_entity="avgChannelData"></div>
    """
```

You can find the code file here:
https://github.com/DTAIEB/Thoughtful-Data-Science/
blob/master/chapter%205/sampleCode9.py

The preceding div is bound to the `avgChannelData` entity via the `pd_entity` attribute and is responsible for creating the real-time chart that is updated every second (*pd_refresh_rate=1000 ms*). In turn, the `avgChannelData` entity is created via a call to `getStreamingChannel()`, which is passed to the `self`. The `computeAverage` function is responsible for updating the average value for all the data being streamed. It is important to note that `avgChannelData` is a class that inherits from `StreamingDataAdapter` and, therefore, can be passed to the `display()` framework for building real-time charts.

The last piece of the puzzle is for the PixieApp to return a `displayHandler` needed by the `display()` framework. This is done by overriding the `newDisplayHandler()` method as follows:

```
def newDisplayHandler(self, options, entity):
    if self.streamingDisplay is None:
        self.streamingDisplay = LineChartStreamingDisplay(options,
entity)
    else:
        self.streamingDisplay.options = options
    return self.streamingDisplay
```

You can find the code file here:
https://github.com/DTAIEB/Thoughtful-Data-Science/
blob/master/chapter%205/sampleCode10.py

In the preceding code, we use it to create an instance of `LineChartStreamingDisplay` provided by PixieDust in the `pixiedust.display.streaming.bokeh` package (https://github.com/pixiedust/pixiedust/blob/master/pixiedust/display/streaming/bokeh/lineChartStreamingDisplay.py), passing the `avgChannelData` entity.

If you want to see this application in action, you need to create a Message Hub service instance on IBM Cloud (`https://console.bluemix.net/catalog/services/message-hub`) and, using its credentials, invoke this PixieApp in a Notebook with the following code:

```
from pixiedust.apps.messageHub import *
MessageHubStreamingApp().run(
    credentials={
        "username": "XXXX",
        "password": "XXXX",
        "api_key" : "XXXX",
        "prod": True
    }
)
```

If you are interested in knowing more about PixieDust streaming, you can find other streaming application examples here:

- A simple PixieApp that demonstrate how to create streaming visualizations from randomly generated data: `https://github.com/pixiedust/pixiedust/blob/master/notebook/pixieapp-streaming/PixieApp%20Streaming-Random.ipynb`

- PixieApp that shows how to build live visualization of stock tickers: `https://github.com/pixiedust/pixiedust/blob/master/notebook/pixieapp-streaming/PixieApp%20Streaming-Stock%20Ticker.ipynb`

The next topic will cover PixieApp events that let you add interactivity between different components of your application.

Adding dashboard drill-downs with PixieApp events

The PixieApp framework supports sending and receiving events between different components using the publish-subscribe pattern available in browsers. The great advantage of using this model, which borrows from the loose coupling pattern (`https://en.wikipedia.org/wiki/Loose_coupling`), is that it allows the sending and receiving components to remain agnostic of each other. Therefore, their implementation can be executed independently from one another and will not be sensitive to changes in requirements. This can be very useful when your PixieApp is using components from different PixieApps built by different teams, or if the events are coming from the user interacting with a chart (for instance, clicking on a map) and you want to provide drill-down features.

Each event carries a JSON payload of arbitrary keys and values. The payload must have at least one of the following keys (or both):

- `targetDivId`: A DOM ID identifying the element sending the event
- `type`: A string identifying the event type

Publishers can trigger events in two ways:

- **Declarative**: Use the `pd_event_payload` attribute to specify the payload content. This attribute follows the same rules as `pd_options`:
    - Each key/value pair must be encoded using the `key=value` notation
    - The event will be triggered by a click or a change event
    - Support must be provided for the `$val()` directive to dynamically inject user-entered input
    - Use the `<pd_event_payload>` child to enter raw JSON

    Example:

    ```
    <button type="submit" pd_event_payload="type=topicA;message=Button
    clicked">
        Send event A
    </button>
    ```

    Alternatively, we can use this:

    ```
    <button type="submit">
        <pd_event_payload>
        {
            "type":"topicA",
            "message":"Button Clicked"
        }
        </pd_event_payload>
        Send event A
    </button>
    ```

 You can find the code file here:

https://github.com/DTAIEB/Thoughtful-Data-Science/
blob/master/chapter%205/sampleCode11.html

- **Programmatic**: In some cases, you may want to directly trigger an event via JavaScript. In this case, you can use the `sendEvent(payload, divId)` method of the `pixiedust` global object. The `divId` is an optional argument that specifies the origin of the event. If the `divId` argument is omitted, then it defaults to the `divId` of the element that is currently sending the event. As a result, you should always use `pixiedust.sendEvent` without a `divId` from a JavaScript handler of a user event such as click, and hover.

Example:

```
<table
onclick="pixiedust.sendEvent({type:'topicB',text:event.srcElement.
innerText})">
    <tr><td>Row 1</td></tr>
    <tr><td>Row 2</td></tr>
    <tr><td>Row 3</td></tr>
</table>
```

You can find the code file here:
`https://github.com/DTAIEB/Thoughtful-Data-Science/`
`blob/master/chapter%205/sampleCode12.html`

Subscribers can listen to an event by declaring a `<pd_event_handler>` element that can accept any of the PixieApp Kernel execution attributes, such as `pd_options` and `pd_script`. It must also use the `pd_source` attribute to filter which events they want to process. The `pd_source` attribute can contain one of the following values:

- `targetDivId`: Only events originating from the element with the specified ID will be accepted
- `type`: Only events with the specified type will be accepted
- `"*"`: Denotes that any event will be accepted

Example:

```
<div class="col-sm-6" id="listenerA{{prefix}}">
    Listening to button event
    <pd_event_handler
        pd_source="topicA"
        pd_script="print(eventInfo)"
        pd_target="listenerA{{prefix}}">
    </pd_event_handler>
</div>
```

You can find the code file here:
https://github.com/DTAIEB/Thoughtful-Data-Science/
blob/master/chapter%205/sampleCode13.html

The following diagram shows how components interact with one another:

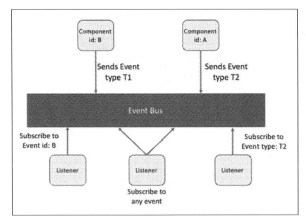

Sending/receiving events between components

In the following code sample, we illustrate the PixieDust eventing system by building two publishers, a button element and a table, where each row is an event source. We also have two listeners implemented as div elements:

```python
from pixiedust.display.app import *
@PixieApp
class TestEvents():
    @route()
    def main_screen(self):
        return """
<div>
    <button type="submit">
        <pd_event_payload>
        {
            "type":"topicA",
            "message":"Button Clicked"
        }
        </pd_event_payload>
        Send event A
    </button>
```

```
    <table onclick="pixiedust.sendEvent({type:'topicB',text:event.
srcElement.innerText})">
        <tr><td>Row 1</td></tr>
        <tr><td>Row 2</td></tr>
        <tr><td>Row 3</td></tr>
    </table>
</div>
<div class="container" style="margin-top:30px">
    <div class="row">
        <div class="col-sm-6" id="listenerA{{prefix}}">
            Listening to button event
            <pd_event_handler pd_source="topicA" pd_
script="print(eventInfo)" pd_target="listenerA{{prefix}}">
            </pd_event_handler>
        </div>
        <div class="col-sm-6" id="listenerB{{prefix}}">
            Listening to table event
            <pd_event_handler pd_source="topicB" pd_
script="print(eventInfo)" pd_target="listenerB{{prefix}}">
            </pd_event_handler>
        </div>
    </div>
</div>
        """
app = TestEvents()
app.run()
```

 You can find the code file here:

> https://github.com/DTAIEB/Thoughtful-Data-Science/
> blob/master/chapter%205/sampleCode14.py

The preceding code produces the following results:

User interaction flow for PixieApp events

PixieApp events enable you to create sophisticated dashboards with drill-down capabilities. It is also good to know that you can leverage events that are automatically published for some of the charts generated by the `display()` framework. For example, built-in renderers, such as Google Maps, Mapbox, and Table, will automatically generate events when the user clicks somewhere on the chart. This is very useful for rapidly building all kinds of interactive dashboards with drill-down capabilities.

In the next topic, we'll discuss how to use the PixieDust extensibility APIs to create custom visualizations.

Extending PixieDust visualizations

PixieDust is designed to be highly extensible. You can create your own visualization and control when it can be invoked, based on the entity being displayed. There are multiple extensibility layers provided by the PixieDust framework. The lowest and most powerful one lets you create your own `Display` class. However, the majority of visualizations have a lot of properties in common, such as standard options (aggregation, max rows, title, and so on), or a caching mechanism to prevent recomputing everything if the user only selected a minor option that doesn't require reprocessing of the data.

To prevent users from reinventing the wheel every time, PixieDust offers a second extensibility layer called **renderer** that includes all the facilities described here.

The following diagram illustrates the different layers:

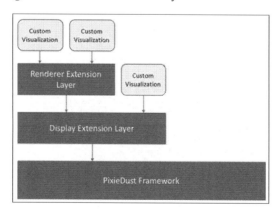

PixieDust extension layers

To start working with the **Display Extension Layer**, you'll need to get your visualization presented in the menu by creating a class that inherits from `pixiedust.display.DisplayHandlerMeta`. This class contains two methods that need to be overridden:

- `getMenuInfo(self,entity,dataHandler)`: Return an empty array if the entity passed as an argument is not supported, otherwise an array containing a set of JSON objects with information about the menu. Each JSON object must contain the following information:
    - `id`: A unique string that identifies your tool.
    - `categoryId`: A unique string that identifies the menu category or group. A full list of all the built-in categories is provided a little later on.
    - `title`: An arbitrary string that describes the menu.
    - `icon`: The name of a font-awesome icon, or a URL for an image.

- `newDisplayHandler(self,options,entity)`: When your menu is activated by the user, the `newDisplayHandler()` method is called. This method must return a class instance that inherits from `pixiedust.display.Display`. The contract is for this class to implement the `doRender()` method, which is responsible for creating the visualization.

Let's take the example of creating a custom table rendering for a pandas DataFrame. We first create the `DisplayHandlerMeta` class that configures the menu and the factory method:

```python
from pixiedust.display.display import *
import pandas
@PixiedustDisplay()
class SimpleDisplayMeta(DisplayHandlerMeta):
    @addId
    def getMenuInfo(self,entity,dataHandler):
        if type(entity) is pandas.core.frame.DataFrame:
            return [
                {"categoryId": "Table", "title": "Simple Table",
"icon": "fa-table", "id": "simpleTest"}
            ]
        return []
    def newDisplayHandler(self,options,entity):
        return SimpleDisplay(options,entity)
```

You can find the code file here:
https://github.com/DTAIEB/Thoughtful-Data-Science/
blob/master/chapter%205/sampleCode15.py

Notice that the preceding `SimpleDisplayMeta` class needs to be decorated with
`@PixiedustDisplay`, which is required to add this class to the internal PixieDust
registry of plugins. In the `getMenuInfo()` method, we first check whether the entity
type is *pandas DataFrame* and, if not, return an empty array signifying that this plugin
doesn't support the current entity and will therefore not contribute anything to the
menu. If the type is correct, we return an array with one JSON object containing the
menu info.

The factory method `newDisplayHandler()` gets passed the `options` and `entity`
as parameters. The `options` argument is a dictionary of key/value pairs containing
the various choices made by the users. As we'll see later, the visualization can define
arbitrary key/value pairs reflecting its capabilities, and the PixieDust framework
will automatically persist them in the cell metadata.

For example, you could add an option for displaying HTTP links as clickable
in the UI. In our example, we return a `SimpleDisplay` instance as defined here:

```
class SimpleDisplay(Display):
    def doRender(self, handlerId):
        self._addHTMLTemplateString("""
<table class="table table-striped">
    <thead>
        {%for column in entity.columns.tolist()%}
        <th>{{column}}</th>
        {%endfor%}
    </thead>
    <tbody>
        {%for _, row in entity.iterrows()%}
        <tr>
            {%for value in row.tolist()%}
            <td>{{value}}</td>
            {%endfor%}
        </tr>
        {%endfor%}
    </tbody>
</table>
        """)
```

You can find the code file here:

```
https://github.com/DTAIEB/Thoughtful-Data-Science/
blob/master/chapter%205/sampleCode16.py
```

As stated before, the `SimpleDisplay` class must inherit from the `Display` class and implement the `doRender()` method. Within the implementation of this method, you have access to the `self.entity` and `self.options` variables to adjust how the information is rendered on screen. In the preceding sample, we use the `self._addHTMLTemplateString()` method to create the HTML fragment that will render the visualization. As is the case for PixieApp routes, the string being passed to `self._addHTMLTemplateString()` can leverage the Jinja2 template engine and have automatic access to variables such as `entity`. If you don't want to hardcode the template string in the Python file, you can extract it into its own file that you must place in a directory called `templates` that must be located in the same directory as the calling Python file. You would then need to use the `self._addHTMLTemplate()` method that takes the name of the file as an argument (without specifying the `templates` directory).

 The other advantage of externalizing the HTML fragment into its own file is that you don't have to restart the kernel every time you make a change, which can save you a lot of time. Because of the way Python works, the same cannot be said if the HTML fragment is embedded in the source code, in which case you would have to restart the kernel for any changes made in the HTML fragment.

It is also important to note that `self._addHTMLTemplate()` and `self._addHTMLTemplateString()` accept keyword arguments that will be passed to the Jinja2 template. For example:

```
self._addHTMLTemplate('simpleTable.html', custom_arg = "Some value")
```

We can now run a cell that displays, for example, the `cars` dataset:

Note: The **Simple Table** extension only works with pandas, not Spark DataFrame. Therefore, you would need to use `forcePandas = True` when calling `sampleData()` if your Notebook is connected to Spark.

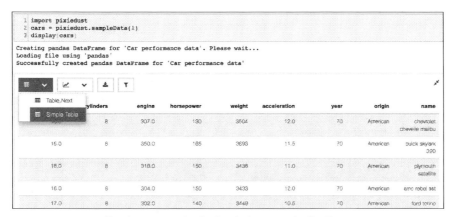

Running a custom visualization plugin on a pandas DataFrame

As shown in the PixieDust extension layer architecture diagram, you can also extend PixieDust using the **Renderer Extension Layer**, which is more prescriptive than the **Display Extension Layer** but provides many more capabilities out of the box, such as options management and interim data computation caching. From the user interface perspective, users can switch between renderers using a **Renderer** drop-down in the upper right-hand corner of the chart area.

PixieDust comes with a few built-in renderers, such as Matplotlib, Seaborn, Bokeh, Mapbox, Brunel, and Google Maps, but it doesn't declare any hard dependency on the underlying visualization libraries, including Bokeh, Brunel, or Seaborn. Therefore, it is incumbent on the user to manually install them, otherwise, they won't show up in the menus.

The following screenshot illustrates the mechanism to switch between renderers for a given chart:

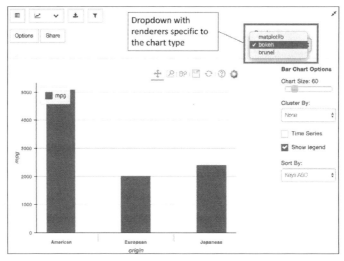

Switching between renderers

Adding a new renderer is similar to adding a display visualization (it's using the same APIs), though it's actually simpler since you only have to build one class (no need to build the metadata class). Here are the steps you need to follow:

1. Create a Display class that inherits from the specialized `BaseChartDisplay` class. Implement the required `doRenderChart()` method.

2. Use the `@PixiedustRenderer` decorator to register the `rendererId` (which must be unique across all renderers) and the type of chart being rendered.

   Note that the same `rendererId` can be reused for all the charts included in the renderer. PixieDust provides a set of core chart types:

   - `tableView`
   - `barChart`
   - `lineChart`
   - `scatterPlot`
   - `pieChart`
   - `mapView`
   - `histogram`

3. *(Optional)* Create a set of dynamic options using the `@commonChartOptions` decorator.

4. *(Optional)* Customize the options dialog by overriding the `get_options_dialog_pixieapp()` method to return the fully qualified name of a PixieApp class inheriting from the `BaseOptions` class in the `pixiedust.display.chart.options.baseOptions` package.

As an example, let's rewrite the preceding custom `SimpleDisplay` table visualization using the renderer extension layer:

```
from pixiedust.display.chart.renderers import PixiedustRenderer
from pixiedust.display.chart.renderers.baseChartDisplay import
BaseChartDisplay

@PixiedustRenderer(rendererId="simpletable", id="tableView")
class SimpleDisplayWithRenderer(BaseChartDisplay):
    def get_options_dialog_pixieapp(self):
        return None #No options needed

    def doRenderChart(self):
        return self.renderTemplateString("""
<table class="table table-striped">
    <thead>
        {%for column in entity.columns.tolist()%}
        <th>{{column}}</th>
        {%endfor%}
    </thead>
    <tbody>
        {%for _, row in entity.iterrows()%}
        <tr>
            {%for value in row.tolist()%}
            <td>{{value}}</td>
            {%endfor%}
        </tr>
        {%endfor%}
    </tbody>
</table>
        """)
```

 You can find the code file here:

https://github.com/DTAIEB/Thoughtful-Data-Science/blob/master/chapter%205/sampleCode17.py

We decorate the class with the `@PixiedustRenderer` decorator, specifying a unique `rendererId` called `simpletable`, and associating it with the `tableView` chart type defined by the PixieDust framework. We return `None` for the `get_options_dialog_pixieapp()` method to signify that this extension does not support custom options. As a result, the **Options** button will not be shown. In the `doRenderChart()` method, we return the HTML fragment. Since we want to use Jinja2, we need to render it using the `self.renderTemplateString` method.

We can now test this new renderer using the `cars` dataset.

Again, when running the code, make sure that you're loading the `cars` dataset as a pandas DataFrame. If you have already run the first implementation of the **Simple Table** and are reusing the Notebook, it is possible that you will still see the old **Simple Table** menu. If that's the case, you will need to restart the kernel and try again.

The following screenshot shows the simple table visualization as a renderer:

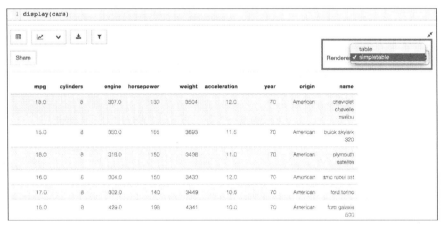

Testing the renderer implementation of the Simple Table

You can find more material about this topic at: `https://pixiedust.github.io/pixiedust/develop.html`. Hopefully, by now, you have a good idea about the type of customization you can write to integrate your own visualization in the `display()` framework.

In the next section, we'll discuss a very important topic for developers: debugging.

Debugging

Being able to rapidly debug an application is critical to the success of your project. If not, most—if not all—of the gains we've made in term of productivity and collaboration, by breaking the silo between data science and engineering, will be lost. It is also important to note that our code runs in different places, that is, Python on the server side, and JavaScript on the client side, and that debugging must take place in both places. For Python code, let's look at two ways to troubleshoot programming errors.

Debugging on the Jupyter Notebook using pdb

pdb (https://docs.python.org/3/library/pdb.html) is an interactive command-line Python debugger that comes as standard with every Python distribution.

There are multiple ways to invoke the debugger:

- At launch, from the command line:

  ```
  python -m pdb <script_file>
  ```

- Programmatically, in the code:

  ```
  import pdb
  pdb.run("<insert a valid python statement here>")
  ```

- By setting an explicit breakpoint in the code with the set_trace() method:

  ```
  import pdb
  def my_function(arg1, arg2):
      pdb.set_trace()
      do_something_here()
  ```

 You can find the code file here:
https://github.com/DTAIEB/Thoughtful-Data-Science/
blob/master/chapter%205/sampleCode18.py

- Post-mortem, after an exception has occurred, by calling pdb.pm().

Once in the interactive debugger, you can invoke commands, inspect variables, run statements, set breakpoints, and so on.

 A complete list of commands can be found here:
https://docs.python.org/3/library/pdb.html

The great news is that Jupyter Notebooks provide first-class support for the interactive debugger. To invoke the debugger, simply use the `%pdb` cell magic command to turn it on/off, and, if an exception is triggered, then the debugger will automatically stop execution at the offending line.

Magic commands (`http://ipython.readthedocs.io/en/stable/interactive/magics.html`) are constructs specific to the IPython kernel. They are language agnostic and therefore can theoretically be available in any language supported by the kernel (for example, Python, Scala, and R).

There are two types of magic commands:

- **Line magics**: The syntax is `%<magic_command_name> [optional arguments]` for example, `%matplotlib inline`, which configures Matplotlib to output the charts inline in the Notebook output cell.

  They can be invoked anywhere in the cell code, and can even return values that can be assigned to Python variables, for example:

  ```
  #call the pwd line magic to get the current working directory
  #and assign the result into a Python variable called pwd
  pwd = %pwd
  print(pwd)
  ```

> You can find a list of all the line magics here:
>
> `http://ipython.readthedocs.io/en/stable/interactive/magics.html#line-magics`

- **Cell magics**: The syntax is `%%<magic_command_name> [optional arguments]`. For example, we call the HTML cell magic to display HTML on the output cell:

  ```
  %%html
  <div>Hello World</div>
  ```

  Cell magics must be located at the top of the cell; any other location would result in an execution error. Everything below the cell magic is passed as an argument to the handler to be interpreted according to the cell magic specification. For example, the HTML cell magic expects the rest of the cell content to be HTML.

The following code example calls a function that raises a `ZeroDivisionError` exception, with `pdb` automatic calling activated:

Note: Once you turn pdb on, it stays on for the duration of the Notebook session.

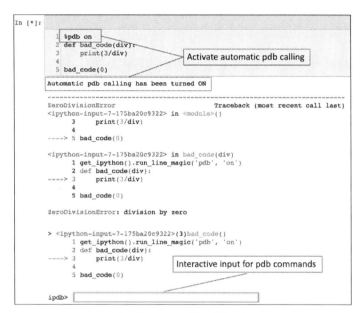

Interactive command-line debugging

Here are some important pdb commands that can be used to troubleshoot an issue:

- s(tep): Step into the function being called and stop at the next statement line.
- n(ext): Continue to the next line, without entering into a nest function.
- l(list): List code surrounding the current line.
- c(ontinue): Keep running the program and stop at the next breakpoint, or if another exception is raised.
- d(own): Move down the stack frame.
- u(p): Move up the stack frame.
- <any expression>: Evaluate and display an expression within the context of the current frame. For example, you can use locals() to get a list of all the local variables scoped to the current frame.

If an exception occurred and you didn't set the automatic `pdb` calling, you can still invoke the debugger after the fact by using `%debug` magic in another cell, as shown in the following screenshot:

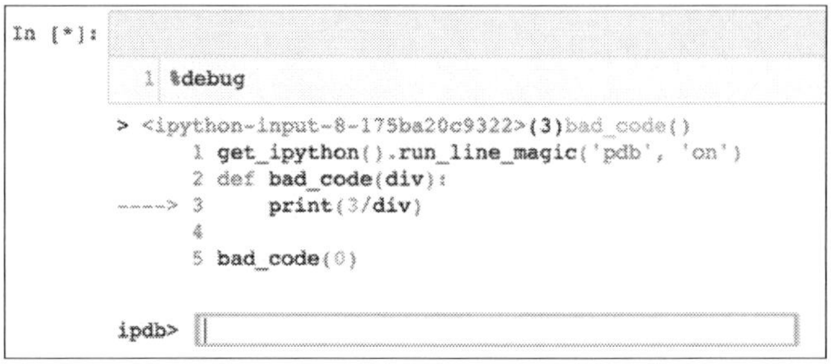

```
In [*]:
    1 %debug

> <ipython-input-8-175ba20c9322>(3)bad_code()
      1 get_ipython().run_line_magic('pdb', 'on')
      2 def bad_code(div):
----> 3     print(3/div)
      4
      5 bad_code(0)

ipdb>
```

Doing a post-mortem debugging session with %debug

Similar to a regular Python script, you can also explicitly set a breakpoint programmatically with the `pdb.set_trace()` method. However, it is recommended using the enhanced version of `set_trace()` provided by the IPython core module that provides syntax coloring:

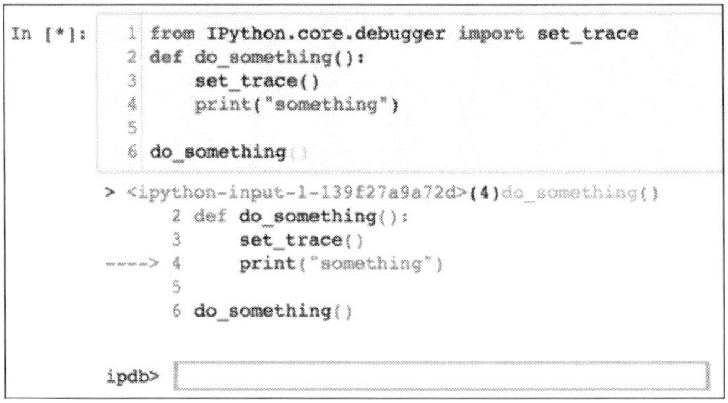

```
In [*]:
    1 from IPython.core.debugger import set_trace
    2 def do_something():
    3     set_trace()
    4     print("something")
    5
    6 do_something()

> <ipython-input-1-139f27a9a72d>(4)do_something()
      2 def do_something():
      3     set_trace()
----> 4     print("something")
      5
      6 do_something()

ipdb>
```

Explicit breakpoint

In the next topic, we look at an enhanced version of the Python debugger provided by PixieDust.

Visual debugging with PixieDebugger

Using the standard command line-oriented Python pdb to debug your code
is a nice tool to have in our tool belt, but it has two major limitations:

- It's command line-oriented, which means that commands have to be entered
  manually and results are sequentially appended to the cell output, making
  it impractical when it comes to advanced debugging
- It doesn't work with PixieApps

The PixieDebugger capability addresses both issues. You can use it with any Python
code running in a Jupyter Notebook cell to visually debug the code. To invoke the
PixieDebugger in a cell, simply add the `%%pixie_debugger` cell magic at the top
of the cell.

 Note: If you have not already done so, don't forget to always import
`pixiedust` in a separate cell before attempting to use `%%pixie_`
`debugger`.

As an example, the following code is trying to compute how many cars have the
name `chevrolet` in the `cars` dataset:

```
%%pixie_debugger
import pixiedust
cars = pixiedust.sampleData(1, forcePandas=True)

def count_cars(name):
    count = 0
    for row in cars.itertuples():
        if name in row.name:
            count += 1
    return count

count_cars('chevrolet')
```

 You can find the code file here:

https://github.com/DTAIEB/Thoughtful-Data-Science/
blob/master/chapter%205/sampleCode19.py

Running the cell with the preceding code will trigger the visual debugger shown in the following screenshot. The user interface lets you step into the code line by line, with the ability to inspect local variables, evaluate Python expressions, and set breakpoints. The code execution toolbar provides buttons for managing code execution: resume execution, step over the current line, step into the code a particular function, run to the end of the current function, and display the stack frame up and down one level:

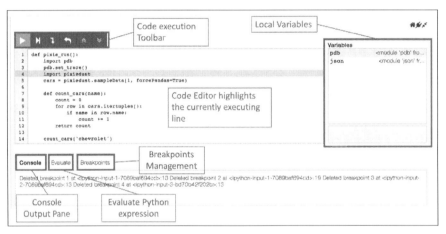

PixieDebugger in action

With no parameter, the `pixie_debugger` cell magic will stop at the first executable statement in the code. However, you can easily configure it to stop at specific locations using the `-b` switch, followed by a list of breakpoints that could be either a line number or a method name.

Starting from the preceding example code, let's add breakpoints at the `count_cars()` method and line **11**:

```
%%pixie_debugger -b count_cars 11
import pixiedust
cars = pixiedust.sampleData(1, forcePandas=True)
```

```
def count_cars(name):
    count = 0
    for row in cars.itertuples():
        if name in row.name:
            count += 1
    return count


count_cars('chevrolet')
```

 You can find the code file here:

https://github.com/DTAIEB/Thoughtful-Data-Science/
blob/master/chapter%205/sampleCode20.py

Running the preceding code will now trigger the PixieDebugger to stop at the first executable statement of the count_cars() method. It also added a breakpoint at line 11, which will cause the execution flow to stop there if the user resumes, as can be seen in the following screenshot:

PixieDebugger with predefined breakpoints

 Note: To run to a specific line of code without setting an explicit breakpoint, simply hover over the line number in the gutter in the left-hand pane and click on the icon that appears.

Like the %debug line magic, you can also invoke the PixieDebugger to do post-mortem debugging by using the %pixie_debugger line magic.

Debugging PixieApp routes with PixieDebugger

PixieDebugger is fully integrated into the PixieApp framework. Whenever an exception happens while triggering a route, the resulting traceback is augmented with two extra buttons:

- **Post Mortem**: Invoke the PixieDebugger to start a post-mortem troubleshooting session that lets you inspect variables and analyses the stack frames
- **Debug Route**: Replay the current route stopping at the first executable statement in the PixieDebugger

As an example, let's consider the following code for implementing a PixieApp that lets the user search the `cars` dataset by providing a column name and a search query:

```
from pixiedust.display.app import *

import pixiedust
cars = pixiedust.sampleData(1, forcePandas=True)

@PixieApp
class DisplayCars():
    @route()
    def main_screen(self):
        return """
        <div>
            <label>Column to search</label>
            <input id="column{{prefix}}" value="name">
            <label>Query</label>
            <input id="search{{prefix}}">
            <button type="submit" pd_options="col=$val(column{{prefix}
});query=$val(search{{prefix}})"
                pd_target="target{{prefix}}">
            Search
            </button>
        </div>
        <div id="target{{prefix}}"></div>
        """
    @route(col="*", query="*")
    def display_screen(self, col, query):
        self.pdf = cars.loc[cars[col].str.contains(query)]
        return """
```

```
        <div pd_render_onload pd_entity="pdf">
            <pd_options>
            {
                "handlerId": "tableView",
                "table_noschema": "true",
                "table_nosearch": "true",
                "table_nocount": "true"
            }
            </pd_options>
        </div>
        """
    app = DisplayCars()
    app.run()
```

 You can find the code file here:

https://github.com/DTAIEB/Thoughtful-Data-Science/
blob/master/chapter%205/sampleCode21.py

The default value for the search column is name, but if the user enters a column name that doesn't exist, a traceback is generated as follows:

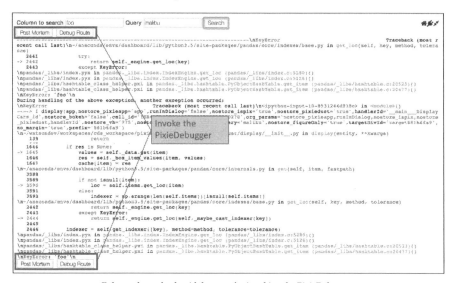

Enhanced traceback with buttons for invoking the PixieDebugger

Clicking on the **Debug Route** will automatically start the PixieDebugger and stop at the first executable statement of the route, as shown in the following screenshot:

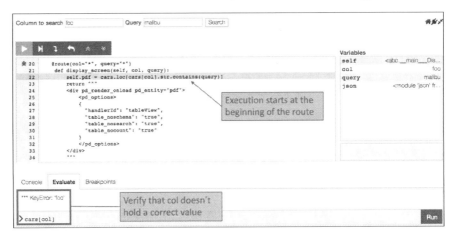

Debugging a PixieApp route

You could also deliberately have the PixieDebugger stop at the `display_screen()` route without waiting for a traceback to happen by using the `debug_route` keyword argument to the `run` method:

```
...
app = DisplayCars()
app.run(debug_route="display_screen")
```

PixieDebugger is the first visual Python debugger for Jupyter Notebook, providing a feature that has long been requested by the Jupyter user community. However, using live debugging is not the only tool that developers use. In the next section, we will look at debugging by inspecting logging messages.

Troubleshooting issues using PixieDust logging

It is always good practice to instrument your code with logging messages, and the PixieDust framework provides an easy way to create and read back logging messages directly from the Jupyter Notebook. To start off, you'll need to create a logger by calling the `getLogger()` method as follows:

```
import pixiedust
my_logger = pixiedust.getLogger(__name__)
```

You can find the code file here:

`https://github.com/DTAIEB/Thoughtful-Data-Science/`
`blob/master/chapter%205/sampleCode22.py`

You can use anything as an argument to the `getLogger()` method. However, to better identify where a particular message comes from, it is recommended using the `__name__` variable, which returns the name of the current module. The `my_logger` variable is a standard Python logger object that provides logging methods with various levels:

- `debug(msg, *args, **kwargs)`: Logs a message with the DEBUG level.
- `info(msg, *args, **kwargs)`: Logs a message with the INFO level.
- `warning(msg, *args, **kwargs)`: Logs a message with the WARNING level.
- `error(msg, *args, **kwargs)`: Logs a message with the ERROR level.
- `critical(msg, *args, **kwargs)`: Logs a message with the CRITICAL level.
- `exception(msg, *args, **kwargs)`: Logs a message with the EXCEPTION level. This method should only be called from within an exception handler.

Note: You can find more information about the Python logging framework here:

`https://docs.python.org/2/library/logging.html`

You can then query the log messages directly from the Jupyter Notebook using the `%pixiedustLog` cell magic, which takes the following parameters:

- `-l`: Filter by log level, for example, CRITICAL, FATAL, ERROR, WARNING, INFO, and DEBUG
- `-f`: Filter a message that contains a given string, for example, `Exception`
- `-m`: Maximum number of log messages returned

In the following example, we use the `%pixiedustLog` magic to display all the debug messages, limiting these to the last five messages:

```
1 %pixiedustLog -l debug -m 5
2018-02-09 15:21:37,341 - pixiedust.display.display.Display - DEBUG - Value Fields: ['mpg']
2018-02-09 15:21:37,341 - pixiedust.utils.template - DEBUG - Template already qualified pixiedust.display.chart.rende
rers.baseChartDisplay:baseChartOptionsDialogBody.html
2018-02-09 15:21:37,359 - pixiedust.display.chart.renderers.baseChartDisplay - DEBUG - Found cache data for 285AC18D1
1294C348C072F891FE5A8D1. Validating integrity...
2018-02-09 15:21:37,359 - pixiedust.display.chart.renderers.baseChartDisplay - DEBUG - Cache data not validated for k
ey filter_options. Expected Value is {'constraint': 'greater_than', 'value': '46', 'field': 'mpg', 'regex': 'False',
'case_matter': 'False'}. Got {'constraint': 'greater_than', 'value': '45', 'field': 'mpg', 'regex': 'False', 'case_ma
tter': 'False'}. Destroying it!...
2018-02-09 15:21:37,480 - pixiedust.display.display.Display - DEBUG - getWorkingPandasDataFrame returns:       accelerat
ion cylinders engine horsepower    mpg
0       17.9         4   86.0          65  46.6
```

Display the last five log messages

For convenience, when working with Python classes, you can also use the `@Logger` decorator, which automatically creates a logger using the class name as its identifier.

Here is a code example that uses the `@Logger` decorator:

```python
from pixiedust.display.app import *
from pixiedust.utils import Logger

@PixieApp
@Logger()
class AppWithLogger():
    @route()
    def main_screen(self):
        self.info("Calling default route")
        return "<div>hello world</div>"

app = AppWithLogger()
app.run()
```

You can find the code file here:
https://github.com/DTAIEB/Thoughtful-Data-Science/blob/master/chapter%205/sampleCode23.py

After running the preceding PixieApp in a cell, you can invoke the `%pixiedustLog` magic to display the messages:

```
1 %pixiedustLog -l info -f Calling
2018-02-10 22:13:06,358 - __main__.AppWithLogger - INFO - Calling default route
```

Querying the log with a specific term

This completes our discussion on server-side debugging. In the next section, we look at a technique for performing client-side debugging

Client-side debugging

One of the design principles of the PixieApp programming model is to minimize the need for developers to write JavaScript. The framework will automatically trigger kernel requests by listening to user input events, such as click or change events. However, there will be cases where writing a little bit of JavaScript is inevitable. These JavaScript snippets are usually part of a particular route HTML fragment and are dynamically injected into the browser, which makes it very difficult to debug.

One popular technique is to sprinkle `console.log` calls in the JavaScript code in order to print messages to the browser developer console.

 Note: Each browser flavor has its own way of invoking the developer console. For example, in Google Chrome, you would use **View** | **Developer** | **JavaScript Console**, or the *Command + Alt + J* shortcut.

One other debugging technique that I particularly like is to programmatically insert in a breakpoint in the JavaScript code using the `debugger;` statement. This statement has no effect unless the browser developer tools are open and source debugging is enabled, in which case, the execution will automatically break at the `debugger;` statement.

The following PixieApp example uses a JavaScript function to resolve a dynamic value referenced by the `$val()` directive:

```
from pixiedust.display.app import *

@PixieApp
class TestJSDebugger():
    @route()
    def main_screen(self):
        return """
<script>
function FooJS(){
    debugger;
    return "value"
}
</script>
<button type="submit" pd_options="state=$val(FooJS)">Call route</
button>
        """
```

```
@route(state="*")
def my_route(self, state):
    return "<div>Route called with state <b>{{state}}</b></div>"

app = TestJSDebugger()
app.run()
```

 You can find the code file here:

https://github.com/DTAIEB/Thoughtful-Data-Science/
blob/master/chapter%205/sampleCode24.py

In the preceding code, the button is dynamically setting the value of a state using
the FooJS JavaScript function that contains a debugger statement. Executing the app
and clicking on the button while the developer tool is open will automatically start
a debugging session on the browser:

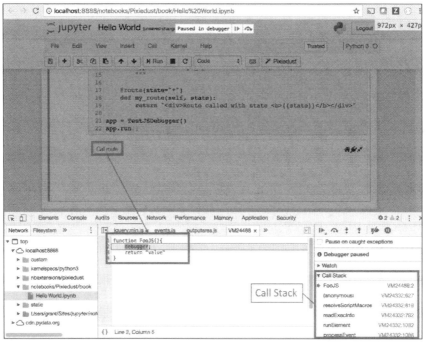

Debugging JavaScript code on the client side with a debugger; statement

Run Node.js inside a Python Notebook

Even though I've clearly stated at the beginning of this book that Python has emerged as a clear leader in the field of data science, it is still only marginally used by the developer community where traditional languages, such as Node.js, are still preferred. Recognizing that, for some developers, learning a new language, such as Python, is a cost of entry to data science that may be too high, I partnered with my IBM colleague, Glynn Bird, to build an extension library to PixieDust called `pixiedust_node` (`https://github.com/pixiedust/pixiedust_node`) that would let developers run Node.js/JavaScript code inside cells in a Python Notebook. The goal of this library is to ease developers into the Python world by allowing them to reuse their favourite Node.js libraries, for example, to load and process data from existing data sources.

To install the `pixiedust_node` library, simply run the following command in its own cell:

```
!pip install pixiedust_node
```

 Note: Don't forget to restart the kernel once the installation is complete.

Important: You need to make sure that a Node.js runtime version 6 or higher is installed on the same machine as the Jupyter Notebook Server.

Once the kernel has restarted, we import the `pixiedust_node` module:

```
import pixiedust_node
```

You should see information about both PixieDust and `pixiedust_node` in the output as follows:

pixiedust_node welcome output

When `pixiedust_node` is imported, a Node subprocess is created from the Python side along with a special thread that reads the output of the subprocess and passes it to the Python side to be displayed in the cell currently executing in the Notebook. This subprocess is responsible for starting an **REPL** session (**Read-Eval-Print Loop**: `https://en.wikipedia.org/wiki/Read-eval-print_loop`) that will execute all the scripts sent from the Notebook and make any created classes, functions, and variables reusable across all executions.

It also defines a set of functions that are designed to interact with the Notebook and the PixieDust `display()` API:

- `print(data)`: Outputs the value of data in the cell currently executing in the Notebook.
- `display(data)`: Calls the PixieDust `display()` API with a pandas DataFrame converted from data. If data cannot be converted into a pandas DataFrame, then it defaults to the `print` method.
- `html(data)`: Displays the data as HTML in the cell currently executing in the Notebook.
- `image(data)`: Expects data to be a URL to an image and displays it in the cell currently executing in the Notebook.
- `help()`: Displays a list of all the preceding methods.

In addition, `pixiedust_node` makes two variables, called `npm` and `node`, globally available in the Notebook:

- `node.cancel()`: Stops the current execution of code in the Node.js subprocess.
- `node.clear()`: Resets the Node.js session; all existing variables will be deleted.
- `npm.install(package)`: Installs an npm package and makes it available to the Node.js session. The package is persisted across sessions.
- `npm.uninstall(package)`: Removes the npm package from the system and the current Node.js session.
- `npm.list()`: Lists all npm packages currently installed.

`pixiedust_node` creates a cell magic that lets you run arbitrary JavaScript code. Simply use the `%%node` magic at the top of the cell and run it as usual. The code will then be executed in the Node.js subprocess REPL session.

The following code displays a string that includes the current datetime using the JavaScript `Date` object (`https://www.w3schools.com/Jsref/jsref_obj_date.asp`):

```
%%node
var date = new Date()
print("Today's date is " + date)
```

This outputs the following:

```
"Today's date is Sun May 27 2018 20:36:35 GMT-0400 (EDT)"
```

The following diagram illustrates the execution flow of the preceding cell:

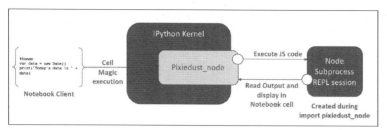

The life cycle of a Node.js script execution

The JavaScript code is processed by the `pixiedust_node` magic and sent to the Node subprocess for execution. As the code is being executed, its output is read by the special thread and displayed back in the cell currently executing in the Notebook. Note that the JavaScript code may make an asynchronous call, in which case the execution will return right away before the asynchronous calls have finished. In this case, the Notebook will indicate that the cell code is done, even though more output may be generated later by the asynchronous code. There is no way to deterministically know when an asynchronous code is done. Therefore it is incumbent upon the developer to manage this state carefully.

`pixiedust_node` also has the ability to share variables between the Python side and the JavaScript side, and vice-versa. Therefore, you could declare a Python variable (such as an array of integers, for example), apply a transformation in JavaScript (perhaps using your favorite library), and have it processed back in Python.

The following code is run in two cells, one in pure Python declaring an array of integers, and one in JavaScript that multiplies each element by 2:

```python
python_ar = [x for x in range(10)]
print(python_ar)
```

```
[0, 1, 2, 3, 4, 5, 6, 7, 8, 9]
```

```
%%node
for (var i = 0; i < python_ar.length; i++ ){
    python_ar[i] *= 2;
}
print(python_ar)
```

```
... ...
[0, 2, 4, 6, 8, 10, 12, 14, 16, 18]
```

The reverse direction also works the same. The following code starts by creating a JSON variable in JavaScript in a node cell, and then creates and displays a pandas DataFrame in the Python cell:

```
%%node
data = {
    "name": ["Bob","Alice","Joan","Christian"],
    "age": [20, 25, 19, 45]
}
print(data)
```

The results are as follows:

```
{"age": [20, 25, 19, 45], "name": ["Bob", "Alice", "Joan",
"Christian"]}
```

Then, in a Python cell, we use PixieDust `display()`:

```
df = pandas.DataFrame(data)
display(df)
```

Using the following options:

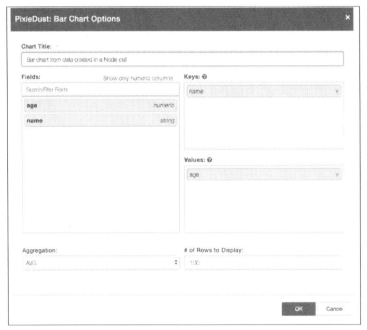

display() options for data created from a node cell

And we get the following results:

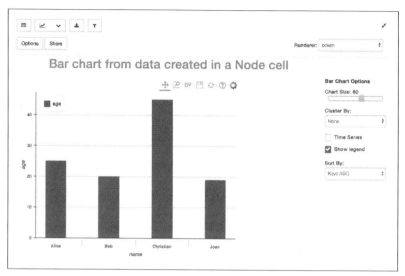

Bar chart from data created in a node cell

We could also have arrived at the same results directly from the Node cell by using the `display()` method made available by `pixiedust_node`, as shown in the following code:

```
%%node
data = {
    "name": ["Bob","Alice","Joan","Christian"],
    "age": [20, 25, 19, 45]
}
display(data)
```

If you are interested in knowing more about `pixiedust_node`, I strongly recommend this blog post: `https://medium.com/ibm-watson-data-lab/nodebooks-node-js-data-science-notebooks-aa140bea21ba`. As always, I encourage the reader to get involved with improving these tools, either by contributing code or ideas for enhancement.

Summary

In this chapter, we've explored various advanced concepts, tools, and best practices that added more tools to our toolbox, ranging from advanced techniques for PixieApps (Streaming, how to implement a route by integrating third-party libraries with `@captureOutput`, PixieApp events, and better modularity with `pd_app`), to essential developer tools like the PixieDebugger. We've also covered the details of how to create your own custom visualization using the PixieDust `display()` API. We also discussed `pixiedust_node`, which is an extension of the PixieDust framework that lets developers who are more comfortable with JavaScript work with data in their favorite language.

Throughout the remainder of this book, we are going to put all these lessons learned to good use by building industry use case data pipelines, starting with a *Deep Learning Visual Recognition* application in *Chapter 6, Image Recognition with TensorFlow*.

A developer quick-reference guide for the PixieApp programming model is provided in *Appendix, PixieApp Quick-Reference* at the end of this book.

6

Image Recognition
with TensorFlow

"Artificial Intelligence, deep learning, machine learning — whatever you're doing if you don't understand it — learn it. Because otherwise, you're going to be a dinosaur within 3 years."

– Mark Cuban

This is the first chapter of a series of sample applications covering popular industry use cases, and it is no coincidence that I start with a use case related to machine learning and, more specifically, deep learning through a image recognition sample application. We're seeing accelerated growth in the field of **Artificial Intelligence (AI)** over the last few years, to the point where many practical applications are becoming a reality, such as self-driving cars, and chatbots with advanced automated speech recognition that, for some tasks, are perfectly able to replace human operators, while more and more people, from academia to industry, are starting to get involved. However, there is a perception that the cost of entry is very high and that mastering the underlying mathematical concepts of machine learning is a prerequisite. In this chapter, we try to demonstrate, through the use of examples, that this is not the case.

We will start this chapter with a quick introduction to machine learning, and a subset of it called deep learning. We will then introduce a very popular deep learning framework called TensorFlow that we'll use to build an image recognition model. In the second part of this chapter, we'll show how to operationalize the model we've built by implementing a sample PixieApp that lets the user enter a link to a website, have all the images scraped, and use as input to the model to categorize them.

At the end of this chapter, you should be convinced that it is possible to build meaningful applications and operationalize them without a Ph.D. in machine learning.

What is machine learning?

One definition that I think captures very well the intuition behind machine learning comes from Andrew Ng, adjunct professor at Stanford University, in his *Machine Learning* class on Coursera (`https://www.coursera.org/learn/machine-learning`):

> *Machine learning is the science of getting computers to learn, without being explicitly programmed.*

The key word from the preceding definition is *learn*, which, in this context, has a meaning that is very similar to how, we, humans learn. To continue with this parallel, from a young age, we were taught how to accomplish a task either by example, or on our own by trial and error. Broadly speaking, machine learning algorithms can be categorized into two types that correspond to the two ways in which humans learn:

- **Supervised**: The algorithm learns from example data that has been properly labeled. This data is also called training data, or sometimes referred to as *ground truth*.

- **Unsupervised**: The algorithm is able to learn on its own from data that has not been labeled.

For each of the two categories described here, the following table gives a high-level overview of the most commonly used machine learning algorithms and the type of problem they solve:

	Continuous Output	Discrete Output

Supervised	• Regression
	  - Linear
	  - Ridge
	  - Lasso
	  - Isotonic
	• Decision Tree
	• RandomForest
	• GradientBoostedTree
		• Classification
		  - Logistic Regression
		  - SVM
		  - NaiveBayes
		• Decision Tree
		• RandomForest
		• GradientBoostedTree
		• K-NN

Unsupervised	• Clustering
	  - KMeans
	  - Gaussian Mixture
	• Dimensionality Reduction
	  - PCA
	  - SVD
		• FP-Growth

List of machine learning algorithms

The output of these algorithms is called a **model** and is used to make predictions on new input data that has not been seen before. The overall end-to-end process for building and deploying these models is very consistent across the different types of algorithms.

The following diagram shows a high-level workflow of this process:

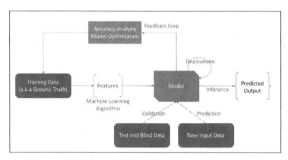

Machine learning model workflow

As always, the workflow starts with data. In the case of supervised learning, the data will be used as an example and therefore must be correctly labeled with the correct answers. The input data is then processed to extract intrinsic properties called **features,** which we can think of as numerical values representing the input data. Subsequently, these features are fed into a machine learning algorithm that builds a model. In typical settings, the original data is split between training, test, and blind data. The test and blind data are used during the model building phase to validate and optimize the model to make sure that it doesn't overfit the training data. Overfitting happens when the model parameters are such that they follow too closely the training data, leading to errors when unseen data is used. When the model produces the desired accuracy level, it is then deployed in production and used against new data as needed by the host application.

In this section, we will provide a very high-level introduction to machine learning with a simplified data pipeline workflow, just enough to give the intuition of how a model is built and deployed. Once again, if you are a beginner, I highly recommend Andrew Ng's *Machine Learning* class on Coursera (which I still revisit from time to time). In the next section, we will introduce a branch of machine learning called deep learning, which we'll use to build the image recognition sample application.

What is deep learning?

Getting computers to learn, reason, and think (make decisions) is a science that is commonly called **cognitive computing,** of which machine learning and deep learning are a big part. The following Venn diagram shows how these fields are related to the overarching field of AI:

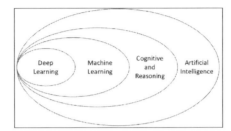

How deep learning fits in to AI

As the diagram suggests, deep learning is one type of machine learning algorithm. What is perhaps not widely known is that the field of deep learning has existed for quite some time, but hasn't really been widely used until very recently. The rekindling in interest is due to the extraordinary advances in computer, cloud, and storage technologies observed in the last few years that have fuelled exponential growth in AI with the development of many new deep learning algorithms, each best suited to solve a particular problem.

As we'll discuss later in this chapter, deep learning algorithms are especially good at learning complex non-linear hypotheses. Their design is actually inspired by how the human brain works, for example, the input data flows through multiple layers of computation units in order to decompose complex model representations (such as an image, for example) into simpler ones, before passing the results to the next layer, and so on and so forth, until reaching the final layer that is responsible for outputting the results. The assembly of these layers is also referred to as **neural networks**, and the computation units that compose a layer are called **neurons**. In essence, a neuron is responsible for taking multiple inputs and transforming them into a single output that can then be fed into other neurons in the next layers.

The following diagram represents a multilayer neural network for image classification:

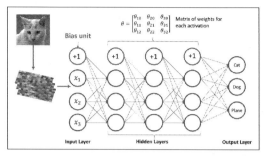

High-level representation of a neural network for image classification

The preceding neural network is also called **feed-forward** because the output of each computation unit is used as input to the next layer, starting with the input layer. The intermediary layers are called the **hidden layers** and contain intermediary features that are automatically learned by the network. In our image example, certain neurons could be responsible for detecting corners, while certain others might focus on edges, and so on. The final output layer is responsible for assigning a confidence level (score) to each of the output classes.

One important question is how does the neuron output get generated from its input? Without diving too deeply in to the mathematics involved, each artificial neuron applies an activation function $g(x)$ on the weighted sum of its inputs to decide whether it should *fire* or not.

The following formula calculates the weighted sum:

$$A = \sum_j \theta^i * input_j + bias$$

Where θ^i is the matrix of weights between the layer i and $i + 1$. These weights are computed during the training phase that we will discuss briefly a little later.

Note: The bias in the preceding formula represents the weight of the bias neuron, which is an extra neuron added to each layer with an x value of +1. The bias neuron is special because it contributes to the input for the next layer, but it is not connected to the previous one. Its weight, however, is still normally learned like any other neuron. The intuition behind the bias neuron is that it provides the constant term b in the linear regression equation:

$$Y = mx + b$$

Of course, applying the neuron activation function $g(x)$ on A cannot simply produce a binary (0 or 1) value, because we wouldn't be able to correctly rank the final candidate answers if multiple classes are given the score of 1. Instead, we use activation functions that provide a non-discrete score between 0 and 1 and set a threshold value (for example, 0.5) to decide whether to activate the neuron or not.

One of the most popular activation functions is the sigmoid function:

$$g(x) = \frac{1}{1+e^{-x}}$$

The following diagram shows how a neuron output is calculated from its input and its weight using a sigmoid activation function:

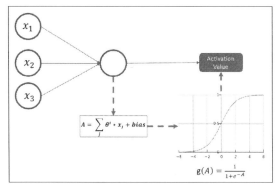

Neuron output calculation using the sigmoid function

Other popular activation functions include the hyperbolic tangent $\tanh(x)$ and the **Rectified Linear Unit (ReLu)**: $\max(0, x)$. ReLu works better when there are a lot of layers because it provides sparsity of *firing* neurons, thereby reducing noise and resulting in faster learning.

Feed-forward propagation is used during scoring of the model, but when it comes to training the weight matrix of the neural network, a popular method used is called **backpropagation** (https://en.wikipedia.org/wiki/Backpropagation).

The following high-level steps describe how the training works:

1. Randomly initialize the weight matrix (preferably using small values, for example, $[-\varepsilon, +\varepsilon]$.

2. Use the forward propagation described earlier on all the training examples to compute the outputs of each neuron using the activation function of your choice.

3. Implement a cost function for your neural network. A **cost function** quantifies the error with respect to the training examples. There are multiple cost functions that can be used with the backpropagation algorithm, such as a mean-square error (`https://en.wikipedia.org/wiki/Mean_squared_error`) and cross-entropy (`https://en.wikipedia.org/wiki/Cross_entropy`).

4. Use backpropagation to minimize your cost function and compute the weight matrix. The idea behind backpropagation is to start with the activation values of the output layer, compute the error with respect to the training data, and pass their errors backward to the hidden layers. These errors are then adjusted to minimize the cost function implemented in step 3.

 Note: Explaining in detail these cost functions and how they are being optimized is beyond the scope of this book. For a deeper dive, I highly recommend looking at the *Deep Learning* book from MIT press (Ian Goodfellow, Yoshua Bengio, and Aaron Courville)

In this section, we've discussed at a high level how neural networks work and how they are trained. Of course, we've only touched the surface of this exciting technology, but you hopefully should have an idea as to how they work. In the next section, we start looking at TensorFlow, which is a programming framework that helps abstract the underlying complexity of implementing a neural network.

Getting started with TensorFlow

There are multiple open source deep learning frameworks besides TensorFlow (`https://www.tensorflow.org`) that I could have chosen for this sample application.

Some of the most popular frameworks are as follows:

- PyTorch (`http://pytorch.org`)
- Caffee2 (`https://caffe2.ai`)
- MXNet (`https://mxnet.apache.org`)

- Keras (`https://keras.io`): A high-level neural network abstraction API capable of running other deep learning frameworks such as TensorFlow, CNTK (`https://github.com/Microsoft/cntk`), and Theano (`https://github.com/Theano/Theano`)

TensorFlow APIs are available in multiple languages: Python, C++, Java, Go, and, more recently, JavaScript. We can distinguish two categories of APIs: high level and low level, represented by this diagram:

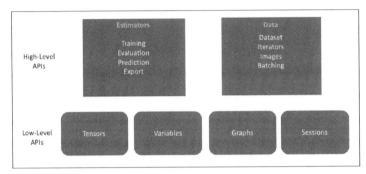

TensorFlow high-level API architecture

To get started with the TensorFlow API, let's build a simple neural network that will learn the XOR transformation.

As a reminder, the XOR operator has only four training examples:

X	Y	Result
0	0	0
0	1	1
1	0	1
1	1	0

It's interesting to note that linear classifiers (`https://en.wikipedia.org/wiki/Linear_classifier`) are not able to learn the XOR transformation. However, we can solve this problem with a simple neural network with two neurons in the input layer, one hidden layer with two neurons, and an output layer with one neuron (binary classification), demonstrated as follows:

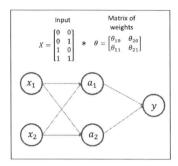

XOR neural network

 Note: You can install TensorFlow directly from the Notebook by using the following command:

`!pip install tensorflow`

As always, don't forget to restart the kernel after any successful install.

To create the input and output layer tensors, we use the `tf.placeholder` API, as shown in the following code:

```
import tensorflow as tf
x_input = tf.placeholder(tf.float32)
y_output = tf.placeholder(tf.float32)
```

Then, we use the `tf.Variable` API (https://www.tensorflow.org/programmers_guide/variables) to initialize the random value for the matrices θ_1 and θ_2, corresponding to the hidden layer and the output layer:

```
eps = 0.01
W1 = tf.Variable(tf.random_uniform([2,2], -eps, eps))
W2 = tf.Variable(tf.random_uniform([2,1], -eps, eps))
```

For the activation function, we use the sigmoid function:

 Note: For simplicity, we omit to introduce the bias.

```
layer1 = tf.sigmoid(tf.matmul(x_input, W1))
output_layer = tf.sigmoid(tf.matmul(layer1, W2))
```

For the cost function, we use the **MSE** (short for, **mean square error**):

```
cost = tf.reduce_mean(tf.square(y_output - output_layer))
```

With all the tensors in place in the graph, we can now proceed with the training by using the `tf.train.GradientDescentOptimizer` with a learning rate of `0.05` to minimize our cost function:

```
train = tf.train.GradientDescentOptimizer(0.05).minimize(cost)
training_data = ([[0,0],[0,1],[1,0],[1,1]], [[0],[1],[1],[0]])
with tf.Session() as sess:
    sess.run(tf.global_variables_initializer())
    for i in range(5000):
        sess.run(train,
            feed_dict={x_input: training_data[0], y_output: training_
data[1]})
```

 You can find the code file here:

https://github.com/DTAIEB/Thoughtful-Data-Science/blob/master/chapter%206/sampleCode1.py

The preceding code introduces the concept of a TensorFlow `Session` for the first time, which is a foundational part of the framework. In essence, any TensorFlow operation must be executed within the context of `Session` by using its `run` method. Sessions also maintain resources that need to be explicitly released using the `close` method. For convenience, the `Session` class supports the context management protocol by providing an `__enter__` and `__exit__` method. This allows the caller to call TensorFlow operations using the `with` statement (https://docs.python.org/3/whatsnew/2.6.html#pep-343-the-with-statement) and have the resources automatically freed.

The following pseudo-code shows a typical structure of a TensorFlow execution:

```
with tf.Session() as sess:
    with-block statement with TensorFlow operations
```

In this section, we quickly explored the low-level TensorFlow APIs to build a simple neural network that learned the XOR transformation. In the next section, we'll explore the higher level estimator APIs that provide an abstraction layer on top of the low-level API.

Simple classification with DNNClassifier

 Note: This section discusses the source code for a sample PixieApp. If you want to follow along, it might be easier to download the complete Notebook at this location:

`https://github.com/DTAIEB/Thoughtful-Data-Science/blob/master/chapter%206/TensorFlow%20classification.ipynb`

Before we look at using Tensors, Graphs, and Sessions from the low-level TensorFlow APIs, it would be good to get familiar with the high-level API provided in the `Estimators` package. In this section, we build a simple PixieApp that takes a pandas DataFrame as input and trains a classification model with the categorical output.

 Note: There are essentially two types of classification output: categorical and continuous. In a categorical classifier model, the output can only be chosen from a list of finite predefined values with or without a logical order. We commonly call binary classification a classification model with only two classes. On the other hand, the continuous output can have any numerical values.

The user is first asked to choose a numerical column to predict on, and a classification model is trained on all the other numerical columns present in the DataFrame.

 Note: Some of the code of this sample app is adapted from `https://github.com/tensorflow/models/tree/master/samples/core/get_started`.

For this example, we'll use built-in sample dataset #7: Boston Crime data, two-week sample, but you could use any other dataset as long it has sufficient data and numerical columns.

As a reminder, you can browse the PixieDust built-in datasets using the following code:

```
import pixiedust
pixiedust.sampleData()
```

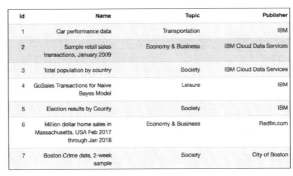

Id	Name	Topic	Publisher
1	Car performance data	Transportation	IBM
2	Sample retail sales transactions, January 2009	Economy & Business	IBM Cloud Data Services
3	Total population by country	Society	IBM Cloud Data Services
4	GoSales Transactions for Naive Bayes Model	Leisure	IBM
5	Election results by County	Society	IBM
6	Million dollar home sales in Massachusetts, USA Feb 2017 through Jan 2018	Economy & Business	Redfin.com
7	Boston Crime data, 2-week sample	Society	City of Boston

List of built-in datasets in PixieDust

The following code loads the *Boston Crime* dataset using the `sampleData()` API:

```
import pixiedust
crimes = pixiedust.sampleData(7, forcePandas=True)
```

As always, we first start by exploring the data using the `display()` command. The goal here is to look for a suitable column to predict on:

```
display(crimes)
```

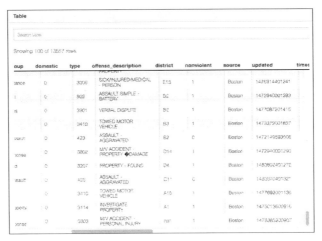

Table view of the crime dataset

It looks like `nonviolent` is a good candidate for binary classification. Let's now bring up a bar chart to make sure we have a good data distribution in this column:

Select the nonviolent column in the option dialog

Clicking **OK** produces the following chart:

Distribution of nonviolent crimes

Unfortunately, the data is skewed toward nonviolent crimes, but we have close to 2,000 data points for violent crimes, which, for the purpose of this sample application, should be OK.

We are now ready to create the `do_training` method that will use a `tf.estimator.DNNClassifier` to create a classification model.

> **Note:** You can find more information on `DNNClassifier` and other high-level TensorFlow estimators here:
>
> https://www.tensorflow.org/api_docs/python/tf/estimator

The `DNNClassifier` constructor takes a lot of optional parameters. In our sample application, we'll only use three of them, but I encourage you to take a look at the other parameters in the documentation:

- `feature_columns`: An iterable of `feature_column._FeatureColumn` model inputs. In our case, we can just create an array from the numerical columns of the pandas DataFrame using Python comprehension.

- `hidden_units`: An iterable of a number of hidden layers per unit. Here, we'll use only two layers with 10 nodes each.

- n_classes: The number of label classes. We'll infer this number by grouping the DataFrame on the predictor columns and count the rows.

Here's the code for the do_training method:

```
def do_training(train, train_labels, test, test_labels, num_classes):
    #set TensorFlow logging level to INFO
    tf.logging.set_verbosity(tf.logging.INFO)

    # Build 2 hidden layer DNN with 10, 10 units respectively.
    classifier = tf.estimator.DNNClassifier(
        # Compute feature_columns from dataframe keys using a list
comprehension
        feature_columns =
            [tf.feature_column.numeric_column(key=key) for key in
train.keys()],
        hidden_units=[10, 10],
        n_classes=num_classes)

    # Train the Model
    classifier.train(
        input_fn=lambda:train_input_fn(train, train_labels,100),
        steps=1000
    )

    # Evaluate the model
    eval_result = classifier.evaluate(
        input_fn=lambda:eval_input_fn(test, test_labels,100)
    )

    return (classifier, eval_result)
```

You can find the code file here:
https://github.com/DTAIEB/Thoughtful-Data-Science/
blob/master/chapter%206/sampleCode2.py

The classifier.train method uses a train_input_fn method that is responsible for providing training input data (a.k.a ground truth) as minibatches, returning either a tf.data.Dataset or a tuple of (features, labels). Our code is also performing a model evaluation using classifier.evaluate to validate the accuracy by scoring the model against the test dataset and comparing the results in the given label. The results are then returned as part of the function output.

This method requires an `eval_input_fn` method that is similar to the `train_input_fn`, with the exception that we do not make the dataset repeatable during evaluation. Since the two methods share most of the same code, we use a helper method called `input_fn` that is called by both methods with the appropriate flag:

```
def input_fn(features, labels, batch_size, train):
    # Convert the inputs to a Dataset and shuffle.
    dataset = tf.data.Dataset.from_tensor_slices((dict(features),
labels)).shuffle(1000)
    if train:
        #repeat only for training
        dataset = dataset.repeat()
    # Return the dataset in batch
    return dataset.batch(batch_size)

def train_input_fn(features, labels, batch_size):
    return input_fn(features, labels, batch_size, train=True)

def eval_input_fn(features, labels, batch_size):
    return input_fn(features, labels, batch_size, train=False)
```

You can find the code file here:
https://github.com/DTAIEB/Thoughtful-Data-Science/blob/master/chapter%206/sampleCode3.py

The next step is to build the PixieApp that will create the classifier from a pandas DataFrame passed as input to the `run` method. The main screen builds a list of all the numerical columns into a drop-down control and asks the user to select a column that will be used as the classifier output. This is done in the following code using a Jinja2 `{%for ...%}` loop iterating over the DataFrame passed as input that is referenced using the `pixieapp_entity` variable.

Note: The following code uses the `[[SimpleClassificationDNN]]` notation to denote that it is incomplete code from the specified class. Do not try to run this code yet until the full implementation is provided.

```
[[SimpleClassificationDNN]]
from pixiedust.display.app import *
@PixieApp
class SimpleClassificationDNN():
    @route()
```

```
        def main_screen(self):
            return """
<h1 style="margin:40px">
    <center>The classificiation model will be trained on all the
numeric columns of the dataset</center>
</h1>
<style>
    div.outer-wrapper {
        display: table;width:100%;height:300px;
    }
    div.inner-wrapper {
        display: table-cell;vertical-align: middle;height: 100%;width:
100%;
    }
</style>
<div class="outer-wrapper">
    <div class="inner-wrapper">
        <div class="col-sm-3"></div>
        <div class="input-group col-sm-6">
          <select id="cols{{prefix}}" style="width:100%;height:30px"
pd_options="predictor=$val(cols{{prefix}})">
                <option value="0">Select a predictor column</option>
                {%for col in this.pixieapp_entity.columns.values.
tolist()%}
                <option value="{{col}}">{{col}}</option>
                {%endfor%}
            </select>
        </div>
    </div>
</div>
        """
```

You can find the code file here:
https://github.com/DTAIEB/Thoughtful-Data-Science/
blob/master/chapter%206/sampleCode4.py

Using the `crimes` dataset, we run the PixieApp with the following code:

```
app = SimpleClassificationDNN()
app.run(crimes)
```

Note: The PixieApp code is incomplete at this time, but we can still see the results of the welcome page, as shown in the following screenshot:

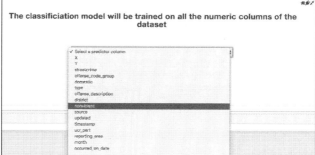

The main screen showing the list of columns in the input pandas DataFrame

When the user selects the prediction column (for example, `nonviolent`), a new `prepare_training` route is triggered by the attribute: `pd_options="predictor=$val(cols{{prefix}})"`. This route will show two bar charts showing the output class distribution for both the training and test sets that are randomly selected using an 80/20 split from the original dataset.

Note: We use an 80/20 split between training and test sets, which, from my experience, is quite common. Of course, this is not an absolute rule and could be adjusted depending on the use case

The screen fragment also includes a button to start training the classifier.

The code for the `prepare_training` route is shown here:

```
[[SimpleClassificationDNN]]
@route(predictor="*")
@templateArgs
def prepare_training(self, predictor):
        #select only numerical columns
        self.dataset = self.pixieapp_entity.dropna(axis=1).select_
dtypes(
                include=['int16', 'int32', 'int64', 'float16', 'float32',
'float64']
                )
        #Compute the number of classed by counting the groups
        self.num_classes = self.dataset.groupby(predictor).size().
```

```
shape[0]
        #Create the train and test feature and labels
        self.train_x=self.dataset.sample(frac=0.8)
        self.full_train = self.train_x.copy()
        self.train_y = self.train_x.pop(predictor)
        self.test_x=self.dataset.drop(self.train_x.index)
        self.full_test = self.test_x.copy()
        self.test_y=self.test_x.pop(predictor)

        bar_chart_options = {
          "rowCount": "100",
          "keyFields": predictor,
          "handlerId": "barChart",
          "noChartCache": "true"
        }

        return """
<div class="container" style="margin-top:20px">
    <div class="row">
        <div class="col-sm-5">
            <h3><center>Train set class distribution</center></h3>
            <div pd_entity="full_train" pd_render_onload>
                <pd_options>{{bar_chart_options|tojson}}</pd_options>
            </div>
        </div>
        <div class="col-sm-5">
            <h3><center>Test set class distribution</center></h3>
            <div pd_entity="full_test" pd_render_onload>
                <pd_options>{{bar_chart_options|tojson}}</pd_options>
            </div>
        </div>
    </div>
</div>

<div style="text-align:center">
    <button class="btn btn-default" type="submit" pd_options="do_
training=true">
        Start Training
    </button>
</div>
"""
```

You can find the code file here:

```
https://github.com/DTAIEB/Thoughtful-Data-Science/
blob/master/chapter%206/sampleCode5.py
```

Note: @templateArgs is used due to the fact that we compute the bar_chart_options variable once and then use it in the Jinja2 template.

Selecting the nonviolent prediction column gives us the following screenshot result:

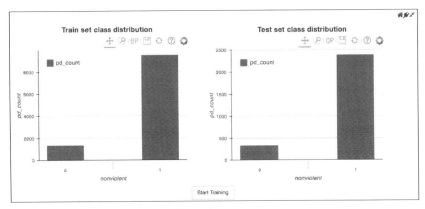

Pretraining screen

The **Start Training** button invokes the do_training route using the attribute pd_options="do_training=true", which invokes the do_training method we created earlier. Note that we use the @captureOutput decorator because, since we set the TensorFlow log level to INFO, we want to capture the log messages and display them to the user. These log messages are sent back to the browser using the *stream* mode, and PixieDust will automatically display them as a specially created <div> element that will append the data to it as it arrives. When the training is done, the route returns an HTML fragment that generates a table with the evaluation metrics returned by the do_training method, as shown in the following code:

```
[[SimpleClassificationDNN]]
@route(do_training="*")
    @captureOutput
def do_training_screen(self):
        self.classifier, self.eval_results = \
        do_training(
self.train_x, self.train_y, self.test_x, self.test_y, self.num_classes
        )
        return """
<h2>Training completed successfully</h2>
<table>
    <thead>
        <th>Metric</th>
        <th>Value</th>
    </thead>
    <tbody>
{%for key,value in this.eval_results.items()%}
<tr>
    <td>{{key}}</td>
    <td>{{value}}</td>
</tr>
{%endfor%}
    </tbody>
</table>
        """
```

 You can find the code file here:

https://github.com/DTAIEB/Thoughtful-Data-Science/blob/master/chapter%206/sampleCode6.py

The following screenshot shows the results after the model has been successfully created and includes the evaluation metrics table for the classification model with an accuracy of 87%:

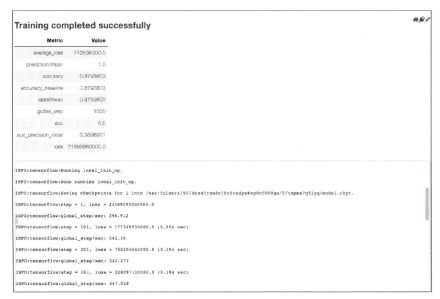

Final screen showing the result of successful training

This PixieApp was run using the `crimes` dataset as an argument, as shown in the following code:

```
app = SimpleClassificationDNN()
app.run(crimes)
```

Once the model is successfully trained, you can access it to classify new data by calling the `predict` method on the `app.classifier` variable. Similar to the `train` and `evaluate` method, `predict` also takes an `input_fn` that constructs the input features.

 Note: More details on the `predict` method are provided here:
https://www.tensorflow.org/api_docs/python/tf/estimator/DNNClassifier#predict

This sample application provides a good starting point for getting familiar with the TensorFlow framework by using the high-level estimator APIs.

 Note: The complete Notebook for this sample application can be found here:

`https://github.com/DTAIEB/Thoughtful-Data-Science/blob/master/chapter%206/TensorFlow%20classification.ipynb`

In the next section, we'll start building our image recognition sample application using the low-level TensorFlow APIs, including Tensors, Graphs, and Sessions.

Image recognition sample application

When it comes to building an open-ended application, you want to start by defining the requirements for an **MVP** (short for, **Minimum Viable Product**) version that contains just enough functionalities to make it usable and valuable to your users. When it comes to making technical decisions for your implementation, making sure that you get a working end-to-end implementation as quickly as possible, without investing too much time, is a very important criteria. The idea is that you want to start small so that you can quickly iterate and improve your application.

For the MVP of our image recognition sample application, we'll use the following requirements:

- Don't build a model from scratch; instead, reuse one of the pretrained generic **convolutional neural network** (**CNN**: `https://en.wikipedia.org/wiki/Convolutional_neural_network`) models that are publicly available, such as MobileNet. We can always retrain these models later with custom training images using transfer learning (`https://en.wikipedia.org/wiki/Transfer_learning`).

- For MVP, while we are focusing on scoring only and not training, we should still make it interesting for the users. So let's build a PixieApp that allows the user to input the URL of a web page and display all the images scraped from the page, including the classification output inferred by our model.

- Since we are learning about deep learning neural networks and TensorFlow, it would be great if we could display the TensorBoard Graph Visualization (`https://www.tensorflow.org/programmers_guide/graph_viz`) in the Jupyter Notebook directly without forcing the user to use another tool. This will provide a better user experience and increase their engagement with the application.

Note: The implementation of the application in this section is adapted from the tutorial:

```
https://codelabs.developers.google.com/codelabs/
tensorflow-for-poets
```

Part 1 – Load the pretrained MobileNet model

Note: You can download the completed Notebook to follow this section discussion here:

```
https://github.com/DTAIEB/Thoughtful-Data-Science/blob/
master/chapter%206/Tensorflow%20VR%20Part%201.ipynb
```

There are plenty of publicly available image classification models, using CNNs, that are pretrained on large image databases such as ImageNet (http://www.image-net.org). ImageNet has started multiple public challenges, such as the **ImageNet Large Scale Visual Recognition Challenge (ILSVRC)** or the *ImageNet Object Localization Challenge* on Kaggle (https://www.kaggle.com/c/imagenet-object-localization-challenge), with very interesting results.

These challenges have produced multiple models, such as ResNet, Inception, SqueezeNet, VGGNet, or Xception, each using a different neural network architecture. Going over each of these architectures is beyond the scope of this book, but even if you are not yet an expert in machine learning (which I am definitely not), I encourage you to read about them online. The model I've selected for this sample application is MobileNet because it is small, fast, and very accurate. It provides an image classification model for 1,000 categories of images, which is sufficient for this sample application.

To ensure the stability of the code, I've made a copy of the model in the GitHub repo: https://github.com/DTAIEB/Thoughtful-Data-Science/tree/master/chapter%206/Visual%20Recognition/mobilenet_v1_0.50_224.

In this directory, you can find the following files:

- `frozen_graph.pb`: A serialized binary version of the TensorFlow graph

- `labels.txt`: A text file that includes a description of the 1,000 image categories and their index

- `quantized_graph.pb`: A compressed form of the model graph that used an 8-bit fixed point representation

Loading the model consists of building a `tf.graph` object and associated labels. Since we may want to load multiple models in the future, we first define a dictionary that provides metadata about the model:

```
models = {
    "mobilenet": {
        "base_url":"https://github.com/DTAIEB/Thoughtful-Data-Science/
raw/master/chapter%206/Visual%20Recognition/mobilenet_v1_0.50_224",
        "model_file_url": "frozen_graph.pb",
        "label_file": "labels.txt",
        "output_layer": "MobilenetV1/Predictions/Softmax"
    }
}
```

 You can find the file here:

```
https://github.com/DTAIEB/Thoughtful-Data-Science/
blob/master/chapter%206/sampleCode7.py
```

Each key in the preceding `models` dictionary represents the metadata of a particular model:

- `base_url`: Points to the URL where the files are stored
- `model_file_url`: The name of the model file that is assumed to be relative to `base_url`
- `label_file`: The name of the labels that are assumed to be relative to `base_url`
- `output_layer`: The name of the output layer that provides final scoring for each category

We implement a `get_model_attribute` helper method to facilitate reading from the `model` metadata, which will be very useful throughout our application:

```
# helper method for reading attributes from the model metadata
def get_model_attribute(model, key, default_value = None):
    if key not in model:
        if default_value is None:
            raise Exception("Require model attribute {} not found".
format(key))
        return default_value
    return model[key]
```

You can find the code file here:

https://github.com/DTAIEB/Thoughtful-Data-Science/
blob/master/chapter%206/sampleCode8.py

To load the graph, we download the binary file, load it into a `tf.GraphDef` object using the `ParseFromString` method, and we then invoke the `tf.import_graph_def` method using the graph as the current content manager:

```python
import tensorflow as tf
import requests
# Helper method for resolving url relative to the selected model
def get_url(model, path):
    return model["base_url"] + "/" + path


# Download the serialized model and create a TensorFlow graph
def load_graph(model):
    graph = tf.Graph()
    graph_def = tf.GraphDef()
    graph_def.ParseFromString(
        requests.get( get_url( model, model["model_file_url"] )
).content
    )
    with graph.as_default():
        tf.import_graph_def(graph_def)
    return graph
```

You can find the code file here:

https://github.com/DTAIEB/Thoughtful-Data-Science/
blob/master/chapter%206/sampleCode9.py

The method that loads the labels returns either a JSON object or an array (we'll see later that both are needed). The following code uses a Python list comprehension to iterate over the lines returned by the `requests.get` call. It then uses the `as_json` flag to format the data as appropriate:

```python
# Load the labels
def load_labels(model, as_json = False):
    labels = [line.rstrip() \
      for line in requests.get(get_url(model, model["label_file"])
).text.split("\n") if line != ""]
    if as_json:
        return [{"index": item.split(":")[0],"label":item.split(":")
[1]} for item in labels]
    return labels
```

You can find the code file here:
`https://github.com/DTAIEB/Thoughtful-Data-Science/`
`blob/master/chapter%206/sampleCode10.py`

The next step is to invoke the model to classify images. To make it simpler and perhaps more valuable, we ask the user to provide a URL to an HTML page that contains the images to be classified. We'll use the BeautifulSoup4 library to help parsing the page. To install BeautifulSoup4, simply run the following command:

`!pip install beautifulsoup4`

Note: As always, don't forget to restart the kernel once installation is complete.

The following `get_image_urls` method takes a URL as an input, downloads the HTML, instantiates a BeautifulSoup parser and extracts all the images found in any `<img>` elements and `background-image` styles. BeautifulSoup has a very elegant and easy-to-use API for parsing HTML. Here, we simply use the `find_all` method to find all `<img>` elements and the `select` method to select all elements with an inline style. The reader will be quick to notice that there are many other ways to create images using HTML that we are not discovering, such as, for example, images declared as CSS classes. As always, if you have the interest and time to improve it, I strongly welcome pull requests in the GitHub repo (see here for instructions on how to create a pull request: `https://help.github.com/articles/creating-a-pull-request`).

The code for `get_image_urls` looks like this:

```
from bs4 import BeautifulSoup as BS
import re

# return an array of all the images scraped from an html page
def get_image_urls(url):
    # Instantiate a BeautifulSoup parser
    soup = BS(requests.get(url).text, "html.parser")

    # Local helper method for extracting url
    def extract_url(val):
        m = re.match(r"url\((.*)\)", val)
        val = m.group(1) if m is not None else val
        return "http:" + val if val.startswith("//") else val
```

```
    # List comprehension that look for <img> elements and backgroud-
image styles
    return [extract_url(imgtag['src']) for imgtag in soup.find_
all('img')] + [ \
        extract_url(val.strip()) for key,val in \
        [tuple(selector.split(":")) for elt in soup.select("[style]")
\
            for selector in elt["style"].strip(" ;").split(";")] \
        if key.strip().lower()=='background-image' \
        ]
```

You can find the code file here:

https://github.com/DTAIEB/Thoughtful-Data-Science/
blob/master/chapter%206/sampleCode11.py

For each of the images discovered, we'll also need a helper function to download the images that will be passed as input to the model for classification.

The following download_image method downloads the image into a temporary file:

```
import tempfile
def download_image(url):
    response = requests.get(url, stream=True)
    if response.status_code == 200:
        with tempfile.NamedTemporaryFile(delete=False) as f:
            for chunk in response.iter_content(2048):
                f.write(chunk)
            return f.name
    else:
        raise Exception("Unable to download image: {}".format(response.
status_code))
```

You can find the code file here:

https://github.com/DTAIEB/Thoughtful-Data-Science/
blob/master/chapter%206/sampleCode12.py

Given a local path to an image, we now need to decode it into a tensor by calling the right decode method from the tf.image package, that is, the decode_png for .png files.

Note: In mathematics, a tensor is a generalization of a vector, which is defined by a direction and a size, to support higher dimensionality. Vectors are tensors of order 1, similarly, scalars are tensors of order 0. Intuitively, we can think of order 2 tensors as a two-dimensional array with values defined as a result of multiplying two vectors. In TensorFlow, tensors are arrays of n-dimensions.

After a few transformations on the image reader tensor (casting to the right decimal representation, resizing, and normalization), we call `tf.Session.run` on the normalizer tensor to execute the steps defined earlier, as shown in the following code:

```
# decode a given image into a tensor
def read_tensor_from_image_file(model, file_name):
    file_reader = tf.read_file(file_name, "file_reader")
    if file_name.endswith(".png"):
        image_reader = tf.image.decode_png(file_reader, channels =
3,name='png_reader')
    elif file_name.endswith(".gif"):
        image_reader = tf.squeeze(tf.image.decode_gif(file_
reader,name='gif_reader'))
    elif file_name.endswith(".bmp"):
        image_reader = tf.image.decode_bmp(file_reader, name='bmp_
reader')
    else:
        image_reader = tf.image.decode_jpeg(file_reader, channels = 3,
name='jpeg_reader')
    float_caster = tf.cast(image_reader, tf.float32)
    dims_expander = tf.expand_dims(float_caster, 0);

    # Read some info from the model metadata, providing default values
    input_height = get_model_attribute(model, "input_height", 224)
    input_width = get_model_attribute(model, "input_width", 224)
    input_mean = get_model_attribute(model, "input_mean", 0)
    input_std = get_model_attribute(model, "input_std", 255)

    resized = tf.image.resize_bilinear(dims_expander, [input_height,
input_width])
    normalized = tf.divide(tf.subtract(resized, [input_mean]),
[input_std])
    sess = tf.Session()
    result = sess.run(normalized)
    return result
```

You can find the code file here:

https://github.com/DTAIEB/Thoughtful-Data-Science/
blob/master/chapter%206/sampleCode13.py

With all the pieces in place, we are now ready to implement the `score_image` method that takes a `tf.graph`, a model metadata, and a URL to an image as input parameters, and returns the top five candidate classifications based on their confidence score, including their labels:

```python
import numpy as np

# classify an image given its url
def score_image(graph, model, url):
    # Get the input and output layer from the model
    input_layer = get_model_attribute(model, "input_layer", "input")
    output_layer = get_model_attribute(model, "output_layer")

    # Download the image and build a tensor from its data
    t = read_tensor_from_image_file(model, download_image(url))

    # Retrieve the tensors corresponding to the input and output
layers
    input_tensor = graph.get_tensor_by_name("import/" + input_layer +
":0");
    output_tensor = graph.get_tensor_by_name("import/" + output_layer
+ ":0");

    with tf.Session(graph=graph) as sess:
        results = sess.run(output_tensor, {input_tensor: t})
    results = np.squeeze(results)
    # select the top 5 candidate and match them to the labels
    top_k = results.argsort()[-5:][::-1]
    labels = load_labels(model)
    return [(labels[i].split(":")[1], results[i]) for i in top_k]
```

You can find the code file here:

https://github.com/DTAIEB/Thoughtful-Data-Science/
blob/master/chapter%206/sampleCode14.py

We can now test the code using the following steps:

1. Pick the `mobilenet` model and load the corresponding graph
2. Get a list of image URLs scraped from the Flickr website
3. Call the `score_image` method for each image URL and print the result

The code is shown here:

```
model = models['mobilenet']
graph = load_graph(model)
image_urls = get_image_urls("https://www.flickr.com/
search/?text=cats")
for url in image_urls:
    results = score_image(graph, model, url)
    print("Result for {}: \n\t{}".format(url, results))
```

You can find the code file here:

https://github.com/DTAIEB/Thoughtful-Data-Science/
blob/master/chapter%206/sampleCode15.py

The results are pretty accurate (except for the first image that is a blank image) as shown in the following screenshot:

```
Results for https://geo.yahoo.com/b?s=792600534:
   [('nail', 0.034935154), ('screw', 0.03144558), ('puck, hockey puck', 0.03032596), ('envelope', 0.0285034),
('Band Aid', 0.027891463)]
Results for http://c1.staticflickr.com/6/5598/14934282524_344c84246b_n.jpg:
   [('Egyptian cat', 0.4644194), ('tiger cat', 0.1485573), ('tabby, tabby cat', 0.09759513), ('plastic bag', 0.0
3814263), ('Siamese cat, Siamese', 0.033892646)]
Results for http://c1.staticflickr.com/4/3677/13545844805_170ec3746b_n.jpg:
   [('tabby, tabby cat', 0.7330132), ('Egyptian cat', 0.14256532), ('tiger cat', 0.11719289), ('plastic bag', 0.
0028653105), ('bow tie, bow-tie, bowtie', 0.00082955)]
Results for http://c1.staticflickr.com/6/5170/5372754294_db6acaale5_n.jpg:
   [('Persian cat', 0.607673), ('Angora, Angora rabbit', 0.20204937), ('hamster', 0.02988311), ('Egyptian cat',
0.027227053), ('lynx, catamount', 0.018035706)]
Results for http://c1.staticflickr.com/6/5589/14818641818_b0058c0cfc_m.jpg:
   [('Egyptian cat', 0.5786173), ('tabby, tabby cat', 0.27942237), ('tiger cat', 0.11966114), ('lynx, catamoun
t', 0.016066141), ('plastic bag', 0.002206809)]
Results for http://c1.staticflickr.com/6/5036/5081933297_7974eaff82_n.jpg:
   [('tiger cat', 0.26617262), ('tabby, tabby cat', 0.2417825), ('Persian cat', 0.18471399), ('lynx, catamount',
0.11543496), ('Egyptian cat', 0.025188642)]
Results for http://c1.staticflickr.com/3/2602/3977203168_b9d02a0233.jpg:
   [('tabby, tabby cat', 0.75482476), ('tiger cat', 0.13780454), ('Egyptian cat', 0.05675489), ('Siamese cat, Si
amese', 0.02073992), ('lynx, catamount', 0.010187127)]
Results for http://c1.staticflickr.com/8/7401/16393044637_72e93d96b6_n.jpg:
   [('Egyptian cat', 0.67294717), ('tiger cat', 0.18149199), ('tabby, tabby cat', 0.0952419), ('lynx, catamoun
t', 0.025225954), ('candle, taper, wax light', 0.003860443)]
Results for http://c1.staticflickr.com/9/8110/8594699278_dd256c10fd_m.jpg:
   [('tabby, tabby cat', 0.5829553), ('Egyptian cat', 0.15930973), ('tiger cat', 0.12964381), ('lynx, catamoun
t', 0.11114485), ('plastic bag', 0.006467772)]
Results for http://c1.staticflickr.com/8/7023/6581178955_7e23af8bf9_m.jpg:
   [('tabby, tabby cat', 0.28574014), ('Egyptian cat', 0.190615), ('plastic bag', 0.17165014), ('lynx, catamoun
t', 0.101593874)]
```

Classification of the images found on a Flickr page related to cats

Part 1 of our image recognition sample application is now complete; you can find the full Notebook at the following location: `https://github.com/DTAIEB/Thoughtful-Data-Science/blob/master/chapter%206/Tensorflow%20VR%20Part%201.ipynb`.

In the next section, we will build a more user-friendly experience by building a user interface with a PixieApp.

Part 2 – Create a PixieApp for our image recognition sample application

> **Note**: You can download the completed Notebook to follow this section discussion here:
>
> `https://github.com/DTAIEB/Thoughtful-Data-Science/blob/master/chapter%206/Tensorflow%20VR%20Part%202.ipynb`

As a reminder, the `setup` method of a PixieApp, if defined, is executed before the app starts running. We use it to select our model and initialize the graph:

```
from pixiedust.display.app import *

@PixieApp
class ScoreImageApp():
    def setup(self):
        self.model = models["mobilenet"]
        self.graph = load_graph( self.model )
    ...
```

> You can find the code file here:
>
> `https://github.com/DTAIEB/Thoughtful-Data-Science/blob/master/chapter%206/sampleCode16.py`

In the main screen of the PixieApp, we use an input box to let the user enter the URL to the web page, as shown in the following code snippet:

```
[[ScoreImageApp]]
@route()
def main_screen(self):
    return """
<style>
    div.outer-wrapper {
        display: table;width:100%;height:300px;
```

```
    }
    div.inner-wrapper {
        display: table-cell;vertical-align: middle;height: 100%;width:
100%;
    }
</style>
<div class="outer-wrapper">
    <div class="inner-wrapper">
        <div class="col-sm-3"></div>
        <div class="input-group col-sm-6">
          <input id="url{{prefix}}" type="text" class="form-control"
             value="https://www.flickr.com/search/?text=cats"
             placeholder="Enter a url that contains images">
          <span class="input-group-btn">
            <button class="btn btn-default" type="button" pd_
options="image_url=$val(url{{prefix}})">Go</button>
          </span>
        </div>
    </div>
</div>
"""
```

You can find the code file here:

`https://github.com/DTAIEB/Thoughtful-Data-Science/`
`blob/master/chapter%206/sampleCode17.py`

For convenience, we initialize the input text with a default value of `https://www.flickr.com/search/?text=cats`.

We can already run the code to test the main screen by using the following code:

```
app = ScoreImageApp()
app.run()
```

The main screen looks like this:

The main screen for the image recognition PixieApp

Note: This is good for testing, but we should keep in mind that the `do_process_url` route has not yet been implemented and, therefore, clicking on the **Go** button will fall back to the default route again.

Let's now implement the `do_process_url` route, which is triggered when the user clicks on the **Go** button. This route first calls the `get_image_urls` method to get the list of image URLs. Using Jinja2, we then build an HTML fragment that displays all the images. For each image, we asynchronously invoke the `do_score_url` route that runs the model and displays the results.

The following code shows the implementation of the `do_process_url` route:

```
[[ScoreImageApp]]
@route(image_url="*")
@templateArgs
def do_process_url(self, image_url):
    image_urls = get_image_urls(image_url)
    return """
<div>
{%for url in image_urls%}
<div style="float: left; font-size: 9pt; text-align: center; width:
30%; margin-right: 1%; margin-bottom: 0.5em;">
<img src="{{url}}" style="width: 100%">
  <div style="display:inline-block" pd_render_onload pd_
options="score_url={{url}}">
  </div>
</div>
{%endfor%}
<p style="clear: both;">
</div>
        """
```

 You can find the code file here:

https://github.com/DTAIEB/Thoughtful-Data-Science/blob/master/chapter%206/sampleCode18.py

Notice the use of the `@templateArgs` decorator, which allows the Jinja2 fragment to reference the local `image_urls` variable.

Finally, in the `do_score_url` route, we call the `score_image` and display the results as a list:

```
[[ScoreImageApp]]
@route(score_url="*")
```

```
@templateArgs
def do_score_url(self, score_url):
    results = score_image(self.graph, self.model, score_url)
    return """
<ul style="text-align:left">
{%for label, confidence in results%}
<li><b>{{label}}</b>: {{confidence}}</li>
{%endfor%}
</ul>
"""
```

 You can find the code file here:
https://github.com/DTAIEB/Thoughtful-Data-Science/
blob/master/chapter%206/sampleCode19.py

The following screenshot shows the results for the Flickr page that contains images of cats:

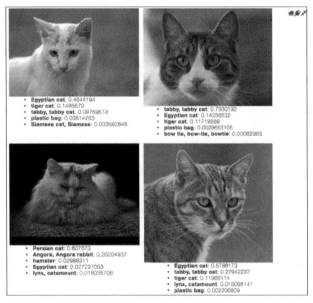

Results of the image classification for cats

As a reminder, you can find the complete Notebook at this location:

```
https://github.com/DTAIEB/Thoughtful-Data-Science/
blob/master/chapter%206/Tensorflow%20VR%20Part%202.
ipynb
```

Our MVP application is almost complete. In the next section, we will integrate the TensorBoard graph visualization directly in the Notebook.

Part 3 – Integrate the TensorBoard graph visualization

Note: Part of the code described in this section is adapted from the deepdream notebook located here:

```
https://github.com/tensorflow/tensorflow/blob/master/
tensorflow/examples/tutorials/deepdream/deepdream.ipynb
```

You can download the completed Notebook to follow this section discussion here:

```
https://github.com/DTAIEB/Thoughtful-Data-Science/blob/
master/chapter%206/Tensorflow%20VR%20Part%203.ipynb
```

TensorFlow comes with a very powerful suite of visualizations that help with debugging and performance optimization of your application. Please take a moment to explore the TensorBoard capabilities here: `https://www.tensorflow.org/programmers_guide/summaries_and_tensorboard`.

One issue here is that configuring the TensorBoard server to work with your Notebook could be difficult, especially if your Notebooks are hosted on the cloud, and you have little to no access to the underlying operating systems. In this case, configuring and starting the TensorBoard server could prove to be an impossible task. In this section, we show how to work around this problem by integrating the model graph visualization directly in your Notebook with zero configuration required. To provide a better user experience, we want to add the TensorBoard visualization to our PixieApp. We do that by changing the main layout to a tab layout and assign the TensorBoard visualization to its own tab. Conveniently, PixieDust provides a base PixieApp called `TemplateTabbedApp` that takes care of building a tabbed layout. When using `TemplateTabbedApp` as the base class, we need to configure the tab in the `setup` method as follows:

```
[[ImageRecoApp]]
from pixiedust.apps.template import TemplateTabbedApp
@PixieApp
class ImageRecoApp(TemplateTabbedApp):
    def setup(self):
        self.apps = [
            {"title": "Score", "app_class": "ScoreImageApp"},
            {"title": "Model", "app_class": "TensorGraphApp"},
            {"title": "Labels", "app_class": "LabelsApp"}
        ]
        self.model = models["mobilenet"]
        self.graph = self.load_graph(self.model)

app = ImageRecoApp()
app.run()
```

 You can find the code file here:
https://github.com/DTAIEB/Thoughtful-Data-Science/
blob/master/chapter%206/sampleCode20.py

It should be noted that in the preceding code, we have added the LabelsApp child
PixieApp to the list of tabs even though it hasn't yet been implemented. Therefore,
as expected, if you run the code as is, the Labels tab will fail.

self.apps contains an array of objects that define the tabs:

- title: Tab title
- app_class: PixieApp to run when the tab is selected

In ImageRecoApp, we configure three tabs associated with three child PixieApps:
the ScoreImageApp that we've already created in *Part 2 – Create a PixieApp for our
image recognition sample application*, the TensorGraphApp for displaying the model
graph, and the LabelsApp to display a table of all the labeled categories used in
the model.

The results are shown in the following screenshot:

Tabbed layout that includes Score, Model, and Labels

What's also nice about using `TemplateTabbedApp` superclass is that the sub-PixieApps are defined separately, which makes the code more maintainable and reusable.

Let's first look at the `TensorGraphApp` PixieApp. Its main route returns an HTML fragment that loads the `tf-graph-basic.build.html` into an Iframe from `https://tensorboard.appspot.com`, and using a JavaScript load listener applies the serialized graph definition that was computed using the `tf.Graph.as_graph_def` method. To make sure the graph definition remains at a reasonable size, and to avoid unnecessary performance degradation on the browser client, we call the `strip_consts` method to remove tensors with constant values that have a large size.

The code for `TensorGraphApp` is shown here:

```
@PixieApp
class TensorGraphApp():
    """Visualize TensorFlow graph."""
    def setup(self):
        self.graph = self.parent_pixieapp.graph

    @route()
    @templateArgs
    def main_screen(self):
        strip_def = self.strip_consts(self.graph.as_graph_def())
        code = """
            <script>
              function load() {{
```

```
                document.getElementById("{id}").pbtxt = {data};
            }}
        </script>
        <link rel="import" href="https://tensorboard.appspot.com/
tf-graph-basic.build.html" onload=load()>
        <div style="height:600px">
          <tf-graph-basic id="{id}"></tf-graph-basic>
        </div>
    """.format(data=repr(str(strip_def)), id='graph'+ self.
getPrefix()).replace('"', '&quot;')


    return """
<iframe seamless style="width:1200px;height:620px;border:0"
srcdoc="{{code}}"></iframe>
"""


def strip_consts(self, graph_def, max_const_size=32):
    """Strip large constant values from graph_def."""
    strip_def = tf.GraphDef()
    for n0 in graph_def.node:
        n = strip_def.node.add()
        n.MergeFrom(n0)
        if n.op == 'Const':
            tensor = n.attr['value'].tensor
            size = len(tensor.tensor_content)
            if size > max_const_size:
                tensor.tensor_content = "<stripped {} bytes>".
format(size).encode("UTF-8")
    return strip_def
```

You can find the code file here:

https://github.com/DTAIEB/Thoughtful-Data-Science/
blob/master/chapter%206/sampleCode21.py

Note: Child PixieApps have access to their parent PixieApp through the
`self.parent_pixieapp` variables.

The resulting screen for the `TensorGraphApp` child PixieApp is shown in the following screenshot. It provides an interactive visualization of the TensorFlow graph for the selected model, allowing the user to navigate through the different nodes and to drill down deeper into the model. However, it is important to note that the visualization runs entirely within the browser, without the TensorBoard server. Therefore, some of the functions available in the full TensorBoard, such as runtime statistics, are disabled.

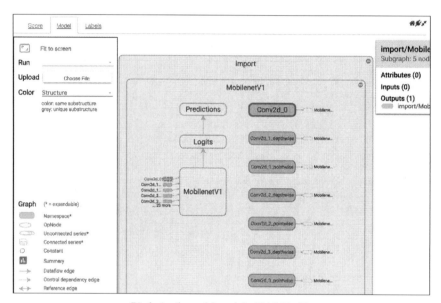

Displaying the model graph for MobileNet V1

In the `LabelsApp` PixieApp, we simply load the labels as JSON format, and display it in a PixieDust table, using the `handlerId=tableView` option:

```
[[LabelsApp]]
@PixieApp
class LabelsApp():
    def setup(self):
        self.labels = self.parent_pixieapp.load_labels(
            self.parent_pixieapp.model, as_json=True
        )

    @route()
    def main_screen(self):
        return """
```

```
<div pd_render_onload pd_entity="labels">
    <pd_options>
    {
        "table_noschema": "true",
        "handlerId": "tableView",
        "rowCount": "10000"
    }
    </pd_options>
</div>
    """
```

You can find the code file here:

https://github.com/DTAIEB/Thoughtful-Data-Science/blob/master/chapter%206/sampleCode22.py

Note: We configure the table to not show the schema by setting `table_noschema` to `true`, but we keep the search bar for convenience.

The results are shown in the following screenshot:

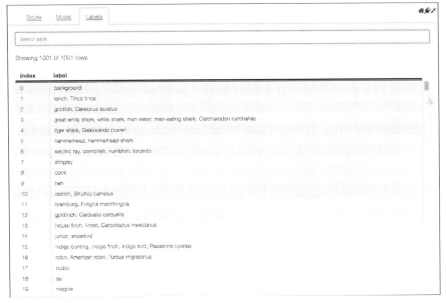

Searchable table for the model categories

Our MVP image recognition sample application is now complete; you can find the full Notebook here: `https://github.com/DTAIEB/Thoughtful-Data-Science/blob/master/chapter%206/Tensorflow%20VR%20Part%203.ipynb`.

In the next section, we will improve the application by allowing the user to retrain the model using custom images.

Part 4 – Retrain the model with custom training data

Note: You can download the completed Notebook to follow this section discussion here:

`https://github.com/DTAIEB/Thoughtful-Data-Science/blob/master/chapter%206/Tensorflow%20VR%20Part%204.ipynb`

The code in this section is quite extensive, and some helper functions that are not directly related to the topic will be omitted. However, as always, refer to the complete Notebook on GitHub for more information on the code.

In this section, we want to retrain the MobileNet model with custom training data and use it to classify images that would have had a low score on the generic model otherwise.

Note: The code in this section is adapted from the *TensorFlow for poets* tutorial:

`https://github.com/googlecodelabs/tensorflow-for-poets-2/blob/master/scripts/retrain.py`

As is the case most of the time, getting quality training data can be one of the most daunting and time-consuming tasks. In our example, we need images in large quantities for each of the classes we want to train. For the sake of simplicity and reproducibility, we are using the ImageNet databases that conveniently provide APIs for getting URLs and associated labels. We also limit the downloaded files to `.jpg` files. Of course, feel free to acquire your own training data if needed.

We first download the list of all the image URLs from the Fall 2011 release that is available here: `http://image-net.org/imagenet_data/urls/imagenet_fall11_urls.tgz`, and unpack the file into a local directory of your choice (for example, I chose `/Users/dtaieb/Downloads/fall11_urls.txt`).We also need to download the mapping between WordNet ID and words for all `synsets` available at `http://image-net.org/archive/words.txt`, which we'll use to find the WordNet IDs containing the URLs that we need to download.

The following code will load both files into a pandas DataFrame respectively:

```
import pandas
wnid_to_urls = pandas.read_csv('/Users/dtaieb/Downloads/fall11_urls.
txt',
                  sep='\t', names=["wnid", "url"],
                  header=0, error_bad_lines=False,
                  warn_bad_lines=False, encoding="ISO-8859-1")
wnid_to_urls['wnid'] = wnid_to_urls['wnid'].apply(lambda x:
x.split("_")[0])
wnid_to_urls = wnid_to_urls.dropna()

wnid_to_words = pandas.read_csv('/Users/dtaieb/Downloads/words.txt',
                  sep='\t', names=["wnid", "description"],
                  header=0, error_bad_lines=False,
                  warn_bad_lines=False, encoding="ISO-8859-1")
wnid_to_words = wnid_to_words.dropna()
```

> You can find the code file here:
>
> `https://github.com/DTAIEB/Thoughtful-Data-Science/blob/master/chapter%206/sampleCode23.py`
>
> Notice that we needed to clean the wnid column in the `wnid_to_urls` dataset because it contains a suffix corresponding to the index of the image in the category.

We can then define a method `get_url_for_keywords` that returns a dictionary containing the categories as keys and an array of URLs as values:

```
def get_url_for_keywords(keywords):
    results = {}
    for keyword in keywords:
        df = wnid_to_words.loc[wnid_to_words['description'] ==
keyword]
        row_list = df['wnid'].values.tolist()
        descriptions = df['description'].values.tolist()
        if len(row_list) > 0:
```

```
                    results[descriptions[0]] = \
                    wnid_to_urls.loc[wnid_to_urls['wnid'] == \
                    row_list[0]]["url"].values.tolist()
           return results
```

You can find the code file here:
`https://github.com/DTAIEB/Thoughtful-Data-Science/`
`blob/master/chapter%206/sampleCode24.py`

We can easily glance at the data distribution by using PixieDust `display`. As always, feel free to do more exploration on your own:

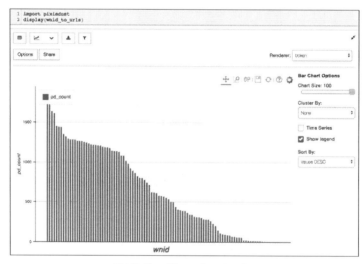

Distribution of images by categories

We can now build the code that will download the images corresponding to a list of categories of our choice. In our case, we chose fruits: `["apple", "orange", "pear", "banana"]`. The images will be downloaded in a subdirectory of the PixieDust home directory (using the PixieDust `Environment` helper class from the `pixiedust.utils` package), limiting the number of images to `500` for speed:

Note: The following code uses methods and imports defined earlier in the Notebook. Make sure to run the corresponding cell before attempting to run the following code.

```
from pixiedust.utils.environment import Environment
root_dir = ensure_dir_exists(os.path.join(Environment.pixiedustHome,
"imageRecoApp")
image_dir = root_dir
image_dict = get_url_for_keywords(["apple", "orange", "pear",
"banana"])
with open(os.path.join(image_dir, "retrained_label.txt"), "w")
as f_label:
    for key in image_dict:
        f_label.write(key + "\n")
        path = ensure_dir_exists(os.path.join(image_dir, key))
        count = 0
        for url in image_dict[key]:
            download_image_into_dir(url, path)
            count += 1
            if count > 500:
                break;
```

You can find the code file here:

```
https://github.com/DTAIEB/Thoughtful-Data-Science/
blob/master/chapter%206/sampleCode25.py
```

The next part of the code processes each of the images in the training set using the following steps:

Note: As mentioned before, the code is quite extensive, and part of it is omitted; only the important parts are explained here. Please do not attempt to run the following code as is and refer to the complete Notebook for full implementation.

1. Decode the .jpeg file using the following code:

```
def add_jpeg_decoding(model):
    input_height = get_model_attribute(model,
                    "input_height")
    input_width = get_model_attribute(model, "input_width")
    input_depth = get_model_attribute(model, "input_depth")
    input_mean = get_model_attribute(model, "input_mean",
                    0)
    input_std = get_model_attribute(model, "input_std",
                255)

    jpeg_data = tf.placeholder(tf.string,
```

```
                  name='DecodeJPGInput')
decoded_image = tf.image.decode_jpeg(jpeg_data,
              channels=input_depth)
decoded_image_as_float = tf.cast(decoded_image,
                    dtype=tf.float32)
decoded_image_4d = tf.expand_dims(
                decoded_image_as_float,
                0)
resize_shape = tf.stack([input_height, input_width])
resize_shape_as_int = tf.cast(resize_shape,
                 dtype=tf.int32)
resized_image = tf.image.resize_bilinear(
              decoded_image_4d,
              resize_shape_as_int)
offset_image = tf.subtract(resized_image, input_mean)
mul_image = tf.multiply(offset_image, 1.0 / input_std)
return jpeg_data, mul_image
```

You can find the code file here:

https://github.com/DTAIEB/Thoughtful-Data-Science/
blob/master/chapter%206/sampleCode26.py

2. Create the bottleneck values (caching them as appropriate) that normalize the
    image by resizing and rescaling it. This is done in the following code:

```
def run_bottleneck_on_image(sess, image_data,
    image_data_tensor,decoded_image_tensor,
    resized_input_tensor,bottleneck_tensor):
    # First decode the JPEG image, resize it, and rescale the
pixel values.
    resized_input_values = sess.run(decoded_image_tensor,
        {image_data_tensor: image_data})
    # Then run it through the recognition network.
    bottleneck_values = sess.run(
        bottleneck_tensor,
        {resized_input_tensor: resized_input_values})
    bottleneck_values = np.squeeze(bottleneck_values)
    return bottleneck_values
```

You can find the code file here:
`https://github.com/DTAIEB/Thoughtful-Data-Science/blob/master/chapter%206/sampleCode27.py`

3. Add the final training operations using the `add_final_training_ops` method, under a common namespace, so that it's easier to manipulate when visualizing the graph. The training steps are as follows:

   1. Generate random weight with the `tf.truncated_normal` API:

   ```
   initial_value = tf.truncated_normal(
       [bottleneck_tensor_size, class_count],
       stddev=0.001)
       layer_weights = tf.Variable(
           initial_value, name='final_weights')
   ```

   2. Add the biases, initialized to zero:

   ```
   layer_biases = tf.Variable(tf.zeros([class_count]),
       name='final_biases')
   ```

   3. Compute the weighted sum:

   ```
   logits = tf.matmul(bottleneck_input, layer_weights) +
       layer_biases
   ```

   4. Add the `cross_entropy` cost function:

   ```
   cross_entropy =
       tf.nn.softmax_cross_entropy_with_logits(
       labels=ground_truth_input, logits=logits)
   with tf.name_scope('total'):
       cross_entropy_mean = tf.reduce_mean(
       cross_entropy)
   ```

   5. Minimize the cost function:

   ```
   optimizer = tf.train.GradientDescentOptimizer(
       learning_rate)
   train_step = optimizer.minimize(cross_entropy_mean)
   ```

To visualize the retrained graph, we first need to update the `TensorGraphApp` PixieApp to let the user select which model to visualize: generic MobileNet or custom. This is done by adding a `<select>` drop-down in the main route and attaching a `pd_script` element to update the state:

```
[[TensorGraphApp]]
return """
{%if this.custom_graph%}
```

```
<div style="margin-top:10px" pd_refresh>
    <pd_script>
self.graph = self.custom_graph if self.graph is not self.custom_graph
else self.parent_pixieapp.graph
    </pd_script>
    <span style="font-weight:bold">Select a model to display:</span>
    <select>
        <option {%if this.graph!=this.custom_graph%}selected{%endif%}
value="main">MobileNet</option>
        <option {%if this.graph==this.custom_graph%}selected{%endif%}
value="custom">Custom</options>
    </select>
{%endif%}
<iframe seamless style="width:1200px;height:620px;border:0"
srcdoc="{{code}}"></iframe>
"""
```

You can find the code file here:

https://github.com/DTAIEB/Thoughtful-Data-Science/
blob/master/chapter%206/sampleCode28.py

Rerunning our `ImageReco` PixieApp produces the following screenshot:

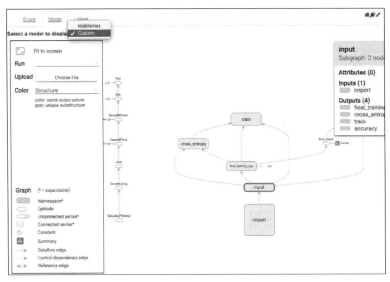

Visualization of the retrained graph

Clicking on the train node will reveal the nested operations that run the backpropagation algorithms to minimize the cross_entropy_mean cost functions specified in the preceding add_final_training_ops:

```
with tf.name_scope('cross_entropy'):
    cross_entropy = tf.nn.softmax_cross_entropy_with_logits(
        labels=ground_truth_input, logits=logits)
    with tf.name_scope('total'):
        cross_entropy_mean = tf.reduce_mean(cross_entropy)
```

> You can find the code file here:
> https://github.com/DTAIEB/Thoughtful-Data-Science/
> blob/master/chapter%206/sampleCode29.py

The following screenshot shows the details of the **train** namespace:

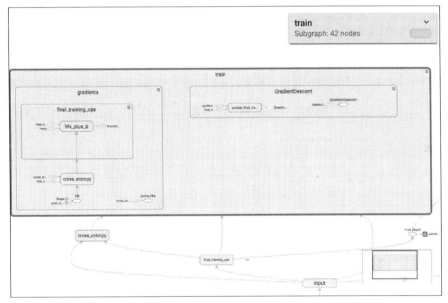

Backpropagation during training

Similarly, we can add the drop-down toggle in the `LabelsApp` to switch
the visualization between the generic MobileNet and custom model:

```
[[LabelsApp]]
@PixieApp
class LabelsApp():
    def setup(self):
        ...

    @route()
    def main_screen(self):
        return """
{%if this.custom_labels%}
<div style="margin-top:10px" pd_refresh>
    <pd_script>
self.current_labels = self.custom_labels if self.current_labels is not
self.custom_labels else self.labels
    </pd_script>
    <span style="font-weight:bold">
        Select a model to display:</span>
    <select>
        <option {%if this.current_labels!=this.labels%}
selected{%endif%} value="main">MobileNet</option>
        <option {%if this.current_labels==this.custom_labels%}
selected{%endif%} value="custom">Custom</options>
    </select>
{%endif%}
<div pd_render_onload pd_entity="current_labels">
    <pd_options>
    {
        "table_noschema": "true",
        "handlerId": "tableView",
        "rowCount": "10000",
        "noChartCache": "true"

    }
    </pd_options>
</div>
        """
```

You can find the code file here:

https://github.com/DTAIEB/Thoughtful-Data-Science/
blob/master/chapter%206/sampleCode30.py

The results are displayed in the following screenshot:

Display labels information for each model

The last step for our Part 4 MVP is to update the `score_image` method to classify the image with both models and add the results in a dictionary with an entry for each model. We define a local method `do_score_image` that returns the top 5 candidates answers.

This method is called for each model, and the results populate a dictionary with the model name as the key:

```
# classify an image given its url
def score_image(graph, model, url):
    # Download the image and build a tensor from its data
    t = read_tensor_from_image_file(model, download_image(url))

    def do_score_image(graph, output_layer, labels):
        # Retrieve the tensors corresponding to the input and output
layers
        input_tensor = graph.get_tensor_by_name("import/" +
            input_layer + ":0");
        output_tensor = graph.get_tensor_by_name( output_layer +
            ":0");

        with tf.Session(graph=graph) as sess:
            # Initialize the variables
            sess.run(tf.global_variables_initializer())
            results = sess.run(output_tensor, {input_tensor: t})
        results = np.squeeze(results)
        # select the top 5 candidates and match them to the labels
        top_k = results.argsort()[-5:][::-1]
        return [(labels[i].split(":")[1], results[i]) for i in top_k]
```

```
        results = {}
        input_layer = get_model_attribute(model, "input_layer",
            "input")
        labels = load_labels(model)
        results["mobilenet"] = do_score_image(graph, "import/" +
            get_model_attribute(model, "output_layer"), labels)
        if "custom_graph" in model and "custom_labels" in model:
            with open(model["custom_labels"]) as f:
                labels = [line.rstrip() for line in f.readlines() if line
!= ""]
                custom_labels = ["{}:{}".format(i, label) for i,label in
zip(range(len(labels)), labels)]
            results["custom"] = do_score_image(model["custom_graph"],
                "final_result", custom_labels)
        return results
```

You can find the code file here:

https://github.com/DTAIEB/Thoughtful-Data-Science/
blob/master/chapter%206/sampleCode31.py

Since we modified the returned values for the `score_image` method, we need to adjust the HTML fragment returned in `ScoreImageApp` to loop over all the model entries of the `results` dictionary:

```
@route(score_url="*")
@templateArgs
def do_score_url(self, score_url):
    scores_dict = score_image(self.graph, self.model, score_url)
    return """
{%for model, results in scores_dict.items()%}
<div style="font-weight:bold">{{model}}</div>
<ul style="text-align:left">
{%for label, confidence in results%}
<li><b>{{label}}</b>: {{confidence}}</li>
{%endfor%}
</ul>
{%endfor%}
    """
```

You can find the code file here:

https://github.com/DTAIEB/Thoughtful-Data-Science/
blob/master/chapter%206/sampleCode32.py

With these changes in place, the PixieApp will automatically invoke the custom models if available and, if that's the case, display the results for both models.

The following screenshot shows the results for images related to *banana*:

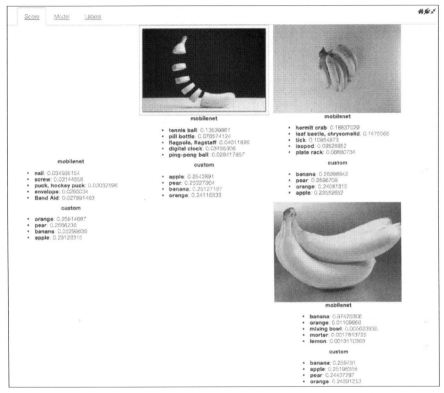

Score with generic MobileNet and custom-trained model

The reader will notice that the scores for the custom models are pretty low. One possible explanation is that the training data acquisition is fully automated and used without human curation. One possible enhancement to this sample application would be to move the training data acquisition and retraining steps into its own tab PixieApp. We should also give the user the opportunity to validate the images and reject the one that is of poor quality. It would also be great to let the user relabel the images that have been wrongly categorized.

The completed Notebook for Part 4 can be found here:
`https://github.com/DTAIEB/Thoughtful-Data-Science/blob/`
`master/chapter%206/Tensorflow%20VR%20Part%204.ipynb`

In this section, we've discussed the incremental approach of building an image recognition sample application in a Jupyter Notebook using TensorFlow, with a special focus on operationalizing the algorithms using PixieApps. We started with building a simple classification model from a pandas DataFrame using the TensorFlow `DNNClassifier` estimator. We then built an MVP version of the image recognition sample application in four parts:

1. We loaded the pretrained MobileNet model
2. We created a PixieApp for our image recognition sample application
3. We integrated the TensorBoard graph visualization into the PixieApp
4. We enabled users to retrain the model with custom training data from ImageNet

Summary

Machine learning is a vast topic that enjoys tremendous growth, both in research and development. In this chapter, we've explored only a tiny fraction of the state of the art in connection with machine learning algorithms, namely, using a deep learning neural network to perform image recognition. For some readers who are just beginning to get familiar with machine learning, the sample PixieApps and associated algorithms code may be too deep to digest at one time. However, the underlying aim was to demonstrate how to iteratively build an application that leverages a machine learning model. We happened to use a convolutional neural network model for image recognition, but any other model would do.

Hopefully, you got a good idea of how PixieDust and the PixieApp programming model can help you with your own project, and I strongly encourage you to use this sample application as a starting point to build your own custom application using the machine learning of your choice. I also recommend deploying your PixieApp as a web application with the PixieGateway microservice and exploring whether it's a viable solution.

In the next chapter, we will cover another important industry use case related to big data and natural language processing. We'll build a sample application that analyzes social media trends using a natural language understanding service.

7
Big Data Twitter Sentiment Analysis

"Data is the new oil."

– Unknown

In this chapter we are going to look at two important fields of AI and data science: **natural language processing (NLP)** and big data analysis. For the supporting sample application, we re-implement the *Sentiment analysis of Twitter hashtags* project described in *Chapter 1, Perspectives on Data Science from a Developer*, but this time we leverage Jupyter Notebooks and PixieDust to build live dashboards that analyze data from a stream of tweets related to a particular entity, such as a product offered by a company, for example, to provide sentiment information as well as information about other trending entities extracted from the same tweets. At the end of this chapter, the reader will learn how to integrate cloud-based NLP services such as *IBM Watson Natural Language Understanding* into their application as well as perform data analysis at (Twitter) scale with frameworks such as Apache Spark.

As always, we'll show how to operationalize the analytics by implementing a live dashboard as a PixieApp that runs directly in the Jupyter Notebook.

Getting started with Apache Spark

The term *big data* can rightly feel vague and imprecise. What is the cut-off for considering any dataset big data? Is it 10 GB, 100 GB, 1 TB or more? One definition that I like is: big data is when the data cannot fit into the memory available in a single machine. For years, data scientists have been forced to sample large datasets, so they could fit into a single machine, but that started to change as parallel computing frameworks that are able to distribute the data into a cluster of machines made it possible to work with the dataset in its entirety, provided of course that the cluster had enough machines. At the same time, advances in cloud technologies made it possible to provision on demand a cluster of machines that are adapted to the size of the dataset.

Today, there are multiple frameworks (most of the time available as open source) that can provide robust, flexible parallel computing capabilities. Some of the most popular include Apache Hadoop (`http://hadoop.apache.org`), Apache Spark (`https://spark.apache.org`) and Dask (`https://dask.pydata.org`). For our *Twitter Sentiment Analysis* application, we'll use Apache Spark, which provides excellent performances in the area of scalability, programmability, and speed. In addition, many cloud providers offer some flavor of Spark as a Service giving the ability to create on demand an appropriately sized Spark cluster in minutes.

Some Spark as a Service cloud providers include:

- Microsoft Azure: `https://azure.microsoft.com/en-us/services/hdinsight/apache-spark`
- Amazon Web Services: `https://aws.amazon.com/emr/details/spark`
- Google Cloud: `https://cloud.google.com/dataproc`
- Databricks: `https://databricks.com`
- IBM Cloud: `https://www.ibm.com/cloud/analytics-engine`

Note: Apache Spark can also be easily installed on a local machine for testing purposes, in which case, the cluster nodes are simulated using threads.

Apache Spark architecture

The following diagram shows the main components of the Apache Spark framework:

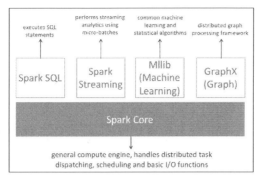

Spark high level architecture

- **Spark SQL**: The core data structure of this component is the Spark DataFrame, which enables users who know the SQL language, to effortlessly work with structured data.

- **Spark Streaming**: Module used to work with streaming data. As we'll see later on, we'll use this module and more specifically Structured Streaming (which was introduced in Spark 2.0) in our sample application.

- **MLlib**: Module that provides a feature-rich machine learning library that works on a Spark scale.

- **GraphX**: Module used for performing the graph-parallel computation.

There are mainly two ways of working with a Spark cluster as illustrated in the following diagram:

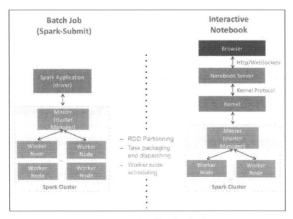

Two ways to work with a Spark cluster

- **spark-submit**: Shell script used to launch Spark applications on a cluster
- **Notebooks**: Interactively execute code statements against a Spark cluster

Covering the `spark-submit` shell script is beyond the scope of this book, but official documentation can be found at: `https://spark.apache.org/docs/latest/submitting-applications.html`. For the rest of this chapter, we'll focus on interacting with the Spark cluster via Jupyter Notebooks.

Configuring Notebooks to work with Spark

The instructions in this section only cover installing Spark locally for development and testing. Manually installing Spark in a cluster is beyond the scope of this book. If a real cluster is needed, it is highly recommended to use a cloud-based service.

By default, local Jupyter Notebooks are installed with plain Python Kernels. To work with Spark, users must use the following steps:

1. Install Spark locally by downloading a binary distribution from `https://spark.apache.org/downloads.html`.

2. Generate a kernel specification in a temporary directory using the following command:

   ```
   ipython kernel install --prefix /tmp
   ```

> **Note:** The preceding command may generate a warning message that can be safely ignored as long as the following message is stated:
>
> ```
> Installed kernelspec python3 in /tmp/share/jupyter/
> kernels/python3
> ```

3. Go to `/tmp/share/jupyter/kernels/python3`, and edit the `kernel.json` file to add the following key to the JSON object (replace `<<spark_root_path>>` with the directory path where you installed Spark and `<<py4j_version>>` with the version installed on your system):

   ```
   "env": {
       "PYTHONPATH": "<<spark_root_path>>/python/:<<spark_root_
   path>>/python/lib/py4j-<<py4j_version>>-src.zip",
       "SPARK_HOME": "<<spark_root_path>>",
       "PYSPARK_SUBMIT_ARGS": "--master local[10] pyspark-shell",
       "SPARK_DRIVER_MEMORY": "10G",
       "SPARK_LOCAL_IP": "127.0.0.1",
       "PYTHONSTARTUP": "<<spark_root_path>>/python/pyspark/shell.py"
   }
   ```

4. You may also want to customize the `display_name` key to make it unique and easily recognizable from the Juptyer UI. If you need to know the list of existing kernels, you can use the following command:

```
jupyter kernelspec list
```

The preceding command will give you a list of kernel names and associated paths on the local filesystem. From the path, you can open the `kernel.json` file to access the `display_name` value. For example:

```
Available kernels:
  pixiedustspark16
/Users/dtaieb/Library/Jupyter/kernels/pixiedustspark16
  pixiedustspark21
/Users/dtaieb/Library/Jupyter/kernels/pixiedustspark21
  pixiedustspark22
/Users/dtaieb/Library/Jupyter/kernels/pixiedustspark22
  pixiedustspark23
/Users/dtaieb/Library/Jupyter/kernels/pixiedustspark23
```

5. Install the kernel with the edited files using the following command:

```
jupyter kernelspec install /tmp/share/jupyter/kernels/python3
```

Note: Depending on the environment, you may receive a "permission denied" error when running the preceding command. In this case, you may want to run the command with the admin privileges using `sudo` or use the `--user` switch as follows:

```
jupyter kernelspec install --user /tmp/share/jupyter/
kernels/python3
```

For more information about install ation options, you can use the `-h` switch. For example:

```
jupyter kernelspec install -h
```

6. Restart the Notebook server and start using the new PySpark kernel.

Fortunately, PixieDust provides an `install` script to automate the preceding manual steps.

> You can find detailed documentation for this script here:
> `https://pixiedust.github.io/pixiedust/install.html`

In short, using the automated PixieDust `install` script requires the following command to be issued and the on-screen instructions to be followed:

```
jupyter pixiedust install
```

We'll dive deeper into the Spark programming model later in this chapter, but for now, let's define in the next section, the MVP requirements for our *Twitter Sentiment Analysis* application.

Twitter sentiment analysis application

As always, we start by defining the requirements for our MVP version:

- Connect to Twitter to get a stream of real-time tweets filtered by a query string provided by the user
- Enrich the tweets to add sentiment information and relevant entities extracted from the text
- Display a dashboard with various statistics about the data using live charts that are updated at specified intervals
- The system should be able to scale up to Twitter data size

The following diagram shows the first version of our application architecture:

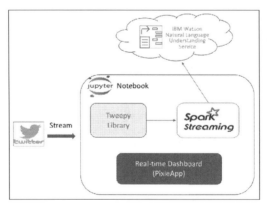

Twitter sentiment architecture version 1

For version 1, the application will be entirely implemented in a single Python Notebook and will call out to an external service for the NLP part. To be able to scale, we will certainly have to externalize some of the processing outside of the Notebook, but for development and testing, I found that being able to contain the whole application in a single Notebook significantly increases productivity.

As for libraries and frameworks, we'll use Tweepy (`http://www.tweepy.org`) for connecting to Twitter, Apache Spark Structured Streaming (`https://spark.apache.org/streaming`) for processing the streaming data in a distributed cluster and the Watson Developer Cloud Python SDK (`https://github.com/watson-developer-cloud/python-sdk`) to access the IBM Watson Natural Language Understanding (`https://www.ibm.com/watson/services/natural-language-understanding`) service.

Part 1 – Acquiring the data with Spark Structured Streaming

To acquire the data, we use Tweepy which provides an elegant Python client library to access the Twitter APIs. The APIs covered by Tweepy are very extensive and covering them in detail is beyond the scope of this book, but you can find the complete API reference at the Tweepy official website: `http://tweepy.readthedocs.io/en/v3.6.0/cursor_tutorial.html`.

You can install the Tweepy library directly from PyPi using the `pip install` command. The following command shows how to install it from a Notebook using the `!` directive:

```
!pip install tweepy
```

 Note: The current Tweepy version used is 3.6.0. Do not forget to restart the kernel after installing the library.

Architecture diagram for the data pipeline

Before we start diving into each component of the data pipeline, it would be good to take a look at its overall architecture and understand the computation flow.

As shown in the following diagram, we start by creating a Tweepy stream that writes raw data in CSV files. We then create a Spark Streaming DataFrame that reads the CSV files and is periodically updated with new data. From the Spark Streaming DataFrame, we create a Spark structured query using SQL and store its results in a Parquet database:

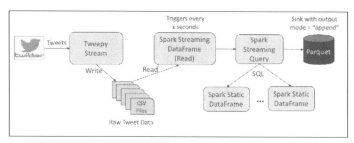

Streaming computation flow

Authentication with Twitter

Before using any of the Twitter APIs, it is recommended to authenticate with the system. One of the most commonly used authentication mechanism is the OAuth 2.0 protocol (`https://oauth.net`) which enables third-party applications to access a service on the web. The first thing you need to do is acquire a set of key strings that are used by the OAuth protocol to authenticate you:

- **Consumer key**: String that uniquely identifies the client app (a.k.a. the API Key).

- **Consumer secret**: Secret string known only to the application and the Twitter OAuth server. It can be thought of like a password.

- **Access token**: String used to authenticate your requests. This token is also used during the authorization phase to determine the level of access for the application.

- **Access token secret**: Similar to the consumer secret, this is a secret string sent with the access token to be used as a password.

To generate the preceding key strings, you need to go to `http://apps.twitter.com`, provide authentication with your regular Twitter user ID and password and follow these steps:

1. Create a new Twitter app using the **Create New App** button.

2. Fill out the application details, agree to the Developer agreement and click on **Create your Twitter application** button.

Note: Make sure that your mobile phone number is added to your profile or you'll get an error when creating the Twitter application.

You can provide a random URL for the mandatory **Website** input and leave the **URL** input blank as this is an optional callback URL.

3. Click on the **Keys and Access Tokens** tab to get the consumer and access token. At any time, you can regenerate these tokens using the buttons available on this page. If you do so, you'll need to also update the value in your application code.

For easier code maintenance, let's put these tokens in their own variables at the top of the Notebook and create the tweepy.OAuthHandler class that we'll use later on:

```
from tweepy import OAuthHandler
# Go to http://apps.twitter.com and create an app.
# The consumer key and secret will be generated for you after
consumer_key="XXXX"
consumer_secret="XXXX"

# After the step above, you will be redirected to your app's page.
# Create an access token under the "Your access token" section
access_token="XXXX"
access_token_secret="XXXX"

auth = OAuthHandler(consumer_key, consumer_secret)
auth.set_access_token(access_token, access_token_secret)
```

Creating the Twitter stream

For implementing our application, we only need to use the Twitter streaming API that is documented here: http://tweepy.readthedocs.io/en/v3.5.0/streaming_how_to.html. In this step, we create a Twitter stream that stores the incoming data into CSV files on the local filesystem. This is done using a custom RawTweetsListener class that inherits from tweepy.streaming.StreamListener. Custom processing of the incoming data is done by overriding the on_data method.

In our case, we want to transform the incoming data from JSON to CSV using DictWriter from the standard Python csv module. Because the Spark Streaming file input source triggers only when new files are created in the input directory, we can't simply append the data into an existing file. Instead, we buffer the data into an array and write it to disk once the buffer has reached capacity.

For simplicity, the implementation doesn't include cleaning up the files once they have been processed. Another minor limitation of this implementation is that we currently wait until the buffer is filled to write the file which theoretically could take a long time if no new tweets appear.

The code for the `RawTweetsListener` is shown here:

```
from six import iteritems
import json
import csv
from tweepy.streaming import StreamListener
class RawTweetsListener(StreamListener):
    def __init__(self):
        self.buffered_data = []
        self.counter = 0

    def flush_buffer_if_needed(self):
        "Check the buffer capacity and write to a new file if needed"
        length = len(self.buffered_data)
        if length > 0 and length % 10 == 0:
            with open(os.path.join( output_dir,
                "tweets{}.csv".format(self.counter)), "w") as fs:
                self.counter += 1
                csv_writer = csv.DictWriter( fs,
                    fieldnames = fieldnames)
                for data in self.buffered_data:
                    csv_writer.writerow(data)
            self.buffered_data = []

    def on_data(self, data):
        def transform(key, value):
            return transforms[key](value) if key in transforms
else value

        self.buffered_data.append(
            {key:transform(key,value) \
                for key,value in iteritems(json.loads(data)) \
                if key in fieldnames}
        )
        self.flush_buffer_if_needed()
        return True

    def on_error(self, status):
        print("An error occured while receiving streaming data: {}".
```

```
format(status))
        return False
```

 You can find the code file here:
https://github.com/DTAIEB/Thoughtful-Data-Science/
blob/master/chapter%207/sampleCode1.py

A few important things to notice from the preceding code are:

- Each tweet coming from the Twitter API contains a lot of data, and we pick which field to keep using the `field_metadata` variable. We also define a global variable `fieldnames` that holds the list of fields to capture from the stream, and a `transforms` variable that contains a dictionary with all the field names that have a transform function as a key and the transform function itself as a value:

```
from pyspark.sql.types import StringType, DateType
from bs4 import BeautifulSoup as BS
fieldnames = [f["name"] for f in field_metadata]
transforms = {
    item['name']:item['transform'] for item in field_metadata
if "transform" in item
}
field_metadata = [
    {"name": "created_at","type": DateType()},
    {"name": "text", "type": StringType()},
    {"name": "source", "type": StringType(),
        "transform": lambda s: BS(s, "html.parser").text.strip()
    }
]
```

 You can find the code file here:
https://github.com/DTAIEB/Thoughtful-Data-Science/
blob/master/chapter%207/sampleCode2.py

- The CSV files are written in `output_dir` which is defined in its own variable. At start time, we first remove the directory and its contents:

```
import shutil
def ensure_dir(dir, delete_tree = False):
    if not os.path.exists(dir):
        os.makedirs(dir)
    elif delete_tree:
```

```
        shutil.rmtree(dir)
        os.makedirs(dir)
    return os.path.abspath(dir)


root_dir = ensure_dir("output", delete_tree = True)
output_dir = ensure_dir(os.path.join(root_dir, "raw"))
```

You can find the code file here:

`https://github.com/DTAIEB/Thoughtful-Data-Science/blob/master/chapter%207/sampleCode3.py`

- The `field_metadata` contains the Spark DataType that we'll use later on to build the schema when creating the Spark streaming query.

- The `field_metadata` also contains an optional transform `lambda` function to cleanse the value before being written to disk. For reference, a lambda function in Python is an anonymous function defined inline (see `https://docs.python.org/3/tutorial/controlflow.html#lambda-expressions`). We use it for the source field that is often returned as an HTML fragment. In this lambda function, we use the BeautifulSoup library (which was also used in the previous chapter) to extract only the text as shown in the following snippet:

```
lambda s: BS(s, "html.parser").text.strip()
```

Now that the `RawTweetsListener` is created, we define a `start_stream` function that we'll use later on in the PixieApp. This function takes an array of search terms as input and starts a new stream using the `filter` method:

```
from tweepy import Stream
def start_stream(queries):
    "Asynchronously start a new Twitter stream"
    stream = Stream(auth, RawTweetsListener())
    stream.filter(track=queries, async=True)
    return stream
```

Notice the `async=True` parameter passed to `stream.filter`. This is needed to make sure that the function doesn't block, which would prevent us from running any other code in the Notebook.

You can find the code file here:

`https://github.com/DTAIEB/Thoughtful-Data-Science/blob/master/chapter%207/sampleCode4.py`

The following code starts the stream that will receive tweets containing the word `baseball` in it:

```
stream = start_stream(["baseball"])
```

When running the preceding code, no output is generated in the Notebook. However, you can see the files (that is, `tweets0.csv`, `tweets1.csv`, and so on.) being generated in the output directory (that is, `../output/raw`) from the path where the Notebook is being run.

To stop the stream, we simply call the `disconnect` method, as shown here:

```
stream.disconnect()
```

Creating a Spark Streaming DataFrame

Referring to the architecture diagram, the next step is to create a Spark Streaming DataFrame `tweets_sdf` that uses the `output_dir` as the source file input. We can think of a Streaming DataFrame as an unbounded table where new rows are continuously added as new data arrives from the stream.

 Note: Spark Structured Streaming supports multiple types of input source including File, Kafka, Socket, and Rate. (Both Socket and Rate are used only for testing.)

The following diagram is taken from the Spark website and does a great job explaining how new data is appended to the Streaming DataFrame:

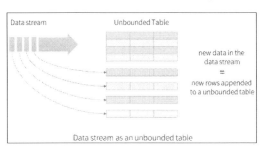

Streaming DataFrame flow

Source: https://spark.apache.org/docs/latest/img/structured-streaming-stream-as-a-table.png

The Spark Streaming Python API provides an elegant way to create the Streaming DataFrame using the `spark.readStream` property which creates a new `pyspark.sql.streamingreamReader` object that conveniently lets you chain method calls with the added benefit of creating clearer code (see `https://en.wikipedia.org/wiki/Method_chaining` for more details on this pattern).

For example, to create a CSV file stream, we call the format method with `csv`, chain the applicable options and call the `load` method with the path of the directory:

```python
schema = StructType(
[StructField(f["name"], f["type"], True) for f in field_metadata]
)
csv_sdf = spark.readStream\
    .format("csv")\
    .option("schema", schema)\
    .option("multiline", True)\
    .option("dateFormat", 'EEE MMM dd kk:mm:ss Z y')\
    .option("ignoreTrailingWhiteSpace", True)\
    .option("ignoreLeadingWhiteSpace", True)\
    .load(output_dir)
```

 You can find the code file here:

`https://github.com/DTAIEB/Thoughtful-Data-Science/blob/master/chapter%207/sampleCode5.py`

`spark.readStream` also provides a convenient high-level `csv` method that takes the path as the first argument and keyword arguments for the options:

```python
csv_sdf = spark.readStream \
    .csv(
        output_dir,
        schema=schema,
        multiLine = True,
        dateFormat = 'EEE MMM dd kk:mm:ss Z y',
        ignoreTrailingWhiteSpace = True,
        ignoreLeadingWhiteSpace = True
    )
```

 You can find the code file here:

`https://github.com/DTAIEB/Thoughtful-Data-Science/blob/master/chapter%207/sampleCode6.py`

You can verify that the csv_sdf DataFrame is indeed a Streaming DataFrame by calling the isStreaming method which should return true. The following code also adds a call to printSchema to verify that the schema follows the field_ metadata configuration as expected:

```
print(csv_sdf.isStreaming)
csv_sdf.printSchema()
```

Returns:

```
root
 |-- created_at: date (nullable = true)
 |-- text: string (nullable = true)
 |-- source: string (nullable = true)
```

Before continuing to the next step, it is important to understand how the csv_sdf Streaming DataFrame fits in the Structured Streaming programming model and what limitations it has. At its core, the Spark low-level APIs define the **Resilient Distributed Dataset (RDD)** data structure which encapsulates all the underlying complexity of managing the distributed data. Features like fault-tolerance (cluster nodes that crashes for any reason are transparently restarted with no intervention from the developer) are automatically handled by the framework. There are two types of RDD operations: transformations and actions. **Transformations** are logical operations on an existing RDD that are not immediately executed on the cluster until an action is invoked (lazy execution). The output of a transformation is a new RDD. Internally, Spark maintains an RDD acyclic directed graph that keeps track of all the lineage resulting in the creation of the RDD, which is useful when recovering from server failure. Example transformations include map, flatMap, filter, sample, and distinct. The same goes for transformations on DataFrames (which internally are backed by RDDs) that have the benefit of including SQL queries. On the other hand, **actions** do not produce other RDDs, but rather perform an operation on the actual distributed data to return a non-RDD value. Examples of actions include reduce, collect, count, and take.

As mentioned before, csv_sdf is a Streaming DataFrame, which means that the data is continuously added to it and as such we are only able to apply transformations to it, not actions. To circumvent this problem, we must first create a streaming query using csv_sdf.writeStream which is a pyspark.sql. streaming.DataStreamWriter object. The streaming query is responsible for sending the results to an output sink. We can then run the streaming query using the start() method.

Spark Streaming supports multiple output sink types:

- **File**: All the classic file formats are supported, including JSON, CSV, and Parquet
- **Kafka**: Write directly to one or more Kafka topics
- **Foreach**: Run arbitrary computations on each element in the collection
- **Console**: Prints the output to the system console (used mainly for debugging)
- **Memory**: Output is stored in memory

In the next section, we'll create and run a structured query on `csv_sdf` with an output sink that stores the output in Parquet format.

Creating and running a structured query

Using the `tweets_sdf` Streaming DataFrame, we create a streaming query `tweet_streaming_query` that writes the data into a Parquet format using the *append* output mode.

 Note: Spark streaming queries support three output modes: **complete** where the entire table is written at each trigger, **append** where only the delta rows since the last trigger are written, and **update** where only the rows that were modified are written.

Parquet is a columnar database format that provides an efficient, scalable storage for distributed analytics. You can find more information about the Parquet format at: `https://parquet.apache.org`.

The following code creates and starts the `tweet_streaming_query` streaming query:

```
tweet_streaming_query = csv_sdf \
    .writeStream \
    .format("parquet") \
    .option("path", os.path.join(root_dir, "output_parquet")) \
    .trigger(processingTime="2 seconds") \
    .option("checkpointLocation", os.path.join(root_dir,
"output_chkpt")) \
    .start()
```

You can find the code file here:

`https://github.com/DTAIEB/Thoughtful-Data-Science/blob/master/chapter%207/sampleCode7.py`

Similarly, you can stop the streaming query by using the `stop()` method as follows:

```
tweet_streaming_query.stop()
```

In the preceding code, we use the `path` option to specify the location of the Parquet files, and the `checkpointLocation` to specify the location of the recovery data that would be used in case of a server failure. We also specify the trigger interval for new data to be read from the stream and new rows to be added to the Parquet database.

For testing purpose, you can also use the `console` sink to see the new rows being read every time a new raw CSV file is generated in the `output_dir` directory:

```
tweet_streaming_query = csv_sdf.writeStream\
    .outputMode("append")\
    .format("console")\
    .trigger(processingTime='2 seconds')\
    .start()
```

You can find the code file here:

`https://github.com/DTAIEB/Thoughtful-Data-Science/blob/master/chapter%207/sampleCode8.py`

You can see the results in the system output of the master node of your Spark cluster (you will need to physically access the master node machine and look at the log files, since, unfortunately, the output is not printed into the Notebook itself because the operation is executed in a different process. Location of the log files depends on the cluster management software; please refer to the specific documentation for more information).

Here are sample results displayed for a particular batch (identifiers have been masked):

```
-------------------------------------------
Batch: 17
-------------------------------------------
+----------+-------------------+-------------------+
|created_at|               text|             source|
+----------+-------------------+-------------------+
|2018-04-12|RT @XXXXXXXXXXXXX...|Twitter for Android|
|2018-04-12|RT @XXXXXXX: Base...| Twitter for iPhone|
```

```
|2018-04-12|That's my roommat...|  Twitter for iPhone|
|2018-04-12|He's come a long ...|  Twitter for iPhone|
|2018-04-12|RT @XXXXXXXX: U s...|  Twitter for iPhone|
|2018-04-12|Baseball: Enid 10...|     PushScoreUpdates|
|2018-04-12|Cubs and Sox aren...|  Twitter for iPhone|
|2018-04-12|RT @XXXXXXXXXX: T...|            RoundTeam|
|2018-04-12|@XXXXXXXX that ri...|  Twitter for iPhone|
|2018-04-12|RT @XXXXXXXXXX: S...|  Twitter for iPhone|
+----------+--------------------+-------------------+
```

Monitoring active streaming queries

When a streaming query is started, cluster resources are allocated by Spark. Therefore, it is important to manage and monitor these queries to make sure that you don't run out of cluster resources. At any time, you can get a list of all the running queries as shown in the following code:

```
print(spark.streams.active)
```

Results:

```
[<pyspark.sql.streaming.StreamingQuery object at 0x12d7db6a0>,
<pyspark.sql.streaming.StreamingQuery object at 0x12d269c18>]
```

You can then dive into the details of each query by using the following query monitoring properties:

- `id`: Returns a unique identifier for the query that persists across restarts from checkpoint data
- `runId`: Returns a unique ID generated for the current session
- `explain()`: Prints detailed explanations of the query
- `recentProgress`: Returns an array of the most recent progress updates
- `lastProgress`: Returns the most recent progress

The following code prints the most recent progress for each active query:

```
import json
for query in spark.streams.active:
    print("-----------")
    print("id: {}".format(query.id))
    print(json.dumps(query.lastProgress, indent=2, sort_keys=True))
```

You can find the code file here:
`https://github.com/DTAIEB/Thoughtful-Data-Science/`
`blob/master/chapter%207/sampleCode9.py`

Results for the first query are shown here:

```
-----------
id: b621e268-f21d-4eef-b6cd-cb0bc66e53c4
{
  "batchId": 18,
  "durationMs": {
    "getOffset": 4,
    "triggerExecution": 4
  },
  "id": "b621e268-f21d-4eef-b6cd-cb0bc66e53c4",
  "inputRowsPerSecond": 0.0,
  "name": null,
  "numInputRows": 0,
  "processedRowsPerSecond": 0.0,
  "runId": "d2459446-bfad-4648-ae3b-b30c1f21be04",
  "sink": {
    "description": "org.apache.spark.sql.execution.streaming.
ConsoleSinkProvider@586d2ad5"
  },
  "sources": [
    {
      "description": "FileStreamSource[file:/Users/dtaieb/cdsdev/
notebookdev/Pixiedust/book/Chapter7/output/raw]",
      "endOffset": {
        "logOffset": 17
      },
      "inputRowsPerSecond": 0.0,
      "numInputRows": 0,
      "processedRowsPerSecond": 0.0,
      "startOffset": {
        "logOffset": 17
      }
    }
  ],
  "stateOperators": [],
  "timestamp": "2018-04-12T21:40:10.004Z"
}
```

As an exercise for the reader, it would be useful to build a PixieApp that provides a live dashboard with updated details about each active streaming query.

 Note: We'll show how to build this PixieApp in *Part 3 – Create a real-time dashboard PixieApp.*

Creating a batch DataFrame from the Parquet files

 Note: For the rest of this chapter, we define a batch Spark DataFrame as a classic Spark DataFrame, that is non-streaming.

The last step of this streaming computation flow is to create one or more batch DataFrames that we can use for building our analytics and data visualizations. We can think of this last step as taking a snapshot of the data for deeper analysis.

There are two ways to programmatically load a batch DataFrame from a Parquet file:

- Using `spark.read` (notice that we don't use `spark.readStream` as we did earlier):

```
parquet_batch_df = spark.read.parquet(os.path.join(root_dir,
"output_parquet"))
```

- Using `spark.sql`:

```
parquet_batch_df = spark.sql(
"select * from parquet.'{}'".format(
os.path.join(root_dir, "output_parquet")
)
)
```

 You can find the code file here:
https://github.com/DTAIEB/Thoughtful-Data-Science/blob/master/chapter%207/sampleCode10.py

The benefit of this method is that we can use any ANSI SQL query to load the data, instead of using the equivalent low-level DataFrame APIs that we would have to use in the first method.

We can then periodically refresh the data by rerunning the preceding code and recreating the DataFrame. We are now ready to create further analysis on the data by, for example, running the PixieDust `display()` method on it in order to create visualizations:

```
import pixiedust
display(parquet_batch_df)
```

We select the **Bar Chart** menu and drag and drop the `source` field in the **Keys** field area. Since we want to show only the top 10 tweets, we set this value in the **# of Rows to Display** field. The following screenshot shows the PixieDust options dialog:

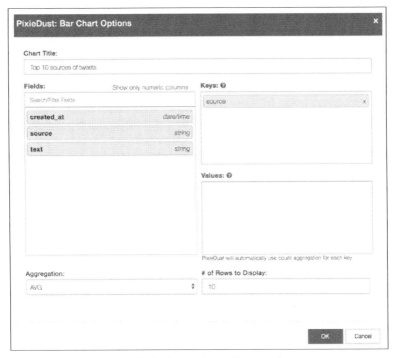

Options dialog for showing the top 10 sources of tweets

After clicking **OK**, we see the following results:

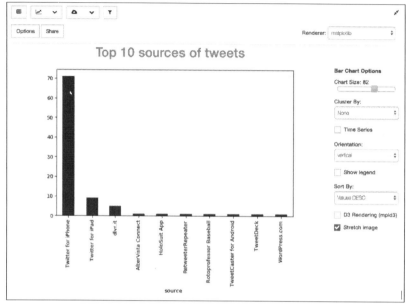

Chart showing the number of tweets related to baseball by source

In this section, we've seen how to use the Tweepy library to create a Twitter stream, clean the raw data and store it in CSV files, create a Spark Streaming DataFrame, run streaming queries on it and store the output in a Parquet database, create a batch DataFrame from the Parquet file, and visualize the data using PixieDust `display()`.

The complete notebook for *Part 1 – Acquiring the data with Spark Structured Streaming* can be found here:

```
https://github.com/DTAIEB/Thoughtful-Data-Science/
blob/master/chapter%207/Twitter%20Sentiment%20
Analysis%20-%20Part%201.ipynb
```

In the next part, we'll look at enriching the data with sentiment and entity extraction using the IBM Watson Natural Language Understanding service.

Part 2 – Enriching the data with sentiment and most relevant extracted entity

In this part, we enrich the Twitter data with sentiment information, for example, *positive*, *negative*, and *neutral*. We also want to extract the most relevant entity from the tweet, for example, sport, organization, and location. This extra information will be analyzed and visualized by the real-time dashboard that we'll build in the next section. The algorithms used to extract sentiment and entity from an unstructured text belong to a field of computer science and artificial intelligence called **natural language processing** (NLP). There are plenty of tutorials available on the web that provide algorithm examples on how to extract sentiment. For example, you can find a comprehensive text analytic tutorial on the scikit-learn repo at `https://github.com/scikit-learn/scikit-learn/blob/master/doc/tutorial/text_analytics/working_with_text_data.rst`.

However, for this sample application, we are not going to build our own NLP algorithm. Instead, we'll choose a cloud-based service that provides text analytics such as sentiment and entity extraction. This approach works very well when you have generic requirements such as do not require training custom models, but even then, most of the service providers now provide tooling to do so. There are major advantages to use a cloud-based provider over creating your own model such as saving on the development time and much better accuracy and performance. With a simple REST call, we'll be able to generate the data we need and integrate it into the flow of our application. Also, it would be very easy to change providers if needed as the code responsible for interfacing with the service is well isolated.

For this sample application, we'll use the **IBM Watson Natural Language Understanding** (NLU) service which is a part of the IBM Watson family of cognitive services, and available on IBM Cloud.

Getting started with the IBM Watson Natural Language Understanding service

The process of provisioning a new service is usually the same for every cloud provider. After logging in, you go to a service catalog page where you can search for a particular service.

To log in to the IBM Cloud, just go to `https://console.bluemix.net` and create a free IBM account if you don't already have one. Once in the dashboard, there are multiple ways to search for the IBM Watson NLU service:

- Click on the top left-hand menu, and select **Watson**, select **Browse services**, and find the **Natural Language Understanding** entry in the list of services.

- Click on the **Create Resource** button in the top-right corner to get to the catalog. Once in the catalog, you can search for `Natural Language Understanding` in the search bar as shown in the following screenshot:

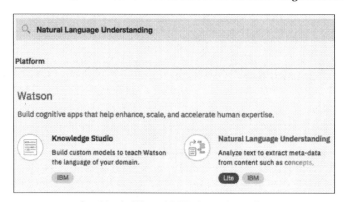

Searching for Watson NLU in the service catalog

You can then click on **Natural Language Understanding** to provision a new instance. It is not unusual that cloud providers offer a free or trial-based plan for some services and fortunately Watson NLU provides one of these, with the limitation that you can train only one custom model with a maximum of 30,000 NLU items processed per month (which is adequate for our sample application). After selecting the **Lite** (free) plan and clicking on the **Create** button, the newly provisioned instance will appear on the dashboard and is ready to accept requests.

 Note: After creating the service, you may be redirected to the NLU service *getting started document*. If so, simply navigate back to the dashboard where you should see the new service instance listed.

The next step is to test the service from our Notebook by making a REST call. Every service provides detailed documentation on how to use it including the API reference. From the Notebook, we could use the requests package to make GET, POST, PUT, or DELETE calls according to the API reference, but it is highly recommended to check whether the service offers SDKs with high-level programmatic access to the APIs.

Fortunately, IBM Watson provides the `watson_developer_cloud` open source library which includes multiple open source SDKs supporting some of the most popular languages, including Java, Python, and Node.js. For this project, we'll use the Python SDK with source code and code examples located here: `https://github.com/watson-developer-cloud/python-sdk`.

The following `pip` command installs the `watson_developer_cloud` package directly from the Jupyter Notebook:

```
!pip install Watson_developer_cloud
```

Notice the `!` in front of the command that signifies that it's a shell command.

Note: Don't forget to restart the kernel once installation is complete.

Most cloud service providers use a common pattern to let consumers authenticate with the service, which consists of generating a set of credentials from the service console dashboard that will be embedded in the client application. To generate the credentials, simply click on the **Service credentials** tab of your Watson NLU instance and click on the **New credential** button.

This will generate a new set of credentials in JSON format as shown in the following screenshot:

Generating new credentials for the Watson NLU service

Now that we have the credentials to our service, we can create a `NaturalLanguageUnderstandingV1` object that will provide programmatic access to the REST APIs, as shown in the following code:

```
from watson_developer_cloud import NaturalLanguageUnderstandingV1
from watson_developer_cloud.natural_language_understanding_v1 import
Features, SentimentOptions, EntitiesOptions

nlu = NaturalLanguageUnderstandingV1(
    version='2017-02-27',
    username='XXXX',
    password='XXXX'
)
```

You can find the code file here:

`https://github.com/DTAIEB/Thoughtful-Data-Science/` `blob/master/chapter%207/sampleCode11.py`

Note: In the preceding code, replace the XXXX text with the appropriate username and password from the service credentials.

The `version` argument refers to a specific version of the API. To know the latest version, go to the official documentation page located here:

`https://www.ibm.com/watson/developercloud/natural-` `language-understanding/api/v1`

Before continuing with building the application, let's take a moment to understand the text analytics capabilities offered by the Watson Natural Language service which include:

- Sentiment
- Entities
- Concepts
- Categories
- Emotion
- Keywords
- Relations
- Semantic roles

In our application, enriching the Twitter data happens in the `RawTweetsListener` where we create an `enrich` method that will be invoked from the `on_data` handler method. In this method, we call the `nlu.analyze` method with the Twitter data and a feature list that includes sentiment and entities only as shown in the following code:

Note: The `[[RawTweetsListener]]` notation means that the following code is part of a class called `RawTweetsListener` and that the user should not attempt to run the code as is without the complete class. As always, you can always refer to the complete notebook for reference.

```
[[RawTweetsListener]]
def enrich(self, data):
    try:
        response = nlu.analyze(
            text = data['text'],
            features = Features(
                sentiment=SentimentOptions(),
                entities=EntitiesOptions()
            )
        )
        data["sentiment"] = response["sentiment"]["document"]["label"]
        top_entity = response["entities"][0] if
len(response["entities"]) > 0 else None
        data["entity"] = top_entity["text"] if top_entity is not None
else ""
        data["entity_type"] = top_entity["type"] if top_entity is not
None else ""
        return data
    except Exception as e:
        self.warn("Error from Watson service while enriching data:
{}".format(e))
```

You can find the code file here:

https://github.com/DTAIEB/Thoughtful-Data-Science/blob/master/chapter%207/sampleCode12.py

The results are then stored in the `data` object which will be written to the CSV files. We also guard against unexpected exceptions skipping the current tweet and logging a warning message instead of letting the exception bubble up which would stop the Twitter stream.

Note: The most common exception happens when the tweet data is in a language that is not supported by the service.

We use the @Logger decorator described in *Chapter 5, Best Practices and Advanced PixieDust Concepts* to log messages against the PixieDust logging framework. As a reminder, you can use the %pixiedustLog magic from another cell to view the log messages.

We still need to change the schema metadata to include the new fields as follows:

```
field_metadata = [
    {"name": "created_at", "type": DateType()},
    {"name": "text", "type": StringType()},
    {"name": "source", "type": StringType(),
        "transform": lambda s: BS(s, "html.parser").text.strip()
    },
    {"name": "sentiment", "type": StringType()},
    {"name": "entity", "type": StringType()},
    {"name": "entity_type", "type": StringType()}
]
```

You can find the code file here:

https://github.com/DTAIEB/Thoughtful-Data-Science/blob/master/chapter%207/sampleCode13.py

Finally, we update on_data handler to invoke the enrich method as follows:

```
def on_data(self, data):
    def transform(key, value):
        return transforms[key](value) if key in transforms else value
    data = self.enrich(json.loads(data))
    if data is not None:
        self.buffered_data.append(
            {key:transform(key,value) \
                for key,value in iteritems(data) \
                if key in fieldnames}
        )
        self.flush_buffer_if_needed()
    return True
```

You can find the code file here:

https://github.com/DTAIEB/Thoughtful-Data-Science/blob/master/chapter%207/sampleCode14.py

When we restart the Twitter stream and create the Spark Streaming DataFrame, we can verify that we have the correct schema using the following code:

```
schema = StructType(
    [StructField(f["name"], f["type"], True) for f in field_metadata]
)
csv_sdf = spark.readStream \
    .csv(
        output_dir,
        schema=schema,
        multiLine = True,
        dateFormat = 'EEE MMM dd kk:mm:ss Z y',
        ignoreTrailingWhiteSpace = True,
        ignoreLeadingWhiteSpace = True
    )
csv_sdf.printSchema()
```

 You can find the code file here:

https://github.com/DTAIEB/Thoughtful-Data-Science/blob/master/chapter%207/sampleCode15.py

Which shows the following results as expected:

```
root
 |-- created_at: date (nullable = true)
 |-- text: string (nullable = true)
 |-- source: string (nullable = true)
 |-- sentiment: string (nullable = true)
 |-- entity: string (nullable = true)
 |-- entity_type: string (nullable = true)
```

Similarly, when we run the structured query with the `console` sink, data is displayed in batches in the console of the Spark master node as shown here:

```
-------------------------------------------
Batch: 2
-------------------------------------------
+----------+---------------+---------------+---------+------------+--
----------+
|created_at|           text|         source|sentiment|      entity|
entity_type|
+----------+---------------+---------------+---------+------------+--
----------+
|2018-04-14|Some little ...| Twitter iPhone| positive|        Drew|
Person|d
```

```
|2018-04-14|RT @XXXXXXXX...| Twitter iPhone|  neutral| @
XXXXXXXXXX|TwitterHandle|
|2018-04-14|RT @XXXXXXXX...| Twitter iPhone|  neutral|    baseball|
Sport|
|2018-04-14|RT @XXXXXXXX...| Twitter Client|  neutral| @
XXXXXXXXXX|TwitterHandle|
|2018-04-14|RT @XXXXXXXX...| Twitter Client| positive| @
XXXXXXXXXX|TwitterHandle|
|2018-04-14|RT @XXXXX: I...|Twitter Android| positive| Greg XXXXXX|
Person|
|2018-04-14|RT @XXXXXXXX...| Twitter iPhone| positive| @
XXXXXXXXXX|TwitterHandle|
|2018-04-14|RT @XXXXX: I...|Twitter Android| positive| Greg XXXXXX|
Person|
|2018-04-14|Congrats to ...|Twitter Android| positive|    softball|
Sport|
|2018-04-14|translation:...| Twitter iPhone|  neutral|        null|
null|
+----------+---------------+---------------+---------+------------+--
-----------+
```

Finally, we run the structured query with the Parquet `output` sink, create a batch DataFrame, and explore the data using the PixieDust `display()` to show, for example, a count of tweets by sentiment (`positive`, `negative`, `neutral`) clustered by the entity as shown in the following chart:

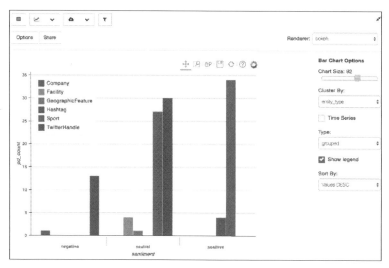

Bar chart showing the number of tweets by sentiment clustered by entities

The complete notebook for *Part 2 – Enrich the data with sentiment and most relevant extracted entity* is located here:

```
https://github.com/DTAIEB/Thoughtful-Data-Science/
blob/master/chapter%207/Twitter%20Sentiment%20
Analysis%20-%20Part%202.ipynb
```

If you are running it, I encourage you to experiment by adding more fields to the schema, run different SQL queries, and visualize the data with PixieDust `display()`.

In the next section, we'll build a dashboard that displays multiple metrics about the Twitter data.

Part 3 – Creating a real-time dashboard PixieApp

As always, we first need to define the requirements for the MVP version of the dashboard. This time we'll borrow a tool from the agile methodology called a **user story** which describes the features we want to build from the perspective of the user. The agile methodology also prescribes fully understanding the context of the different users that will interact with the software by categorizing them into personas. In our case, we will only use one persona: *Frank the marketing director who wants to get real-time insights from what consumers are talking about on social media.*

The user story goes like this:

- Frank enters a search query like for example a product name
- A dashboard is then presented that displays a set of charts showing metrics about user sentiments (positive, negative, neutral)
- The dashboard also contains a word cloud of all the entities being uttered in the tweets
- Additionally, the dashboard has an option to display the real-time progress of all the Spark Streaming queries that are currently active

Note: The last feature is not really needed for Frank, but we show it here anyway as an example implementation of the exercise given earlier.

Refactoring the analytics into their own methods

Before we start, we need to refactor the code that starts the Twitter stream and creates the Spark Streaming DataFrame into their own method that we will invoke in the PixieApp.

The `start_stream`, `start_streaming_dataframe`, and `start_parquet_streaming_query` methods are as follows:

```
def start_stream(queries):
    "Asynchronously start a new Twitter stream"
    stream = Stream(auth, RawTweetsListener())
    stream.filter(track=queries, languages=["en"], async=True)
    return stream
```

 You can find the code file here:

https://github.com/DTAIEB/Thoughtful-Data-Science/
blob/master/chapter%207/sampleCode16.py

```
def start_streaming_dataframe(output_dir):
    "Start a Spark Streaming DataFrame from a file source"
    schema = StructType(
        [StructField(f["name"], f["type"], True) for f in field_
metadata]
    )
    return spark.readStream \
        .csv(
            output_dir,
            schema=schema,
            multiLine = True,
            timestampFormat = 'EEE MMM dd kk:mm:ss Z yyyy',
            ignoreTrailingWhiteSpace = True,
            ignoreLeadingWhiteSpace = True
        )
```

 You can find the code file here:

https://github.com/DTAIEB/Thoughtful-Data-Science/
blob/master/chapter%207/sampleCode17.py

```
def start_parquet_streaming_query(csv_sdf):
    """
    Create and run a streaming query from a Structured DataFrame
    outputing the results into a parquet database
    """
    streaming_query = csv_sdf \
      .writeStream \
      .format("parquet") \
      .option("path", os.path.join(root_dir, "output_parquet")) \
      .trigger(processingTime="2 seconds") \
      .option("checkpointLocation", os.path.join(root_dir, "output_
chkpt")) \
      .start()
    return streaming_query
```

You can find the code file here:

https://github.com/DTAIEB/Thoughtful-Data-Science/
blob/master/chapter%207/sampleCode18.py

As part of the preparation work, we also need to manage the life cycle of the
different streams that will be created by the PixieApp and make sure that the
underlying resources are correctly stopped when the user restarts the dashboard.
To help with that, we create a StreamsManager class that encapsulates the Tweepy
twitter_stream and the CSV Streaming DataFrame. This class has a reset method
that will stop the twitter_stream, stop all the active streaming queries, delete all
the output files created from the previous queries, and start a new one with a new
query string. If the reset method is called without a query string, then we don't
start new streams.

We also create a global streams_manager instance that will keep track of the
current state even if the dashboard is restarted. Since the user can rerun the cell that
contains the global streams_manager we need to make sure that the reset method
is automatically invoked when the current global instance is deleted. For that, we
override the object's __del__ method, which is Python's way of implementing
a destructor and call reset.

The code for StreamsManager is shown here:

```
class StreamsManager():
    def __init__(self):
        self.twitter_stream = None
        self.csv_sdf = None

    def reset(self, search_query = None):
```

```
        if self.twitter_stream is not None:
            self.twitter_stream.disconnect()
        #stop all the active streaming queries and re_initialize the
directories
        for query in spark.streams.active:
            query.stop()
        # initialize the directories
        self.root_dir, self.output_dir = init_output_dirs()
        # start the tweepy stream
        self.twitter_stream = start_stream([search_query]) if search_
query is not None else None
        # start the spark streaming stream
        self.csv_sdf = start_streaming_dataframe(output_dir) if
search_query is not None else None

    def __del__(self):
        # Automatically called when the class is garbage collected
        self.reset()

streams_manager = StreamsManager()
```

You can find the code file here:

https://github.com/DTAIEB/Thoughtful-Data-Science/
blob/master/chapter%207/sampleCode19.py

Creating the PixieApp

Like in *Chapter 6, Image Recognition with TensorFlow*, we'll use the
TemplateTabbedApp class again to create a tab layout with two PixieApps:

- TweetInsightApp: Lets the user specify a query string and shows the
  real-time dashboard associated with it
- StreamingQueriesApp: Monitors the progress of the active structured
  queries

In the default route of the TweetInsightApp, we return a fragment that asks the user
for the query string as follows:

```
from pixiedust.display.app import *
@PixieApp
class TweetInsightApp():
    @route()
```

```
    def main_screen(self):
        return """
<style>
    div.outer-wrapper {
        display: table;width:100%;height:300px;
    }
    div.inner-wrapper {
        display: table-cell;vertical-align: middle;height: 100%;width:
100%;
    }
</style>
<div class="outer-wrapper">
    <div class="inner-wrapper">
        <div class="col-sm-3"></div>
        <div class="input-group col-sm-6">
          <input id="query{{prefix}}" type="text" class="form-control"
            value=""
            placeholder="Enter a search query (e.g. baseball)">
          <span class="input-group-btn">
            <button class="btn btn-default" type="button"
            pd_options="search_query=$val(query{{prefix}})">
                Go
            </button>
          </span>
        </div>
    </div>
</div>
        """


TweetInsightApp().run()
```

You can find the code file here:

https://github.com/DTAIEB/Thoughtful-Data-Science/
blob/master/chapter%207/sampleCode20.py

The following screenshot shows the results of running the preceding code:

 Note: We'll create the main `TwitterSentimentApp` PixieApp that has the tabbed layout and includes this class later on in this section. For now, we are only showing the `TweetInsightApp` child app in isolation.

Welcome screen for the Twitter Sentiment Dashboard

In the `Go` button, we invoke the `search_query` route with the query string provided by the user. In this route, we first start the various streams and create a batch DataFrame stored in a class variable called `parquet_df` from the output directory where the Parquet database is located. We then return the HTML fragment that is composed of three widgets showing the following metrics:

- Bar chart for each of the three sentiments clustered by entities
- Line chart subplots showing the distribution of the tweets by sentiment
- A word cloud for the entities

Each of the widgets is calling a specific route at a regular interval using the `pd_refresh_rate` attribute documented in *Chapter 5, Best Practices and Advanced PixieDust Concepts*. We also make sure to reload the `parquet_df` variable to pick up the new data that has arrived since the last time. This variable is then referenced in the `pd_entity` attribute for displaying the chart.

The following code shows the implementation for the `search_query` route:

```
import time
[[TweetInsightApp]]
@route(search_query="*")
    def do_search_query(self, search_query):
        streams_manager.reset(search_query)
        start_parquet_streaming_query(streams_manager.csv_sdf)
        while True:
```

```
            try:
                parquet_dir = os.path.join(root_dir,
                    "output_parquet")
                self.parquet_df = spark.sql("select * from
parquet.'{}'".format(parquet_dir))
                break
            except:
                time.sleep(5)
        return """
<div class="container">
    <div id="header{{prefix}}" class="row no_loading_msg"
        pd_refresh_rate="5000" pd_target="header{{prefix}}">
        <pd_script>
print("Number of tweets received: {}".format(streams_manager.twitter_
stream.listener.tweet_count))
        </pd_script>
    </div>
    <div class="row" style="min-height:300px">
        <div class="col-sm-5">
            <div id="metric1{{prefix}}" pd_refresh_rate="10000"
                class="no_loading_msg"
                pd_options="display_metric1=true"
                pd_target="metric1{{prefix}}">
            </div>
        </div>
        <div class="col-sm-5">
            <div id="metric2{{prefix}}" pd_refresh_rate="12000"
                class="no_loading_msg"
                pd_options="display_metric2=true"
                pd_target="metric2{{prefix}}">
            </div>
        </div>
    </div>

    <div class="row" style="min-height:400px">
        <div class="col-sm-offset-1 col-sm-10">
            <div id="word_cloud{{prefix}}" pd_refresh_rate="20000"
                class="no_loading_msg"
                pd_options="display_wc=true"
                pd_target="word_cloud{{prefix}}">
            </div>
        </div>
    </div>
        """
```

You can find the code file here:
`https://github.com/DTAIEB/Thoughtful-Data-Science/`
`blob/master/chapter%207/sampleCode21.py`

There are multiple things to notice from the preceding code:

- The output directory for the Parquet files may not be ready when we try to load the `parquet_df` batch DataFrame, which would cause an exception. To solve this timing issue, we wrap the code into a `try...except` statement and wait for 5 seconds using `time.sleep(5)`.

- We also display the current count of tweets in the header. To do this we add a `<div>` element that refreshes every 5 seconds, with a `<pd_script>` that prints the current count of tweets using `streams_manager.twitter_stream.listener.tweet_count` which is a variable we added to the `RawTweetsListener` class. We also updated the `on_data()` method to increment the `tweet_count` variable every time a new tweet arrives as shown in the following code:

```
[[TweetInsightApp]]
def on_data(self, data):
        def transform(key, value):
                return transforms[key](value) if key in transforms
else value
        data = self.enrich(json.loads(data))
        if data is not None:
            self.tweet_count += 1
            self.buffered_data.append(
                {key:transform(key,value) \
                    for key,value in iteritems(data) \
                    if key in fieldnames}
            )
            self.flush_buffer_if_needed()
        return True
```

Also, to avoid flickering, we prevent the displaying of the *loading spinner* image using `class="no_loading_msg"` in the `<div>` element.

- We invoke three different routes (`display_metric1`, `display_metric2`, and `display_wc`) that are responsible for displaying the three widgets respectively.

The `display_metric1` and `display_metric2` routes are very similar. They return a div with `parquet_df` as the `pd_entity` and a custom `<pd_options>` child element that contains the JSON configuration passed to the PixieDust `display()` layer.

The following code shows the implementation for the `display_metric1` route:

```
[[TweetInsightApp]]
@route(display_metric1="*")
    def do_display_metric1(self, display_metric1):
        parquet_dir = os.path.join(root_dir, "output_parquet")
        self.parquet_df = spark.sql("select * from parquet.'{}'".
format(parquet_dir))
        return """
<div class="no_loading_msg" pd_render_onload pd_entity="parquet_df">
    <pd_options>
    {
      "legend": "true",
      "keyFields": "sentiment",
      "clusterby": "entity_type",
      "handlerId": "barChart",
      "rendererId": "bokeh",
      "rowCount": "10",
      "sortby": "Values DESC",
      "noChartCache": "true"
    }
    </pd_options>
</div>
        """
```

You can find the code file here:

https://github.com/DTAIEB/Thoughtful-Data-Science/
blob/master/chapter%207/sampleCode22.py

The `display_metric2` route follows a similar pattern but with a different set of `pd_options` attributes.

The last route is `display_wc` and is responsible for displaying the word cloud for the entities. This route uses the `wordcloud` Python library that you can install with the following command:

```
!pip install wordcloud
```

Note: As always, don't forget to restart the kernel once installation is complete.

We use the @captureOutput decorator documented in *Chapter 5, Best Practices and Advanced PixieDust Concepts* as shown here:

```
import matplotlib.pyplot as plt
from wordcloud import WordCloud

[[TweetInsightApp]]
@route(display_wc="*")
@captureOutput
def do_display_wc(self):
    text = "\n".join(
        [r['entity'] for r in self.parquet_df.select("entity").
collect() if r['entity'] is not None]
    )
    plt.figure( figsize=(13,7) )
    plt.axis("off")
    plt.imshow(
        WordCloud(width=750, height=350).generate(text),
        interpolation='bilinear'
    )
```

 You can find the code file here:

https://github.com/DTAIEB/Thoughtful-Data-Science/
blob/master/chapter%207/sampleCode23.py

The text passed to the WordCloud class is generated from collecting all the entities in the parquet_df batch DataFrame.

The following screenshot shows the dashboard after letting a Twitter stream, created with the search query baseball, run for a little while:

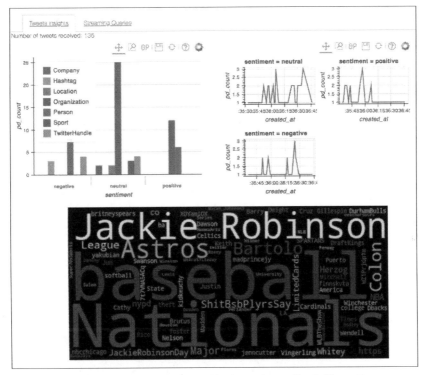

Twitter Sentiment Dashboard for the search query "baseball"

The second PixieApp is used to monitor the streaming queries that are actively running. The main route returns an HTML fragment that has a `<div>` element that invokes the `show_progress` route at regular intervals (5000 ms) as shown in the following code:

```
@PixieApp
class StreamingQueriesApp():
    @route()
    def main_screen(self):
        return """
<div class="no_loading_msg" pd_refresh_rate="5000" pd_options="show_
progress=true">
</div>
    """
```

You can find the code file here:

https://github.com/DTAIEB/Thoughtful-Data-Science/
blob/master/chapter%207/sampleCode24.py

In the `show_progress` route we use the `query.lastProgress` monitoring API described earlier in this chapter, iterate over the JSON object using Jinja2 `{%for%}` loop and display the results in a table as shown in the following code:

```
@route(show_progress="true")
    def do_show_progress(self):
        return """
{%for query in this.spark.streams.active%}
    <div>
    <div class="page-header">
        <h1>Progress Report for Spark Stream: {{query.id}}</h1>
    <div>
    <table>
        <thead>
          <tr>
              <th>metric</th>
              <th>value</th>
          </tr>
        </thead>
        <tbody>
            {%for key, value in query.lastProgress.items()%}
            <tr>
                <td>{{key}}</td>
                <td>{{value}}</td>
            </tr>
            {%endfor%}
        </tbody>
    </table>
{%endfor%}
        """
```

You can find the code file here:

https://github.com/DTAIEB/Thoughtful-Data-Science/
blob/master/chapter%207/sampleCode25.py

The following screenshot shows the streaming query monitoring PixieApp:

Live monitoring of the active Spark streaming queries

The last step is to put together the complete application using the `TemplateTabbedApp` class as shown in the following code:

```
from pixiedust.display.app import *
from pixiedust.apps.template import TemplateTabbedApp


@PixieApp
class TwitterSentimentApp(TemplateTabbedApp):
    def setup(self):
        self.apps = [
            {"title": "Tweets Insights", "app_class":
"TweetInsightApp"},
            {"title": "Streaming Queries", "app_class":
"StreamingQueriesApp"}
        ]

app = TwitterSentimentApp()
app.run()
```

 You can find the code file here:

https://github.com/DTAIEB/Thoughtful-Data-Science/
blob/master/chapter%207/sampleCode26.py

Part 3 of our sample application is now complete; you can find the fully-built Notebook here:

```
https://github.com/DTAIEB/Thoughtful-Data-Science/
blob/master/chapter%207/Twitter%20Sentiment%20
Analysis%20-%20Part%203.ipynb
```

In the next section, we discuss ways to make the data pipeline of our application more scalable by using Apache Kafka for event streaming and IBM Streams Designer for data enrichment of the streaming data.

Part 4 – Adding scalability with Apache Kafka and IBM Streams Designer

Note: This section is optional. It demonstrates how to re-implement parts of the data pipeline with cloud-based streaming services to achieve greater scalability

Implementing the entire data pipeline in a single Notebook gave us high productivity during development and testing. We can experiment with the code and test the changes very rapidly with a very small footprint. Also, performances have been reasonable because we have been working with a relatively small amount of data. However, it is quite obvious that we wouldn't use this architecture in production and the next question we need to ask ourselves is where are the bottlenecks that would prevent the application from scaling as the quantity of streaming data coming from Twitter increases dramatically.

In this section, we identify two areas for improvement:

- In the Tweepy stream, the incoming data is sent to the `RawTweetsListener` instance for processing using the `on_data` method. We need to make sure to spend as little time as possible in this method otherwise the system will fall behind as the amount of incoming data increases. In the current implementation, the data is enriched synchronously by making an external call to the Watson NLU service; it is then buffered and eventually written to disk. To fix this issue, we send the data to a Kafka service, which is a highly scalable, fault tolerant streaming platform using a publish/subscribe pattern for processing a high volume of data. We also use the Streaming Analytics service, which will consume data from Kafka and enrich it by invoking the Watson NLU service. Both services are available on the IBM Cloud.

Note: There are alternative open source frameworks that we could have used for processing the streaming data, such as, for example, Apache Flink (`https://flink.apache.org`) or Apache Storm (`http://storm.apache.org`).

- In the current implementation, the data is stored as CSV files, and we create a Spark Streaming DataFrame with the output directory as the source. This step consumes time and resources on the Notebook and the local environment. Instead, we can have the Streaming Analytics write back the enriched events in a different topic and create a Spark Streaming DataFrame with the Message Hub service as the Kafka input source.

The following diagram shows the updated architecture for our sample application:

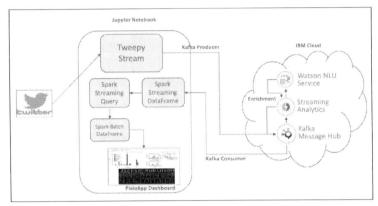

Scaling the architecture with Kafka and Streams Designer

In the next few sections, we will implement the updated architecture, starting with streaming the tweets to Kafka.

Streaming the raw tweets to Kafka

Provisioning a Kafka / Message Hub service instance on IBM Cloud follows the same pattern as the steps we used to provision the Watson NLU service. We first locate and select the service in the catalog, pick a pricing plan and click **Create**. We then open the service dashboard and select the **Service credentials** tab to create new credentials as shown in the following screenshot:

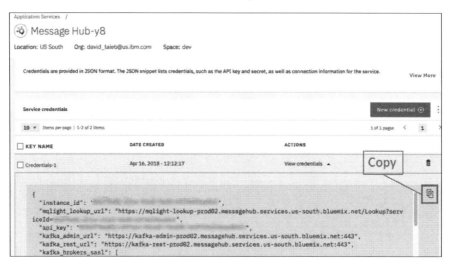

Creating new credentials for the Message Hub service

As is the case for all the services available on IBM Cloud, the credentials come in the form of a JSON object that we'll need to store in its own variable in the Notebook as shown in the following code (again, don't forget to replace the xxxx text with your username and password from the service credentials):

```
message_hub_creds = {
    "instance_id": "XXXXX",
    "mqlight_lookup_url": "https://mqlight-lookup-prod02.messagehub.
services.us-south.bluemix.net/Lookup?serviceId=XXXX",
    "api_key": "XXXX",
    "kafka_admin_url": "https://kafka-admin-prod02.messagehub.services.
us-south.bluemix.net:443",
    "kafka_rest_url": "https://kafka-rest-prod02.messagehub.services.us-
south.bluemix.net:443",
    "kafka_brokers_sasl": [
        "kafka03-prod02.messagehub.services.us-south.bluemix.net:9093",
        "kafka01-prod02.messagehub.services.us-south.bluemix.net:9093",
```

```
        "kafka02-prod02.messagehub.services.us-south.bluemix.net:9093",
        "kafka05-prod02.messagehub.services.us-south.bluemix.net:9093",
        "kafka04-prod02.messagehub.services.us-south.bluemix.net:9093"
    ],
    "user": "XXXX",
    "password": "XXXX"
}
```

 You can find the code file here:
https://github.com/DTAIEB/Thoughtful-Data-Science/
blob/master/chapter%207/sampleCode27.py

As for interfacing with Kafka, we have a choice between multiple good client libraries. I have tried many of them, but the one I ended up using most often is kafka-python (https://github.com/dpkp/kafka-python) which has the advantage of being a pure Python implementation and is thereby easier to install.

To install it from the Notebook, use the following command:

```
!pip install kafka-python
```

 Note: As always, do not forget to restart the kernel after installing any libraries.

The kafka-python library provides a KafkaProducer class for writing the data as messages into the service, which we'll need to configure with the credentials we created earlier. There are multiple Kafka configuration options available and going over all of them is beyond the scope of this book. The required options are related to authentication, host servers, and API version.

The following code is implemented in the __init__ constructor of RawTweetsListener class. It creates a KafkaProducer instance and stores it as a class variable:

```
[[RawTweetsListener]]
context = ssl.create_default_context()
context.options &= ssl.OP_NO_TLSv1
context.options &= ssl.OP_NO_TLSv1_1
kafka_conf = {
    'sasl_mechanism': 'PLAIN',
    'security_protocol': 'SASL_SSL',
    'ssl_context': context,
    "bootstrap_servers": message_hub_creds["kafka_brokers_sasl"],
```

```
        "sasl_plain_username": message_hub_creds["user"],
        "sasl_plain_password": message_hub_creds["password"],
        "api_version":(0, 10, 1),
        "value_serializer" : lambda v: json.dumps(v).encode('utf-8')
    }
    self.producer = KafkaProducer(**kafka_conf)
```

You can find the code file here:
https://github.com/DTAIEB/Thoughtful-Data-Science/
blob/master/chapter%207/sampleCode28.py

We configure a lambda function for the `value_serializer` key that serializes JSON objects which is the format we'll be using for our data.

Note: We need to specify the `api_version` key because otherwise, the library would try to autodiscover its value which would cause a `NoBrokerAvailable` exception to be raised due to a bug in the `kafka-python` library reproducible only on Macs. A fix for this bug has not yet been provided at the time of writing this book.

We now need to update the `on_data` method to send the tweets data to Kafka using the `tweets` topic. A Kafka topic is like a channel that applications can publish or subscribe to. It is important to have the topic already created before attempting to write into it otherwise an exception will be raised. This is done in the following `ensure_topic_exists` method:

```
import requests
import json

def ensure_topic_exists(topic_name):
    response = requests.post(
                message_hub_creds["kafka_rest_url"] +
                "/admin/topics",
                data = json.dumps({"name": topic_name}),
                headers={"X-Auth-Token": message_hub_creds["api_key"]}
            )
    if response.status_code != 200 and \
        response.status_code != 202 and \
        response.status_code != 422 and \
        response.status_code != 403:
        raise Exception(response.json())
```

You can find the code file here:

https://github.com/DTAIEB/Thoughtful-Data-Science/
blob/master/chapter%207/sampleCode29.py

In the preceding code, we make a POST request into the path /admin/topic
with a JSON payload that contains the name of the topic we want to create. The
request must be authenticated using the API key provided in the credentials and
the X-Auth-Token header. We also make sure to ignore HTTP error codes 422 and
403 which indicate that the topic already exists.

The code for the on_data method now looks much simpler as shown here:

```
[[RawTweetsListener]]
def on_data(self, data):
    self.tweet_count += 1
    self.producer.send(
        self.topic,
        {key:transform(key,value) \
            for key,value in iteritems(json.loads(data)) \
            if key in fieldnames}
    )
    return True
```

You can find the code file here:

https://github.com/DTAIEB/Thoughtful-Data-Science/
blob/master/chapter%207/sampleCode30.py

As we can see, with this new code, we're spending as little time as possible in the
on_data method, which is the goal we wanted to achieve. The tweet data is now
flowing into the Kafka tweets topic, ready to be enriched by the Streaming Analytics
service which we'll discuss in the next section.

Enriching the tweets data with the Streaming Analytics service

For this step, we'll need to use Watson Studio which is an integrated cloud-based
IDE that provides various tools for working with data, including machine learning
/ deep learning models, Jupyter Notebooks, stream flows, and more. Watson Studio
is a companion tool to IBM Cloud accessible at https://datascience.ibm.com,
and therefore no extra sign up is required.

Once logged in to Watson Studio, we create a new project which we'll call
`Thoughtful Data Science`.

 Note: It is OK to select the default options when creating a project.

We then go to the **Settings** tab to create a Streaming Analytics service, which will
be the engine that powers our enrichment process and associate it with the project.
Note that we could also have created the service in the IBM Cloud catalog as we did
for the other services used in this chapter, but since we still have to associate it with
the project, we might as well do the creation in Watson Studio too.

In the **Settings** tab, we scroll to the **Associated services** section and click on the
Add service drop-down to select **Streaming Analytics**. In the next page, you have
the choice between **Existing** and **New**. Select **New** and follow the steps to create the
service. Once done, the newly created service should be associated with the project
as shown in the following screenshot:

 Note: If there are multiple free options, it is OK to pick any one of them.

Associating the Streaming Analytics service with the project

We are now ready to create the stream flow that defines the enrichment processing
of our tweet data.

We go to the **Assets** tab, scroll down to the **Streams flows** section and click on the
New streams flow button. In the next page, we give a name, select the Streaming
Analytics service, select **Manually** and click on the **Create** button.

We are now in the Streams Designer which is composed of a palette of operators
on the left and a canvas where we can graphically build our stream flow. For our
sample application, we'll need to pick three operators from the palette and drag
and drop them into the canvas:

- **Message Hub from the Sources section of the palette**: Input source for our data. Once in the canvas, we rename it `Source Message Hub` (by double-clicking on it to enter edit mode).

- **Code from the Processing and analytics section**: It will contain the data enrichment Python code that invokes the Watson NLU service. We rename the operator to `Enrichment`.

- **Message Hub from the Targets section of the palette**: Output source for the enriched data. We rename it to `Target Message Hub`.

Next, we create a connection between the **Source Message Hub** and **Enrichment** and between **Enrichment** and the **Target Message Hub**. To create a connection between two operators, simply grab the output port at the end of the first operator and drag it to the input port of the other operator. Notice that a source operator has only one output port on the right of the box to denote that it only supports outgoing connections, while a target operator has only one input port on the left to denote that it only supports incoming connections. Any operator from the **PROCESSING AND ANALYTICS** section has two ports on the left and right as they accept both incoming and outgoing connections.

The following screenshot shows the fully completed canvas:

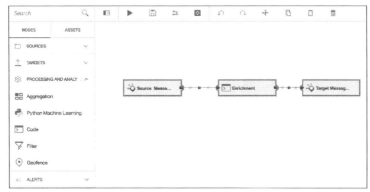

Tweet enrichment stream flow

Let's now look at the configuration of each of these three operators.

Note: To complete this section, make sure to run the code that generates topics to the Message Hub instance that we discussed in the previous section. Otherwise, the Message Hub instance will be empty, and no schema will be detected.

Click on the source Message Hub. An animated pane on the right appears with the options to select the Message Hub instance that contains the tweets. The first time, you'll need to create a connection to the Message Hub instance. Select tweets as the topic. Click on the **Edit Output Schema** and then **Detect Schema** to have the schema autopopulated from the data. You can also preview the live streaming data using the **Show Preview** button as shown in the following screenshot:

Setting the schema and previewing the live streaming data

Now select the **Code** operator to implement the code that invokes the Watson NLU. The animated contextual right-hand pane contains a Python code editor with boilerplate code that includes the required functions to implement, namely init(state) and process(event, state).

In the init method, we instantiate the NaturalLanguageUnderstandingV1 instance as shown in the following code:

```
import sys
from watson_developer_cloud import NaturalLanguageUnderstandingV1
```

```
from watson_developer_cloud.natural_language_understanding_v1 import
Features, SentimentOptions, EntitiesOptions

# init() function will be called once on pipeline initialization
# @state a Python dictionary object for keeping state. The state
object is passed to the process function
def init(state):
    # do something once on pipeline initialization and save in the
state object
    state["nlu"] = NaturalLanguageUnderstandingV1(
        version='2017-02-27',
        username='XXXX',
        password='XXXX'
    )
```

You can find the code file here:

https://github.com/DTAIEB/Thoughtful-Data-Science/
blob/master/chapter%207/sampleCode31.py

Note: We need to install the `Watson_developer_cloud` library via
the **Python packages** link located above the Python editor window
in the right-hand contextual pane as shown in the following screenshot:

Adding the watson_cloud_developer package to the stream flow

The process method is invoked on every event data. We use it to invoke the Watson NLU and add the extra information to the event object as shown in the following code:

```python
# @event a Python dictionary object representing the input event tuple
as defined by the input schema
# @state a Python dictionary object for keeping state over subsequent
function calls
# return must be a Python dictionary object. It will be the output of
this operator.
# Returning None results in not submitting an output tuple for this
invocation.
# You must declare all output attributes in the Edit Schema window.
def process(event, state):
    # Enrich the event, such as by:
    # event['wordCount'] = len(event['phrase'].split())
    try:
        event['text'] = event['text'].replace('"', "'")
        response = state["nlu"].analyze(
            text = event['text'],
            features=Features(sentiment=SentimentOptions(),
entities=EntitiesOptions())
        )
        event["sentiment"] = response["sentiment"]["document"]
["label"]
        top_entity = response["entities"][0] if
len(response["entities"]) > 0 else None
        event["entity"] = top_entity["text"] if top_entity is not None
else ""
        event["entity_type"] = top_entity["type"] if top_entity is not
None else ""
    except Exception as e:
        return None
    return event
```

You can find the code file here:

```
https://github.com/DTAIEB/Thoughtful-Data-Science/
blob/master/chapter%207/sampleCode32.py
```

Note: We must also declare all output variables by using the
Edit Output Schema link as shown in the following screenshot:

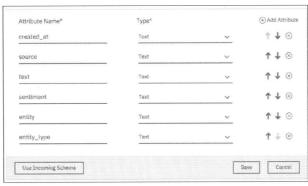

Declaring all output variables for the Code operator

Finally, we configure the target Message Hub to use the `enriched_tweets` topic.
Note that you'll need to manually create the topic the first time by going into the
dashboard of the Message Hub instance on the IBM Cloud and clicking on the **Add
Topic** button.

We then save the stream flow using the **Save** button in the main toolbar. Any errors
in the flow, whether it be a compile error in the code, a service configuration error
or any other errors, will be shown in the notification pane. After we make sure that
there is no error, we can run the flow using the **Run** button which takes us to the
streams flow live monitoring screen. This screen is composed of multiple panes.
The main pane shows the different operators with the data represented as little
balls flowing in a virtual pipe between operators. We can click on a pipe to show
the events payload in a pane on the right. This is really useful for debugging as
we can visualize how the data is transformed through each operator.

Note: Streams Designer also supports adding Python logging messages in the code operator which can then be downloaded on your local machine for analysis. You can learn more about this functionality here:

`https://dataplatform.cloud.ibm.com/docs/content/`
`streaming-pipelines/downloading_logs.html`

The following screenshot shows the stream flow live monitoring screen:

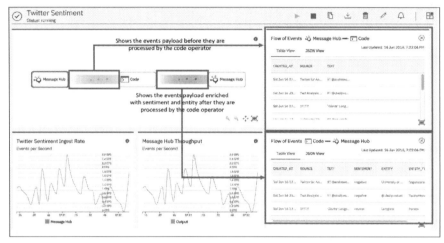

Live monitoring screen for the Twitter Sentiment Analysis stream flow

We now have our enriched tweets flowing in the Message Hub instance using the `enriched_tweets` topic. In the next section, we show how to create a Spark Streaming DataFrame using the Message Hub instance as the input source.

Creating a Spark Streaming DataFrame with a Kafka input source

In this final step, we create a Spark Streaming DataFrame that consumes the enriched tweets from the `enriched_tweets` Kafka topic of the Message Hub service. For this, we use the built-in Spark Kafka connector specifying the topic we want to subscribe to in the `subscribe` option. We also need to specify the list of Kafka servers in the `kafka.bootstrap.servers` option, by reading it from the global `message_hub_creds` variable that we created earlier.

Note: You have probably noticed that different systems use different names for this option making it more error prone. Fortunately, in case of a misspelling, an exception with an explicit root cause message will be displayed.

The preceding options are for Spark Streaming, and we still need to configure the Kafka credentials so that the lower level Kafka consumer can be properly authenticated with the Message Hub service. To properly pass these consumer properties to Kafka, we do not use the `.option` method, but rather we create a `kafka_options` dictionary that we pass to the load method as shown in the following code:

```python
def start_streaming_dataframe():
    "Start a Spark Streaming DataFrame from a Kafka Input source"
    schema = StructType(
        [StructField(f["name"], f["type"], True) for f in field_
metadata]
    )
    kafka_options = {
        "kafka.ssl.protocol":"TLSv1.2",
        "kafka.ssl.enabled.protocols":"TLSv1.2",
        "kafka.ssl.endpoint.identification.algorithm":"HTTPS",
        'kafka.sasl.mechanism': 'PLAIN',
        'kafka.security.protocol': 'SASL_SSL'
    }
    return spark.readStream \
        .format("kafka") \
        .option("kafka.bootstrap.servers", ",".join(message_hub_
creds["kafka_brokers_sasl"])) \
        .option("subscribe", "enriched_tweets") \
        .load(**kafka_options)
```

 You can find the code file here:

https://github.com/DTAIEB/Thoughtful-Data-Science/blob/master/chapter%207/sampleCode33.py

You would think that we're done with the code at this point since the rest of the Notebook should work unchanged from *Part 3 – Create a real-time dashboard PixieApp*. This would be correct until we run the Notebook and start seeing exceptions with Spark complaining that the Kafka connector cannot be found. This is because the Kafka connector is not included in the core distribution of Spark and must be installed separately.

Unfortunately, these types of problems which are infrastructural in nature and are not directly related to the task at hand, happen all the time and we end up spending a lot of time trying to fix them. Searching on Stack Overflow or any other technical site usually yields a solution rapidly, but in some cases, the answer is not obvious. In this case, because we are running in a Notebook and not in a `spark-submit` script, there isn't much help available, and we have to experiment ourselves until we find the solution. To install the `spark-sql-kafka`, we need to edit the `kernel.json` file discussed earlier in this chapter, and add the following option to the `"PYSPARK_SUBMIT_ARGS"` entry:

```
--packages org.apache.spark:spark-sql-kafka-0-10_2.11:2.3.0
```

When the kernel restarts, this configuration will automatically download the dependencies and cache them locally.

It should all work now right? Well, not yet. We still have to configure Kafka security to use the credentials to our Message Hub service which uses SASL as the security protocol. For that, we need to provide a **JAAS** (short for, **Java Authentication and Authorization Service**) configuration file that will contain the username and password for the service. The latest version of Kafka provides a flexible mechanism to programmatically configure the security using a consumer property called `sasl.jaas.config`. Unfortunately, the latest version of Spark (2.3.0 as of the time of writing) has not yet updated to the latest version of Kafka. So, we have to fall back to the other way of configuring JAAS which is to set a JVM system property called `java.security.auth.login.config` with the path to a `jaas.conf` configuration file.

We first create the `jaas.conf` in a directory of our choice and add the following content to it:

```
KafkaClient {
    org.apache.kafka.common.security.plain.PlainLoginModule required
    username="XXXX"
    password="XXXX";
};
```

In the preceding content, replace the XXXX text with the username and password taken from the Message Hub service credentials.

We then add the following configuration to the `"PYSPARK_SUBMIT_ARGS"` entry of `kernel.json`:

```
--driver-java-options=-Djava.security.auth.login.config=<<jaas.conf
path>>
```

For reference, here is a sample `kernel.json` that contains these configurations:

```
{
 "language": "python",
 "env": {
  "SCALA_HOME": "/Users/dtaieb/pixiedust/bin/scala/scala-2.11.8",
  "PYTHONPATH": "/Users/dtaieb/pixiedust/bin/spark/spark-2.3.0-bin-
hadoop2.7/python/:/Users/dtaieb/pixiedust/bin/spark/spark-2.3.0-bin-
hadoop2.7/python/lib/py4j-0.10.6-src.zip",
  "SPARK_HOME": "/Users/dtaieb/pixiedust/bin/spark/spark-2.3.0-bin-
hadoop2.7",
  "PYSPARK_SUBMIT_ARGS": "--driver-java-options=-Djava.security.auth.
login.config=/Users/dtaieb/pixiedust/jaas.conf --jars /Users/dtaieb/
pixiedust/bin/cloudant-spark-v2.0.0-185.jar --driver-class-path /
Users/dtaieb/pixiedust/data/libs/* --master local[10] --packages org.
apache.spark:spark-sql-kafka-0-10_2.11:2.3.0 pyspark-shell",
  "PIXIEDUST_HOME": "/Users/dtaieb/pixiedust",
  "SPARK_DRIVER_MEMORY": "10G",
  "SPARK_LOCAL_IP": "127.0.0.1",
  "PYTHONSTARTUP": "/Users/dtaieb/pixiedust/bin/spark/spark-2.3.0-bin-
hadoop2.7/python/pyspark/shell.py"
 },
 "display_name": "Python with Pixiedust (Spark 2.3)",
 "argv": [
  "python",
  "-m",
  "ipykernel",
  "-f",
  "{connection_file}"
 ]
}
```

 You can find the code file here:
https://github.com/DTAIEB/Thoughtful-Data-Science/
blob/master/chapter%207/sampleCode34.json

Note: We should always restart the Notebook server when modifying `kernel.json` to make sure that all new configurations are properly reloaded.

The rest of the Notebook code doesn't change, and the PixieApp dashboard should work the same.

We have now completed Part 4 of our sample application; you can find the complete notebook here:

```
https://github.com/DTAIEB/Thoughtful-Data-Science/
blob/master/chapter%207/Twitter%20Sentiment%20
Analysis%20-%20Part%204.ipynb
```

The extra code we had to write at the end of this section reminds us that the journey of working with data is never a straight line. We have to be prepared to deal with obstacles that can be different in nature: a bug in a dependency library or a limitation in an external service. Surmounting these obstacles doesn't have to stop the project for a long time. Since we're using mostly open-source components, we can leverage a large community of like-minded developers on social sites such as Stack Overflow, get new ideas and code samples, and experiment quickly on a Jupyter Notebook.

Summary

In this chapter, we've built a data pipeline that analyzes large quantities of streaming data containing unstructured text and applies NLP algorithms coming from external cloud services to extract sentiment and other important entities found in the text. We also built a PixieApp dashboard that displays live metrics with insights extracted from the tweets. We've also discussed various techniques for analyzing data at scale, including Apache Spark Structured Streaming, Apache Kafka, and IBM Streaming Analytics. As always, the goal of these sample applications is to show the art of the possible in building data pipelines with a special focus on leveraging existing frameworks, libraries, and cloud services.

In the next chapter, we'll discuss time series analysis, which is another great data science topic with a lot of industry applications, which we'll illustrate by building a *Financial Portfolio* analysis application.

8

Financial Time Series Analysis and Forecasting

"When making important decisions, it's ok to trust your instincts but always verify with data"

– David Taieb

The study of time series is a very important field of data science with multiple applications in industry, including the weather, medicine, sales, and, of course, finance. It is a broad and complex subject and covering it in detail would be outside the scope of this book, but we'll try to touch upon a few of the important concepts in this chapter, staying sufficiently high level as not to require any particular specific knowledge from the reader. We also show how Python is particularly well adapted to time series analysis from data manipulation with libraries like pandas (`https://pandas.pydata.org`) for data analysis and NumPy (`http://www.numpy.org`) for scientific computation, to visualization with Matplotlib (`https://matplotlib.org`) and Bokeh (`https://bokeh.pydata.org`).

This chapter starts with an introduction to the NumPy library and its most important APIs that will be put to good use when building descriptive analytics to analyze time series representing stock historical financial data. Using Python libraries such as `statsmodels` (`https://www.statsmodels.org/stable/index.html`), we'll show how to do statistical exploration and find properties like stationarity, **autocorrelation function (ACF)**, and **partial autocorrelation function (PACF)**. which will be useful to find trends in the data and creating forecasting models. We'll then operationalize these analytics by building a PixieApp that summarizes all the important statistics and visualizations about stock historical financial data.

In the second part, we'll attempt to build a time series forecasting model that predicts future trends of a stock. We'll use an autoregressive model with Integrated Moving Average called **ARIMA** where we use previous values in the time series to predict the next value. ARIMA is one of the most popular models currently used, although new models based on recurrent neural networks are starting to gain in popularity.

As usual, we'll conclude the chapter by incorporating the building of an ARIMA time series forecasting model in the `StockExplorer` PixieApp.

Getting started with NumPy

The NumPy library is one of the main reasons why Python has gained so much traction in the data scientist community. It is a foundational library upon which a lot of the most popular libraries, such as pandas (`https://pandas.pydata.org`), Matplotlib (`https://matplotlib.org`), SciPy (`https://www.scipy.org`), and scikit-learn (`http://scikit-learn.org`) are built.

The key capabilities provided by NumPy are:

- A very powerful multidimensional NumPy array called ndarray with very high-performance mathematical operations (at least compared to regular Python lists and arrays)
- Universal functions also called `ufunc` for short, for providing very efficient and easy-to-use element by element operations on one or more ndarray
- Powerful ndarray slicing and selection capabilities
- Broadcasting functions that make it possible to apply arithmetic operations on ndarray of different shapes provided that some rules are respected

Before we start exploring the NumPy APIs, there is one API that is absolutely essential to know: `lookfor()`. With this method, you can find a function using a query string, which is very useful considering the hundreds of powerful APIs provided by NumPy.

For example, I can look for a function that computes the average mean of an array:

```
import numpy as np
np.lookfor("average")
```

The results are as follows:

```
Search results for 'average'
---------------------------
numpy.average
    Compute the weighted average along the specified axis.
```

numpy.irr
    Return the Internal Rate of Return (IRR).
numpy.mean
    Compute the arithmetic mean along the specified axis.
numpy.nanmean
    Compute the arithmetic mean along the specified axis, ignoring
NaNs.
numpy.ma.average
    Return the weighted average of array over the given axis.
numpy.ma.mean
    Returns the average of the array elements along given axis.
numpy.matrix.mean
    Returns the average of the matrix elements along the given axis.
numpy.chararray.mean
    Returns the average of the array elements along given axis.
numpy.ma.MaskedArray.mean
    Returns the average of the array elements along given axis.
numpy.cov
    Estimate a covariance matrix, given data and weights.
numpy.std
    Compute the standard deviation along the specified axis.
numpy.sum
    Sum of array elements over a given axis.
numpy.var
    Compute the variance along the specified axis.
numpy.sort
    Return a sorted copy of an array.
numpy.median
    Compute the median along the specified axis.
numpy.nanstd
    Compute the standard deviation along the specified axis, while
numpy.nanvar
    Compute the variance along the specified axis, while ignoring
NaNs.
numpy.nanmedian
    Compute the median along the specified axis, while ignoring NaNs.
numpy.partition
    Return a partitioned copy of an array.
numpy.ma.var
    Compute the variance along the specified axis.
numpy.apply_along_axis
    Apply a function to 1-D slices along the given axis.
numpy.ma.apply_along_axis
    Apply a function to 1-D slices along the given axis.

```
numpy.ma.MaskedArray.var
    Compute the variance along the specified axis.
```

Within seconds, I can find a few candidate functions without having to leave my Notebook to consult the documentation. In the preceding case, I can spot a few functions that are interesting— `np.average` and `np.mean`—for which I still need to know their arguments. Again, instead of looking up the documentation which takes time and breaks the flow of what I was doing, I use a little-known capability of Jupyter Notebooks that provides me with the signature and docstring of the function inline. To invoke the inline help of a function, simply position the cursor at the end of the function and use the *Shift* + *Tab* combination. Calling *Shift* + *Tab* a second time will expand the pop-up window to show more of the text as shown in the following screenshot:

Note: *Shift* + *Tab* only applies to a function.

Inline help in Jupyter Notebook.

Using this method, I can rapidly iterate over the candidate functions until I find the one that fits my needs.

It is important to note that `np.lookfor()` is not limited to querying the NumPy module; you could search in other modules as well. For example, the following code searches for `acf` (autocorrelation function) related methods in the `statsmodels` package:

```
import statsmodels
np.lookfor("acf", module = statsmodels)
```

You can find the code file here:
`https://github.com/DTAIEB/Thoughtful-Data-Science/`
`blob/master/chapter%208/sampleCode1.py`

This produces the following results:

```
Search results for 'acf'
-----------------------
statsmodels.tsa.vector_ar.var_model.var_acf
    Compute autocovariance function ACF_y(h) up to nlags of
stable VAR(p)
statsmodels.tsa.vector_ar.var_model._var_acf
    Compute autocovariance function ACF_y(h) for h=1,...,p
statsmodels.tsa.tests.test_stattools.TestPACF
    Set up for ACF, PACF tests.
statsmodels.sandbox.tsa.fftarma.ArmaFft.acf2spdfreq
    not really a method
statsmodels.tsa.stattools.acf
    Autocorrelation function for 1d arrays.
statsmodels.tsa.tests.test_stattools.TestACF_FFT
    Set up for ACF, PACF tests.
...
```

Creating a NumPy array

There are many ways to create a NumPy array. Here are the methods most commonly used:

- From a Python list or tuple using `np.array()`, for example, `np.array([1, 2, 3, 4])`.
- From one of the NumPy factory functions:
  - `np.random`: A module that provides a very rich set of functions for randomly generating values. This module is composed of the following categories:

    Simple random data: `rand`, `randn`, `randint`, and so on

    Permutations: `shuffle`, `permutation`

    Distributions: `geometric`, `logistic`, and so on

 You can find more information on the `np.random` module here:
`https://docs.scipy.org/doc/numpy-1.14.0/reference/`
`routines.random.html`

- ° `np.arange`: Return an ndarray with evenly spaced values within a given interval.

    Signature: `numpy.arange([start, ]stop, [step, ]dtype=None)`

    For example: `np.arange(1, 100, 10)`

    Results: `array([ 1, 11, 21, 31, 41, 51, 61, 71, 81, 91])`

- ° `np.linspace`: Similar to `np.arange`, it returns an ndarray with evenly spaced values within a given interval, the difference being that with `linspace` you specify the number of samples you want instead of the number of steps.

    For example: `np.linspace(1,100,8, dtype=int)`

    Results: `array([ 1, 15, 29, 43, 57, 71, 85, 100])`

- ° `np.full`, `np.full_like`, `np.ones`, `np.ones_like`, `np.zeros`, `np.zeros_like`: Create an ndarray initialized with a constant value.

    For example: `np.ones( (2,2), dtype=int)`

    Results: `array([[1, 1], [1, 1]])`

- ° `np.eye`, `np.identity`, `np.diag`: Creates an ndarray with constant values in the diagonal:

    For example: `np.eye(3,3)`

    Results: `array([[1, 0, 0],[0, 1, 0],[0, 0, 1]])`

> **Note**: When the `dtype` argument is not provided, NumPy tries to infer it from the input argument. However, it may happen that the type returned is not the correct one; for example, float is returned when it should be an integer. In this case, you should use the `dtype` argument to force the type. For example:
>
> `np.arange(1, 100, 10, dtype=np.integer)`

Why NumPy arrays are so much faster than their Python lists and arrays counterpart?

As mentioned before, operations on NumPy arrays run much faster than their Python counterpart. This is because Python is a dynamic language that doesn't know, a priori, the type it's dealing with and therefore has to constantly query the metadata associated with it to dispatch it to the right method. On the other hand, NumPy is highly optimized to deal with large multidimensional arrays of data by, among other things, delegating the execution of the CPU-intensive routine to external highly optimized C libraries that have been precompiled.

To be able to do that, NumPy places two important constraints on ndarrays:

- **ndarrays are immutable**: Therefore, if you want to change the shape or the size of an ndarray or if you want to add/delete elements, you always must create a new one. For example, the following code creates an ndarray using the `arange()` function which returns a one-dimensional array with evenly spaced values, and then reshapes it to fit a 4 by 5 matrix:

```
ar = np.arange(20)
print(ar)
print(ar.reshape(4,5))
```

You can find the code file here:

`https://github.com/DTAIEB/Thoughtful-Data-Science/blob/master/chapter%208/sampleCode2.py`

The results are as follows:

```
before:
 [ 0  1  2  3  4  5  6  7  8  9 10 11 12 13 14 15 16 17 18 19]
after:
 [[ 0  1  2  3  4]
 [ 5  6  7  8  9]
 [10 11 12 13 14]
 [15 16 17 18 19]]
```

- **Elements in an ndarray must be of the same type**: ndarray carries the element type in the `dtype` member. When creating a new ndarray using the `nd.array()` function, NumPy will automatically infer a type that is suitable for all elements.

  For example: `np.array([1,2,3]).dtype` will be `dtype('int64')`.

  `np.array([1,2,'3']).dtype` will be `dtype('<U21')` where `<` means little endian (see `https://en.wikipedia.org/wiki/Endianness`) and `U21` means a 21-character Unicode string.

Note: You can find detailed information about all the supported data types here:

`https://docs.scipy.org/doc/numpy/reference/arrays.dtypes.html`

Operations on ndarray

Most often, we have the need to summarize data over an ndarray. Fortunately, NumPy provides a very rich set of functions (also called **reduction functions**) that provide out-of-the-box summarization over an ndarray or an axis of the ndarray.

For reference, a NumPy axis corresponds to a dimension of the array. For example, a two-dimensional ndarray has two axes: one running across rows, which is referred to as axis 0 and one running across columns which is called axis 1.

The following diagram illustrates the axes in a two-dimensional array:

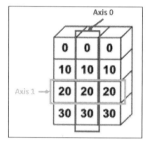

Axes in a two-dimensional array

Most of the reduction functions we'll discuss next take an axis as an argument. They fall into the following categories:

- **Mathematical functions**:
    - Trigonometric: `np.sin`, `np.cos`, and so on
    - Hyperbolic: `np.sinh`, `np.cosh`, and so on
    - Rounding: `np.around`, `np.floor`, and so on
    - Sums, products, differences: `np.sum`, `np.prod`, `np.cumsum`, and so on
    - Exponents and logarithms: `np.exp`, `np.log`, and so on
    - Arithmetic: `np.add`, `np.multiply`, and so on
    - Miscellaneous: `np.sqrt`, `np.absolute`, and so on

Note: All these unary functions (functions that take only one argument) work directly at the ndarray level. For example, we can use np.square to square all the values in an array at once:

Code: `np.square(np.arange(10))`

Results: `array([ 0,  1,  4,  9, 16, 25, 36, 49, 64, 81])`

You can find more information on NumPy mathematical functions here:

`https://docs.scipy.org/doc/numpy/reference/routines.math.html`

- **Statistical functions**:

    ○ Order statistics: `np.amin`, `np.amax`, `np.percentile`, and so on

    ○ Averages and variances: `np.median`, `np.var`, `np.std`, and so on

    ○ Correlating: `np.corrcoef`, `np.correlate`, `np.cov`, and so on

    ○ Histograms: `np.histogram`, `np.bincount`, and so on

Note: pandas provides very tight integration with NumPy and lets you apply these NumPy operations on pandas DataFrames. We'll use this capability quite a bit when analyzing time series in the rest of this chapter.

The following code example creates a pandas DataFrame and computes the square on all the columns:

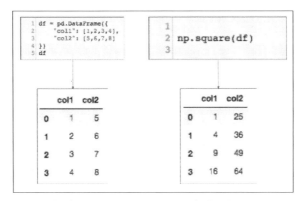

Applying NumPy operations to pandas DataFrames

Selections on NumPy arrays

NumPy arrays support similar slicing operations as Python arrays and lists. So, using an ndarray created with the `np.arrange()` method, we can do the following:

```
sample = np.arange(10)
print("Sample:", sample)
print("Access by index: ", sample[2])
print("First 5 elements: ", sample[:5])
print("From 8 to the end: ", sample[8:])
print("Last 3 elements: ", sample[-3:])
print("Every 2 elements: ", sample[::2])
```

 You can find the code file here:

https://github.com/DTAIEB/Thoughtful-Data-Science/blob/master/chapter%208/sampleCode3.py

Which produces the following results:

```
Sample: [0 1 2 3 4 5 6 7 8 9]
Access by index:  2
First 5 elements:  [0 1 2 3 4]
From index 8 to the end:  [8 9]
Last 3 elements:  [7 8 9]
Every 2 elements:  [0 2 4 6 8]
```

Selections using slices also work with NumPy arrays that have multiple dimensions. We can use slices for every dimension in the array. This is not the case for Python arrays and lists which only allow indexing using integers of slices.

 Note: For reference a slice in Python has the following syntax:

```
start:end:step
```

As an example, let's create a NumPy array with the shape `(3,4)`, that is, 3 rows * 4 columns:

```
my_nparray = np.arange(12).reshape(3,4)
print(my_nparray)
```

Returns:

```
array([[ 0,  1,  2,  3],
       [ 4,  5,  6,  7],
       [ 8,  9, 10, 11]])
```

Suppose that I want to select only the middle of the matrix, that is, [5, 6]. I can simply apply slices on rows and columns, for example, [1:2] to select the second row and [1:3] to select the second and third values in the second row:

```
print(my_nparray[1:2, 1:3])
```

Returns:

```
array([[5, 6]])
```

Another interesting NumPy feature is that we can also use predicates to index an ndarray with Boolean values.

For example:

```
print(sample > 5 )
```

Returns:

```
[False False False False False False  True  True  True  True]
```

We can then use the Boolean ndarray to select subsets of data with a simple and elegant syntax.

For example:

```
print( sample[sample > 5] )
```

Returns:

```
[6 7 8 9]
```

This is only a small preview of all the selection capabilities of NumPy. For more information on NumPy selection, you can visit:

https://docs.scipy.org/doc/numpy-1.13.0/reference/arrays.indexing.html

Broadcasting

Broadcasting is a very convenient feature of NumPy. It lets you perform arithmetic operations on ndarrays having different shapes. The term **broadcasting** comes from the fact that the smaller array is automatically duplicated to fit the bigger array so that they have compatible shapes. There are however a set of rules that govern how broadcasting works.

You can find more information on broadcasting here:
`https://docs.scipy.org/doc/numpy/user/basics.broadcasting.html`

The simplest form of NumPy broadcasting is **scalar broadcasting**, which lets you perform element-wise arithmetic operations between an ndarray and a scalar (that is, a number).

For example:

```
my_nparray * 2
```

Returns:

```
array([[ 0,  2,  4,  6],
       [ 8, 10, 12, 14],
       [16, 18, 20, 22]])
```

 Note: In the following discussion, we assume that we want to operate on two ndarrays which do not have the same dimensions.

Broadcasting with smaller arrays needs to follow only one rule: one of the arrays must have at least one of its dimensions equal to 1. The idea is to duplicate the smaller array along the dimensions that don't match until they do.

The following diagram, taken from the `http://www.scipy-lectures.org/` website, illustrates very nicely the different cases for adding two arrays:

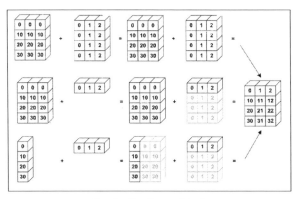

Broadcasting flow explained

Source: http://www.scipy-lectures.org/_images/numpy_broadcasting.png

The three use cases demonstrated in the preceding diagram are:

- **The array's dimensions match**: Perform the sum element-wise as usual.

- **The smaller array has only 1 row**: Duplicate the rows until the dimensions fit the first array. The same algorithm would be used if the smaller array had only 1 column.

- **The first array has only 1 column and the second array only 1 row**:
    - Duplicate the columns in the first array until we have the same number of columns as the second array
    - Duplicate the rows in the second array until we have the same number of rows as the first array

The following code sample shows NumPy broadcasting in action:

```
my_nparray + np.array([1,2,3,4])
```

Results:

```
array([[ 1,  3,  5,  7],
       [ 5,  7,  9, 11],
       [ 9, 11, 13, 15]])
```

In this section, we provided a basic introduction to NumPy, at least enough to get us started and follow the code samples that we'll cover in the rest of this chapter. In the next section, we will start the discussion on time series with statistical data exploration to find patterns that will help us to identify underlying structures in the data.

Statistical exploration of time series

For the sample application, we'll use stock historical financial data provided by the Quandl data platform financial APIs (https://www.quandl.com/tools/api) and the quandl Python library (https://www.quandl.com/tools/python).

To get started, we need to install the quandl library by running the following command in its own cell:

```
!pip install quandl
```

 Note: As always, don't forget to restart the kernel after the installation is complete.

Access to the Quandl data is free but limited to 50 calls a day, but you can bypass this limit by creating a free account and get an API key:

1. Go to `https://www.quandl.com` and create a new account by clicking on the **SIGN UP** button on the top right.

2. Fill up the form in three steps of the sign-up wizard. (I chose **Personal**, but depending on your situation, you may want to choose **Business** or **Academic**.)

3. At the end of the process, you should receive an email confirmation with a link to activate the account.

4. Once the account is activated, log in to the Quandl platform website and click on **Account Settings** in the top right-hand menu, and then go to the **API KEY** tab.

5. Copy the API key provided in this page. This value will be used to programmatically set the key in the `quandl` Python library as shown in the following code:

```
import quandl
quandl.ApiConfig.api_key = "YOUR_KEY_HERE"
```

The `quandl` library is mainly composed of two APIs:

- `quandl.get(dataset, **kwargs)`: This returns a pandas DataFrame or a NumPy array for the requested dataset(s). The `dataset` argument can be either a string (single dataset) or a list of strings (multi dataset). Each dataset follows the syntax `database_code/dataset_code` when `database_code` is a data publisher and `dataset_code` related to the resource. (See next how to get a full list of all the `database_code` and `dataset_code`).

  The keyword arguments enable you to refine the query. You can find the full list of supported arguments in the `quandl` code on GitHub: `https://github.com/quandl/quandl-python/blob/master/quandl/get.py`.

  One interesting keyword argument called `returns` controls the data structure returned by the method and can take the following two values:

  - `pandas`: Returns a pandas DataFrame
  - `numpy`: Returns a NumPy array

- quandl.get_table(datatable_code, **kwargs): Returns a non-time series dataset (called datatable) about a resource. We will not be using this method in this chapter, but you can find out more about it by looking at the code: https://github.com/quandl/quandl-python/blob/master/quandl/get_table.py.

To get the list of database_code, we use the Quandl REST API: https://www.quandl.com/api/v3/databases?api_key=YOUR_API_KEY&page=n which uses pagination.

> **Note**: In the preceding URL, replace the YOUR_API_KEY value with your actual API key.

The returned payload is in the following JSON format:

```
{
  "databases": [{
        "id": 231,
        "name": "Deutsche Bundesbank Data Repository",
        "database_code": "BUNDESBANK",
        "description": "Data on the German economy, ...",
        "datasets_count": 49358,
        "downloads": 43209922,
        "premium": false,
        "image": "https://quandl--upload.s3.amazonaws/...thumb_
bundesbank.png",
        "favorite": false,
        "url_name": "Deutsche-Bundesbank-Data-Repository"
      },...
  ],
  "meta": {
    "query": "",
    "per_page": 100,
    "current_page": 1,
    "prev_page": null,
    "total_pages": 3,
    "total_count": 274,
    "next_page": 2,
    "current_first_item": 1,
    "current_last_item": 100
  }
}
```

You can find the code file here:

https://github.com/DTAIEB/Thoughtful-Data-Science/
blob/master/chapter%208/sampleCode4.json

We use a `while` loop to load all the available pages relying on the `payload['meta']` `['next_page']` value to know when to stop. At each iteration, we append the list of `database_code` information into an array called `databases` as shown in the following code:

```
import requests
databases = []
page = 1
while(page is not None):
    payload = requests.get("https://www.quandl.com/api/v3/
databases?api_key={}&page={}"\
                        .format(quandl.ApiConfig.api_key, page)).json()
    databases += payload['databases']
    page = payload['meta']['next_page']
```

You can find the code file here:

https://github.com/DTAIEB/Thoughtful-Data-Science/
blob/master/chapter%208/sampleCode5.py

The `databases` variable now contains an array of JSON objects containing the metadata about each `database_code`. We use the PixieDust `display()` API to look at the data in a nice searchable table:

```
import pixiedust
display(databases)
```

In the following screenshot of the PixieDust table, we use the **Filter** button described in *Chapter 2, Data Science at Scale with Jupyter Notebooks and PixieDust*, to access the statistics about the count of datasets available in each database, for example, min, max and mean:

List of Quandl database codes

After searching for a database that contains stock information from the
New York Stock Exchange (NYSE), I found the XNYS database as shown here:

 Note: Make sure to increase the number of the value displayed to
300 in the chart options dialog, so all the results are shown in the table.

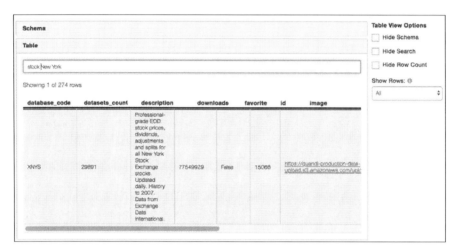

Looking for a database with stock data from NYSE

Unfortunately, the XNYS database is not public and requires a paid subscription.
I ended up using the WIKI database code, which for some reason was not part of the
list returned by the preceding API request, but which I found in some code examples.

I then used the https://www.quandl.com/api/v3/databases/{database_code}/
codes REST API to get the list of datasets. Fortunately, this API returns a CSV
compressed in a ZIP file, which the PixieDust sampleData() method can handle
easily, as shown in the following code:

```
codes = pixiedust.sampleData( "https://www.quandl.com/api/v3/
databases/WIKI/codes?api_key=" + quandl.ApiConfig.api_key)
display(codes)
```

 You can find the code file here:

https://github.com/DTAIEB/Thoughtful-Data-Science/
blob/master/chapter%208/sampleCode6.py

In the PixieDust table interface, we click on the **Options** dialog to increase
the number of values displayed to 4000 so that we can fit the entire dataset
(which is 3,198) and use the search bar to look for particular stocks as shown
in the following screenshot:

Note: The search bar only searches for the rows that are displayed in the
browser, which can be a smaller set when the dataset is too large. Since
in this case, the dataset is too large, it would be impractical to increase
the number of rows to display; it is recommended to use the **Filter**
instead which guarantees to query the entire dataset.

The CSV file returned by the quandl API doesn't have a header,
but PixieDust.sampleData() expects one to be there. This
is currently a limitation that will be addressed in the future.

List of datasets for the WIKI database

For the rest of this section, we load the Microsoft stock (ticker symbol MSFT) historical time series data for the last several years and start exploring its statistical properties. In the following code, we use `quandl.get()` with the `WIKI/MSFT` dataset. We add a column called `daily_spread` that computes the daily gain/loss by calling the pandas `diff()` method, which returns the difference between the current and previous adjusted close price. Note that the returned pandas DataFrame uses the dates as an index, but PixieDust does not support plotting time series by the index at this time. Therefore, in the following code, we call `reset_index()` to convert the `DateTime` index into a new column called `Date` that contains the dates information:

```
msft = quandl.get('WIKI/MSFT')
msft['daily_spread'] = msft['Adj. Close'].diff()
msft = msft.reset_index()
```

 You can find the code file here:
https://github.com/DTAIEB/Thoughtful-Data-Science/blob/master/chapter%208/sampleCode7.py

For our first data exploration, we use `display()` to create a line chart of the stock adjusted closing price over time using the Bokeh renderer.

The following screenshot shows the **Options** configuration and the resulting line chart:

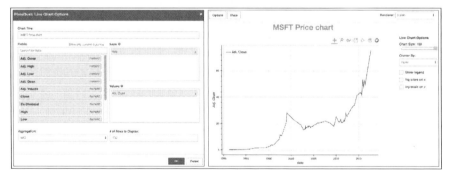

MSFT Price over time, adjusted for dividend distribution, stock split, and other corporate actions

We can also generate a chart that shows the daily spread for each day of the period, as shown in the following screenshot:

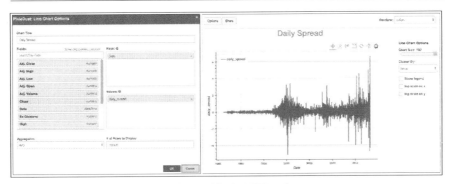

Daily Spread for the MSFT stock

Hypothetical investment

As an exercise, let's try to create a chart that shows how a hypothetical investment of $10,000 in the selected stock (MSFT) would fare over time. To do this, we must compute a DataFrame that contains the total investment value for each day of the period, factoring in the daily spread that we calculated in the previous paragraph and use the PixieDust `display()` API to visualize the data.

We use pandas ability to select rows using a predicate based on dates to first filter the DataFrame to select only the data points in the period we are interested in. We then calculate the number of shares bought by dividing the initial investment of $10,000 by the closing price on the first day of the period and add the initial investment value. All this computation is made very easy, thanks to the efficient series computation of pandas and the underlying NumPy foundational library. We use the `np.cumsum()` method (https://docs.scipy.org/doc/numpy-1.14.0/reference/generated/numpy.cumsum.html) to compute the cumulative sum of all the daily gains adding the initial investment value of $10,000.

Finally, we make the chart easier to read by using the `resample()` method that converts the frequency from daily to monthly computing the new values using the average for the month.

The following code computes the growth DataFrame using a period starting in May 2016:

```
import pandas as pd
tail = msft[msft['Date'] > '2016-05-16']
investment = np.cumsum((10000 / tail['Adj. Close'].values[0]) *
tail['daily_spread']) + 10000
investment = investment.astype(int)
```

```
investment.index = tail['Date']
investment = investment.resample('M').mean()
investment = pd.DataFrame(investment).reset_index()
display(investment)
```

 You can find the code file here:
`https://github.com/DTAIEB/Thoughtful-Data-Science/`
`blob/master/chapter%208/sampleCode8.py`

The following screenshot shows the graph generated by the `display()`
API including the configuration options:

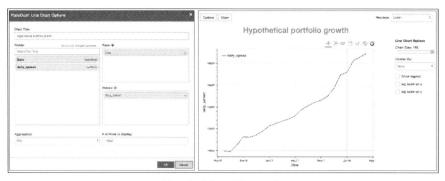

Hypothetical portfolio growth

Autocorrelation function (ACF) and partial autocorrelation function (PACF)

Before trying to generate predictive models, it is essential to understand whether
the time series has identifiable patterns, such as seasonality or trends. One popular
technique is to look at how data points correlate with previous data points according
to a specified time lag. The intuition is that the autocorrelation would reveal internal
structures, such as for example, identifying periods when high correlation (positive
or negative) occurs. You can experiment with different lag values (that is, for each
data point, how many previous points are you taking into account) to find the right
periodicity.

Computing the ACF usually requires calculating the Pearson R correlation
coefficient for the set of data points (`https://en.wikipedia.org/wiki/Pearson_`
`correlation_coefficient`) which is not a trivial thing to do. The good news is
that the `statsmodels` Python library has a `tsa` package (**tsa** stands for **time series**
analysis) that provides helper methods for computing the ACF, that are tightly
integrated with pandas Series.

Note: If not already done, we install the `statsmodels` package using the following command, restarting the kernel after completion:

```
!pip install statsmodels
```

The following code uses `plot_acf()` from the `tsa.api.graphics` package to compute and visualize the ACF for the adjusted close price of the MSFT stock time series:

```
import statsmodels.tsa.api as smt
import matplotlib.pyplot as plt
smt.graphics.plot_acf(msft['Adj. Close'], lags=100)
plt.show()
```

The following is the result:

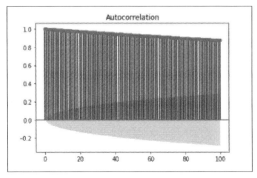

ACF for MSFT with lags = 100

The preceding chart shows the autocorrelation of the data at a number of previous data points (lag) given by the *x* abscissa. So, at lag 0, you always have an autocorrelation of 1.0 (you always correlate perfectly with yourself), lag 1 shows the autocorrelation with the previous data point, lag 2 shows the autocorrelation with the data point that is two steps behind. We can clearly see that the autocorrelation decreases as the lags increase. In the preceding chart, we used only 100 lags, and we see that the autocorrelation still remains statistically significant at around 0.9, which tells us that data separated by long periods of time is not correlated. This suggests that the data has a trend, which is quite obvious when glancing at the overall price chart.

To confirm this hypothesis, we plot the ACF chart with a bigger `lags` argument, say `1000` (which is not unreasonable given the fact that our series has more than 10,000 data points), as shown in the following screenshot:

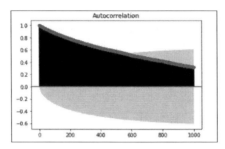

ACF for MSFT with lags = 1000

We now clearly see that the autocorrelation falls below the significance level at around `600` lags.

To better illustrate how the ACF works, let's generate a time series that is periodic, without a trend and see what we can learn. For example, we can use `np.cos()` on a series of evenly spaced points generated with `np.linspace()`:

```
smt.graphics.plot_acf(np.cos(np.linspace(0, 1000, 100)), lags=50)
plt.show()
```

    You can find the code file here:
https://github.com/DTAIEB/Thoughtful-Data-Science/
blob/master/chapter%208/sampleCode9.py

The results are as follows:

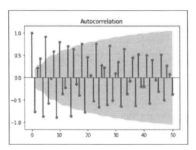

ACF for a periodic series with no trends

In the preceding chart, we can see that the autocorrelation spikes again at regular intervals (every 5 lags or so), clearly showing periodicity (also called seasonality when dealing with real-world data).

Using ACF to detect structure in your time series can sometimes lead to problems, especially when you have strong periodicity. In this case, you'll always see a spike in autocorrelation at a multiple of the period, no matter how far back you try to autocorrelate your data and this could lead to the wrong interpretation. To work around this problem, we use the PACF which uses a shorter lag and unlike ACF, doesn't reuse correlations previously found in shorter time periods. The math for ACF and PACF is rather complex, but the reader only needs to understand the intuition behind it and happily use libraries such as statsmodels to do the heavy lifting computation. One resource I used to get more information on ACF and PACF can be found here: https://www.mathworks.com/help/econ/autocorrelation-and-partial-autocorrelation.html.

Back to our MSFT stock time series, the following code shows how to plot its PACF using the smt.graphics package:

```
import statsmodels.tsa.api as smt
smt.graphics.plot_pacf(msft['Adj. Close'], lags=50)
plt.show()
```

You can find the code file here:

https://github.com/DTAIEB/Thoughtful-Data-Science/blob/master/chapter%208/sampleCode10.py

The results are shown in the following screenshot:

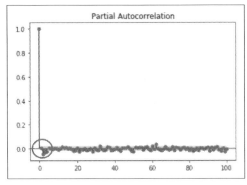

Partial autocorrelation for the MSFT stock time series

We'll get back to ACF and PACF later on in this chapter when we discuss time series forecasting with the ARIMA model.

In this section, we've discussed multiple ways to explore the data. It is of course by no means exhaustive, but we get the idea of how tools such as Jupyter, pandas, NumPy, and PixieDust make it easier to experiment and fail fast if necessary. In the next section, we will build a PixieApp that brings all these charts together.

Putting it all together with the StockExplorer PixieApp

For the first version of our `StockExplorer` PixieApp, we want to operationalize the data exploration of a stock data time series selected by the user. Similar to the other PixieApps we've built, the first screen has a simple layout with an input box where the user can enter a list of stock tickers separated by commas, and an **Explore** button to start data exploration. The main screen is composed of a vertical navigator bar with a menu for each type of data exploration. To make the PixieApp code more modular and easier to maintain and extend, we implement each data exploration screen in its own child PixieApp which is triggered by the vertical navigation bar. Also, each child PixieApp inherits from a base class called `BaseSubApp` that provides common functionalities useful to all the subclasses. The following diagram shows the overall UI layout as well as a class diagram for all the child PixieApps:

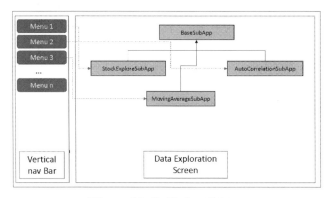

UI layout of the StockExplorer PixieApp

Let's first look at the implementation for the welcome screen. It is implemented in the default route for the `StockExplorer` PixieApp class. The following code shows a partial implementation of the `StockExplorer` class to include the default route only.

Note: Do not try to run this code yet, until the full implementation is provided.

```python
@PixieApp
class StockExplorer():
    @route()
    def main_screen(self):
        return """
<style>
    div.outer-wrapper {
        display: table;width:100%;height:300px;
    }
    div.inner-wrapper {
        display: table-cell;vertical-align: middle;height: 100%;width:
100%;
    }
</style>
<div class="outer-wrapper">
    <div class="inner-wrapper">
        <div class="col-sm-3"></div>
        <div class="input-group col-sm-6">
          <input id="stocks{{prefix}}" type="text"
              class="form-control"
              value="MSFT,AMZN,IBM"
              placeholder="Enter a list of stocks separated by comma
e.g MSFT,AMZN,IBM">
          <span class="input-group-btn">
            <button class="btn btn-default" type="button" pd_
options="explore=true">
                <pd_script>
self.select_tickers('$val(stocks{{prefix}})'.split(','))
                </pd_script>
                Explore
            </button>
          </span>
        </div>
    </div>
</div>
"""
```

You can find the code file here:
`https://github.com/DTAIEB/Thoughtful-Data-Science/blob/master/chapter%208/sampleCode11.py`

The preceding code is very similar to the other sample PixieApps we've seen so far. The **Explore** button contains the following two PixieApp attributes:

- A `pd_script` child element, which calls a Python snippet to set the stock tickers. We also use the `$val` directive to retrieve the user-entered value for the stock tickers:

```
<pd_script>
    self.select_tickers('$val(stocks{{prefix}})'.split(','))
</pd_script>
```

- The `pd_options` attribute, which points to the `explore` route:

```
pd_options="explore=true"
```

The `select_tickers` helper method stores the list of tickers in a dictionary member variable and selects the first one as the active ticker. For performance reasons, we only load the data when needed, that is, when setting the active ticker for the first time or when the user clicks on a particular ticker in the UI.

 Note: As in previous chapters, the `[[StockExplorer]]` notation indicates that the code that follows is part of the `StockExplorer` class.

```
[[StockExplorer]]
def select_tickers(self, tickers):
        self.tickers = {ticker.strip():{} for ticker in tickers}
        self.set_active_ticker(tickers[0].strip())

def set_active_ticker(self, ticker):
    self.active_ticker = ticker
    if 'df' not in self.tickers[ticker]:
        self.tickers[ticker]['df'] = quandl.get('WIKI/{}'.
format(ticker))
        self.tickers[ticker]['df']['daily_spread'] = self.
tickers[ticker]['df']['Adj. Close'] - self.tickers[ticker]['df']['Adj.
Open']
        self.tickers[ticker]['df'] = self.tickers[ticker]['df'].
reset_index()
```

You can find the code file here:

`https://github.com/DTAIEB/Thoughtful-Data-Science/`
`blob/master/chapter%208/sampleCode12.py`

The lazy loading of the stock data for a particular ticker symbol into a pandas DataFrame is done in `set_active_ticker()`. We first check whether the DataFrame has already been loaded by looking if the `df` key is present and, if not, we call the `quandl` API with the `dataset_code: 'WIKI/{ticker}'`. We also add a column that computes the daily spread of the stock that will be displayed in the basic exploration screen. Finally, we need to call `reset_index()` (`https://pandas.` `pydata.org/pandas-docs/stable/generated/pandas.DataFrame.reset_index.` `html`) on the DataFrame to convert the index which is a `DateTimeIndex` into its own column called `Date`. The reason is that the PixieDust `display()` doesn't yet support visualization of DataFrame with a `DateTimeIndex`.

In the `explore` route, we return an HTML fragment that builds the layout for the whole screen. As shown in the preceding mock-up, we use the `btn-group-vertical` and `btn-group-toggle` bootstrap classes to create the vertical navigation bar. The list of menus and associated child PixieApp are defined in the `tabs` Python variable, and we use Jinja2 `{%for loop%}` to build the content. We also add a placeholder `<div>` element with `id ="analytic_screen{{prefix}}"` that will be the recipient of the child PixieApp screen.

The `explore` route implementation is shown here:

```
[[StockExplorer]]
@route(explore="*")
@templateArgs
def stock_explore_screen(self):
    tabs = [("Explore","StockExploreSubApp"),
            ("Moving Average", "MovingAverageSubApp"),
            ("ACF and PACF", "AutoCorrelationSubApp")]
    return """
<style>
    .btn:active, .btn.active {
        background-color:aliceblue;
    }
</style>
<div class="page-header">
    <h1>Stock Explorer PixieApp</h1>
</div>
<div class="container-fluid">
    <div class="row">
        <div class="btn-group-vertical btn-group-toggle col-sm-2"
```

```
                data-toggle="buttons">
            {%for title, subapp in tabs%}
            <label class="btn btn-secondary {%if loop.first%}
    active{%endif%}"
                pd_options="show_analytic={{subapp}}"
                pd_target="analytic_screen{{prefix}}">
                <input type="radio" {%if loop.first%}checked{%endif%}>
                    {{title}}
            </label>
            {%endfor%}
        </div>
        <div id="analytic_screen{{prefix}}" class="col-sm-10">
    </div>
</div>
"""
```

You can find the code file here:

`https://github.com/DTAIEB/Thoughtful-Data-Science/`
`blob/master/chapter%208/sampleCode13.py`

In the preceding code, notice that we use the @templateArgs decorator because we want to use the tabs variable, which is created locally to the method implementation, in the Jinja2 template.

Each menu in the vertical navigation bar points to the same `analytic_screen{{prefix}}` target and invokes the `show_analytic` route with the selected child PixieApp class name referenced by `{{subapp}}`.

In turn, the `show_anatytic` route simply returns an HTML fragment with a `<div>` element that has a `pd_app` attribute referencing the child PixieApp class name. We also use the `pd_render_onload` attribute to ask PixieApp to render the content of the `<div>` element as soon as it is loaded in the browser DOM.

The following code is for the `show_analytic` route:

```
    @route(show_analytic="*")
    def show_analytic_screen(self, show_analytic):
        return """
<div pd_app="{{show_analytic}}" pd_render_onload></div>
"""
```

You can find the code file here:
`https://github.com/DTAIEB/Thoughtful-Data-Science/`
`blob/master/chapter%208/sampleCode14.py`

BaseSubApp – base class for all the child PixieApps

Let's now look at the implementation for each of the child PixieApps and how the base class `BaseSubApp` is used to provide common functionalities. For each child PixieApp we want the user to be able to select a stock ticker through a tabbed interface as shown in the following screenshot:

Tab widget for MSFT, IBM, AMZN tickers

Instead of repeating the HTML fragment for every child PixieApp, we use a technique that I particularly like which consists of creating a Python decorator called `add_ticker_selection_markup` that dynamically changes how the function behaves (for more information on Python decorators, see `https://wiki.python.org/moin/PythonDecorators`). This decorator is created in the `BaseSubApp` class and will automatically prepend the tab selection widget HTML markup for the route, as shown in the following code:

```
[[BaseSubApp]]
def add_ticker_selection_markup(refresh_ids):
    def deco(fn):
        def wrap(self, *args, **kwargs):
            return """
<div class="row" style="text-align:center">
    <div class="btn-group btn-group-toggle"
        style="border-bottom:2px solid #eeeeee"
        data-toggle="buttons">
        {%for ticker, state in this.parent_pixieapp.tickers.items()%}
        <label class="btn btn-secondary {%if this.parent_pixieapp.
active_ticker == ticker%}active{%endif%}"
            pd_refresh=\"""" + ",".join(refresh_ids) + """\" pd_
script="self.parent_pixieapp.set_active_ticker('{{ticker}}')">
            <input type="radio" {%if this.parent_pixieapp.active_
ticker == ticker%}checked{%endif%}>
                {{ticker}}
```

```
        </label>
        {%endfor%}
    </div>
</div>
            """ + fn(self, *args, **kwargs)
        return wrap
    return deco
```

 You can find the code file here:
https://github.com/DTAIEB/Thoughtful-Data-Science/
blob/master/chapter%208/sampleCode15.py

At first glance, the preceding code may appear very hard to read as the add_ticker_
selection_markup decorator method contains two levels of anonymous nested
methods. Let's try to explain the purpose for each of them including the main add_
ticker_selection_markup decorator method:

- add_ticker_selection_markup: This is the main decorator method that
  takes one argument called refresh_ids which will be used in the generated
  markup. This method returns an anonymous function called deco that takes
  a function argument.

- deco: This is the wrapper method that takes one argument called fn which
  is a pointer to the original function to which the decorator is applied. This
  method returns an anonymous function called wrap which will be called
  in lieu of the original function when it is called in the user code.

- wrap: This is the final wrapper method that takes three arguments:

    ○ self: Pointer to the host class for the function

    ○ *args: Any variable arguments that the original method defines
      (could be empty)

    ○ **kwargs: Any keyword arguments that the original method defines
      (could be empty)

The wrap method can access the variables that are outside its scope through
the Python closure mechanism. In this case, it uses the refresh_ids to
generate the tab widget markup, and then calls the fn function with the
self, args, and kwargs arguments.

Note: Do not worry if the preceding explanation is still confusing, even after reading it multiple times. You can just use the decorator for now, and it won't affect your ability to understand the rest of the chapter.

StockExploreSubApp – first child PixieApp

We can now implement the first child PixieApp called StockExploreSubApp. In the main screen, we create two <div> elements that each have a pd_options attribute that calls the show_chart route with Adj. Close and daily_spread as values. In turn, the show_chart route returns a <div> element with a pd_entity attribute pointing to the parent_pixieapp.get_active_df() method with a <pd_options> element that contains a JSON payload for displaying a Bokeh line chart with Date as the *x* abscissa and whatever value is passed as an argument as the column for the *y* ordinate. We also decorate the route with the BaseSubApp. add_ticker_selection_markup decorator using the ID of the preceding two <div> elements as the refresh_ids argument.

The following code shows the implementation for the StockExplorerSubApp child PixieApp:

```
@PixieApp
class StockExploreSubApp(BaseSubApp):
    @route()
    @BaseSubApp.add_ticker_selection_markup(['chart{{prefix}}',
'daily_spread{{prefix}}'])
    def main_screen(self):
        return """
<div class="row" style="min-height:300px">
    <div class="col-xs-6" id="chart{{prefix}}" pd_render_onload pd_
options="show_chart=Adj. Close">
    </div>
    <div class="col-xs-6" id="daily_spread{{prefix}}" pd_render_onload
pd_options="show_chart=daily_spread">
    </div>
</div>
"""

    @route(show_chart="*")
    def show_chart_screen(self, show_chart):
        return """
<div pd_entity="parent_pixieapp.get_active_df()" pd_render_onload>
    <pd_options>
    {
```

```
        "handlerId": "lineChart",
        "valueFields": "{{show_chart}}",
        "rendererId": "bokeh",
        "keyFields": "Date",
        "noChartCache": "true",
        "rowCount": "10000"
    }
    </pd_options>
</div>
        """
```

You can find the code file here:

https://github.com/DTAIEB/Thoughtful-Data-Science/
blob/master/chapter%208/sampleCode16.py

In the preceding `show_chart` route, the `pd_entity` uses the `get_active_df()`
method from the `parent_pixieapp` which is defined in the `StockExplorer` main
class as follows:

```
[[StockExplorer]]
def get_active_df(self):
    return self.tickers[self.active_ticker]['df']
```

You can find the code file here:

https://github.com/DTAIEB/Thoughtful-Data-Science/
blob/master/chapter%208/sampleCode17.py

As a reminder, the `StockExploreSubApp` is associated with the menu through
a tuple in the `tabs` array variable declared in the `Explore` route of the
`StockExplorer` route:

```
tabs = [("Explore","StockExploreSubApp"), ("Moving Average",
"MovingAverageSubApp"),("ACF and PACF", "AutoCorrelationSubApp")]
```

You can find the code file here:

https://github.com/DTAIEB/Thoughtful-Data-Science/
blob/master/chapter%208/sampleCode18.py

The following screenshot shows the `StockExploreSubApp`:

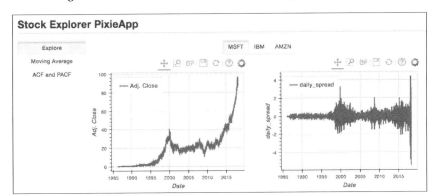

StockExploreSubApp main screen

MovingAverageSubApp – second child PixieApp

The second child PixieApp is `MovingAverageSubApp` which displays a line chart of the moving average for the selected stock ticker with a lag that is configurable through a slider control. Similar to the ticker selection tab, the lag slider will be needed in another child PixieApp. We could use the same decorator technique we use for the ticker selection tab control, but here we want to be able to position the lag slider anywhere on the page. So instead, we'll use a `pd_widget` control called `lag_slider` that we define in the `BaseSubApp` class and return an HTML fragment for the slider control. It also adds a `<script>` element that uses the jQuery `slider` method available in the jQuery UI module (see https://api.jqueryui.com/slider for more information). We also add a `change` handler function that is called when the user has selected a new value. In this handler, we call the `pixiedust.sendEvent` function to publish an event of the `lagSlider` type and a payload containing the new value for the lag. It is the responsibility of the caller to add a `<pd_event_handler>` element to listen to that event and process the payload.

The following code shows the implementation of the `lag_slider pd_widget`:

```
[[BaseSubApp]]
@route(widget="lag_slider")
def slider_screen(self):
    return """
<div>
    <label class="field">Lag:<span id="slideval{{prefix}}">50</span></label>
    <i class="fa fa-info-circle" style="color:orange"
```

```
        data-toggle="pd-tooltip"
        title="Selected lag used to compute moving average, ACF or
PACF"></i>
    <div id="slider{{prefix}}" name="slider" data-min=30
        data-max=300
        data-default=50 style="margin: 0 0.6em;">
    </div>
</div>
<script>
$("[id^=slider][id$={{prefix}}]").each(function() {
    var sliderElt = $(this)
    var min = sliderElt.data("min")
    var max = sliderElt.data("max")
    var val = sliderElt.data("default")
    sliderElt.slider({
        min: isNaN(min) ? 0 : min,
        max: isNaN(max) ? 100 : max,
        value: isNaN(val) ? 50 : val,
        change: function(evt, ui) {
            $("[id=slideval{{prefix}}]").text(ui.value);
            pixiedust.sendEvent({type:'lagSlider',value:ui.value})
        },
        slide: function(evt, ui) {
            $("[id=slideval{{prefix}}]").text(ui.value);
        }
    });
})
</script>
    """
```

You can find the code file here:

https://github.com/DTAIEB/Thoughtful-Data-Science/
blob/master/chapter%208/sampleCode19.py

In the MovingAverageSubApp we use the add_ticker_selection_markup decorator with chart{{prefix}} as an argument in the default route to add the ticker selection tab and add a <div> element with pd_widget named lag_slider, including a <pd_event_handler> to set the self.lag variable and refresh the chart div. The chart div uses a pd_entity attribute with the get_moving_average_df() method that calls the rolling method (https://pandas.pydata.org/pandas-docs/stable/generated/pandas.Series.rolling.html) on the pandas Series returned from the selected pandas DataFrame and calls the mean() method on it. Because the PixieDust display() does not yet support pandas Series, we build a pandas DataFrame using the series index as a column called x and return it in the get_moving_average_df() method.

The following code shows the implementation of the MovingAverageSubApp child PixieApp

```
@PixieApp
class MovingAverageSubApp(BaseSubApp):
    @route()
    @BaseSubApp.add_ticker_selection_markup(['chart{{prefix}}'])
    def main_screen(self):
        return """
<div class="row" style="min-height:300px">
    <div class="page-header text-center">
        <h1>Moving Average for {{this.parent_pixieapp.active_
ticker}}</h1>
    </div>
    <div class="col-sm-12" id="chart{{prefix}}" pd_render_onload
pd_entity="get_moving_average_df()">
        <pd_options>
        {
           "valueFields": "Adj. Close",
           "keyFields": "x",
           "rendererId": "bokeh",
           "handlerId": "lineChart",
           "rowCount": "10000"
        }
        </pd_options>
    </div>
</div>
<div class="row">
    <div pd_widget="lag_slider">
        <pd_event_handler
            pd_source="lagSlider"
            pd_script="self.lag = eventInfo['value']"
            pd_refresh="chart{{prefix}}">
```

```
        </pd_event_handler>
      </div>
  </div>
  """
      def get_moving_average_df(self):
          ma = self.parent_pixieapp.get_active_df()['Adj. Close'].
  rolling(window=self.lag).mean()
          ma_df = pd.DataFrame(ma)
          ma_df["x"] = ma_df.index
          return ma_df
```

 You can find the code file here:
`https://github.com/DTAIEB/Thoughtful-Data-Science/`
`blob/master/chapter%208/sampleCode20.py`

The following screenshot shows the chart displayed by the `MovingAverageSubApp`:

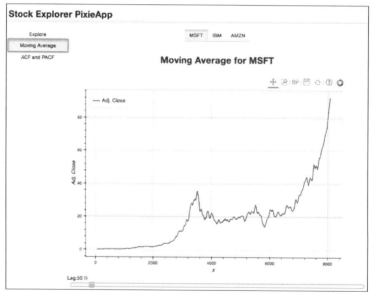

MovingAverageSubApp screenshot

AutoCorrelationSubApp – third child PixieApp

For the third child, PixieApp called `AutoCorrelationSubApp`; we display the ACF and PACF of the selected stock DataFrame, which are computed using the `statsmodels` package.

The following code shows the implementation of the `AutoCorrelationSubApp` which also uses the `add_ticker_selection_markup` decorator and the `pd_widget` named `lag_slider`:

```
import statsmodels.tsa.api as smt
@PixieApp
class AutoCorrelationSubApp(BaseSubApp):
    @route()
    @BaseSubApp.add_ticker_selection_markup(['chart_acf{{prefix}}',
'chart_pacf{{prefix}}'])
    def main_screen(self):
        return """
<div class="row" style="min-height:300px">
    <div class="col-sm-6">
        <div class="page-header text-center">
            <h1>Auto-correlation Function</h1>
        </div>
        <div id="chart_acf{{prefix}}" pd_render_onload
pd_options="show_acf=true">
        </div>
    </div>
    <div class="col-sm-6">
        <div class="page-header text-center">
            <h1>Partial Auto-correlation Function</h1>
        </div>
        <div id="chart_pacf{{prefix}}" pd_render_onload
pd_options="show_pacf=true">
        </div>
    </div>
</div>

<div class="row">
    <div pd_widget="lag_slider">
        <pd_event_handler
            pd_source="lagSlider"
            pd_script="self.lag = eventInfo['value']"
            pd_refresh="chart_acf{{prefix}},chart_pacf{{prefix}}">
        </pd_event_handler>
    </div>
```

```
</div>
"""
    @route(show_acf='*')
    @captureOutput
    def show_acf_screen(self):
        smt.graphics.plot_acf(self.parent_pixieapp.get_active_df()
['Adj. Close'], lags=self.lag)

    @route(show_pacf='*')
    @captureOutput
    def show_pacf_screen(self):
        smt.graphics.plot_pacf(self.parent_pixieapp.get_active_df()
['Adj. Close'], lags=self.lag)
```

 You can find the code file here:

https://github.com/DTAIEB/Thoughtful-Data-Science/
blob/master/chapter%208/sampleCode21.py

In the preceding code, we define two routes: show_acf and show_pacf which respectively call the plot_acf and plot_pacf methods of the smt.graphics package. We also use the @captureOutput decorator to signal the PixieApp framework to capture the output generated by plot_acf and plot_pacf.

The following screenshot shows the charts displayed by AutoCorrelationSubApp:

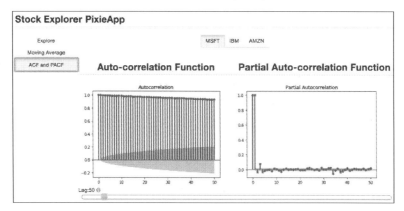

AutoCorrelationSubApp screenshot

In this section, we showed how to put together a sample PixieApp that does basic data exploration on a time series and display various statistical charts. The complete Notebook can be found here: `https://github.com/DTAIEB/Thoughtful-Data-Science/blob/master/chapter%208/StockExplorer%20-%20Part%201.ipynb`.

In the next section, we try to build a time series forecast model using a very popular model called **Autoregressive Integrated Moving Average (ARIMA)**.

Time series forecasting using the ARIMA model

ARIMA is one of the most popular time series forecasting models and as its name indicates is made up of three terms:

- **AR**: Stands for **autoregression**, which is nothing more than applying a linear regression algorithm using one observation and its own lagged observations as training data.

The AR model uses the following formula:

$$Y_t = \phi_1 Y_{t-1} + \phi_2 Y_{t-2} + \ldots + \phi_p Y_{t-p} + \varepsilon_t$$

Where ϕ_i are the weights of the models learned from the previous observations and ε_t is the residual error for observation t.

We also call p the order of the autoregression model, which is defined as the number of lag observations included in the preceding formula.

For example:

AR(2) is defined as:

$$Y_t = \phi_1 Y_{t-1} + \phi_2 Y_{t-2} + \varepsilon_t$$

AR(1) is defined as:

$$Y_t = \phi_1 Y_{t-1} + \varepsilon_t$$

- **I**: Stands for **integrated**. For the ARIMA model to work, it is assumed that the time series is stationary or can be made stationary. A series is said to be stationary (`https://en.wikipedia.org/wiki/Stationary_process`) if its mean and variance doesn't change over time.

Note: There is also the notion of strict stationarity which requires that the joint probability distribution of a subset of observations doesn't change when shifted in time.

Using mathematical notation, strict stationarity translates to:

$F\left(y_t, y_{t+1}, \ldots, y_{t+k}\right)$ and $F\left(y_{t+m}, y_{t+m+1}, \ldots, y_{t+m+k}\right)$ are the same for any t, m, and k, with F being the joint probability distribution.

In practice, this condition is too strong, and the preceding weaker definition provided is preferred.

We can make a time series stationary through a transformation that uses differencing of the log between an observation and the one before that, as shown in the following equation:

$$Z_t = \log Y_t - \log Y_{t-1}$$

It is possible that multiple log differencing transformations are needed before the time series is actually made stationary. We call d the number of times we transform the series using log differencing.

For example:

I(0) is defined as no log differencing needed (the model is then called ARMA).

I(1) is defined as 1 log differencing needed.

I(2) is defined as 2 log differencing needed.

Note: It is important to remember to do the reverse transformation for as many integrations that were made, after predicting a value.

- **MA**: Stands for **moving average**. The MA model uses the residual error from the mean of the current observation and the weighted residual errors of the lagged observations. We can define the model using the following formula:

$$Y_t = \mu + \varepsilon_t + \theta_1\varepsilon_{t-1} + \theta_2\varepsilon_{t-2} + \ldots + \theta_q\varepsilon_{t-q}$$

Where μ is the mean of the time series, ε_t are the residual errors in the series and θ_q are the weights for the lagged residual errors.

We call q the size of the moving average window.

For example:

MA(0) is defined as no moving average needed (the model is then called AR).

MA(1) is defined as using a moving average window of 1. The formula becomes:

$$Y_t = \mu + \varepsilon_t + \theta_1\varepsilon_{t-1}$$

As per the preceding definition, we use the notation *ARIMA(p,d,q)* to define an ARIMA model with an autoregression model of order p, an integration/differencing of order d, and a moving average window of size q.

Implementing all the code to build an ARIMA model can be very time-consuming. Fortunately, the `statsmodels` library implements an ARIMA class in the `statsmodels.tsa.arima_model` package that provides all the computation needed to train a model with the `fit()` method and predict values with the `predict()` method. It also takes care of the log differencing to make the time series stationary. The trick is to find the parameters p, d, and q for building the optimal ARIMA model. For this, we use the ACF and PACF chart as follows:

- The p value corresponds to the number of lags (on the x abscissa) where the ACF chart crosses the statistical significance threshold for the first time.
- Similarly, the q value corresponds to the number of lags (on the x abscissa) where the PACF chart crosses the statistical significance threshold for the first time.

Build an ARIMA model for the MSFT stock time series

As a reminder, the price chart for the MSFT stock time series looks like this:

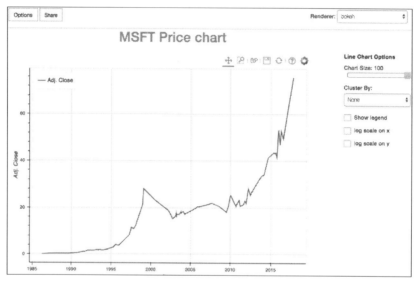

MSFT stock series chart

Before we start building our model, let's first withhold the last 14 days of the data for testing and use the rest for training.

The following code defines two new variables: `train_set` and `test_set`:

```
train_set, test_set = msft[:-14], msft[-14:]
```

 Note: If you're still not familiar with the preceding slicing notation, please refer to the section on NumPy at the beginning of this chapter

From the preceding chart, we can clearly observe a growth trend starting in 2012 but no clear seasonality. Therefore, we can safely assume that there is no stationarity. Let's first try to apply a log differencing transformation once and plot the corresponding ACF and PACF chart.

In the following code, we build the `logmsft` pandas Series by using `np.log()` on the `Adj. Close` column and then build the `logmsft_diff` pandas DataFrame using the difference between `logmsft` and the lag of 1 (using the `shift()` method). As was done before, we also call `reset_index()` to convert the `Date` index into a column so that the PixieDust `display()` can process it:

```
logmsft = np.log(train_set['Adj. Close'])
logmsft.index = train_set['Date']
logmsft_diff = pd.DataFrame(logmsft - logmsft.shift()).reset_index()
logmsft_diff.dropna(inplace=True)
display(logmsft_diff)
```

> You can find the code file here:
> https://github.com/DTAIEB/Thoughtful-Data-Science/
> blob/master/chapter%208/sampleCode22.py

The results are shown in the following screenshot:

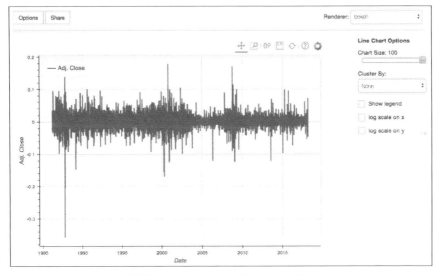

MSFT stock series after log differencing applied

From looking at the preceding graph, we can reasonably think that we've succeeded at making the time series stationary with 0 as the mean. We can also use a more rigorous way to test for stationarity by using the Dickey-Fuller test (https://en.wikipedia.org/wiki/Dickey%E2%80%93Fuller_test) which tests the null hypothesis that a unit root is present in an *AR(1)* model.

Note: In statistics, statistical hypothesis testing consists of challenging whether a proposed hypothesis is true, by taking a sample and deciding whether the claim remains true. We look at the p-value (`https://en.wikipedia.org/wiki/P-value`) which helps determine the significance of the results. More details on statistical hypothesis testing can be found here:

`https://en.wikipedia.org/wiki/Statistical_hypothesis_testing`

The following code uses the `adfuller` method from the `statsmodels.tsa.stattools` package:

```
from statsmodels.tsa.stattools import adfuller
import pprint

ad_fuller_results = adfuller(
logmsft_diff['Adj. Close'], autolag = 'AIC', regression = 'c'
)
labels = ['Test Statistic','p-value','#Lags Used','Number of
Observations Used']
pp = pprint.PrettyPrinter(indent=4)
pp.pprint({labels[i]: ad_fuller_results[i] for i in range(4)})
```

You can find the code file here:

`https://github.com/DTAIEB/Thoughtful-Data-Science/blob/master/chapter%208/sampleCode23.py`

We use the pprint package which is very useful for *pretty-printing* any Python data structures. More info on pprint can be found here:

`https://docs.python.org/3/library/pprint.html`

The results (explained in detail at: `http://www.statsmodels.org/devel/generated/statsmodels.tsa.stattools.adfuller.html`) are shown here:

```
{
    'Number of lags used': 3,
    'Number of Observations Used': 8057,
    'Test statistic': -48.071592138591136,
    'MacKinnon's approximate p-value': 0.0
}
```

You can find the code file here:
`https://github.com/DTAIEB/Thoughtful-Data-Science/`
`blob/master/chapter%208/sampleCode24.json`

The p-value is below the significance level; therefore, we can reject the null hypothesis that a unit root is present in the *AR(1)* model, which gives us confidence that the time series is stationary.

We then plot the ACF and PACF chart which will give us the *p* and *q* parameters of the ARIMA model:

The following code builds the ACF chart:

```
import statsmodels.tsa.api as smt
smt.graphics.plot_acf(logmsft_diff['Adj. Close'], lags=100)
plt.show()
```

 You can find the code file here:
`https://github.com/DTAIEB/Thoughtful-Data-Science/`
`blob/master/chapter%208/sampleCode25.py`

The results are shown in the following screenshot:

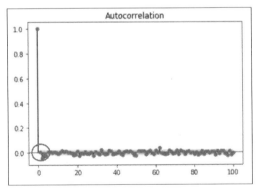

ACF for the log difference MSFT DataFrame

From the preceding ACF graph, we can see that the correlation crosses the statistical significance threshold for the first time at a lag of 1. Therefore, we'll use *p = 1* as the AR order of our ARIMA model.

We do the same for the PACF:

```
smt.graphics.plot_pacf(logmsft_diff['Adj. Close'], lags=100)
plt.show()
```

 You can find the code file here:
https://github.com/DTAIEB/Thoughtful-Data-Science/
blob/master/chapter%208/sampleCode26.py

The results are shown in the following screenshot:

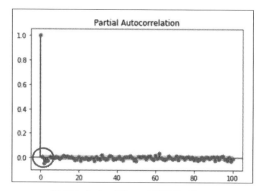

PACF for the log difference MSFT DataFrame

From the preceding PACF graph, we can also see that the correlation crosses the statistical significance threshold for the first time at a lag of 1. Therefore, we'll use $q = 1$ as the MA order of our ARIMA model.

We also had to apply the log differencing transformation only once. Therefore we'll use $d = 1$ for the integrated part of the ARIMA model.

 Note: When calling the ARIMA class, if you use $d = 0$, then you may have to do the log differencing manually and, in this case, you'll need to revert the transformation yourself on the predicted values. If not, the statsmodels package will take care of reverting the transformation before returning the predicted value.

The following code trains an ARIMA model on the train_set time series using $p = 1$, $d = 1$, and $q=1$ as values to the order tuple argument of the ARIMA constructor. We then call the fit() method to proceed with the training and obtain a model:

```
from statsmodels.tsa.arima_model import ARIMA

import warnings
with warnings.catch_warnings():
    warnings.simplefilter("ignore")
    arima_model_class = ARIMA(train_set['Adj. Close'], dates=train_
set['Date'], order=(1,1,1))
    arima_model = arima_model_class.fit(disp=0)

print(arima_model.resid.describe())
```

You can find the code file here:

https://github.com/DTAIEB/Thoughtful-Data-Science/
blob/master/chapter%208/sampleCode27.py

Note: We use the `warnings` package to avoid getting the mutiple deprecation warnings that may happen if you are using older versions of NumPy and pandas.

In the preceding code, we use `train_set['Adj. Close']` as an argument to the ARIMA constructor. Since we are using a Series for the data, we also need to pass the `train_set['Date']` series for the `dates` argument. Note that if we passed a pandas DataFrame instead with a `DateIndex` index, then we wouldn't have to use the `dates` argument. The final argument to the ARIMA constructor is the `order` argument which is a tuple of three values indicating the p, d, and q order, as discussed at the beginning of this section.

We then call the `fit()` method that returns the actual ARIMA model that we'll use to predict values. For information purposes, we print statistics about the residual errors of the model using `arima_model.resid.describe()`.

The results are shown here:

```
count    8.061000e+03
mean    -5.785533e-07
std      4.198119e-01
min     -5.118915e+00
25%     -1.061133e-01
50%     -1.184452e-02
75%      9.848486e-02
max      5.023380e+00
dtype: float64
```

The mean residual error is $-5.7*10^{-7}$ which is very close to zero and therefore shows that the model may be overfitting the training data.

Now that we have a model let's try to diagnose it. We define a method called `plot_predict` that takes a model, a series of dates and a number indicating how far back we want to look. We then call the ARIMA `plot_predict()` method to create a chart with both the predicted and observed values.

The following code shows the implementation for the `plot_predict()` method, including calling it twice with `100` and `10`:

```
def plot_predict(model, dates_series, num_observations):
    fig = plt.figure(figsize = (12,5))
    model.plot_predict(
        start = str(dates_series[len(dates_series)-num_observations]),
        end = str(dates_series[len(dates_series)-1])
    )
    plt.show()

plot_predict(arima_model, train_set['Date'], 100)
plot_predict(arima_model, train_set['Date'], 10)
```

 You can find the code file here:

https://github.com/DTAIEB/Thoughtful-Data-Science/blob/master/chapter%208/sampleCode28.py

The results are shown here:

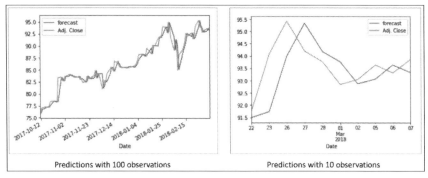

Observations versus Forecast chart

The preceding charts show how close the predictions are to the actual observations from the training set. We now use the test set that was withheld before to further diagnose the model. For this part, we use the forecast() method which predicts the next data point. For each value of the test_set, we build a new ARIMA model from an array of observations called history that contains the training data augmented with each predicted value.

The following code shows the implementation for the compute_test_set_predictions() method that takes a train_set and a test_set as arguments and returns a pandas DataFrame with a forecast column containing all the predicted values and a test column containing the corresponding actual observed values:

```
def compute_test_set_predictions(train_set, test_set):
    with warnings.catch_warnings():
        warnings.simplefilter("ignore")
        history = train_set['Adj. Close'].values
        forecast = np.array([])
        for t in range(len(test_set)):
            prediction = ARIMA(history, order=(1,1,0)).fit(disp=0).
forecast()
            history = np.append(history, test_set['Adj. Close'].
iloc[t])
            forecast = np.append(forecast, prediction[0])
        return pd.DataFrame(
          {"forecast": forecast,
           "test": test_set['Adj. Close'],
           "Date": pd.date_range(start=test_set['Date'].iloc
[len(test_set)-1], periods = len(test_set))
          }
        )

results = compute_test_set_predictions(train_set, test_set)
display(results)
```

 You can find the code file here:

https://github.com/DTAIEB/Thoughtful-Data-Science/
blob/master/chapter%208/sampleCode29.py

The following screenshot shows the result chart:

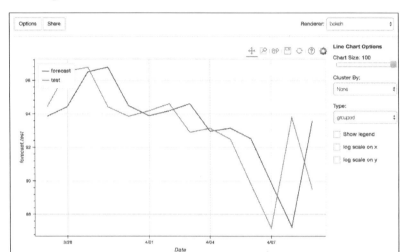

Chart of predicted versus acutal values

We can measure the error using the popular `mean_squared_error` method (`https://en.wikipedia.org/wiki/Mean_squared_error`) of the scikit-learn package (`http://scikit-learn.org`) which is defined as follows:

$$MSE = \frac{1}{n} \sum_{i=1}^{n} \left(Y_i - \hat{Y}_i \right)^2$$

Where Y_i is the actual value and $\hat{Y}_i$ is the predicted value.

The following code defines a `compute_mean_squared_error` method that takes a test and a forecast series and returns the value of the mean squared error:

```
from sklearn.metrics import mean_squared_error
def compute_mean_squared_error(test_series, forecast_series):
    return mean_squared_error(test_series, forecast_series)

print('Mean Squared Error: {}'.format(
compute_mean_squared_error( test_set['Adj. Close'], results.forecast))
)
```

You can find the code file here:
https://github.com/DTAIEB/Thoughtful-Data-Science/
blob/master/chapter%208/sampleCode30.py

The result is shown here:

```
Mean Squared Error: 6.336538843075749
```

StockExplorer PixieApp Part 2 – add time series forecasting using the ARIMA model

In this section, we improve the `StockExplorer` PixieApp by adding a menu that provides time series forecasting for the selected stock ticker using an ARIMA model. We create a new class called `ForecastArimaSubApp` and update the `tabs` variable in the main `StockExplorer` class.

```
[[StockExplorer]]
@route(explore="*")
@templateArgs
def stock_explore_screen(self):
    tabs = [("Explore","StockExploreSubApp"),
            ("Moving Average", "MovingAverageSubApp"),
            ("ACF and PACF", "AutoCorrelationSubApp"),
            ("Forecast with ARIMA", "ForecastArimaSubApp")]
    ...
```

 You can find the code file here:
https://github.com/DTAIEB/Thoughtful-Data-Science/
blob/master/chapter%208/sampleCode31.py

The `ForecastArimaSubApp` child PixieApp is composed of two screens. The first screen displays the time series chart as well as the ACF and the PACF charts. The goal of this screen is to provide the user with the necessary data exploration to figure out what are the values for the p, d, and q order of the ARIMA model, as explained in the previous section. By looking at the time series chart, we can figure out whether the time series is stationary (which, as a reminder, is a requirement for building the ARIMA model). If not, the user can click on the **Add differencing** button to try to make the DataFrame stationery by using a log differencing transformation. The three charts are then updated using the transformed DataFrame.

The following code shows the default route for the `ForecastArimaSubApp` child PixieApp:

```python
from statsmodels.tsa.arima_model import ARIMA

@PixieApp
class ForecastArimaSubApp(BaseSubApp):
    def setup(self):
        self.entity_dataframe = self.parent_pixieapp.get_active_df().copy()
        self.differencing = False

    def set_active_ticker(self, ticker):
        BaseSubApp.set_active_ticker(self, ticker)
        self.setup()

    @route()
    @BaseSubApp.add_ticker_selection_markup([])
    def main_screen(self):
        return """
<div class="page-header text-center">
    <h2>1. Data Exploration to test for Stationarity
        <button class="btn btn-default"
                pd_script="self.toggle_differencing()" pd_refresh>
            {%if this.differencing%}Remove differencing{%else%}Add
differencing{%endif%}
        </button>
        <button class="btn btn-default"
                pd_options="do_forecast=true">
            Continue to Forecast
        </button>
    </h2>
</div>

<div class="row" style="min-height:300px">
    <div class="col-sm-10" id="chart{{prefix}}" pd_render_onload
pd_options="show_chart=Adj. Close">
    </div>
</div>

<div class="row" style="min-height:300px">
    <div class="col-sm-6">
        <div class="page-header text-center">
            <h3>Auto-correlation Function</h3>
        </div>
```

```
        <div id="chart_acf{{prefix}}" pd_render_onload
pd_options="show_acf=true">
        </div>
    </div>
    <div class="col-sm-6">
        <div class="page-header text-center">
            <h3>Partial Auto-correlation Function</h3>
        </div>
        <div id="chart_pacf{{prefix}}" pd_render_onload
pd_options="show_pacf=true">
        </div>
    </div>
</div>
        """
```

You can find the code file here:

`https://github.com/DTAIEB/Thoughtful-Data-Science/`
`blob/master/chapter%208/sampleCode32.py`

The preceding code follows a pattern that we should now be familiar with:

- Define a `setup` method that is guaranteed to be called when the PixieApp starts. In this method, we make a copy of the selected DataFrame obtained from the parent PixieApp. We also maintain a variable called `self.differencing` that tracks whether the user clicked on the **Add differencing** button.

- We create a default route that shows the first screen that is composed of the following components:
    - A header with two buttons: `Add differencing` for making the time series stationary and `Continue to forecast` to display the second screen which we'll discuss later. The `Add differencing` button toggles to `Remove differencing` when the differencing has been applied.
    - A `<div>` element that invokes the `show_chart` route to display the time series chart.
    - A `<div>` element that invokes the `show_acf` route to display the ACF chart.
    - A `<div>` element that invokes the `show_pacf` route to display the PACF chart.

- We use an empty array [] as an argument to the `@BaseSubApp.add_ticker_selection_markup` decorator to make sure that the entire screen is refreshed when the user selects another stock ticker, and to restart from the first screen. We also need to reset the internal variables. To achieve this, we made a change to the `add_ticker_selection_markup` to define a new method in `BaseSubApp` called `set_active_ticker` that is a wrapper method to the `set_active_ticker` from the parent PixieApp. The idea is to let subclasses override this method and inject extra code if needed. We also change the `pd_script` attribute for the tab element to invoke this method when the user selects a new ticker symbol as shown in the following code:

```
[[BaseSubApp]]
def add_ticker_selection_markup(refresh_ids):
        def deco(fn):
            def wrap(self, *args, **kwargs):
                return """
<div class="row" style="text-align:center">
    <div class="btn-group btn-group-toggle"
        style="border-bottom:2px solid #eeeeee"
        data-toggle="buttons">
        {%for ticker, state in this.parent_pixieapp.tickers.
items()%}
        <label class="btn btn-secondary {%if this.parent_pixieapp.
active_ticker == ticker%}active{%endif%}"
            pd_refresh=\"""" + ",".join(refresh_ids) + """\"
pd_script="self.set_active_ticker('{{ticker}}')">
            <input type="radio" {%if this.parent_pixieapp.active_
ticker == ticker%}checked{%endif%}>
                {{ticker}}
        </label>
        {%endfor%}
    </div>
</div>
                """ + fn(self, *args, **kwargs)
            return wrap
        return deco

    def set_active_ticker(self, ticker):
        self.parent_pixieapp.set_active_ticker(ticker)
```

You can find the code file here:

`https://github.com/DTAIEB/Thoughtful-Data-Science/`
`blob/master/chapter%208/sampleCode33.py`

In the `ForecastArimaSubApp` child PixieApp, we then override the `set_active_tracker` method, first calling the super and then calling the `self.setup()` to reinitialize the internal variables:

```
[[ForecastArimaSubApp]]
def set_active_ticker(self, ticker):
        BaseSubApp.set_active_ticker(self, ticker)
        self.setup()
```

You can find the code file here:

`https://github.com/DTAIEB/Thoughtful-Data-Science/`
`blob/master/chapter%208/sampleCode34.py`

The route implementation for the first forecast screen is pretty straightforward. The `Add differencing` / `Remove differencing` button has a `pd_script` attribute that calls the `self.toggle_differencing()` method and the `pd_refresh` attribute to update the entire page. It also defines the three `<div>` elements that respectively call the `show_chart`, `show_acf`, and `show_pacf` routes as shown in the following code:

```
[[ForecastArimaSubApp]]
@route()
    @BaseSubApp.add_ticker_selection_markup([])
    def main_screen(self):
        return """
<div class="page-header text-center">
  <h2>1. Data Exploration to test for Stationarity
    <button class="btn btn-default"
            pd_script="self.toggle_differencing()" pd_refresh>
    {%if this.differencing%}Remove differencing{%else%}Add
differencing{%endif%}
    </button>
    <button class="btn btn-default" pd_options="do_forecast=true">
        Continue to Forecast
    </button>
  </h2>
</div>

<div class="row" style="min-height:300px">
  <div class="col-sm-10" id="chart{{prefix}}" pd_render_onload
pd_options="show_chart=Adj. Close">
```

```
        </div>
    </div>

    <div class="row" style="min-height:300px">
        <div class="col-sm-6">
            <div class="page-header text-center">
                <h3>Auto-correlation Function</h3>
            </div>
            <div id="chart_acf{{prefix}}" pd_render_onload
pd_options="show_acf=true">
            </div>
        </div>
        <div class="col-sm-6">
            <div class="page-header text-center">
                <h3>Partial Auto-correlation Function</h3>
            </div>
            <div id="chart_pacf{{prefix}}" pd_render_onload
pd_options="show_pacf=true">
            </div>
        </div>
    </div>
        """
```

 You can find the code file here:

https://github.com/DTAIEB/Thoughtful-Data-Science/
blob/master/chapter%208/sampleCode35.py

The `toggle_differencing()` method tracks the current differencing state with
the `self.differencing` variable and either makes a copy of the active DataFrame
from the `parent_pixieapp` or applies a log differencing transformation to the `self.`
`entity_dataframe` variable as shown in the following code:

```
def toggle_differencing(self):
    if self.differencing:
        self.entity_dataframe = self.parent_pixieapp.get_active_df().
copy()
```

```
          self.differencing = False
      else:
          log_df = np.log(self.entity_dataframe['Adj. Close'])
          log_df.index = self.entity_dataframe['Date']
          self.entity_dataframe = pd.DataFrame(log_df - log_df.shift()).
reset_index()
          self.entity_dataframe.dropna(inplace=True)
          self.differencing = True
```

You can find the code file here:

```
https://github.com/DTAIEB/Thoughtful-Data-Science/
blob/master/chapter%208/sampleCode36.py
```

The show_acf and show_pacf routes are pretty straightforward. They respectively call the smt.graphics.plot_acf and smt.graphics.plot_pacf methods. They also use the @captureOutput decorator to pass through the chart image to the target widget:

```
@route(show_acf='*')
@captureOutput
def show_acf_screen(self):
    smt.graphics.plot_acf(self.entity_dataframe['Adj. Close'],
lags=50)

@route(show_pacf='*')
@captureOutput
def show_pacf_screen(self):
    smt.graphics.plot_pacf(self.entity_dataframe['Adj. Close'],
lags=50)
```

You can find the code file here:

```
https://github.com/DTAIEB/Thoughtful-Data-Science/
blob/master/chapter%208/sampleCode37.py
```

The following screenshot shows the data exploration page of the forecast child PixieApp without the differencing:

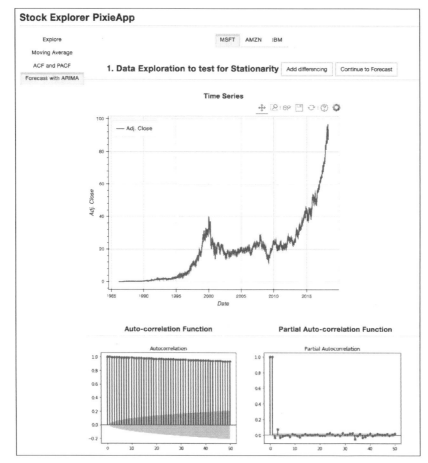

First forecast screen without applying differencing

As expected, the charts are consistent with a time series that is not stationary.
When the user clicks on the **Add differencing** button, the following screen is shown:

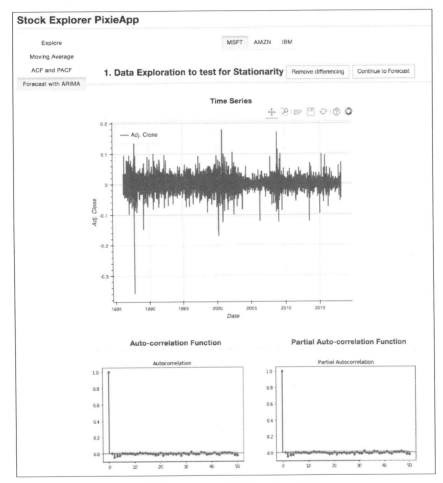

First forecast screen with differencing applied

The next step is to implement the `do_forecast` route that is invoked by the **Continue to Forecast** button. This route is responsible for building the ARIMA model; it starts by showing a configuration page with three input texts that let the user enter the *p*, *d*, and *q* orders, which have been inferred by looking at the charts in the data exploration screen. We add a `Go` button to proceed with the model building using the `build_arima_model` route which we'll discuss later in this section. The header also has a `Diagnose Model` button that invokes another page responsible for evaluating the accuracy of the model.

The implementation of the `do_forecast` route is shown here. Note that we use the `add_ticker_selection_markup` with an empty array to refresh the entire page when the user selects another stock ticker:

```
[[ForecastArimaSubApp]]
@route(do_forecast="true")
    @BaseSubApp.add_ticker_selection_markup([])
    def do_forecast_screen(self):
        return """
<div class="page-header text-center">
    <h2>2. Build Arima model
        <button class="btn btn-default"
                pd_options="do_diagnose=true">
            Diagnose Model
        </button>
    </h2>
</div>
<div class="row" id="forecast{{prefix}}">
    <div style="font-weight:bold">Enter the p,d,q order for the ARIMA
model you want to build</div>

    <div class="form-group" style="margin-left: 20px">
        <label class="control-label">Enter the p order for the
AR model:</label>
        <input type="text" class="form-control"
                id="p_order{{prefix}}"
                value="1" style="width: 100px;margin-left:10px">

        <label class="control-label">Enter the d order for the
Integrated step:</label>
        <input type="text" class="form-control"
                id="d_order{{prefix}}" value="1"
                style="width: 100px;margin-left:10px">

        <label class="control-label">Enter the q order for the
MA model:</label>
```

```
        <input type="text" class="form-control"
                id="q_order{{prefix}}" value="1"
                style="width: 100px;margin-left:10px">
    </div>

    <center>
        <button class="btn btn-default"
                pd_target="forecast{{prefix}}"
            pd_options="p_order=$val(p_order{{prefix}});d_
order=$val(p_order{{prefix}});q_order=$val(p_order{{prefix}})">
        Go
        </button>
    </center>
</div>
"""
```

 You can find the code file here:

https://github.com/DTAIEB/Thoughtful-Data-Science/
blob/master/chapter%208/sampleCode38.py

The following screenshot shows the configuration page of the **Build ARIMA model** page:

Configuration page of the Build Arima model page

The **Go** button has a `pd_options` attribute that invokes a route with three states: `p_order`, `d_order`, and `q_order` with values taken from the three input boxes associated with each attribute.

The route for building the ARIMA model is shown in the following code. It starts by splitting the active DataFrame into a training and test set, withholding 14 observations for the test set. It then builds the model and computes the residual errors. Once the model is successfully built, we return an HTML markup that contains a chart showing the predicted values for the training set versus the actual values in the training set. This is done by calling the `plot_predict` route. Finally, we also show statistics about the residual errors for the model by creating a `<div>` element with a `pd_entity` attribute pointing to the residuals variable with a `<pd_options>` child element that configures a table view of all the statistics

The chart showing the predictions versus the actual training set is using the `plot_predict` route which calls the `plot_predict` method we created earlier in the Notebook. We also use the `@captureOutput` decorator to dispatch the chart image to the correct widget.

The implementation of the `plot_predict` route is shown here:

```
@route(plot_predict="true")
@captureOutput
def plot_predict(self):
    plot_predict(self.arima_model, self.train_set['Date'], 100)
```

You can find the code file here:
https://github.com/DTAIEB/Thoughtful-Data-Science/blob/master/chapter%208/sampleCode39.py

The `build_arima_model` route implementation is shown here:

```
@route(p_order="*",d_order="*",q_order="*")
def build_arima_model_screen(self, p_order, d_order, q_order):
    #Build the arima model
    self.train_set = self.parent_pixieapp.get_active_df()[:-14]
    self.test_set = self.parent_pixieapp.get_active_df()[-14:]
    self.arima_model = ARIMA(
        self.train_set['Adj. Close'], dates=self.train_set['Date'],
        order=(int(p_order),int(d_order),int(q_order))
```

```
    ).fit(disp=0)
    self.residuals = self.arima_model.resid.describe().to_frame().
reset_index()
    return """
<div class="page-header text-center">
    <h3>ARIMA Model succesfully created</h3>
<div>
<div class="row">
    <div class="col-sm-10 col-sm-offset-3">
        <div pd_render_onload pd_options="plot_predict=true">
        </div>
        <h3>Predicted values against the train set</h3>
    </div>
</div>
<div class="row">
    <div pd_render_onload pd_entity="residuals">
        <pd_options>
        {
          "handlerId": "tableView",
          "table_noschema": "true",
          "table_nosearch": "true",
          "table_nocount": "true"
        }
        </pd_options>
    </div>
    <h3><center>Residual errors statistics</center></h3>
<div>
        """
```

You can find the code file here:

https://github.com/DTAIEB/Thoughtful-Data-Science/
blob/master/chapter%208/sampleCode40.py

The following screenshot shows the result for the **Build Arima model** page:

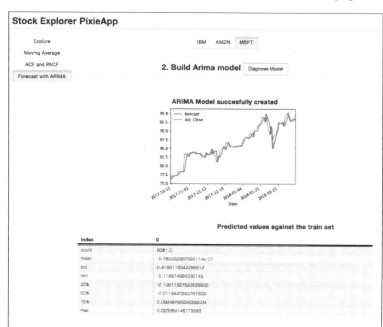

Model building page

The final screen of the forecast child app is the *diagnose model* screen invoked by the do_diagnose route. In this screen, we simply display a line chart for the DataFrame returned by the `compute_test_set_predictions` method we created earlier in the Notebook with the `train_set` and `test_set` variables. The `<div>` element for this chart is using a `pd_entity` attribute that calls an intermediary class method called `compute_test_set_predictions`. It also has a `<pd_options>` child element with the `display()` options for showing the line chart.

The following code shows the implementation of the do_diagnose_screen route:

```
    def compute_test_set_predictions(self):
        return compute_test_set_predictions(self.train_set,
self.test_set)


    @route(do_diagnose="true")
    @BaseSubApp.add_ticker_selection_markup([])
    def do_diagnose_screen(self):
        return """
<div class="page-header text-center"><h2>3. Diagnose the model against
the test set</h2></div>
<div class="row">
    <div class="col-sm-10 center" pd_render_onload pd_entity=
"compute_test_set_predictions()">
        <pd_options>
        {
          "keyFields": "Date",
          "valueFields": "forecast,test",
          "handlerId": "lineChart",
          "rendererId": "bokeh",
          "noChartCache": "true"
        }
        </pd_options>
    </div>
</div>
"""
```

You can find the code file here:

https://github.com/DTAIEB/Thoughtful-Data-Science/
blob/master/chapter%208/sampleCode41.py

The following screenshot shows the results of the diagnose page:

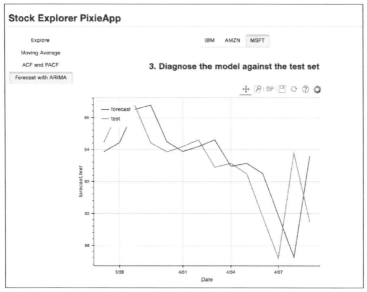

Model diagnose screen

In this section, we have shown how to improve the StockExplorer sample PixieApp to include forecasting capabilities using the ARIMA model. Incidentally, we've demonstrated how to use the PixieApp programming model to create a three-step wizard that first performs some data exploration, then configures the parameters of the model and builds it and finally diagnoses the model against the test set.

The complete implementation of the notebook can be found here:

https://github.com/DTAIEB/Thoughtful-Data-Science/blob/master/chapter%208/StockExplorer%20-%20Part%202.ipynb

Summary

In this chapter, we touched upon the topic of time series analysis and forecasting. Of course, we've only scratched the surface, and there is certainly much more to explore. It is also a very important field for the industry, especially in the finance world, with very active research. For example, we see more and more data scientists trying to build time series forecasting models based on recurrent neural network (`https://en.wikipedia.org/wiki/Recurrent_neural_network`) algorithms, with great success. We've also demonstrated how Jupyter Notebooks combined with PixieDust and the ecosystem of libraries, such as `pandas`, `numpy`, and `statsmodels`, help accelerate the development of analytics as well as its operationalization into applications that are consumable by the line of business user.

In the next chapter, we will look at another important data science use case: graphs. We'll build a sample application related to flight travel and discuss how and when we should apply graph algorithms to solve data problems.

9
US Domestic Flight Data Analysis Using Graphs

"It is a capital mistake to theorize before one has data."

– Sherlock Holmes

In this chapter, we focus on a fundamental computer science data model called graphs and the different types of algorithm commonly used on them. As a data scientist or developer, it is very important to be familiar with graphs and quickly recognize when they provide the right solution to solve a particular data problem. For example, graphs are very well suited to GPS-based applications such as Google Maps, to find the best route from point A to point B, taking into account all kinds of parameters, including whether the user is driving, walking or taking public transport, or whether the user wants the shortest route or one that maximizes the use of highways regardless of overall distance. Some of these parameters can also be real-time parameters, such as traffic conditions, and the weather. Another important class of applications that uses graphs is social networks, such as Facebook or Twitter, where vertices represent individuals and edges represent relationships, such as *is a friend*, and *follows*.

We'll start this chapter with a high-level introduction to graphs and associated graph algorithms. We'll then introduce `networkx` which is a Python library that makes it easy to load, manipulate, and visualize graph data structures as well as provide a rich set of graph algorithms. We'll continue the discussion by building sample analytics that analyzes US flight data using various graph algorithms where airports are used as vertices and flights as edges. As always, we'll also operationalize these analytics by building a simple dashboard PixieApp. We'll finish this chapter by building a forecasting model applying time series techniques we've learned in *Chapter 8, Financial Time Series Analysis and Forecasting* to historical flight data.

Introduction to graphs

The introduction of graphs and the associated graph theory is widely attributed to Leonhard Euler in 1736 when he worked on the problem of the *Seven Bridges of Königsberg* (https://en.wikipedia.org/wiki/Seven_Bridges_of_K%C3%B6nigsberg).

The city was divided by the Pregel river which at some point formed two islands, and seven bridges were built according to the layout shown in the following diagram. The problem was to find a way for a person to walk across each and every bridge once and only once and come back to the starting point. Euler proved that there was no solution to this problem and while doing this gave birth to graph theory. The fundamental idea was to transform the city diagram into a graph where each land mass is a vertex, and each bridge is an edge that linked two vertices (that is, land mass). The problem was then reduced to finding a path, which is a continuous sequence of edges and vertices, that contains each and every bridge only once.

The following diagram shows how Euler simplified the *Seven Bridges of Königsberg* problem into a graph problem:

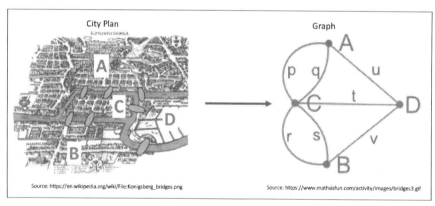

Simplifying the Seven Bridges of Königsberg problem into a graph problem

Using a more formal definition, **graphs** are the data structures that represent pairwise relationships (called **edges**) between objects (called **vertices** or **nodes**). It is common to use the following notation to represent a graph: $G = (V, E)$ where V is the set of vertices and E is the set of edges.

There are mainly two broad categories of graphs:

- **Directed graphs (called digraphs)**: The order in the pairwise relationship matters, that is, the edge (A-B) going from vertex **A** to vertex **B** is different from the edge (B-A) going from vertex **B** to vertex **A**.

- **Undirected graphs**: The order in the pairwise relationship doesn't matter, that is, edge (A-B) is the same as an edge (B-A).

The following diagram shows the representation of a sample graph both as undirected (edges have no arrows) and directed (edges have arrows):

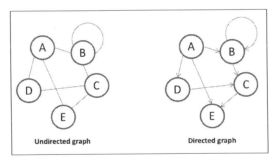

Undirected graph   Directed graph

Graph representations

There are mainly two ways of representing a graph:

- **Adjacency matrix**: Represents the graph using an n by n matrix (we'll call it A), where n is the number of vertices in the graph. The vertices are indexed using 1 to n integers. We use $A_{i,j} = 1$ to denote that an edge exists between vertex i and vertex j and $A_{i,j} = 0$ to denote that no edge exists between vertex i and vertex j. In the case of undirected graphs, we would always have $A_{i,j} = A_{j,i}$ because the order doesn't matter. However, in the case of digraphs where order matters, $A_{i,j}$ may be different from $A_{j,i}$.

The following example shows how to represent a sample graph in an adjacency matrix both directed and undirected:

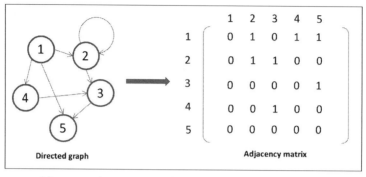

Directed graph   Adjacency matrix

Adjacency matrix representation of a graph (both directed and undirected)

It is important to note that the adjacency matrix representation has a constant space complexity which is $O(n^2)$ where n is the number of vertices, but it has a time complexity of $O(1)$ which is constant time to compute whether two vertices are connected with an edge between them. The high space complexity might be OK when the graph is dense (lots of edges) but could be a waste of space when the graph is sparse, in which case we might prefer the following adjacency list representation.

Note: The big O notation (https://en.wikipedia.org/wiki/Big_O_notation) is commonly used in code analysis to represent the performance of an algorithm by evaluating its behavior as the input size grows. It is used both for evaluating running time (number of instructions needed to run the algorithm) and space requirements (how much storage will it need over time).

- **Adjacency list**: For each vertex, we maintain a list of all the vertices connected by an edge. In the case of an undirected graph, each edge is represented twice, one for each endpoint, which is not the case for a digraph where the order matters.

The following figure shows the adjacency list representation of a graph, both directed and undirected:

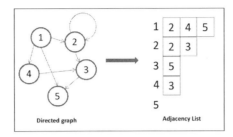

Adjacency list representation of a graph (both directed and undirected)

Contrary to the adjacency matrix representation, the adjacency list representation has a smaller space complexity which is $O\ (m + n)$ where m is the number of edges and n is the number of vertices. However, the time complexity increases to $O(m)$ compared to $O(1)$ for the adjacency matrix. For these reasons, it is preferable to use the adjacency list representation when the graph is sparsely connected (that is, doesn't have a lot of edges).

As hinted in the preceding discussion, which graph representation to use depends heavily on the graph density but also on the type of algorithms we are planning to use. In the next section, we discuss the most commonly used graph algorithms.

Graph algorithms

The following is a list of the most commonly used graph algorithms:

- **Search**: In the context of the graph, searching means finding paths between two vertices. A path is defined as a continuous sequence of edges and vertices. The motivation for searching paths in a graph can be multiple; it could be that you're interested in finding the shortest path according to some predefined distance criteria, such as the minimum number of edges (for example, GPS route mapping) or you simply want to know that a path between two vertices exists (for example, ensure that every machine in a network is reachable from any other machine). A generic algorithm to search for a path is to start from the given vertex, *discover* all the vertices that are connected to it, mark the discovered vertices as explored (so we don't find them twice) and continue the same exploration for each discovered vertex until we find the target vertex, or we run out of vertices. There are two commonly used flavors of this search algorithm: Breadth First Search and Depth First Search, each having their own use cases for which they are better suited. The difference between these two algorithms consists of the way we find the unexplored vertices:

○ **Breadth First Search (BFS)**: The unexplored nodes that are immediate neighbors are explored first. When the immediate neighborhood has been explored, start exploring the neighborhood of each node in the layer, until the end of the graph is reached. Because we are exploring all vertices that are directly connected first, this algorithm guarantees to find the shortest path which corresponds to the number of neighborhoods found. An extension to BFS is the famous Dijkstra shortest path algorithm where each edge is associated with a non-negative weight. In this case, the shortest path may not be the one with the least number of hops but rather a path that minimizes the sum of all weights. One example application of the Dijkstra shortest path is to find the shortest route between two points on a map.

○ **Depth First Search (DFS)**: For each immediate neighbor vertex, aggressively explore its neighbors first going as deeply as you can and then start backtracking when you run out of neighbors. Example of applications for DFS include finding the topological sort and strongly connected components of a digraph. For reference, a topological sort is a linear ordering of the vertices such that each vertex in the linear order follows the edge direction of the next one (that is, it doesn't move backward). See `https://en.wikipedia.org/wiki/Topological_sorting` for more information.

The following diagram demonstrates the differences in finding the unexplored nodes between BFS and DFS:

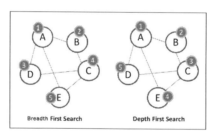

Order of finding unexplored vertices in BFS and DFS

• **Connected components and strongly connected components**: Connected components of a graph are groups of vertices where there is a path between any two vertices. Note that the definition only specifies that a path must exist which means that two vertices do not have to have an edge between them as long as a path exists. In the case of a digraph, the connected component is called a **strongly connected component** because of the additional direction constraint that requires that not only should any vertex A have a path to any other vertex B, but that B must also have a path to A.

The following diagram shows the strongly connected components or a sample directed graph:

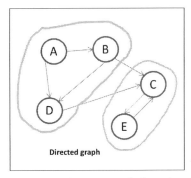

Strongly connected components of a directed graph

- **Centrality**: The centrality indicator of a vertex provides an indication of how important the vertex is with regard to the other vertices in the graph. There are multiple important applications for these centrality indices. For example, identifying the most influential person in a social network or ranking a web search by pages that are the most important, and so on.

  There are multiple indices of centrality, but we'll focus on the following four that we'll use later in this chapter:

  - **Degree**: The degree of a vertex is the number of edges for which the vertex is one of the endpoints. In the case of a digraph, it's the number of edges for which the vertex is either a source or a target, and we call **indegree** the number of edges for which the vertex is a target and **outdegree** the number of edges for which the vertex is a source.

  - **PageRank**: This is the famous algorithm developed by the founders of Google, Larry Page, and Sergey Brin. PageRank is used to rank the search results by providing a measure of importance for a given website that includes counting the number of links to that website from other websites. It also factors in an estimation of the quality of these links (that is, how trustworthy is the site linking to yours).

  - **Closeness**: Closeness centrality is inversely proportional to the average length of the shortest path between the given vertex and all the other vertices in the graph. The intuition is that the closer a vertex is to all the other nodes, the more important it is.

The closeness centrality can be calculated with the following simple equation:

$$C(x) = \frac{1}{\sum_y d(y,x)}$$

(Source: https://en.wikipedia.org/wiki/Centrality#Closeness_centrality)

Where $d(y,x)$ is the length of the edge between node x and y.

- **Shortest path betweenness**: Measure based on how many times the given vertex is part of the shortest path between any two nodes. The intuition is that the more a vertex contributes to shortest paths, the more important it is. The mathematical equation for shortest path betweenness is provided here:

$$Given\ a\ graph\ G = (V, E), then\ C_B(v) = \sum_{s \neq v \neq t \in V} \frac{\sigma_{st}(v)}{\sigma_{st}}$$

(Source: https://en.wikipedia.org/wiki/Centrality#Betweenness_centrality)

Where σ_{st} is the total number of shortest paths from vertex s to vertex t and $\sigma_{st}(v)$ is the subset of σ_{st} that pass through v.

 Note: More information on centrality can be found here: https://en.wikipedia.org/wiki/Centrality

Graph and big data

Our graph discussion has so far focused on data that can fit into a single machine, but what happens when we have very large graphs with billions of vertices and edges where loading the entire data into memory would not be possible? A natural solution would be to distribute the data across a cluster of multiple nodes which process the data in parallel and have the individual results merged to form the final answer. Fortunately, there are multiple frameworks that provide such graph-parallel capabilities, and they pretty much all include the implementation for most of the commonly-used graph algorithms. Examples of popular open-source frameworks are Apache Spark GraphX (https://spark.apache.org/graphx) and Apache Giraph (http://giraph.apache.org) which is currently used by Facebook to analyze its social network.

Without diving into too much detail, it's important to know that these frameworks are all inspired from the **bulk synchronous parallel (BSP)** model of distributed computation (`https://en.wikipedia.org/wiki/Bulk_synchronous_parallel`) which uses messages between machines to find vertices across the cluster. The key point to remember is that these frameworks are usually very easy to use, for example, it would have been fairly easy to write this chapter's analytics using Apache Spark GraphX.

In this section, we've reviewed only a fraction of all the graph algorithms available and going deeper would be beyond the scope of this book. Implementing these algorithms yourself would take a considerable amount of time, but fortunately, there are plenty of open source libraries that provide fairly complete implementations of the graph algorithms and that are easy to use and integrate into your application. In the rest of this chapter, we'll use the `networkx` open source Python library.

Getting started with the networkx graph library

Before we start, if not already done, we need to install the `networkx` library using the `pip` tool. Execute the following code in its own cell:

```
!pip install networkx
```

 Note: As always, don't forget to restart the kernel after the installation is complete.

Most of the algorithms provided by `networkx` are directly callable from the main module. Therefore a user will only need the following `import` statement:

```
import networkx as nx
```

Creating a graph

As a starting point, let's review the different types of graphs supported by `networkx` and the constructors that create empty graphs:

- `Graph`: An undirected graph with only one edge between vertices allowed. Self-loop edges are permitted. Constructor example:

    ```
    G = nx.Graph()
    ```

- `Digraph`: Subclass of `Graph` that implements a directed graph. Constructor example:

    ```
    G = nx.DiGraph()
    ```

- `MultiGraph`: Undirected graph that allows multiple edges between vertices. Constructor example:

    ```
    G = nx.MultiGraph()
    ```

- `MultiDiGraph`: Directed graph that allows multiples edges between vertices. Constructor example:

    ```
    G = nx.MultiDiGraph()
    ```

The `Graph` class provides many methods for adding and removing vertices and edges. Here is a subset of the available methods:

- `add_edge(u_of_edge, v_of_edge, **attr)`: Add an edge between vertex u and vertex v, with optional additional attributes that will be associated with the edge. The vertices u and v will automatically be created if they don't already exist in the graph.

- `remove_edge(u, v)`: Remove the edge between u and v.

- `add_node(self, node_for_adding, **attr)`: Add a node to the graph with optional additional attributes.

- `remove_node(n)`: Remove the node identified by the given argument n.

- `add_edges_from(ebunch_to_add, **attr)`: Add multiple edges in bulk with optional additional attributes. The edges must be given as a list of two-tuples (u, v) or three-tuples (u, v, d) where d is the dictionary that contains edge data.

- `add_nodes_from(self, nodes_for_adding, **attr)`: Add multiple nodes in bulk with optional additional attributes. The nodes can be provided as a list, dict, set, array, and so on.

As an exercise, let's build the directed graph we've been using as a sample from the beginning:

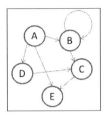

Sample graph to be created programmatically using networkx

The following code starts by creating a `DiGraph()` object, adds all the nodes in one call using the `add_nodes_from()` method, and then starts adding the edges using, for illustration, a combination of `add_edge()` and `add_edges_from()`:

```
G = nx.DiGraph()
G.add_nodes_from(['A', 'B', 'C', 'D', 'E'])
G.add_edge('A', 'B')
G.add_edge('B', 'B')
G.add_edges_from([('A', 'E'),('A', 'D'),('B', 'C'),('C', 'E'),
('D', 'C')])
```

 You can find the code file here:
https://github.com/DTAIEB/Thoughtful-Data-Science/blob/master/chapter%209/sampleCode1.py

The `Graph` class also provides easy access to its properties through variable class views. For example, you can iterate over the vertices and edges of a graph using `G.nodes` and `G.edges`, but also access an individual edge with the following notation: `G.edges[u,v]`.

The following code iterates over the nodes of a graph and prints them:

```
for n in G.nodes:
    print(n)
```

The `networkx` library also provides a rich set of prebuilt graph generators that can be useful for testing your algorithms. For example, you can easily generate a complete graph using the `complete_graph()` generator as shown in the following code:

```
G_complete = nx.complete_graph(10)
```

You can find a complete list of all the available graph generators here:
`https://networkx.github.io/documentation/networkx-2.1/`
`reference/generators.html#generators`

Visualizing a graph

NetworkX supports multiple rendering engines including Matplotlib, Graphviz AGraph (`http://pygraphviz.github.io`) and Graphviz with pydot (`https://github.com/erocarrera/pydot`). Even though Graphviz provides very powerful drawing capabilities, I found it very hard to install. Matplotlib, however, is already preinstalled in Jupyter Notebooks which gets you started very quickly.

The core drawing function is called `draw_networkx` which takes a graph as an argument and a bunch of optional keyword arguments that let you style the graph, such as color, width, and the label font of the nodes and edges. The overall layout of the graph drawing is configured by passing the `GraphLayout` object through the `pos` keyword argument. The default layout is `spring_layout` (which uses a force-directed algorithm), but NetworkX supports many others, including `circular_layout`, `random_layout`, and `spectral_layout`. You can find a list of all the available layouts here: `https://networkx.github.io/documentation/networkx-2.1/reference/drawing.html#module-networkx.drawing.layout`.

For convenience, `networkx` encapsulates each of these layouts into its own high-level drawing methods that call reasonable default values so that the caller doesn't have to deal with the intricacies of each of these layouts. For example, the `draw()` method will draw the graph with a `sprint_layout`, `draw_circular()` with a `circular_layout`, and `draw_random()` with a `random_layout`.

In the following sample code, we use the `draw()` method to visualize the `G_complete` graph we created earlier:

```
%matplotlib inline
import matplotlib.pyplot as plt
nx.draw(G_complete, with_labels=True)
plt.show()
```

You can find the code file here:
`https://github.com/DTAIEB/Thoughtful-Data-Science/`
`blob/master/chapter%209/sampleCode2.py`

The results are shown in the following output:

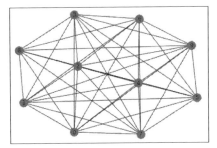

Drawing of a complete graph with 10 nodes

Drawing graphs with `networkx` is both easy and fun, and because it's using Matplotlib, you can beautify them even further using the Matplotlib drawing capabilities. I encourage the reader to experiment further by visualizing different graphs in a Notebook. In the next section, we'll start implementing a sample application that analyzes flight data using graph algorithms.

Part 1 – Loading the US domestic flight data into a graph

To initialize the Notebook, let's run the following code, in its own cell, to import the packages which we'll be using quite heavily in the rest of this chapter:

```
import pixiedust
import networkx as nx
import pandas as pd
import matplotlib.pyplot as plt
```

We'll also be using the *2015 Flight Delays and Cancellations* dataset available on the Kaggle website at this location: `https://www.kaggle.com/usdot/datasets`. The dataset is composed of three files:

- `airports.csv`: List of all U.S. airports including their **IATA** code (**International Air Transport Association**: `https://openflights.org/data.html`), city, state, longitude, and latitude.

- `airlines.csv`: List of U.S. airlines including their IATA code.

- `flights.csv`: List of flights that occurred in 2015. This data includes date, origin and destination airports, scheduled and actual times, and delays.

The `flights.csv` file contains close to 6 million records, which need to be cleaned up to remove all flights that do not have an IATA three letter code in the origin or destination airport. We also want to remove the rows that have a missing value in the `ELAPSED_TIME` column. Failure to do so would cause problems when we load the data into a graph structure. Another issue is that the dataset contains a few time columns, such as `DEPARTURE_TIME`, and `ARRIVAL_TIME`, and to save space, these columns only store the time in HHMM format, while the actual date is stored in the YEAR, MONTH, and DAY column. One of the analyses we will do in this chapter will need a complete datetime for the `DEPARTURE_TIME`, and since it is a time-consuming operation to do this transformation, we do it now and store it in the processed version of `flights.csv` that we'll store on GitHub. This operation uses the pandas `apply()` method that is called with the `to_datetime()` function and `axis=1` (indicating that the transformation is applied on each row).

Another issue is that we want to store the files on GitHub, but there is a maximum file size limitation of 100 M. So, to make the file smaller than 100 M, we also remove some of the columns that won't be needed in the analysis we're trying to build and then zip the file before storing it on GitHub. Of course, another benefit is that the DataFrame will load faster with a smaller file.

After downloading the files from the Kaggle website, we run the following code which first loads the CSV file into a pandas DataFrame, remove the unwanted rows and columns, and write the data back to a file:

Note: The original data is stored in a file called `flights.raw.csv`.

Running the following code may take some time due to the large size of the file which contains 6 million records.

```
import pandas as pd
import datetime
import numpy as np

# clean up the flights data in flights.csv
flights = pd.read_csv('flights.raw.csv', low_memory=False)

# select only the rows that have a 3 letter IATA code in the ORIGIN
and DESTINATION airports
mask = (flights["ORIGIN_AIRPORT"].str.len() == 3) &
(flights["DESTINATION_AIRPORT"].str.len() == 3)
flights = flights[ mask ]

# remove the unwanted columns
dropped_columns=["SCHEDULED_DEPARTURE","SCHEDULED_TIME",
```

```
"CANCELLATION_REASON","DIVERTED","DIVERTED","TAIL_NUMBER",
"TAXI_OUT","WHEELS_OFF","WHEELS_ON",
"TAXI_IN","SCHEDULED_ARRIVAL", "ARRIVAL_TIME", "AIR_SYSTEM_
DELAY","SECURITY_DELAY",
"AIRLINE_DELAY","LATE_AIRCRAFT_DELAY", "WEATHER_DELAY"]
flights.drop(dropped_columns, axis=1, inplace=True)

# remove the row that have NA in the ELAPSED_TIME column
flights.dropna(subset=["ELAPSED_TIME"], inplace=True)

# remove the row that have NA in the DEPARTURE_TIME column
flights.dropna(subset=["ELAPSED_TIME"], inplace=True)

# Create a new DEPARTURE_TIME columns that has the actual datetime
def to_datetime(row):
    departure_time = str(int(row["DEPARTURE_TIME"])).zfill(4)
    hour = int(departure_time[0:2])
    return datetime.datetime(year=row["YEAR"], month=row["MONTH"],
                             day=row["DAY"],
                             hour = 0 if hour >= 24 else hour,
                             minute=int(departure_time[2:4])
                             )
flights["DEPARTURE_TIME"] = flights.apply(to_datetime, axis=1)

# write the data back to file without the index
flights.to_csv('flights.csv', index=False)
```

 You can find the code file here:

https://github.com/DTAIEB/Thoughtful-Data-Science/
blob/master/chapter%209/sampleCode3.py

 Note: As documented in the pandas.read_csv documentation
(http://pandas.pydata.org/pandas-docs/version/0.23/
generated/pandas.read_csv.html), we use the keyword argument
low_memory=False to make sure the data is not loaded in chunks
which could cause problems with type inference, especially with very
large files.

For convenience, the three files are stored at the following GitHub location:
https://github.com/DTAIEB/Thoughtful-Data-Science/tree/master/
chapter%209/USFlightsAnalysis.

The following code uses the `pixiedust.sampleData()` method to load the data into three pandas DataFrames corresponding to `airlines`, `airports`, and `flights`:

```
airports = pixiedust.sampleData("https://github.com/DTAIEB/Thoughtful-
Data-Science/raw/master/chapter%209/USFlightsAnalysis/airports.csv")
airlines = pixiedust.sampleData("https://github.com/DTAIEB/Thoughtful-
Data-Science/raw/master/chapter%209/USFlightsAnalysis/airlines.csv")
flights = pixiedust.sampleData("https://github.com/DTAIEB/Thoughtful-
Data-Science/raw/master/chapter%209/USFlightsAnalysis/flights.zip")
```

You can find the code file here:

https://github.com/DTAIEB/Thoughtful-Data-Science/
blob/master/chapter%209/sampleCode4.py

Note: The GitHub URL uses the `/raw/` segment which indicates that we want to download the raw file as opposed to the HTML for the corresponding GitHub page.

The next step is to load the data into a `networkx` directed weighted graph object using the `flights` DataFrame as the `edge` list and the values from the `ELAPSED_TIME` column as the weight. We first deduplicate all the flights that have the same airports as origin and destination, by grouping them using the `pandas.groupby()` method with a multi-index that has `ORIGIN_AIRPORT` and `DESTINATION_AIRPORT` as the keys. We then select the `ELAPSED_TIME` column from the `DataFrameGroupBy` object and aggregate the results using the `mean()` method. This will give us a new DataFrame that has the mean average `ELAPSED_TIME` for each flight with the same origin and destination airport:

```
edges = flights.groupby(["ORIGIN_AIRPORT","DESTINATION_AIRPORT"])
[["ELAPSED_TIME"]].mean()
edges
```

You can find the code file here:

https://github.com/DTAIEB/Thoughtful-Data-Science/
blob/master/chapter%209/sampleCode5.py

The results are shown in the following screenshot:

ORIGIN_AIRPORT	DESTINATION_AIRPORT	ELAPSED_TIME
ABE	ATL	127.415350
	DTW	101.923741
	ORD	130.298762
ABI	DFW	53.951591
ABQ	ATL	174.822278
	BWI	215.028112
	CLT	193.168421
	DAL	95.107051
	DEN	75.268199
	DFW	103.641714
	HOU	115.464363
	IAH	125.548387
	JFK	232.306273
	LAS	88.696897
	LAX	120.412549
	MCI	106.373802
	MCO	213.412371
	MDW	155.709375
	MSP	147.079070

Flights grouped by origin and destination with mean average ELAPSED_TIME

Before using this DataFrame to create the directed graph, we need to reset the index from a multi-index to a regular single index converting the index columns into regular columns. For that, we simply use the `reset_index()` method as shown here:

```
edges = edges.reset_index()
edges
```

You can find the code file here:

https://github.com/DTAIEB/Thoughtful-Data-Science/blob/master/chapter%209/sampleCode6.py

We now have a DataFrame with the right shape, ready to be used to create the directed graph, as shown in the following screenshot:

	ORIGIN_AIRPORT	DESTINATION_AIRPORT	ELAPSED_TIME
0	ABE	ATL	127.415350
1	ABE	DTW	101.923741
2	ABE	ORD	130.298762
3	ABI	DFW	53.951591
4	ABQ	ATL	174.822278
5	ABQ	BWI	215.028112
6	ABQ	CLT	193.168421
7	ABQ	DAL	95.107051
8	ABQ	DEN	75.268199
9	ABQ	DFW	103.641714
10	ABQ	HOU	115.464363
11	ABQ	IAH	125.548387
12	ABQ	JFK	232.306273
13	ABQ	LAS	88.696897
14	ABQ	LAX	120.412549
15	ABQ	MCI	106.373802
16	ABQ	MCO	213.412371

Flights grouped by origin and destination with mean average ELAPSED_TIME and a single index

To create the directed weighted graph, we use the NetworkX `from_pandas_edgelist()` method which takes a pandas DataFrame as the input source. We also specify the source and target columns, as well as the weight column (in our case ELAPSED_TIME). Finally, we tell NetworkX that we want to create a directed graph by using the `create_using` keyword arguments, passing an instance of DiGraph as a value.

The following code shows how to call the `from_pandas_edgelist()` method:

```
flight_graph = nx.from_pandas_edgelist(
    flights, "ORIGIN_AIRPORT","DESTINATION_AIRPORT",
    "ELAPSED_TIME",
    create_using = nx.DiGraph() )
```

You can find the code file here:

```
https://github.com/DTAIEB/Thoughtful-Data-Science/
blob/master/chapter%209/sampleCode7.py
```

 Note: NetworkX supports the creation of graphs by converting from multiple formats including dictionaries, lists, NumPy and SciPy matrices and of course pandas. You can find more information about these conversion capabilities here:

```
https://networkx.github.io/documentation/networkx-2.1/
reference/convert.html
```

We can quickly validate that our graph has the right values by directly printing its nodes and edges:

```
print("Nodes: {}".format(flight_graph.nodes))
print("Edges: {}".format(flight_graph.edges))
```

 You can find the code file here:

```
https://github.com/DTAIEB/Thoughtful-Data-Science/
blob/master/chapter%209/sampleCode8.py
```

Which produces the following output (truncated):

```
Nodes: ['BOS', 'TYS', 'RKS', 'AMA', 'BUF', 'BHM', 'PPG', …,
'CWA', 'DAL', 'BFL']
Edges: [('BOS', 'LAX'), ('BOS', 'SJC'), ..., ('BFL', 'SFO'),
('BFL', 'IAH')]
```

We can also create better visualization by using the built-in drawing APIs available in networkx which support multiple rendering engines including Matplotlib, Graphviz AGraph (http://pygraphviz.github.io) and Graphviz with pydot (https://github.com/erocarrera/pydot).

For simplicity, we'll use the NetworkX draw() method which uses the readily available Matplotlib engine. To beautify the visualization, we configure it with proper width and height (12, 12) and add a colormap with vivid color (we use the cool and spring colormap from matplolib.cm, see: https://matplotlib.org/2.0.2/examples/color/colormaps_reference.html).

The following code shows the implementation of the graph visualization:

```
import matplotlib.cm as cm
fig = plt.figure(figsize = (12,12))
nx.draw(flight_graph, arrows=True, with_labels=True,
```

```
        width = 0.5,style="dotted",
        node_color=range(len(flight_graph)),
        cmap=cm.get_cmap(name="cool"),
        edge_color=range(len(flight_graph.edges)),
        edge_cmap=cm.get_cmap(name="spring")
    )
plt.show()
```

> You can find the code file here:
>
> https://github.com/DTAIEB/Thoughtful-Data-Science/
> blob/master/chapter%209/sampleCode9.py

Which produces the following results:

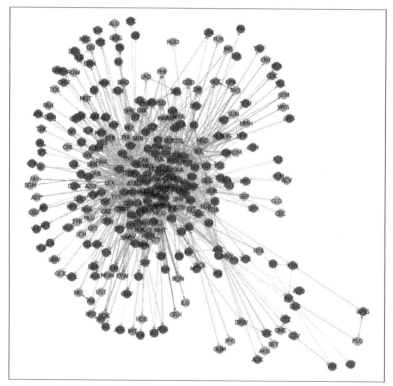

Quick visualization of our directed graph using Matplotlib

In the preceding chart, the nodes are positioned using a default graph layout called `spring_layout`, which is a force-directed layout. One benefit of this layout is that it quickly reveals the nodes with the most edge connections which are located at the center of the graph. We can change the graph layout by using the `pos` keyword argument when calling the `draw()` method. `networkx` supports other types of layout including `circular_layout`, `random_layout`, `shell_layout`, and `spectral_layout`.

For example, using a `random_layout`:

```
import matplotlib.cm as cm
fig = plt.figure(figsize = (12,12))
nx.draw(flight_graph, arrows=True, with_labels=True,
        width = 0.5,style="dotted",
        node_color=range(len(flight_graph)),
        cmap=cm.get_cmap(name="cool"),
        edge_color=range(len(flight_graph.edges)),
        edge_cmap=cm.get_cmap(name="spring"),
        pos = nx.random_layout(flight_graph)
        )
plt.show()
```

 You can find the code file here:

https://github.com/DTAIEB/Thoughtful-Data-Science/
blob/master/chapter%209/sampleCode10.py

We get the following results:

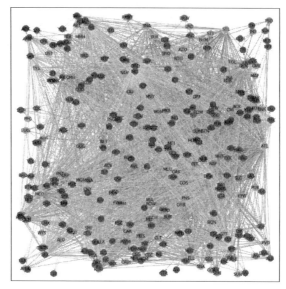

Flight data graph using a random_layout

 Note: You can find more information about these layouts here:
`https://networkx.github.io/documentation/networkx-2.1/`
`reference/drawing.html`

Graph centrality

The next interesting thing to analyze about the graph is its centrality indices which allow us to discover which nodes are the most important vertices. As an exercise, we'll compute four types of centrality index: **degree, PageRank, closeness**, and **shortest path betweenness**. We'll then augment the airports DataFrame to add a column for each of the centrality indices and visualize the results in a Mapbox map using PixieDust `display()`.

Computing the degree of the digraph is very easy with `networkx`; simply use the `degree` property of the `flight_graph` object as follows:

```
print(flight_graph.degree)
```

This outputs an array of tuples with the airport code and the degree index as follows:

```
[('BMI', 14), ('RDM', 8), ('SBN', 13), ('PNS', 18), .........., ('JAC', 26),
('MEM', 46)]
```

We now want to add a DEGREE column to the airport DataFrame that contains the degree value from the preceding array for each of the airport rows. To do that, we'll need to create a new DataFrame that has two columns: IATA_CODE and DEGREE and perform a pandas merge() operation on the IATA_CODE.

The merge operation is illustrated in the following diagram:

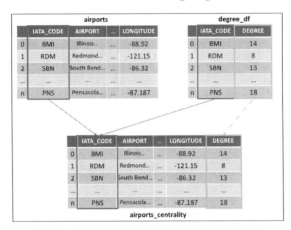

Merging the degree DataFrame to the airports DataFrame

The following code shows how to implement the aforementioned steps. We first create a JSON payload by iterating over the flight_path.degree output and use the pd.DataFrame() constructor to create the DataFrame. We then use pd.merge() using airports and degree_df as arguments. We also use the on argument with value IATA_CODE which is the key column we'll want to do the join on:

```
degree_df = pd.DataFrame([{"IATA_CODE":k, "DEGREE":v} for k,v in
flight_graph.degree], columns=["IATA_CODE", "DEGREE"])
airports_centrality = pd.merge(airports, degree_df, on='IATA_CODE')
airports_centrality
```

You can find the code file here:

https://github.com/DTAIEB/Thoughtful-Data-Science/
blob/master/chapter%209/sampleCode11.py

The results are shown in the following screenshot:

	IATA_CODE	AIRPORT	CITY	STATE	COUNTRY	LATITUDE	LONGITUDE	DEGREE
0	ABE	Lehigh Valley International Airport	Allentown	PA	USA	40.65236	-75.44040	7
1	ABI	Abilene Regional Airport	Abilene	TX	USA	32.41132	-99.68190	2
2	ABQ	Albuquerque International Sunport	Albuquerque	NM	USA	35.04022	-106.60919	46
3	ABR	Aberdeen Regional Airport	Aberdeen	SD	USA	45.44906	-98.42183	2
4	ABY	Southwest Georgia Regional Airport	Albany	GA	USA	31.53552	-84.19447	2
5	ACK	Nantucket Memorial Airport	Nantucket	MA	USA	41.25305	-70.06018	6
6	ACT	Waco Regional Airport	Waco	TX	USA	31.61129	-97.23052	2
7	ACV	Arcata Airport	Arcata/Eureka	CA	USA	40.97812	-124.10862	2
8	ACY	Atlantic City International Airport	Atlantic City	NJ	USA	39.45758	-74.57717	20
9	ADK	Adak Airport	Adak	AK	USA	51.87796	-176.64603	2
10	ADQ	Kodiak Airport	Kodiak	AK	USA	57.74997	-152.49386	2
11	AEX	Alexandria International Airport	Alexandria	LA	USA	31.32737	-92.54856	6
12	AGS	Augusta Regional Airport (Bush Field)	Augusta	GA	USA	33.36996	-81.96450	5

Airport DataFrame augmented with the DEGREE column

To visualize the data in a Mapbox map, we simply use `PixieDust.display()` on the `airport_centrality` DataFrame:

```
display(airports_centrality)
```

The following screenshot shows the options dialog:

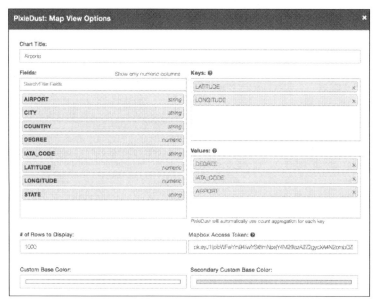

Mapbox options for displaying the airports

After clicking **OK** on the options dialog, we get the following results:

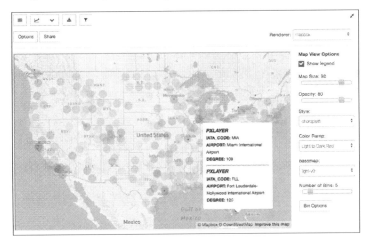

Showing the airport with degree centrality

For the other centrality indices, we can notice that the corresponding computation functions all return a JSON output (as opposed to an array for the degree attribute) with the IATA_CODE airport code as key and the centrality index as value.

For example, if we are computing the PageRank using the following code:

```
nx.pagerank(flight_graph)
```

We get the following results:

```
{'ABE': 0.0011522441195896051,
 'ABI': 0.0006671948649909588,
 ...
 'YAK': 0.001558809391270303,
 'YUM': 0.0006214341604372096}
```

With this in mind, instead of repeating the same steps as we did for degree, we can implement a generic function called compute_centrality() that takes the function that computes the centrality and a column name as arguments, create a temporary DataFrame that contains the computed centrality values, and merge it with the airports_centrality DataFrame.

The following code shows the implementation for compute_centrality():

```
from six import iteritems
def compute_centrality(g, centrality_df, compute_fn, col_name, *args,
```

```
**kwargs):
    # create a temporary DataFrame that contains the computed
centrality values
    temp_df = pd.DataFrame(
        [{"IATA_CODE":k, col_name:v} for k,v in iteritems
(compute_fn(g, *args, **kwargs))],
        columns=["IATA_CODE", col_name]
    )
    # make sure to remove the col_name from the centrality_df
is already there
    if col_name in centrality_df.columns:
        centrality_df.drop([col_name], axis=1, inplace=True)
    # merge the 2 DataFrame on the IATA_CODE column
    centrality_df = pd.merge(centrality_df, temp_df, on='IATA_CODE')
    return centrality_df
```

You can find the code file here:

```
https://github.com/DTAIEB/Thoughtful-Data-Science/
blob/master/chapter%209/sampleCode12.py
```

We can now simply call the compute_centrality() method with the three compute functions nx.pagerank(), nx.closeness_centrality(), and nx.betweenness_centrality() with the columns PAGE_RANK, CLOSENESS, and BETWEENNESS respectively as shown in the following code:

```
airports_centrality = compute_centrality(flight_graph, airports_
centrality, nx.pagerank, "PAGE_RANK")
airports_centrality = compute_centrality(flight_graph, airports_
centrality, nx.closeness_centrality, "CLOSENESS")
airports_centrality = compute_centrality(
    flight_graph, airports_centrality, nx.betweenness_centrality,
"BETWEENNESS", k=len(flight_graph))
airports_centrality
```

You can find the code file here:

```
https://github.com/DTAIEB/Thoughtful-Data-Science/
blob/master/chapter%209/sampleCode13.py
```

The `airports_centrality` DataFrame now has the extra columns as shown in the following output:

	IATA_CODE	AIRPORT	CITY	STATE	COUNTRY	LATITUDE	LONGITUDE	DEGREE	PAGE_RANK	CLOSENESS	BETWEENNESS
0	ABE	Lehigh Valley International Airport	Allentown	PA	USA	40.65236	-75.44040	7	0.001152	0.423483	0.000000e+00
1	ABI	Abilene Regional Airport	Abilene	TX	USA	32.41132	-99.68190	2	0.000667	0.392901	0.000000e+00
2	ABQ	Albuquerque International Sunport	Albuquerque	NM	USA	35.04022	-106.60919	46	0.004145	0.497674	6.023268e-05
3	ABR	Aberdeen Regional Airport	Aberdeen	SD	USA	45.44906	-98.42183	2	0.000647	0.379433	0.000000e+00
4	ABY	Southwest Georgia Regional Airport	Albany	GA	USA	31.53552	-84.19447	2	0.000655	0.402760	0.000000e+00
5	ACK	Nantucket Memorial Airport	Nantucket	MA	USA	41.25305	-70.06018	6	0.000912	0.382302	0.000000e+00
6	ACT	Waco Regional Airport	Waco	TX	USA	31.61129	-97.23052	2	0.000667	0.392901	0.000000e+00
7	ACV	Arcata Airport	Arcata/Eureka	CA	USA	40.97812	-124.10862	2	0.000638	0.382712	0.000000e+00
8	ACY	Atlantic City International Airport	Atlantic City	NJ	USA	39.45758	-74.57717	20	0.002094	0.432615	1.968172e-05
9	ADK	Adak Airport	Adak	AK	USA	51.87796	-176.64603	2	0.000753	0.337539	0.000000e+00
10	ADQ	Kodiak Airport	Kodiak	AK	USA	57.74997	-152.49386	2	0.000753	0.337539	0.000000e+00

Airports DataFrame augmented with PAGE_RANK, CLOSENESS and BETWEENNESS values

As an exercise, we can verify that the four centrality indices provide consistent results for the top airports. Using the pandas `nlargest()` method, we can get the top 10 airports for the four indices as shown in the following code:

```
for col_name in ["DEGREE", "PAGE_RANK", "CLOSENESS", "BETWEENNESS"]:
    print("{} : {}".format(
        col_name,
        airports_centrality.nlargest(10, col_name)["IATA_CODE"].
values)
    )
```

You can find the code file here:
https://github.com/DTAIEB/Thoughtful-Data-Science/
blob/master/chapter%209/sampleCode14.py

Which produces the following results:

```
DEGREE : ['ATL' 'ORD' 'DFW' 'DEN' 'MSP' 'IAH' 'DTW' 'SLC' 'EWR' 'LAX']
PAGE_RANK : ['ATL' 'ORD' 'DFW' 'DEN' 'MSP' 'IAH' 'DTW' 'SLC' 'SFO'
'LAX']
CLOSENESS : ['ATL' 'ORD' 'DFW' 'DEN' 'MSP' 'IAH' 'DTW' 'SLC' 'EWR'
'LAX']
BETWEENNESS : ['ATL' 'DFW' 'ORD' 'DEN' 'MSP' 'SLC' 'DTW' 'ANC'
'IAH' 'SFO']
```

As we can see, Atlanta airport comes up as the top airport for all centrality indices. As an exercise, let's create a generic method called `visualize_neighbors()` that visualizes all the neighbors of a given node and call it with the Atlanta node. In this method, we create a subgraph centered around the parent node by adding an edge from itself to all its neighbors. We use the NetworkX `neighbors()` method to get all the neighbors of a specific node.

The following code shows the implementation of the `visualize_neighbors()` method:

```
import matplotlib.cm as cm
def visualize_neighbors(parent_node):
    fig = plt.figure(figsize = (12,12))
    # Create a subgraph and add an edge from the parent node to all
its neighbors
    graph = nx.DiGraph()
    for neighbor in flight_graph.neighbors(parent_node):
        graph.add_edge(parent_node, neighbor)
    # draw the subgraph
    nx.draw(graph, arrows=True, with_labels=True,
            width = 0.5,style="dotted",
            node_color=range(len(graph)),
            cmap=cm.get_cmap(name="cool"),
            edge_color=range(len(graph.edges)),
            edge_cmap=cm.get_cmap(name="spring"),
        )
    plt.show()
```

You can find the code file here:
https://github.com/DTAIEB/Thoughtful-Data-Science/
blob/master/chapter%209/sampleCode15.py

We then call the `visualize_neighbors()` method on the ATL node:

```
visualize_neighbors("ATL")
```

Which produces the following output:

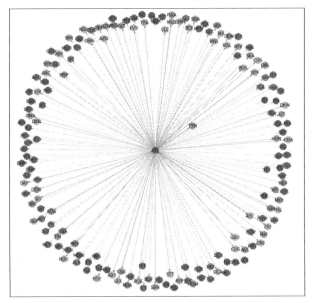

Visualization of the top node ATL and its neighbors

We complete this *Part 1* section by computing the shortest path between two nodes using the famous Dijkstra algorithm (https://en.wikipedia.org/wiki/ Dijkstra%27s_algorithm). We'll experiment with different weight attributes to check if we are getting different results.

As an example, let's compute the shortest path between Boston Logan Airport in Massachusetts (BOS) and Pasco Tri-Cities Airport in Washington (PSC) using the NetworkX dijkstra_path() method (https://networkx.github.io/ documentation/networkx-2.1/reference/algorithms/generated/networkx. algorithms.shortest_paths.weighted.dijkstra_path.html).

We first use the ELAPSED_TIME column as the weight attribute:

Note: As a reminder, ELAPSED_TIME is the average flight time for each of the flights with the same origin and destination airports that we computed earlier in this section.

```
nx.dijkstra_path(flight_graph, "BOS", "PSC", weight="ELAPSED_TIME")
```

Which returns:

```
['BOS', 'MSP', 'PSC']
```

Unfortunately, the centrality indices we computed earlier are not part of the
`flight_graph` DataFrame, so using it as the column name for the `weight` attribute
won't work. However, the `dijkstra_path()` also allows us to use a function
to dynamically compute the weight. Since we want to try for different centrality
indices, we need to create a factory method (`https://en.wikipedia.org/wiki/`
`Factory_method_pattern`) that will create a function for a given centrality index
passed as an argument. This argument is used as a closure for a nested wrapper
function that conforms to the `dijkstra_path()` method's `weight` argument. We also
use a `cache` dictionary to remember the computed weights for a given airport, since
the algorithm will call the function multiple times for the same airport. If the weight
is not in the cache, we look it up in the `airports_centrality` DataFrame using the
`centrality_indice_col` parameter. The final weight is computed by getting the
inverse of the centrality value, since the Dijkstra algorithm favors paths with shorter
distances.

The following code shows the implementation of the `compute_weight` factory
method:

```
# use a cache so we don't recompute the weight for the same airport
every time
cache = {}
def compute_weight(centrality_indice_col):
    # wrapper function that conform to the dijkstra weight argument
    def wrapper(source, target, attribute):
        # try the cache first and compute the weight if not there
        source_weight = cache.get(source, None)
        if source_weight is None:
            # look up the airports_centrality for the value
            source_weight = airports_centrality.loc[airports_
centrality["IATA_CODE"] == source][centrality_indice_col].values[0]
            cache[source] = source_weight
        target_weight = cache.get(target, None)
        if target_weight is None:
            target_weight = airports_centrality.loc[airports_
centrality["IATA_CODE"] == target][centrality_indice_col].values[0]
            cache[target] = target_weight
        # Return weight is inversely proportional to the computed
weighted since
        # the Dijkstra algorithm give precedence to shorter distances
```

```
        return float(1/source_weight) + float(1/target_weight)
    return wrapper
```

 You can find the code file here:

`https://github.com/DTAIEB/Thoughtful-Data-Science/`
`blob/master/chapter%209/sampleCode16.py`

We can now call the NetworkX `dijkstra_path()` method for each of the centrality indices. Note that we don't use BETWEENNESS because some of the values are equal to zero which can't be used as a weight. We also need to clear the cache before calling the `dijkstra_path()` method because using different centrality indices will produce different values for each airport.

The following code shows how to compute the shortest path for each centrality index:

```
for col_name in ["DEGREE", "PAGE_RANK", "CLOSENESS"]:
    #clear the cache
    cache.clear()
    print("{} : {}".format(
        col_name,
        nx.dijkstra_path(flight_graph, "BOS", "PSC",
                        weight=compute_weight(col_name))
    ))
```

 You can find the code file here:

`https://github.com/DTAIEB/Thoughtful-Data-Science/`
`blob/master/chapter%209/sampleCode17.py`

The following result is produced:

```
DEGREE : ['BOS', 'DEN', 'PSC']
PAGE_RANK : ['BOS', 'DEN', 'PSC']
CLOSENESS : ['BOS', 'DEN', 'PSC']
```

It is interesting to note that, as expected, the computed shortest path is the same for the three centrality indices, going through Denver airport which is a top central airport. However, it is not the same as the one computed using the ELAPSED_TIME weight which would have us go through Minneapolis instead.

In this section, we have shown how to load US flight data into a graph data structure, compute different centrality indices and use them to compute the shortest path between airports. We also discussed different ways of visualizing the graph data.

The complete Notebook for *Part 1* can be found here:

```
https://github.com/DTAIEB/Thoughtful-Data-Science/
blob/master/chapter%209/USFlightsAnalysis/US%20
Flight%20data%20analysis%20-%20Part%201.ipynb
```

In the next section, we'll create the USFlightsAnalysis PixieApp that operationalizes these analytics.

Part 2 – Creating the USFlightsAnalysis PixieApp

For the first iteration of our USFlightsAnalysis, we want to implement a simple user story that leverages the analytics created in *Part 1*:

- The welcome screen will show two drop-down controls for selecting an origin and a destination airport
- When an airport is selected, we show a graph showing the selected airports and its immediate neighbors
- When both airports are selected, the user clicks on the **Analyze** button to show a Mapbox map with all the airports
- The user can select one of the centrality indices available as checkboxes to show the shortest flight path according to the selected centrality

Let's first look at the implementation for the welcome screen which is implemented in the default route of the USFlightsAnalysis PixieApp. The following code defines the USFlightsAnalysis class which is decorated with the @PixieApp decorator to make it a PixieApp. It contains a main_screen() method that is decorated with the @route() decorator to make it the default route. This method returns an HTML fragment that will be used as the welcome screen when the PixieApp starts. The HTML fragment is composed of two parts: one that shows the drop-down control for selecting the origin airport and one that contains the drop-down control for selecting the destination airport. We use a Jinja2 {%for...%} loop that goes over each of the airports (returned by the get_airports() method) to generate a set of <options> elements. Under each of these controls, we add a placeholder <div> element that will host the graph visualization when an airport is selected.

> **Note**: As always, we use the [[USFlightsAnalysis]] notation to denote that the code shows only a partial implementation and therefore the reader should not attempt to run it as is until the full implementation is provided.
>
> We'll explain later on why the USFlightsAnalysis class inherits from the MapboxBase class.

[[USFlightsAnalysis]]

```
from pixiedust.display.app import *
from pixiedust.apps.mapboxBase import MapboxBase
from collections import OrderedDict


@PixieApp
class USFlightsAnalysis(MapboxBase):
    ...
    @route()
    def main_screen(self):
        return """
<style>
    div.outer-wrapper {
        display: table;width:100%;height:300px;
    }
    div.inner-wrapper {
        display: table-cell;vertical-align: middle;height: 100%;width:
100%;
    }
</style>
<div class="outer-wrapper">
    <div class="inner-wrapper">
        <div class="col-sm-6">
            <div class="rendererOpt" style="font-weight:bold">
                Select origin airport:
            </div>
            <div>
                <select id="origin_airport{{prefix}}"
                        pd_refresh="origin_graph{{prefix}}">
                    <option value="" selected></option>
                    {%for code, airport in this.get_airports() %}
                    <option value="{{code}}">{{code}} - {{airport}}</
option>
                    {%endfor%}
                </select>
            </div>
            <div id="origin_graph{{prefix}}" pd_options="visualize_
```

```
graph=$val(origin_airport{{prefix}})"></div>
        </div>
        <div class="input-group col-sm-6">
            <div class="rendererOpt" style="font-weight:bold">
                Select destination airport:
            </div>
            <div>
                <select id="destination_airport{{prefix}}"
                        pd_refresh="destination_graph{{prefix}}">
                    <option value="" selected></option>
                    {%for code, airport in this.get_airports() %}
                    <option value="{{code}}">{{code}} - {{airport}}</
option>
                    {%endfor%}
                </select>
            </div>
            <div id="destination_graph{{prefix}}"
pd_options="visualize_graph=$val(destination_airport{{prefix}})">
            </div>
        </div>
    </div>
</div>
<div style="text-align:center">
    <button class="btn btn-default" type="button"
pd_options="org_airport=$val(origin_airport{{prefix}});dest_
airport=$val(destination_airport{{prefix}})">
        <pd_script type="preRun">
            if ($("#origin_airport{{prefix}}").val() == "" ||
$("#destination_airport{{prefix}}").val() == ""){
                alert("Please select an origin and destination
airport");
                return false;
            }
            return true;
        </pd_script>
        Analyze
    </button>
</div>
"""


def get_airports(self):
    return [tuple(l) for l in airports_centrality[["IATA_CODE",
"AIRPORT"]].values.tolist()]
```

You can find the code file here:

https://github.com/DTAIEB/Thoughtful-Data-Science/
blob/master/chapter%209/sampleCode18.py

When the user selects the origin airport, a `pd_refresh` targetted at the placeholder `<div>` element with ID origin_graph{{prefix}}, is triggered. In turn, this `<div>` element triggers a route using the state: visualize_graph=$val(origin_airport{{prefix}}. As a reminder, the $val() directive is resolved at runtime by fetching the airport value of the origin_airport{{prefix}} drop-down element. A similar implementation is used for the destination airport.

The code for the `visualize_graph` route is provided here. It simply calls the `visualize_neighbors()` method that we implemented in *Part 1*, which we slightly change in *Part 2* to add an optional figure size parameter to accommodate the size of the host `<div>` element. As a reminder, we also use the @captureOutput decorator since the `visualize_neighbors()` method is directly writing to the output of the selected cell:

```
[[USFlightsAnalysis]]
@route(visualize_graph="*")
@captureOutput
def visualize_graph_screen(self, visualize_graph):
    visualize_neighbors(visualize_graph, (5,5))
```

You can find the code file here:

https://github.com/DTAIEB/Thoughtful-Data-Science/
blob/master/chapter%209/sampleCode19.py

The `Analyze` button is triggering the `compute_path_screen()` route which is associated with the `org_airport` and `dest_airport` state parameters. We also want to make sure that both airports are selected before allowing the `compute_path_screen()` route to proceed. To do that, we use a `<pd_script>` child element with type="preRun" that contains JavaScript code that will be executed before the route is triggered. The contract is for this code to return the Boolean `true` if we want to let the route proceed, or to return `false` otherwise.

For the `Analyze` button we check that both drop-downs have a value and return `true` if that's the case or else raise an error message and return `false`:

```
<button class="btn btn-default" type="button" pd_options="org_
airport=$val(origin_airport{{prefix}});dest_airport=$val(destination_
airport{{prefix}})">
```

```
<pd_script type="preRun">
    if ($("#origin_airport{{prefix}}").val() == "" ||
$("#destination_airport{{prefix}}").val() == ""){
        alert("Please select an origin and destination airport");
        return false;
    }
    return true;
</pd_script>
    Analyze
</button>
```

 You can find the code file here:

https://github.com/DTAIEB/Thoughtful-Data-Science/
blob/master/chapter%209/sampleCode20.html

The following output shows the end results when selecting BOS as the origin airport and PSC as the destination:

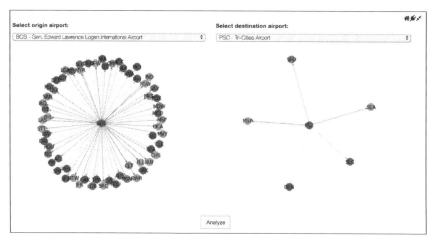

Welcome screen with both airports selected

Let's now look at the implementation of the `compute_path_screen()` route which is responsible for showing the Mapbox map of all the airports and the shortest path based on the selected centrality index as a layer which is an extra visualization superimposed on the overall map.

The following code shows its implementation:

```
[[USFlightsAnalysis]]
@route(org_airport="*", dest_airport="*")
def compute_path_screen(self, org_airport, dest_airport):
    return """
<div class="container-fluid">
    <div class="form-group col-sm-2" style="padding-right:10px;">
        <div><strong>Centrality Indices</strong></div>
        {% for centrality in this.centrality_indices.keys() %}
        <div class="rendererOpt checkbox checkbox-primary">
            <input type="checkbox"
                    pd_refresh="flight_map{{prefix}}"
pd_script="self.compute_toggle_centrality_layer('{{org_airport}}',
'{{dest_airport}}', '{{centrality}}')">
            <label>{{centrality}}</label>
        </div>
        {%endfor%}
    </div>
    <div class="form-group col-sm-10">
        <h1 class="rendererOpt">Select a centrality index to show
the shortest flight path
        </h1>
        <div id="flight_map{{prefix}}" pd_entity="self.airports_
centrality" pd_render_onload>
            <pd_options>
            {
                "keyFields": "LATITUDE,LONGITUDE",
                "valueFields": "AIRPORT,DEGREE,PAGE_RANK,ELAPSED_
TIME,CLOSENESS",
                "custombasecolorsecondary": "#fffb00",
                "colorrampname": "Light to Dark Red",
                "handlerId": "mapView",
                "quantiles": "0.0,0.1,0.2,0.3,0.4,0.5,0.6,0.7,0.8,
0.9,1.0",
                "kind": "choropleth",
                "rowCount": "1000",
                "numbins": "5",
                "mapboxtoken": "pk.
eyJ1IjoibWFwYm94IiwiYSI6ImNpejY4M29iazA2Z2gycXA4N2pmbDZmangifQ.-g_
vE53SD2WrJ6tFX7QHmA",
                "custombasecolor": "#ffffff"
            }
            </pd_options>
        </div>
```

```
    </div>
  </div>
  """
```

You can find the code file here:

https://github.com/DTAIEB/Thoughtful-Data-Science/
blob/master/chapter%209/sampleCode21.py

The central `<div>` element of this screen is the Mapbox map which by default shows the Mapbox map of all the airports. As shown in the code above, the `<pd_options>` child element is taken directly from the corresponding cell metadata where we configured the map in *Part 1*.

On the left-hand side, we generate a set of checkboxes corresponding to each centrality index, using a Jinja2 `{%for ...%}` loop over the `centrality_indices` variable. We initialize this variable in the `setup()` method of the `USFlightsAnalysis` PixieApp which is guaranteed to be called when the PixieApp starts. This variable is an OrderedDict (https://docs.python.org/3/library/collections.html#collections.OrderedDict) with keys as the centrality index and values as a color scheme that will be used in the Mapbox rendering:

```
[[USFlightsAnalysis]]
def setup(self):
    self.centrality_indices = OrderedDict([
        ("ELAPSED_TIME","rgba(256,0,0,0.65)"),
        ("DEGREE", "rgba(0,256,0,0.65)"),
        ("PAGE_RANK", "rgba(0,0,256,0.65)"),
        ("CLOSENESS", "rgba(128,0,128,0.65)")
    ])
```

You can find the code file here:

https://github.com/DTAIEB/Thoughtful-Data-Science/
blob/master/chapter%209/sampleCode22.py

The following output shows the analysis screen with no centrality index selected:

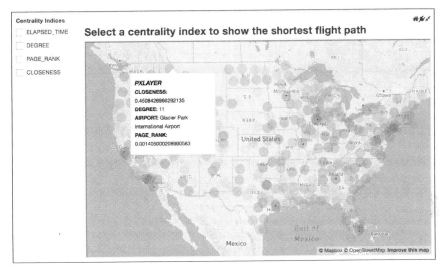

Analysis screen with no centrality index selected

We now arrive at the step where the user selects a centrality index to trigger a shortest path search. Each of the checkboxes have a pd_script attribute that calls the compute_toggle_centrality_layer() method. This method is responsible for calling the NetworkX dijkastra_path() method with a weight argument generated by calling the compute_weight() method that we discussed in *Part 1*. This method returns an array with each airport that constitutes the shortest path. Using this path, we then create a JSON object that contains the GeoJSON payload as a set of lines to be displayed on the map.

At this point, it's worth pausing to discuss what a layer is. A **layer** is defined using the GeoJSON format (http://geojson.org) which we briefly discussed in *Chapter 5, Best Practices and Advanced PixieDust Concepts*. As a reminder, a GeoJSON payload is a JSON object with a specific schema that includes among other things a geometry element that defines the shape of the object being drawn.

For example, we can define a line using the LineString type and an array of longitude and latitude coordinates for both ends of the line:

```
{
    "geometry": {
        "type": "LineString",
        "coordinates": [
```

```
          [-93.21692, 44.88055],
          [-119.11903000000001, 46.26468]
        ]
      },
      "type": "Feature",
      "properties": {}
}
```

 You can find the code file here:

https://github.com/DTAIEB/Thoughtful-Data-Science/
blob/master/chapter%209/sampleCode23.json

Assuming we can generate this GeoJSON payload from the shortest path, we may
wonder how to pass it to the PixieDust Mapbox renderer so that it can be displayed.
Well, the mechanism is pretty simple: the Mapbox renderer will introspect the
host PixieApp for any class variable that conforms to a specific format and use it
to generate the Mapbox layer to be displayed. To help with conforming with this
mechanism, we use the MapboxBase utility class that we briefly introduced earlier.
This class has a get_layer_index() method that takes a unique name (we use
the centrality index) as an argument and returns its index. It also takes an extra
optional argument that creates the layer in case it doesn't already exist. We then call
the toggleLayer() method passing the layer index as an argument to turn the layer
on and off.

The following code shows the implementation of the compute_toggle_
centrality_layer() method that implements the aforementioned steps:

```
[[USFlightsAnalysis]]
def compute_toggle_centrality_layer(self, org_airport, dest_airport,
centrality):
    cache.clear()
    cities = nx.dijkstra_path(flight_graph, org_airport, dest_airport,
weight=compute_weight(centrality))
    layer_index = self.get_layer_index(centrality, {
        "name": centrality,
        "geojson": {
            "type": "FeatureCollection",
            "features":[
                {"type":"Feature",
                 "properties":{"route":"{} to {}".format(cities[i],
cities[i+1])},
                    "geometry":{
                        "type":"LineString",
                        "coordinates":[
```

```
                        self.get_airport_location(cities[i]),
                        self.get_airport_location(cities[i+1])
                    ]
                }
            } for i in range(len(cities) - 1)
        ]
    },
    "paint":{
        "line-width": 8,
        "line-color": self.centrality_indices[centrality]
    }
})
self.toggleLayer(layer_index)
```

You can find the code file here:

```
https://github.com/DTAIEB/Thoughtful-Data-Science/
blob/master/chapter%209/sampleCode24.py
```

The coordinates in the geometry object are computed using the `get_airport_location()` method that queries the `airports_centrality` DataFrame that we created in *Part 1*, as shown in the following code:

```
[[USFlightsAnalysis]]
def get_airport_location(self, airport_code):
    row = airports_centrality.loc[airports["IATA_CODE"] == airport_code]
    if row is not None:
        return [row["LONGITUDE"].values[0], row["LATITUDE"].values[0]]
    return None
```

You can find the code file here:

```
https://github.com/DTAIEB/Thoughtful-Data-Science/
blob/master/chapter%209/sampleCode25.py
```

The layer object passed to the `get_layer_index()` method has the following properties:

- `name`: String that uniquely identifies the layer.
- `geojson`: GeoJSON object that defines the features and geometry of the layer.
- `url`: Used only if `geojson` is not present. Points at a URL that returns a GeoJSON payload.

- `paint`: Optional extra properties specific to Mapbox specification that defines how the layer data is styled, for example, color, width, and opacity.

- `layout`: Optional extra properties specific to Mapbox specification that defines how the layer data is drawn, for example, fill, visibility, and symbol.

 Note: You can find more information about Mapbox layout and paint properties here:

`https://www.mapbox.com/mapbox-gl-js/style-spec/#layers`

In the preceding code, we specify extra `paint` properties to configure the `line-width` and the `line-color` which we take from the `centrality_indices` JSON object defined in the `setup()` method.

The following output shows the shortest path for a flight from BOS to PSC using the **ELAPSED_TIME** (in red) and the **DEGREE** (in green) centrality indices:

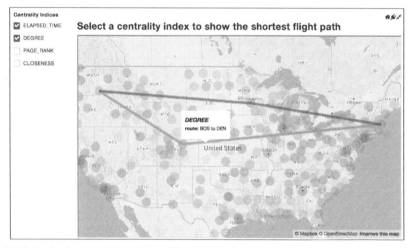

Displaying the shortest path from BOS to PSC using the ELAPSED_TIME and DEGREE centrality indices

In this section, we've built a PixieApp that provides visualization of the shortest path between two airports using the PixieDust Mapbox renderer. We've shown how to create a new layer to enrich the map with extra information using the `MapboxBase` utility class.

You can find the completed Notebook for *Part 2* here:

```
https://github.com/DTAIEB/Thoughtful-Data-Science/
blob/master/chapter%209/USFlightsAnalysis/US%20
Flight%20data%20analysis%20-%20Part%202.ipynb
```

In the next section, we'll add additional data exploration related to flight delays and associated airlines.

Part 3 – Adding data exploration to the USFlightsAnalysis PixieApp

In this section, we want to extend the route analysis screen of the USFlightsAnalysis PixieApp to add two charts showing the historical arrival delay for each airline that flies out of the selected origin airport: one for all the flights coming out of the origin airport and one for all the flights regardless of airport. This will give us a way to compare visually whether the delay for a particular airport is better or worse than for all the other airports.

We start by implementing a method that selects the flights for a given airline. We also add an optional airport argument that can be used to control whether we include all flights or only the one that originates from this airport. The returned DataFrame should have two columns: DATE and ARRIVAL_DELAY.

The following code shows the implementation of this method:

```
def compute_delay_airline_df(airline, org_airport=None):
    # create a mask for selecting the data
    mask = (flights["AIRLINE"] == airline)
    if org_airport is not None:
        # Add the org_airport to the mask
        mask = mask & (flights["ORIGIN_AIRPORT"] == org_airport)
    # Apply the mask to the Pandas dataframe
    df = flights[mask]
    # Convert the YEAR, MONTH and DAY column into a DateTime
    df["DATE"] = pd.to_datetime(flights[['YEAR','MONTH', 'DAY']])
    # Select only the columns that we need
    return df[["DATE", "ARRIVAL_DELAY"]]
```

You can find the code file here:
`https://github.com/DTAIEB/Thoughtful-Data-Science/`
`blob/master/chapter%209/sampleCode26.py`

We can test the preceding code by using it with Delta flights from Boston. We can then call the PixieDust `display()` method to create a line chart that we'll use in the PixieApp:

```
bos_delay = compute_delay_airline_df("DL", "BOS")
display(bos_delay)
```

In the PixieDust output we select the **Line Chart** menu and configure the options dialog as follows:

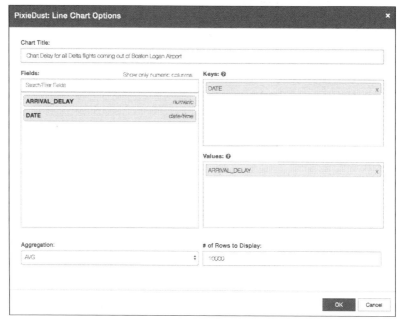

The options dialog for generating an arrival delay line chart for Delta flights out of Boston

When clicking **OK**, we get the following chart:

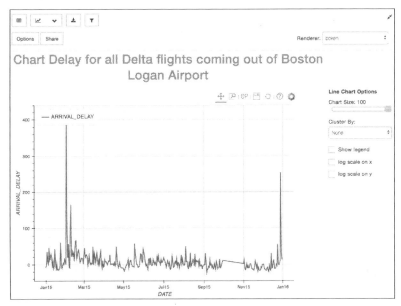

Chart delay for all Delta flights coming out of Boston

As we are going to use this chart in the PixieApp, it is a good idea to copy the JSON configuration from the **Edit Cell Metadata** dialog box:

Edit Cell Metadata

Manually edit the JSON below to manipulate the metadata for this cell. We recommend putting custom metadata attributes in an appropriately named substructure, so they don't conflict with those of others.

```
 1  {
 2    "pixiedust": {
 3      "displayParams": {
 4        "keyFields": "DATE",
 5        "handlerId": "lineChart",
 6        "title": "Chart Delay for all Delta flights coming out of Boston Loga
 7        "aggregation": "AVG",
 8        "rowCount": "10000",
 9        "valueFields": "ARRIVAL_DELAY"
10      }
11    }
12  }
```

Cancel Edit

PixieDust display() configuration for the delay chart that needs to be copied for the PixieApp

Now that we know how to generate a delay chart, we can start designing the PixieApp. We start by changing the layout of the main screen to use the `TemplateTabbedApp` helper class that gives us the tabbed layout for free. The overall analysis screen is now driven by the `RouteAnalysisApp` child PixieApp that contains two tabs: the `Search Shortest Route` tab associated with the `SearchShortestRouteApp` child PixieApp and the `Explore Airlines` tab associated with the `AirlinesApp` child PixieApp.

The following diagram provides a high-level flow of all the classes involved in the new layout:

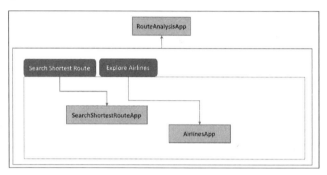

New tabbed layout class diagram

The implementation for the `RouteAnalysisApp` is pretty straightforward using the `TemplateTabbedApp` as shown in the following code:

```
from pixiedust.apps.template import TemplateTabbedApp

@PixieApp
class RouteAnalysisApp(TemplateTabbedApp):
    def setup(self):
        self.apps = [
            {"title": "Search Shortest Route",
             "app_class": "SearchShortestRouteApp"},
            {"title": "Explore Airlines",
             "app_class": "AirlinesApp"}
        ]
```

 You can find the code file here:
https://github.com/DTAIEB/Thoughtful-Data-Science/blob/master/chapter%209/sampleCode27.py

The `SearchShortestRouteApp` child PixieApp is basically a copy of the main PixieApp class we created in *Part 2*. The only difference is that it is a child PixieApp of the `RouteAnalysisApp` which itself is a child PixieApp of the `USFlightsAnalysis` main PixieApp. Therefore, we need a mechanism for passing the origin and destination airport down to the respective child PixieApps. To achieve this, we use the `pd_options` attribute when instantiating the `RouteAnalysisApp` child PixieApp.

In the `USFlightAnalysis` class, we change the `analyze_route` method to return a simple `<div>` element that triggers the `RouteAnalysisApp`. We also add a `pd_options` attribute with the `org_airport` and `dest_airport`, as shown in the following code:

```
[[USFlightsAnalysis]]
@route(org_airport="*", dest_airport="*")
def analyze_route(self, org_airport, dest_airport):
    return """
<div pd_app="RouteAnalysisApp"
pd_options="org_airport={{org_airport}};dest_airport={{dest_airport}}"
    pd_render_onload>
</div>
    """
```

You can find the code file here:

```
https://github.com/DTAIEB/Thoughtful-Data-Science/
blob/master/chapter%209/sampleCode28.py
```

Conversely, in the `setup()` method of the `SearchShortestRouteApp` child PixieApp, we read the values for `org_airport` and `dest_airport` from the options dictionary of the `parent_pixieapp`, as shown in the following code:

```
[[SearchShortestRouteApp]]
from pixiedust.display.app import *
from pixiedust.apps.mapboxBase import MapboxBase
from collections import OrderedDict

@PixieApp
class SearchShortestRouteApp(MapboxBase):
    def setup(self):
        self.org_airport = self.parent_pixieapp.options.get
("org_airport")
        self.dest_airport = self.parent_pixieapp.options.get
("dest_airport")
        self.centrality_indices = OrderedDict([
            ("ELAPSED_TIME","rgba(256,0,0,0.65)"),
```

```
            ("DEGREE", "rgba(0,256,0,0.65)"),
            ("PAGE_RANK", "rgba(0,0,256,0.65)"),
            ("CLOSENESS", "rgba(128,0,128,0.65)")
    ])
    ...
```

You can find the code file here:

`https://github.com/DTAIEB/Thoughtful-Data-Science/blob/master/chapter%209/sampleCode29.py`

Note: The rest of the implementation of the `SearchShortestRouteApp` has been ommitted for brevity since it's exactly the same as in *Part 2*. To access the implementation, please refer to the completed *Part 3* Notebook.

The last PixieApp class to implement is the `AirlinesApp`, which that will display all the delay charts. Similar to the `SearchShortestRouteApp`, we store `org_airport` and `dest_airport` from the `parent_pixieapp` options dictionary. We also compute a list of tuples (code and name) for all the airlines that have flights out of the given `org_airport`. To do that, we use the pandas `groupby()` method on the `AIRLINE` column and get a list of the index values as shown in the following code:

```
[[AirlinesApp]]
@PixieApp
class AirlinesApp():
    def setup(self):
        self.org_airport = self.parent_pixieapp.options.get
("org_airport")
        self.dest_airport = self.parent_pixieapp.options.get
("dest_airport")
        self.airlines = flights[flights["ORIGIN_AIRPORT"] == self.
org_airport].groupby("AIRLINE").size().index.values.tolist()
        self.airlines = [(a, airlines.loc[airlines["IATA_CODE"] ==
a]["AIRLINE"].values[0]) for a in self.airlines]
```

You can find the code file here:

`https://github.com/DTAIEB/Thoughtful-Data-Science/blob/master/chapter%209/sampleCode30.py`

In the main screen of the AirlinesApp, we generate a set of rows for each of the airlines using the Jinja2 {%for...%} loop. In each row, we add two <div> elements that will hold the delay line chart for the given airline: one for flights coming out of the origin airport and one for all the flights for this airline. Each <div> element has a pd_options attribute, with the org_airport and dest_airport as state attributes, which triggers the delay_airline_screen route. We also add a delay_org_airport Boolean state attribute to denote which type of delay chart we want to display. To make sure the <div> element is rendered immediately, we add the pd_render_onload attribute as well.

The following code shows the implementation of the AirlinesApp default route:

```
[[AirlinesApp]]
@route()
    def main_screen(self):
        return """
<div class="container-fluid">
    {%for airline_code, airline_name in this.airlines%}
    <div class="row" style="max-e">
        <h1 style="color:red">{{airline_name}}</h1>
        <div class="col-sm-6">
            <div pd_render_onload pd_options="delay_org_
airport=true;airline_code={{airline_code}};airline_name=
{{airline_name}}"></div>
        </div>
        <div class="col-sm-6">
            <div pd_render_onload pd_options="delay_org_
airport=false;airline_code={{airline_code}};airline_name=
{{airline_name}}"></div>
        </div>
    </div>
    {%endfor%}
</div>
        """
```

You can find the code file here:
https://github.com/DTAIEB/Thoughtful-Data-Science/
blob/master/chapter%209/sampleCode31.py

The `delay_airline_screen()` route has three parameters:

- `delay_org_airport`: `true` if we only want the flights coming out of the origin airport, and `false` if we want all the flights for the given airline. We use this flag to build the mask for filtering the data out of the flights DataFrame.

- `airline_code`: The IATA code for the given airline.

- `airline_name`: The full name of the airline. We'll use this when building the UI in the Jinja2 template.

In the body of the `delay_airline_screen()` method, we also compute the average delay for the selected data in the `average_delay` local variable. As a reminder, in order to use this variable in the Jinja2 template, we use the `@templateArgs` decorator, which automatically makes all local variables available in the Jinja2 template.

The `<div>` element that holds the chart has a `pd_entity` attribute that uses the `compute_delay_airline_df()` method that we created at the beginning of this section. However, we needed to rewrite this method as a member of the class since the arguments have changed: `org_airport` is now a class variable, and `delay_org_airport` is now a String Boolean. We also add a `<pd_options>` child element with the PixieDust `display()` JSON configuration that we copied from the **Edit Cell Metadata** dialog.

The following code shows the implementation of the `delay_airline_screen()` route:

```
[[AirlinesApp]]
@route(delay_org_airport="*",airline_code="*", airline_name="*")
    @templateArgs
    def delay_airline_screen(self, delay_org_airport, airline_code,
airline_name):
        mask = (flights["AIRLINE"] == airline_code)
        if delay_org_airport == "true":
            mask = mask & (flights["ORIGIN_AIRPORT"] == self.
org_airport)
        average_delay = round(flights[mask]["ARRIVAL_DELAY"].
mean(), 2)
        return """
{%if delay_org_airport == "true" %}
<h4>Delay chart for all flights out of {{this.org_airport}}</h4>
{%else%}
<h4>Delay chart for all flights</h4>
{%endif%}
<h4 style="margin-top:5px">Average delay: {{average_delay}}
```

```
minutes</h4>
<div pd_render_onload pd_entity="compute_delay_airline_df
('{{airline_code}}', '{{delay_org_airport}}')">
    <pd_options>
    {
      "keyFields": "DATE",
      "handlerId": "lineChart",
      "valueFields": "ARRIVAL_DELAY",
      "noChartCache": "true"
    }
    </pd_options>
</div>
            """
```

You can find the code file here:

`https://github.com/DTAIEB/Thoughtful-Data-Science/blob/master/chapter%209/sampleCode32.py`

The `compute_delay_airline_df()` method has two arguments: airlines that correspond to the IATA code and the `delay_org_airport` String Boolean. We already covered implementation of this method, but the new adapted code is provided here:

```
[[AirlinesApp]]
def compute_delay_airline_df(self, airline, delay_org_airport):
        mask = (flights["AIRLINE"] == airline)
        if delay_org_airport == "true":
            mask = mask & (flights["ORIGIN_AIRPORT"] == self.
org_airport)
        df = flights[mask]
        df["DATE"] = pd.to_datetime(flights[['YEAR','MONTH', 'DAY']])
        return df[["DATE", "ARRIVAL_DELAY"]]
```

You can find the code file here:

`https://github.com/DTAIEB/Thoughtful-Data-Science/blob/master/chapter%209/sampleCode33.py`

Running the `USFlightsAnalysis` PixieApp with BOS and PSC as the origin and destination airports respectively, we click on the **Explore Airlines** tab.

The results are shown in the following screenshot:

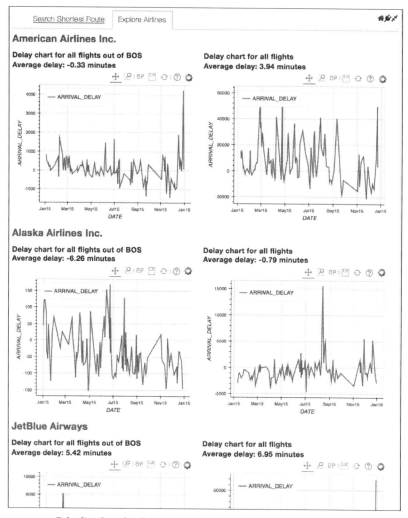

Delay line charts for all the airlines that provide services from Boston airport

In this section, we provide another example of how to use the PixieApp programming model to build powerful dashboards that provide visualization and insights into the output of the analytics developed in the Notebook.

The completed Notebook for *Part 3* of the `USFlightsAnalysis` PixieApp can be found here:

```
https://github.com/DTAIEB/Thoughtful-Data-Science/
blob/master/chapter%209/USFlightsAnalysis/US%20
Flight%20data%20analysis%20-%20Part%203.ipynb
```

In the next section, we'll build an ARIMA model that tries to predict flight delays.

Part 4 – Creating an ARIMA model for predicting flight delays

In *Chapter 8*, *Financial Time Series Analysis and Forecasting*, we used time series analysis to build a forecasting model for predicting financial stocks. We can actually use the same technique in flight delays since, after all, we are also dealing here with time series, and so in this section, we'll follow the exact same steps. For each destination airport and optional airline, we'll build a pandas DataFrame that contains matching flight information.

Note: We'll use the `statsmodels` library again. Make sure to install it if you haven't done so already and refer to *Chapter 8*, *Financial Time Series Analysis and Forecasting* for more information.

As an example, let's focus on all the Delta (DL) flights with BOS as the destination:

```
df = flights[(flights["AIRLINE"] == "DL") & (flights["ORIGIN_AIRPORT"]
== "BOS")]
```

Using the `ARRIVAL_DELAY` column as a value for our time series, we plot the ACF and PACF plots to identify trends and seasonality as shown in the following code:

```
import statsmodels.tsa.api as smt
smt.graphics.plot_acf(df['ARRIVAL_DELAY'], lags=100)
plt.show()
```

You can find the code file here:

```
https://github.com/DTAIEB/Thoughtful-Data-Science/
blob/master/chapter%209/sampleCode34.py
```

The result is shown in the following screenshot:

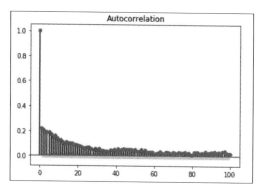

Autocorrelation function for the ARRIVAL_DELAY data

Similarly, we also plot the partial autocorrelation function using the following code:

```
import statsmodels.tsa.api as smt
smt.graphics.plot_pacf(df['ARRIVAL_DELAY'], lags=50)
plt.show()
```

 You can find the code file here:

https://github.com/DTAIEB/Thoughtful-Data-Science/
blob/master/chapter%209/sampleCode35.py

The results are shown here:

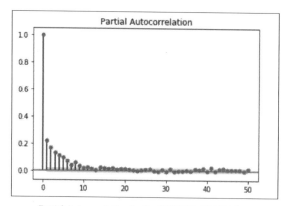

Partial Autocorrelation for the ARRIVAL_DELAY data

From the preceding charts, we can hypothesize that the data has a trend and/or seasonality, and that it is not stationary. Using the log difference technique that we explained in *Chapter 8, Financial Time Series Analysis and Forecasting*, we transform the series and visualize it with the PixieDust `display()` method, as shown in the following code:

 Note: We also make sure to remove the rows with NA and Infinite values by first calling the `replace()` method to replace `np.inf` and `-np.inf` with `np.nan`, and then call the `dropna()` method to remove all the rows with the `np.nan` value.

```
import numpy as np
train_set, test_set = df[:-14], df[-14:]
train_set.index = train_set["DEPARTURE_TIME"]
test_set.index = test_set["DEPARTURE_TIME"]
logdf = np.log(train_set['ARRIVAL_DELAY'])
logdf.index = train_set['DEPARTURE_TIME']
logdf_diff = pd.DataFrame(logdf - logdf.shift()).reset_index()
logdf_diff.replace([np.inf, -np.inf], np.nan, inplace=True)
logdf_diff.dropna(inplace=True)
display(logdf_diff)
```

 You can find the code file here:

https://github.com/DTAIEB/Thoughtful-Data-Science/blob/master/chapter%209/sampleCode36.py

The following screenshot shows the PixieDust option dialog:

Options dialog for the log difference of the ARRIVAL_DELAY data

After clicking **OK**, we get the following results:

Note: When running the preceding code, you may not get the exact same chart as shown in the following screenshot. This is because we configure the **# of Rows to Display** in the options dialog to be 100 which means that PixieDust will take a sample of size 100 before creating the chart.

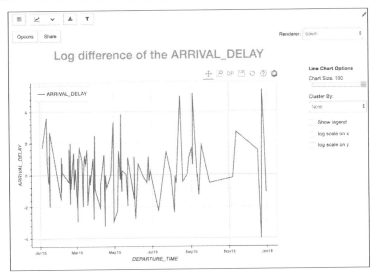

Log difference line chart of the ARRIVAL_DELAY data

The preceding chart looks stationary; we can reinforce this hypothesis by plotting the ACF and PACF again on the log difference as shown in the following code:

```
smt.graphics.plot_acf(logdf_diff["ARRIVAL_DELAY"], lags=100)
plt.show()
```

You can find the code file here:
https://github.com/DTAIEB/Thoughtful-Data-Science/
blob/master/chapter%209/sampleCode37.py

The results are as follows:

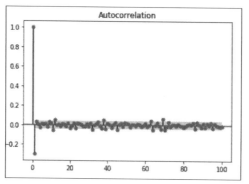

ACF chart for the log difference of the ARRIVAL_DELAY data

In the following code, we do the same thing for the PACF:

```
smt.graphics.plot_pacf(logdf_diff["ARRIVAL_DELAY"], lags=100)
plt.show()
```

 You can find the code file here:

https://github.com/DTAIEB/Thoughtful-Data-Science/blob/master/chapter%209/sampleCode38.py

The results are as follows:

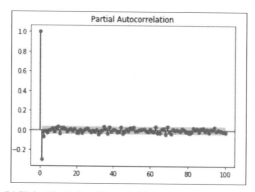

PACF chart for the log difference of the ARRIVAL_DELAY data

As a reminder from *Chapter 8, Financial Time Series Analysis and Forecasting,*
an ARIMA model is composed of three orders: *p, d,* and *q.* From the preceding
two charts, we can infer these orders for the ARIMA model we want to build:

- **Autoregression order p is 1**: Corresponds to the first time the ACF crosses
  the significance level
- **Integration order d is 1**: We had to do a log difference once
- **Moving average order q is 1**: Corresponds to the first time the PACF crosses
  the significance level

Based on these hypotheses, we can build an ARIMA model using the `statsmodels`
package and get information about its residual error, as shown in the following code:

```
from statsmodels.tsa.arima_model import ARIMA

import warnings
with warnings.catch_warnings():
    warnings.simplefilter("ignore")
    arima_model_class = ARIMA(train_set['ARRIVAL_DELAY'],
                              dates=train_set['DEPARTURE_TIME'],
                              order=(1,1,1))
    arima_model = arima_model_class.fit(disp=0)
    print(arima_model.resid.describe())
```

 You can find the code file here:
https://github.com/DTAIEB/Thoughtful-Data-Science/
blob/master/chapter%209/sampleCode39.py

The results are shown as follows:

```
count    13882.000000
mean         0.003116
std         48.932043
min       -235.439689
25%        -17.446822
50%         -5.902274
75%          6.746263
max       1035.104295
dtype: float64
```

As we can see, the mean error is only 0.003 which is pretty good, so we're ready
to run the model with values from the `train_set` and visualize the discrepencies
with the actual values.

The following code uses the ARIMA `plot_predict()` method to create the chart:

```
def plot_predict(model, dates_series, num_observations):
    fig,ax = plt.subplots(figsize = (12,8))
    model.plot_predict(
        start = dates_series[len(dates_series)-num_observations],
        end = dates_series[len(dates_series)-1],
        ax = ax
    )
    plt.show()
plot_predict(arima_model, train_set['DEPARTURE_TIME'], 100)
```

You can find the code file here:

https://github.com/DTAIEB/Thoughtful-Data-Science/
blob/master/chapter%209/sampleCode40.py

The results are shown as follows:

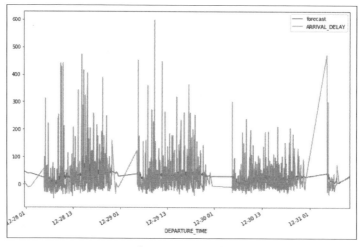

Forecast versus actual

In the preceding chart, we can clearly see that the forecast line is much smoother than the actual values. This makes sense since, in reality, there are always unexpected reasons for delays that can be treated as outliers and therefore hard to model.

We still need to use the `test_set` to validate the model with data not yet seen by the model. The following code creates a `compute_test_set_predictions()` method to compare forecast and test data and visualize the results using the PixieDust `display()` method:

```python
def compute_test_set_predictions(train_set, test_set):
    with warnings.catch_warnings():
        warnings.simplefilter("ignore")
        history = train_set['ARRIVAL_DELAY'].values
        forecast = np.array([])
        for t in range(len(test_set)):
            prediction = ARIMA(history, order=(1,1,0)).fit(disp=0).forecast()
            history = np.append(history, test_set['ARRIVAL_DELAY'].iloc[t])
            forecast = np.append(forecast, prediction[0])
        return pd.DataFrame(
          {"forecast": forecast,
           "test": test_set['ARRIVAL_DELAY'],
           "Date": pd.date_range(start=test_set['DEPARTURE_TIME'].iloc[len(test_set)-1], periods = len(test_set))
          }
        )

results = compute_test_set_predictions(train_set, test_set)
display(results)
```

 You can find the code file here:

https://github.com/DTAIEB/Thoughtful-Data-Science/blob/master/chapter%209/sampleCode41.py

The PixieDust options dialog is shown here:

Options dialog for the forecast versus test comparison line chart

After clicking **OK**, we get the following results:

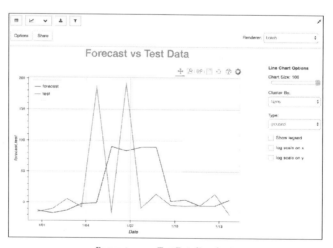

Forecast versus Test Data line chart

We are now ready to integrate this model into our USFlightsAnalysis PixieApp, by adding a third tab to the RouteAnalysisApp main screen called Flight Delay Prediction. This tab will be driven by a new child PixieApp called PredictDelayApp that will let the user select a flight segment of the shortest path computed using the Dijkstra shortest path algorithm with DEGREE as the centrality index. The user will also be able to select an airline, in which case the training data will be limited to flights operated by the selected airline.

In the following code, we create the PredictDelayApp child PixieApp and implement the setup() method that computes the Dijkstra shortest path for the selected origin and destination airports:

```
[[PredictDelayApp]]
import warnings
import numpy as np
from statsmodels.tsa.arima_model import ARIMA


@PixieApp
class PredictDelayApp():
    def setup(self):
        self.org_airport = self.parent_pixieapp.options.get
("org_airport")
        self.dest_airport = self.parent_pixieapp.options.get
("dest_airport")
        self.airlines = flights[flights["ORIGIN_AIRPORT"] ==
self.org_airport].groupby("AIRLINE").size().index.values.tolist()
        self.airlines = [(a, airlines.loc[airlines["IATA_CODE"] ==
a]["AIRLINE"].values[0]) for a in self.airlines]
        path = nx.dijkstra_path(flight_graph, self.org_airport,
self.dest_airport, weight=compute_weight("DEGREE"))
        self.paths = [(path[i], path[i+1]) for i in range
(len(path) - 1)]
```

In the default route of the PredictDelayApp, we use the Jinja2 {%for..%} loop to build two drop-down boxes that display the flight segment and the airlines, as shown in the following code:

```
[[PredictDelayApp]]
@route()
    def main_screen(self):
        return """
<div class="container-fluid">
    <div class="row">
        <div class="col-sm-6">
            <div class="rendererOpt" style="font-weight:bold">
                Select a flight segment:
```

```
            </div>
            <div>
                <select id="segment{{prefix}}" pd_refresh="
prediction_graph{{prefix}}">
                    <option value="" selected></option>
                    {%for start, end in this.paths %}
                    <option value="{{start}}:{{end}}">{{start}} ->
{{end}}</option>
                    {%endfor%}
                </select>
            </div>
        </div>
        <div class="col-sm-6">
            <div class="rendererOpt" style="font-weight:bold">
                Select an airline:
            </div>
            <div>
                <select id="airline{{prefix}}" pd_refresh="
prediction_graph{{prefix}}">
                    <option value="" selected></option>
                    {%for airline_code, airline_name in this.
airlines%}
                    <option value="{{airline_code}}">{{airline_
name}}</option>
                    {%endfor%}
                </select>
            </div>
        </div>
    </div>
    <div class="row">
        <div class="col-sm-12">
            <div id="prediction_graph{{prefix}}"
                pd_options="flight_segment=$val(segment{{prefix}});
airline=$val(airline{{prefix}})">
            </div>
        </div>
    </div>
</div>
        """
```

You can find the code file here:

`https://github.com/DTAIEB/Thoughtful-Data-Science/blob/master/chapter%209/sampleCode42.py`

The two drop-downs have a `pd_refresh` attribute that points to the `<div>` element with ID `prediction_graph{{prefix}}`. When triggered, this `<div>` element invokes the `predict_screen()` route using the `flight_segment` and `airline` state attributes.

In the `predict_screen()` route, we use the `flight_segment` and `airline` arguments to create the training dataset, build an ARIMA model that forecasts the model, and visualize the results in a line chart that compares the forecast and the actual values.

 Time series forecast models are limited to predictions that are close to the actual data, and since we only have data from 2015, we can't really use this model to predict more recent data. Of course, in a production application, it is assumed that we have flight data that is current and therefore this wouldn't be a problem.

The following code shows the implementation of the `predict_screen()` route:

```
[[PredictDelayApp]]
@route(flight_segment="*", airline="*")
    @captureOutput
    def predict_screen(self, flight_segment, airline):
        if flight_segment is None or flight_segment == "":
            return "<div>Please select a flight segment</div>"
        airport = flight_segment.split(":")[1]
        mask = (flights["DESTINATION_AIRPORT"] == airport)
        if airline is not None and airline != "":
            mask = mask & (flights["AIRLINE"] == airline)
        df = flights[mask]
        df.index = df["DEPARTURE_TIME"]
        df = df.tail(50000)
        df = df[~df.index.duplicated(keep='first')]
        with warnings.catch_warnings():
            warnings.simplefilter("ignore")
            arima_model_class = ARIMA(df["ARRIVAL_DELAY"],
dates=df['DEPARTURE_TIME'], order=(1,1,1))
            arima_model = arima_model_class.fit(disp=0)
            fig, ax = plt.subplots(figsize = (12,8))
            num_observations = 100
            date_series = df["DEPARTURE_TIME"]
            arima_model.plot_predict(
                start = str(date_series[len(date_series)-num_
observations]),
```

```
        end = str(date_series[len(date_series)-1]),
        ax = ax
    )
    plt.show()
```

You can find the code file here:

https://github.com/DTAIEB/Thoughtful-Data-Science/
blob/master/chapter%209/sampleCode43.py

In the following code, we also wanted to make sure that the dataset index is deduplicated to avoid errors when plotting the results. This is done by filtering the duplicated indices using `df = df[~df.index.duplicated(keep='first')]`.

The last thing left to do is to wire the `PredictDelayApp` child PixieApp to the `RouteAnalysisApp` as shown in the following code:

```
from pixiedust.apps.template import TemplateTabbedApp

@PixieApp
class RouteAnalysisApp(TemplateTabbedApp):
    def setup(self):
        self.apps = [
            {"title": "Search Shortest Route",
             "app_class": "SearchShortestRouteApp"},
            {"title": "Explore Airlines",
             "app_class": "AirlinesApp"},
            {"title": "Flight Delay Prediction",
             "app_class": "PredictDelayApp"}
        ]
```

You can find the code file here:

https://github.com/DTAIEB/Thoughtful-Data-Science/
blob/master/chapter%209/sampleCode44.py

When we run the `USFlightsAnalysis` PixieApp using BOS and PSC as we did in the previous sections. In the **Flight Delay Prediction** tab, we select the **BOS->DEN** flight segment.

The results are shown as follows:

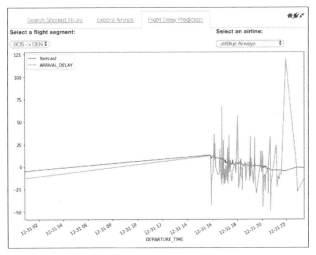

Forecast for the Boston to Denver flight segment

In this section, we've shown how to use time series forecasting models to predict flight delays based on historical data.

You can find the complete Notebook here:

```
https://github.com/DTAIEB/Thoughtful-Data-Science/
blob/master/chapter%209/USFlightsAnalysis/US%20
Flight%20data%20analysis%20-%20Part%204.ipynb
```

As a reminder, while this is only a sample application which has a lot of room for improvement, the techniques for operationalizing data analytics using the PixieApp programming model would apply just the same in any other project.

Summary

In this chapter, we've discussed graphs and its associated graph theory, exploring its data structure and algorithms. We've also briefly introduced the `networkx` Python library that provides a rich set of APIs for manipulating and visualizing graphs. We then applied these techniques toward building a sample application that analyzes flight data by treating it as a graph problem with airports being the vertices and flights the edges. As always, we've also shown how to operationalize these analytics into a simple yet powerful dashboard that can run directly in the Jupyter Notebook and then optionally be deployed as a web analytics application with the PixieGateway microservice.

This chapter completes the series of sample applications that cover many important industry use cases. In the next chapter, I offer some final thoughts about the theme of this book which is to bridge the gap between data science and engineering by making working with data simple and accessible to all.

10
Final Thoughts

"We are creating and hiring to fill "new collar" jobs – entirely new roles in areas such as cybersecurity, data science, artificial intelligence and cognitive business."

– Ginni Rometty, IBM Chairman, and CEO

Once again, let me thank you and congratulate you, the reader, for the long journey of reading through these long chapters and perhaps trying some or all of the sample code provided. I tried to provide a good mix between diving into the fundamentals of a particular topic, such as deep learning or time series analysis, and giving comprehensive example code for the practitioner. I especially hope that you found the idea of tightly integrating the data science analytics with the PixieApp application programming model in a single Jupyter Notebook interesting and novel. But, most importantly, I hope that you found it useful and something you can reuse in your own projects and with your own teams.

At the beginning of *Chapter 1, Perspectives on Data Science from a Developer*, I use the Drew's Conway Venn Diagram (which is one of my favorites) as a representation of what is data science and why data scientists are widely considered unicorns. With all respect to Drew Conway, I'd like to extend this diagram to denote the important and growing role of developers in the field of data science, as shown in the following diagram:

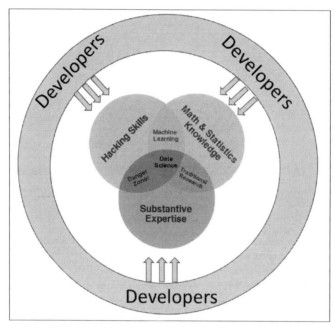

Drew's Conway Venn Diagram for data science that now includes developers

I'd now like to take advantage of this last chapter to provide my views for the future and what to expect when it comes to AI and data science.

Forward thinking – what to expect for AI and data science

This is the part I like a lot as I get to express forward-looking opinions without being held accountable for accuracy since, by definition, these are only my opinions ☺.

As I explained in *Chapter 1, Perspectives on Data Science from a Developer*, I believe that AI and data science are here to stay, and they will continue to cause disruption to existing industries for the foreseeable future, most likely at an accelerating rate. This will certainly have an effect on the overall number of jobs and, similar to other technological revolutions we've seen in the past (agricultural, industrial, information, and many more), some will disappear, while new ones will be created.

In 2016, Ginny Rometty, IBM Chairman, and CEO, in a letter to President Donald Trump (`https://www.ibm.com/blogs/policy/ibm-ceo-ginni-romettys-letter-u-s-president-elect`), talks about the need to better prepare for the AI revolution by creating new types of jobs that she calls "new collar," as shown in the following excerpt:

> *"Getting a job at today's IBM does not always require a college degree; at some of our centers in the United States, as many as one third of employees have less than a four-year degree. What matters most is relevant skills, sometimes obtained through vocational training. In addition, we are creating and hiring to fill "new collar" jobs – entirely new roles in areas such as cybersecurity, data science, artificial intelligence and cognitive business."*

These "new collar" jobs can only be created in sufficient numbers if we are successful in our quest to democratize data science, because data science is the lifeblood of AI and everyone needs to be involved in some capacity; developers, line of business users, data engineers, and so on. It is easy to imagine that the demand for these new types of jobs will be so high that traditional academic tracks will not be able to fill the needs. Rather, it will be incumbent upon the industry to fill the void by creating new programs designed to retrain all existing workers whose jobs may be at risk of becoming redundant. New programs similar to the *Everyone Can Code* program from Apple (`https://www.apple.com/everyone-can-code`) will emerge; perhaps something like *Anyone can do Data Science*. I also think that **MOOCs** (short for, **Massive Open Online Courses**) will play an even greater role that we already see today with the many partnerships being formed between key MOOC players such as Coursera and edX, and companies like IBM (see `https://www.coursera.org/ibm`).

There are other things companies can do in order to better prepare for the AI and data science revolution. In *Chapter 1, Perspectives on Data Science from a Developer*, I talk about three pillars for a data science strategy that can help us with this ambitious goal: data, services, and tools.

On the services side, high growth in public clouds is substantially contributing to the overall increase in high-quality services in multiple fields: data persistence, cognitive, streaming, and so on. Providers such as Amazon, Facebook, Google, IBM, and Microsoft are taking a leading role in building innovative capabilities with a service-first approach backed by a strong platform that provides a consistent experience for developers. This trend will continue to accelerate, with more and more powerful services being released at an increasingly rapid rate.

A good example is Google self-learning AI called AlphaZero (`https://en.wikipedia.org/wiki/AlphaZero`), which taught itself chess in 4 hours and went on to beat a champion chess program. Another great example comes from IBM's recently announced project debater (`https://www.research.ibm.com/artificial-intelligence/project-debater`), which is the first AI system that can debate a human on complex topics. These types of advances will continue to fuel the availability of more and more powerful services that can be accessed by everyone, including developers. Chatbots are another example of services that have been successfully democratized as it has never been easier for developers to create applications that contain conversational capabilities. I believe that consuming these services will become easier and easier over time, enabling developers to build amazing new applications that we can't even begin to imagine today.

On the data side, we need to make accessing high-quality data much easier than it is today. One model I have in mind is coming from a television show called *24*. Full disclosure; I love watching, and binging on, TV series and I think that some of them provide a good indicator of where technology is headed. In *24*, Jack Bauer, a counter-terrorism agent, has 24 hours to stop bad guys from causing catastrophic events. Watching that show, I'm always amazed at how easy the data circulates from the analyst back at the command center to the mobile phone of Jack Bauer, or how, given a data problem with only minutes to solve, the analyst is able to summon the data from different systems (satellite images, system of records, and so on) to zero-in on the bad guys; for example, we're looking for someone who bought this type of chemicals in the last 2 months and within a given radius. Wow! from my perspective, this is how easy and frictionless it should be for data scientists to access and process data. I believe we are making great progress toward this goal with tools such as Jupyter Notebooks that act as a control plane for connecting data sources with services and analytics that process them. Jupyter Notebooks bring tools to the data instead of the opposite, thus lowering greatly the cost of entry for anyone who wants to get involved in data science.

References

- DeepQA (IBM): `https://researcher.watson.ibm.com/researcher/view_group_subpage.php?id=2159`

- *Deep parsing in Watson, McCord, Murdock, Boguraev*: `http://brenocon.com/watson_special_issue/03%20Deep%20parsing.pdf`

- *Jupyter for Data Science, Dan Toomey, Packt Publishing*: `https://www.packtpub.com/big-data-and-business-intelligence/jupyter-data-science`

- PixieDust documentation: `https://pixiedust.github.io/pixiedust/`

- *The Visual Python Debugger for Jupyter Notebooks You've Always Wanted, David Taieb*: `https://medium.com/ibm-watson-data-lab/the-visual-python-debugger-for-jupyter-notebooks-youve-always-wanted-761713babc62`

- *Share Your Jupyter Notebook Charts on the Web, David Taieb*: `https://medium.com/ibm-watson-data-lab/share-your-jupyter-notebook-charts-on-the-web-43e190df4adb`

- *Deploy Your Analytics as Web Apps Using PixieDust's 1.1 Release, David Taieb*: `https://medium.com/ibm-watson-data-lab/deploy-your-analytics-as-web-apps-using-pixiedusts-1-1-release-d08067584a14`

- Kubernetes: `https://kubernetes.io/docs/home/`

- WordCloud: `https://amueller.github.io/word_cloud/index.html`

- *Neural Networks and Deep Learning, Michael Nielsen*: `http://neuralnetworksanddeeplearning.com/index.html`

- *Deep Learning, Ian Goodfellow, Yoshua Bengio,* and *Aaron Courville, An MIT Press book*: `http://www.deeplearningbook.org/`

- TensorFlow documentation site: `https://www.tensorflow.org/`

- *TensorFlow For Poets*: `https://codelabs.developers.google.com/codelabs/tensorflow-for-poets`

- *Tensorflow and deep learning - without a PhD, Martin Görner*: `https://www.youtube.com/watch?v=vq2nnJ4g6N0`

- Apache Spark: `https://spark.apache.org/`

- Tweepy library documentation: `http://tweepy.readthedocs.io/en/latest/`

- *Watson Developer Cloud Python SDK*: `https://github.com/watson-developer-cloud/python-sdk`

- Kafka-Python: `https://kafka-python.readthedocs.io/en/master/usage.html`

- *Sentiment Analysis of Twitter Hashtags with Spark, David Taieb*: `https://medium.com/ibm-watson-data-lab/real-time-sentiment-analysis-of-twitter-hashtags-with-spark-7ee6ca5c1585`

- *Time Series Forecasting using Statistical and Machine Learning Models, Jeffrey Yau*: `https://www.youtube.com/watch?v=_vQ0W_qXMxk`

- *Time Series Forecasting Theory, Analytics University*: `https://www.youtube.com/watch?v=Aw77aMLj9uM`

- *Time Series Analysis - PyCon 2017, Aileen Nielsen*: `https://www.youtube.com/watch?v=zmfe2RaX-14`

- Quandl Python documentation: `https://docs.quandl.com/docs/python`

- Statsmodels documentation: `https://www.statsmodels.org/stable/index.html`

- NetworkX: `https://networkx.github.io/documentation/networkx-2.1/index.html`

- GeoJSON Specification: `http://geojson.org/`

- *Beautiful Soup Documentation*: `https://www.crummy.com/software/BeautifulSoup/bs4/doc`

PixieApp Quick-Reference

This appendix is a developer quick-reference guide that provides a summary of all the PixieApp attributes.

Annotations

- `@PixieApp`: Class annotation that must be added to any class that is a PixieApp.

    Arguments: None

    Example:

    ```
    from pixiedust.display.app import *
    @PixieApp
    class MyApp():
        pass
    ```

- `@route`: Method annotation required to denote that a method — which can have any name — is associated with a route.

    Arguments: `**kwargs`. Keyword arguments (key-value pairs) representing the route definition. The PixieApp dispatcher will match the current kernel request with a route according to the following rules:

    - The route with the highest number of arguments get evaluated first.

    - All arguments must match for a route to be selected. Argument values can use `*` to denote that any value will match.

    - If a route is not found, then the default route (the one with no argument) is selected.

    - Each key of the route argument can be either a transient state (defined by the `pd_options` attribute) or persisted (field of the PixieApp class that remains present until explicitly changed).

    - The method can have any number of arguments. When invoking the method, the PixieApp dispatcher will try to match the method argument with the route arguments with the same name.

Return: The method must return an HTML fragment (except if the @ captureOutput annotation is used) that will be injected in the frontend. The method can leverage the Jinja2 template syntax to generate the HTML. The HTML template has access to a certain number of variables:

- ○ **this**: Reference to the PixieApp class (Note that we use this instead of self because self is already used by the Jinja2 framework itself)
- ○ **prefix**: String ID that is unique to the PixieApp instance
- ○ **entity**: The current data entity for the request
- ○ **Method arguments**: All arguments of the method can be accessed as a variable in the Jinja2 template

Example:

```
from pixiedust.display.app import *
@PixieApp
class MyApp():
    @route(key1="value1", key2="*")
    def myroute_screen(self, key1, key2):
        return "<div>fragment: Key1 = {{key1}} - Key2 = {{key2}}"
```

You can find the code file here:

https://github.com/DTAIEB/Thoughtful-Data-Science/
blob/master/chapter%205/sampleCode25.py

- @templateArgs: Annotation that enables any local variable to be used within the Jinja2 template. Note that @templateArgs cannot be used in combination with @captureOutput:

Arguments: None

Example:

```
from pixiedust.display.app import *
@PixieApp
class MyApp():
    @route(key1="value1", key2="*")
    @templateArgs
    def myroute_screen(self, key1, key2):
        local_var = "some value"
        return "<div>fragment: local_var = {{local_var}}"
```

You can find the code file here:

```
https://github.com/DTAIEB/Thoughtful-Data-Science/
blob/master/chapter%205/sampleCode26.py
```

- @captureOutput: Annotation that changes the contract with the route method, so that it doesn't have to return an HTML fragment anymore. Instead, the method body can simply output the results as it would in a Notebook cell. The framework will capture the output and return it as HTML. Note that you cannot use Jinja2 template in this case.

Arguments: None

Example:

```
from pixiedust.display.app import *
import matplotlib.pyplot as plt
@PixieApp
class MyApp():
    @route()
    @captureOutput
    def main_screen(self):
        plt.plot([1,2,3,4])
        plt.show()
```

You can find the code file here:

```
https://github.com/DTAIEB/Thoughtful-Data-Science/
blob/master/chapter%205/sampleCode27.py
```

- @Logger: Add logging capabilities by adding logging methods to the class: debug, warn, info, error, critical, exception.

Arguments: None

Example:

```
from pixiedust.display.app import *
from pixiedust.utils import Logger
@PixieApp
@Logger()
class MyApp():
    @route()
    def main_screen(self):
        self.debug("In main_screen")
        return "<div>Hello World</div>"
```

You can find the code file here:

https://github.com/DTAIEB/Thoughtful-Data-Science/
blob/master/chapter%205/sampleCode28.py

Custom HTML attributes

These can be used with any regular HTML elements to configure kernel requests.
The PixieApp framework can trigger these requests when the element receives
a click or change event, or right after the HTML fragment has completed loading.

- pd_options: List of key-value pairs that define transient states for the
  kernel request, according to the following format: pd_options="key1=va
  lue1;key2=value2;...". When used in combination with the pd_entity
  attribute, the pd_options attribute invokes the PixieDust display() API.
  In this case, you can get the values from the metadata of a separate Notebook
  cell in which you have used the display() API. When using pd_options
  in display() mode, it is recommended for convenience, to use the JSON
  notation of pd_options by creating a child element called <pd_options>
  and include the JSON values as text.

Example with pd_options as child element invoking display():

```
<div pd_entity>
    <pd_options>
        {
            "mapboxtoken": "XXXXX",
            "chartsize": "90",
            "aggregation": "SUM",
            "rowCount": "500",
            "handlerId": "mapView",
            "rendererId": "mapbox",
            "valueFields": "IncidntNum",
            "keyFields": "X,Y",
            "basemap": "light-v9"
        }
    </pd_options>
</div>
```

You can find the code file here:

https://github.com/DTAIEB/Thoughtful-Data-Science/
blob/master/chapter%205/sampleCode29.html

Example with `pd_options` as HTML attribute:

```
<!-- Invoke a route that displays a chart -->
<button type="submit" pd_options="showChart=true"
pd_target="chart{{prefix}}">
    Show Chart
</button>
```

 You can find the code file here:

```
https://github.com/DTAIEB/Thoughtful-Data-Science/
blob/master/chapter%205/sampleCode30.html
```

- `pd_entity`: Used only to invoke the `display()` API on specific data. Must be used in combination with `pd_options` where key-value pairs will be used as arguments to `display()`. If no value is specified for the `pd_entity` attribute, then it is assumed to be the entity passed to the `run` method that starts the PixieApp. The `pd_entity` value can be either a variable defined in the Notebook or a field of the PixieApp (for example, `pd_entity="df"`), or a field to an object using the dot notation (for example, `pd_entity="obj_instance.df"`).

- `pd_target`: By default, the output of a kernel request is injected in the overall output cell or dialog (if you use `runInDialog="true"` as an argument to the `run` method). However, you can use `pd_target="elementId"` to specify a target element that will receive the output. (Note that the `elementId` must exist in the current view.)

Example:

```
<div id="chart{{prefix}}">
<button type="submit" pd_options="showChart=true"
pd_target="chart{{prefix}}">
    Show Chart
</button>
</div>
```

 You can find the code file here:

```
https://github.com/DTAIEB/Thoughtful-Data-Science/
blob/master/chapter%205/sampleCode31.html
```

- pd_script: This invokes arbitrary Python code as part of the kernel request. This can be used in combination with other attributes like pd_entity and pd_options. It's important to note that the Python indentation rules (https://docs.python.org/2.0/ref/indentation.html) must be respected to avoid a runtime error.

  If the Python code contains multiple lines, it is recommended to use pd_script as a child element and store the code as text.

  Example:

```
<!-- Invoke a method to load a dataframe before visualizing it -->
<div id="chart{{prefix}}">
<button type="submit"
    pd_entity="df"
    pd_script="self.df = self.load_df()"
    pd_options="handlerId=dataframe"
    pd_target="chart{{prefix}}">
    Show Chart
</button>
</div>
```

You can find the code file here:

```
https://github.com/DTAIEB/Thoughtful-Data-Science/
blob/master/chapter%205/sampleCode32.html
```

- pd_app: This dynamically invokes a separate PixieApp by its fully qualified class name. The pd_options attribute can be used to pass route arguments to invoke a specific route of the PixieApp.

  Example:

```
<div pd_render_onload
    pd_option="show_route_X=true"
    pd_app="some.package.RemoteApp">
</div>
```

You can find the code file here:

```
https://github.com/DTAIEB/Thoughtful-Data-Science/
blob/master/chapter%205/sampleCode33.html
```

- pd_render_onload: This should be used to trigger a kernel request upon loading, as opposed to when a user clicks on an element or when a change event occurs. The pd_render_onload attribute can be combined with any other attribute that defines the request, like pd_options or pd_script. Note that this attribute should only be used with a div element.

  Example:

  ```
  <div pd_render_onload>
      <pd_script>
  print('hello world rendered on load')
      </pd_script>
  </div>
  ```

   You can find the code file here:

  https://github.com/DTAIEB/Thoughtful-Data-Science/
  blob/master/chapter%205/sampleCode34.html

- pd_refresh: This is used to force the HTML element to execute a kernel request even if no event (click or change event) has occurred. If no value is specified, then the current element is refreshed, otherwise, the element with the ID specified in the value will be refreshed.

  Example:

  ```
  <!-- Update state before refreshing a chart -->
  <button type="submit"
      pd_script="self.show_line_chart()"
      pd_refresh="chart{{prefix}}">
      Show line chart
  </button>
  ```

   You can find the code file here:

  https://github.com/DTAIEB/Thoughtful-Data-Science/
  blob/master/chapter%205/sampleCode35.html

- pd_event_payload: This emits a PixieApp event with the specified payload content. This attribute follows the same rules as pd_options:
  - Each key-value pair must be encoded using the key=value notation
  - The event will be triggered on a click or a change event
  - Support for $val() directive to dynamically inject user entered input
  - Use <pd_event_payload> child to enter raw JSON.

Example:

```
<button type="submit" pd_event_payload="type=topicA;message=Button
clicked">
    Send event A
</button>
<button type="submit">
    <pd_event_payload>
    {
        "type":"topicA",
        "message":"Button Clicked"
    }
    </pd_event_payload>
    Send event A
</button>
```

 You can find the code file here:

```
https://github.com/DTAIEB/Thoughtful-Data-Science/
blob/master/chapter%205/sampleCode36.html
```

- pd_event_handler: Subscribers can listen to an event by declaring a <pd_event_handler> child element which can accept any of the PixieApp kernel execution attributes like pd_options and pd_script. This element must use the pd_source attribute to filter which events they want to process. The pd_source attribute can contain one of the following values:

    ○ targetDivId: Only events originating from the element with the specified ID will be accepted

    ○ type: Only events with the specified type will be accepted

Example:

```
<div class="col-sm-6" id="listenerA{{prefix}}">
    Listening to button event
    <pd_event_handler
        pd_source="topicA"
        pd_script="print(eventInfo)"
        pd_target="listenerA{{prefix}}">
    </pd_event_handler>
</div>
```

You can find the code file here:

```
https://github.com/DTAIEB/Thoughtful-Data-Science/
blob/master/chapter%205/sampleCode37.html
```

Note: Using * for pd_source denotes that all events will be accepted.

- pd_refresh_rate: This is used to repeat the execution of an element at a specified interval expressed in milliseconds. This is useful for when you want to poll the state of a particular variable and show the result in the UI.

Example:

```
<div pd_refresh_rate="3000"
    pd_script="print(self.get_status())">
</div>
```

You can find the code file here:

```
https://github.com/DTAIEB/Thoughtful-Data-Science/
blob/master/chapter%205/sampleCode38.html
```

Methods

- setup: This is an optional method implemented by the PixieApp to initialize its state. Will be automatically invoked before the PixieApp runs.

Arguments: None

Example:

```
def setup(self):
    self.var1 = "some initial value"
    self.pandas_dataframe = pandas.DataFrame(data)
```

You can find the code file here:

```
https://github.com/DTAIEB/Thoughtful-Data-Science/
blob/master/chapter%205/sampleCode39.py
```

- run: This starts the PixieApp.

Arguments:

  ○ **entity**: [Optional] Dataset passed as input to the PixieApp. Can be referenced with the pd_entity attribute or directly as a field called pixieapp_entity.

-        °   ****kwargs**: Keyword arguments to be passed to the PixieApp when it runs. For example, using `runInDialog="true"` will start the PixieApp in a dialog.

Example:

```
app = MyPixieApp()
app.run(runInDialog="true")
```

- `invoke_route`: This is used to programmatically invoke a route.

  Arguments:

  -     °   **Route method**: Method to be invoked.
  -     °   ****kwargs**: Keyword arguments to be passed to the route method.

Example:

```
app.invoke_route(app.route_method, arg1 = "value1", arg2 = "value2")
```

- `getPixieAppEntity`: This is used to retrieve the current PixieApp entity (which can be None) passed when calling the `run()` method. `getPixieAppEntity()` is typically called from within the PixieApp itself, that is:

```
self.getPixieAppEntity()
```

Other Books You May Enjoy

If you enjoyed this book, you may be interested in these other books by Packt:

Statistics for Data Science

James D. Miller

ISBN: 978-1-78829-067-8

- Analyze the transition from a data developer to a data scientist mindset
- Get acquainted with the R programs and the logic used for statistical computations
- Understand mathematical concepts such as variance, standard deviation, probability, matrix calculations, and more
- Learn to implement statistics in data science tasks such as data cleaning, mining, and analysis
- Learn the statistical techniques required to perform tasks such as linear regression, regularization, model assessment, boosting, SVMs, and working with neural networks
- Get comfortable with performing various statistical computations for data science programmatically

Practical Data Science Cookbook - Second Edition

Prabhanjan Tattar, Tony Ojeda, Sean Patrick Murphy, Benjamin Bengfort,
Abhijit Dasgupta

ISBN: 978-1-78712-962-7

- Learn and understand the installation procedure and environment required for R and Python on various platforms
- Prepare data for analysis by implement various data science concepts such as acquisition, cleaning and munging through R and Python
- Build a predictive model and an exploratory model
- Analyze the results of your model and create reports on the acquired data
- Build various tree-based methods and Build random forest

Leave a review – let other readers know what you think

Please share your thoughts on this book with others by leaving a review on the site that you bought it from. If you purchased the book from Amazon, please leave us an honest review on this book's Amazon page. This is vital so that other potential readers can see and use your unbiased opinion to make purchasing decisions, we can understand what our customers think about our products, and our authors can see your feedback on the title that they have worked with Packt to create. It will only take a few minutes of your time, but is valuable to other potential customers, our authors, and Packt. Thank you!

Index

using 63, 64, 67
widget, creating with pd_widget 148, 149
PixieApp events
 used, for adding dashboard drill-downs 156,
  158, 159, 161
PixieApp routes
 debugging, with PixieDebugger 176-178
PixieDebugger
 used, for debugging PixieApp routes 176-178
 used, for visual debugging 173-175
PixieDust
 about 32, 34, 35
 data streaming 150-152
 reference link 25
PixieDust logging
 issues, troubleshooting 178, 179, 181
pixiedust_rosie
 used, for data wrangling 42, 44, 46-49
PixieDust visualizations
 extending 161-168
PixieGateway
 admin console 134-136
 reference link 36
PixieGateway Docker image
 reference link 115
PixieGateway server
 admin console credentials 117
 application, publishing 124, 126, 127
 architecture 120-123
 charts sharing, by publishing as web pages
  129-132, 134
 configuring 116
 Python console 137
 remote kernels 118
 state, encoding in PixieApp URL 128, 129
 storage connector 117
 warmup and run code, displaying for
  PixieApp 138
PixieGateway server, REST interface
 browser client, used for executing admin
  console 120
 browser client, used for executing
  PixieApp 120
 Jupyter Notebook Server 120
Platform as a Service (PaaS) 4
Python
 advantages 28-32

magic commands 170
Python Debugger
 reference link 169
Python decorators
 reference link 75, 333
Python, logging facility
 reference link 179
Python Notebook
 Node.js, executing 183-187

Q

Question Answering (QA) 12

R

React
 reference link 67
Rectified Linear Unit (ReLu) 194
reduction functions 310, 311
REPL (Read-Eval-Print-Loop)
 about 22
 reference link 183
Representational State Transfer (REST)
 reference link 19
Resilient Distributed Dataset (RDD) 33, 257
Rosie Pattern Language (RPL) 43

S

SampleData
 used, for loading data into Notebook 36, 38-
  40, 42
scalability
 adding, with Apache Kafka 286, 287
 adding, with IBM Streams Designer 286, 287
scikit learn package
 reference link 29
scopes, data science
 descriptive analytics 2
 predictive analytics 2
 prescriptive analytics 2

Made in the USA
Lexington, KY
25 August 2018